ROUTLEDGE LIBRARY EDITIONS: COLONIALISM AND IMPERIALISM

Volume 8

BRITISH INDIA'S RELATIONS WITH THE KINGDOM OF NEPAL, 1857–1947

BRITISH INDIA'S RELATIONS WITH THE KINGDOM OF NEPAL, 1857–1947

A Diplomatic History of Nepal

ASAD HUSAIN

Routledge
Taylor & Francis Group

LONDON AND NEW YORK

First published in 1970 by George Allen and Unwin Ltd

This edition first published in 2023
by Routledge
4 Park Square, Milton Park, Abingdon, Oxon OX14 4RN

and by Routledge
605 Third Avenue, New York, NY 10158

Routledge is an imprint of the Taylor & Francis Group, an informa business

© 1970 Asad Husain

All rights reserved. No part of this book may be reprinted or reproduced or utilised in any form or by any electronic, mechanical, or other means, now known or hereafter invented, including photocopying and recording, or in any information storage or retrieval system, without permission in writing from the publishers.

Trademark notice: Product or corporate names may be trademarks or registered trademarks, and are used only for identification and explanation without intent to infringe.

British Library Cataloguing in Publication Data
A catalogue record for this book is available from the British Library

ISBN: 978-1-032-41054-8 (Set)
ISBN: 978-1-032-41968-8 (Volume 8) (hbk)
ISBN: 978-1-032-41969-5 (Volume 8) (pbk)
ISBN: 978-1-003-36062-9 (Volume 8) (ebk)

DOI: 10.4324/9781003360629

Publisher's Note
The publisher has gone to great lengths to ensure the quality of this reprint but points out that some imperfections in the original copies may be apparent.

Disclaimer
The publisher has made every effort to trace copyright holders and would welcome correspondence from those they have been unable to trace.

BRITISH INDIA'S RELATIONS WITH THE KINGDOM OF NEPAL
1857–1947

A DIPLOMATIC HISTORY OF NEPAL

ASAD HUSAIN
Assistant Professor, Asian Studies
Northeastern Illinois State College

London
GEORGE ALLEN AND UNWIN LTD
RUSKIN HOUSE   MUSEUM STREET

FIRST PUBLISHED IN 1970

This book is copyright under the Berne Convention. All rights are reserved. Apart from any fair dealing for the purpose of private study, research, criticism or review, as permitted under the Copyright Act, 1956, no part of this publication may be reproduced, stored in a retrieval system, or transmitted, in any form or by any means, electronic, electrical, chemical, mechanical, optical, photocopying recording or otherwise, without the prior permission of the copyright owner. Enquiries should be addressed to the publishers.

© *Asad Husain 1970*

ISBN 0 04 954014 9

PRINTED IN GREAT BRITAIN
in 10 on 11pt *Plantin* type
BY UNWIN BROTHERS LTD
LONDON AND WOKING

TO MY PARENTS

PREFACE

The idea to undertake the study of the British Government of India's relations with Nepal during the nineteenth and twentieth centuries came initially from the fact, that as recently as 1960, there was not a single good, scholarly, documented work available on this subject. Yet Nepal, the only surviving Hindu kingdom in Asia, has occupied an extremely important strategic position, situated as it is between the two giants of Asia—China and India. Also, it could be interesting to see how Nepal managed to maintain its freedom in the past against strong outside pressures when other countries have failed. These, and other factors, have increased the interest in the earlier history of Nepal–India–China relations, including relations with Tibet.

The first study of Nepal's foreign relations was made by Dr K. C. Chaudhuri, in his doctoral dissertation *Anglo-Nepalese Relations*, published in 1960, covering the period from the earliest times of the British rule in India until the Gurkha war of 1814–16. Another Ph.D. dissertation, *Indo-Nepalese Relations, 1816–1877* was written in the same year by Dr Ramakant. A third Ph.D. dissertation titled *Indo-Nepalese Relations, 1837–1877* was completed by Dr Kanchanmoy Majumdar in 1962. Dr Satish Kumar's doctoral dissertation, *Political System of Nepal Under the Ranas, 1845–1901*, although a political history, is a valuable contribution to the understanding of Nepal. Two recent publications, *Politics in Nepal* (1964) by Dr Anirudha Gupta on the present domestic problems of Nepal, and B. D. Sanwal's *Nepal and the East India Company* (1965) were also useful. I am glad to acknowledge my debt to Dr Margaret Fisher and Dr Leo Rose who are working in this subject area at the University of California at Berkeley. The Indian School of International Studies in New Delhi, India, is also paying considerable attention to the study of Nepalese affairs. None of the foregoing studies or individuals, however, cover the whole history of Nepal's foreign relations during the nineteenth and twentieth centuries, and none of the authors were able to obtain access to the Nepalese and Indian archives for recent documents.

The present study, which is a Ph.D. dissertation submitted to the University of Minnesota Department of International Relations, covers British India's relations with the Kingdom of Nepal from 1857 to 1947. This would, in effect, complete the study of the history of Nepal's foreign relations to the end of the British period.

PREFACE

This dissertation is based mostly on original documents and secret papers from the National Archives of India, New Delhi; the British Commonwealth Relations Library, London (better known as the India Office Library); and the Foreign Office of the Government of Nepal, Kathmandu, Nepal; also, other libraries, published materials and public records offices in India, England and Nepal, such as the British Museum and the Central Records Office at Patna, Bihar.

For convenience, the dissertation has been divided into four parts and ten chapters. The Introduction deals with the earlier history of Nepal's foreign relations up to 1856. This discussion is based mostly on histories of Nepal that have already been published by well-known European, American and Asian scholars and that contain scattered references to Nepal's foreign relations. Also, I have used some primary unpublished materials in this section. At the suggestion of Professor Burton Stein, Professor of History at the University of Minnesota and member of my Ph.D. Committee, I have also attempted to give a brief history of the foreign relations of Thailand and of Hyderabad (formerly the largest princely state of India), in the hope that this material will make more clear the proximate position of Nepal in the field of International Affairs. There are many interesting contrasts in the diplomatic activities of these three states.

The second chapter of this dissertation contains the discussion of the Indian Mutiny and Jung Bahadur's prime ministership (1857–77). This chapter is based mostly on the primary original sources gathered from the India Office Library, the National Archives of India and other libraries in India and Nepal. In addition to these original documents, most of the published materials cited previously have been used in this chapter. The unpublished doctoral dissertation of Dr Majumdar has also been of help here.

The third Chapter, 'Frustration and Compromise', which begins in 1877 and ends in 1901, is based mainly on original documents, but also makes use of a few published books. From this period forward, little research has previously been done on Nepal's foreign affairs. From Chapters four to seven, the entire study is based on the original materials collected from the libraries already mentioned. These three chapters discuss the period from 1901 to 1938, which was one of the most important in Nepal's relations with British India.

Chapter seven, which is termed the 'Last Phase' is entirely based on Nepal Foreign Office papers, since other documents on this period were not available. This chapter discusses, among other issues, Nepal's co-operation with the allied powers during World War II. Gurkha recruitment is treated separately in Chapter eight because the British efforts to obtain Gurkha enlistments played a major role in shaping

PREFACE

British–Nepalese relations. Chapter nine is devoted to the relations of Nepal with China and Tibet. It describes how the suzerainty of China over Nepal was maintained for reasons of personal profit long after it had become purely nominal. In the final chapter an attempt is made to define the diplomatic status of Nepal in its relations with British India and with other Asian countries, together with a comparison of Nepal's status with that of Thailand and Hyderabad. In the light of these discussions, a final conclusion has been drawn about the actual status of Nepal in the community of nations during the period under study.

It has been considered proper that from the many unpublished documents collected during this research from London, New Delhi and Kathmandu, a few of the more significant and important ones should be placed in the Appendix of this paper; and this has been done.

As scholars in this subject area are well aware, there is considerable variation in the spellings of names and places involving Nepal. The author has attempted to standardize on the name spellings used by Dr Margaret Fisher and Dr Leo Rose, cited earlier. The place spellings have been based on the authors' experience as to the most accepted spellings used by the people in the area.

Throughout this dissertation, certain abbreviations have been used. These are listed below:

B.E.K.—British Embassy, Kathmandu
N.A.I.—National Archives of India
N.F.O.K.—Nepal Foreign Office, Kathmandu
B.M.M.M.—British Museum Manuscript Microfilm
I.O.L.—India Office Library
B.C.R.O.—Bihar Central Records Office

This study of the foreign relations of Nepal during the nineteenth and twentieth centuries cannot completely exhaust the subject. There are still many avenues to explore. But at least it is hoped that this study might be of some help to others who are searching to find the facts. In spite of its deficiencies, if scholars and students consider it worthwhile to use it in any way for reaching an understanding of the politics of this area, then the purpose of this study is served.

Minneapolis, Minn.   ASAD HUSAIN
December, 1965

ACKNOWLEDGMENTS

Many institutions, organizations and individuals have helped me since I began working on this project three years ago. During this period, I have received financial grants, verbal advice and friendly suggestions and have had the benefit of arguments and discussions about my material, all of which has contributed to the writing of this dissertation. For all, I am grateful.

First, I wish to thank the Graduate School of the University of Minnesota for a special research grant awarded me in 1962. This was followed by a two-year grant from the Ford Foundation which enabled me to travel to Nepal, India and England in search of supporting materials. Upon my return to the University of Minnesota this year, the Graduate School again gave me financial assistance to make possible the writing of the thesis. Without these grants, I could not have completed my project.

I am grateful to many in the United States, India, Nepal and Great Britain. In the United States, I wish especially to thank President O. Meredith Wilson of the University of Minnesota. It was his letter which introduced me to His Majesty, King Mahendra of Nepal. I also owe thanks to Dean Bryce Crawford and Associate Dean Francis Boddy of the Graduate School of the University of Minnesota for taking an interest in my project and extending me financial assistance. University Vice President Stanley Wenberg and former Vice President Malcolm Willey also gave me much encouragement. Mr Henry Scholberg and the staffs of the Ames and Walter Libraries of the University have been most helpful. I also wish to thank Dr Burton Stein of the University's Department of History upon whose suggestion I incorporated the brief comparison of Nepal's status with that of Thailand and Hyderabad. I am especially indebted to my advisors, Professors Lennox A. Mills and Charles H. McLaughlin who read my dissertation and gave me valuable criticism and advice.

In personal terms, I am grateful to Mr A. Harold Peterson of Chicago City, Minnesota for his constant encouragement and support to Mr William Hambley, Jr., whose meticulous reading of parts of this manuscript and competent advice on literary form were particularly helpful, and to Mr S. M. Master for help on the Bibliography. I am also grateful for the friendly advice given to me by Dr Leo Rose when he was in India.

In Great Britain, I am greatly indebted to the staff of the India

ACKNOWLEDGMENTS

Office Library in London who furnished every available material which I needed for my research.

In India, my first thanks go to my own Government for granting permission to me to study its archives to as late a date as 1935. I must especially thank Mr M. Rasgotra, Deputy Secretary, Ministry of Foreign Affairs, who in spite of his crowded schedule, took time to read all of the documents before they were released to me. His intimate knowledge of Nepalese affairs and keen interest in the area added much to the pleasure of my study. The staff members of the National Archives of India, including Miss David, Mr Sareen and Mr Suraj Prakash gave me full co-operation and help. Special thanks go to Dr Bhargave, the Director, and to Mr S. C. Joshi, now with the Indian School of Public Administration.

I wish to thank the library staff of the Indian School of International Studies, including my friends, Dr Satish Kumar and Dr Bimla Prasad, for their useful advice, ideas and suggestions. In Patna, Bihar, I owe much to many. I am grateful to Dr K. K. Dutta, now Vice Chancellor of Patna University and Director of the Central Records Office at Patna, for granting permission to me to make copies of the archives without delay. The staff of his office was most cordial and helpful to me. My thanks are also due to Professor Hasan Askari, Director of the K. P. Jayaswal Research Institute, and to my friend Dr Qyeam Uddin Ahmed for their great assistance. I also remember with gratitude the help given me by the Librarian and staff of the Khuda Buxsh Oriental Library at Patna.

I am grateful to many individuals in India, among them Dr Syed Mahmud, former Minister of State for Foreign Affairs, Government of India; Sir C. P. N. Singh, former Indian Ambassador to Nepal; Shri Sri Prakash, former Governor of the Punjab; Mr Hira Lal Jalan, a close friend of the Rana family; Mr Hasan Naim, now on the staff of India's permanent mission to the United Nations; Dr R. S. Sharma, Head of the Department of History, Patna University; Mr Yadunath Khanal, Nepal's Ambassador to India; Mr Anand, former President of the Indo-Nepalese Association, Delhi; and Dr Tara Chand, MP, all of whom gave generously of their time in order to tell me of their experiences in Nepal.

I take pleasure in expressing my thanks to His Highness, the Maharajah of Banares who kindly permitted me to examine his private library of Persian and Urdu manuscripts, one of the best collections of its kind in India. My thanks also go to the staff of the National Library of India, Calcutta, for their help in finding for me all of the newspapers needed for my research.

In Nepal, I was permitted to carry on research in the Foreign Office

ACKNOWLEDGMENTS

of Nepal, a privilege for which I am grateful to the Government of His Majesty, the King. I am under obligation to Major General Padma Bahadur Khatri, former Defense and Foreign Secretary of Nepal and the present Ambassador of Nepal to the United States; Dr Tulsi Giri, former Chairman of the Council of Ministers; Mr Prakash Chand Thakur, Chief of Protocol, and the entire staff of the Foreign Office who were always ready to help me. My thanks go to the staff of the Bir Library, Kathmandu, and to the staff of the Madan Purskar Memorial Pushtakaylia, Patan, Nepal. I also wish to thank General Samrajyai Shamsher, the late Field Marshal Kaiser Shamsher, Mr M. C. Regmi, author of two monographs on Nepal's economic system, Mr Balchandra Sharma, Vice Chancellor of Nepal Academy; Mr Rashi Kesh Shah, former Ambassador of Nepal to the United States; Mr Ahmed Din, President of Anjuman-e-Islam, Babu Ram, Acharyai; Dr D. R. Regmi, the famous Nepalese historian and former Minister; Mr Lydon Clough, the British Consul; Dr Merrill Goodall of the United Nations; Dr Gokul Chand Shastri, Professor of History, Tribhuvan University; Dr William O. Thwett of the Ford Foundation for allowing the use of its Kathmandu office; and the then Ambassador of Britain to Nepal for the privilege of using his personal library.

The typing and preparation of this dissertation has taken many hours and much patience on the part of my typists. In this regard, I want to thank Mrs Margaret Jensen and Mrs Bernice Berg.

My task of producing extra copies of this dissertation was made significantly easier by the co-operation of Mr Karl E. Kaufmann, District Manager, Thermofax Sales, Minnesota Mining and Manufacturing Company, Minneapolis, Minnesota, who permitted me to use the facilities of his agency for this purpose. I thank him for this assistance.

It hardly seems necessary to add that none of the individuals or institutions mentioned here bear any responsibility for the views—or errors—of this dissertation.

Finally, I would like to thank a friend and well-wisher whose ideas and understanding were an unfailing source of inspiration to me and without whose sympathetic encouragement and persuasion this work would not have been completed.

A.H.

CONTENTS

	page
PREFACE	9
ACKNOWLEDGMENTS	13
MAP: NEPAL AND NEIGHBORING REGIONS	18
MAP: MODERN POLITICAL NEPAL	19

PART I BRITISH–NEPALESE RELATIONS TO THE END OF THE NINETEENTH CENTURY

1	A General Survey (to 1857)	23
2	The Indian Mutiny and Jung Bahadur's Prime Ministership	69
3	Frustration and Compromise	112

PART II ANGLO–NEPALESE RELATIONS IN THE FIRST HALF OF THE TWENTIETH CENTURY

4	Chandra Shamsher and his Foreign Policy	149
5	Nepalese–British Co-operation in World War I	183
6	Nepalese–British Relations between the World Wars	198

PART III THE LAST PHASE AND OTHER PROBLEMS

7	The Last Phase	219
8	Gurkha Recruitment and the Government of India	234
9	Nepal, China, Tibet	255
10	The International Status of Nepal	285

PART IV BIBLIOGRAPHY AND APPENDICES   317

INDEX	400

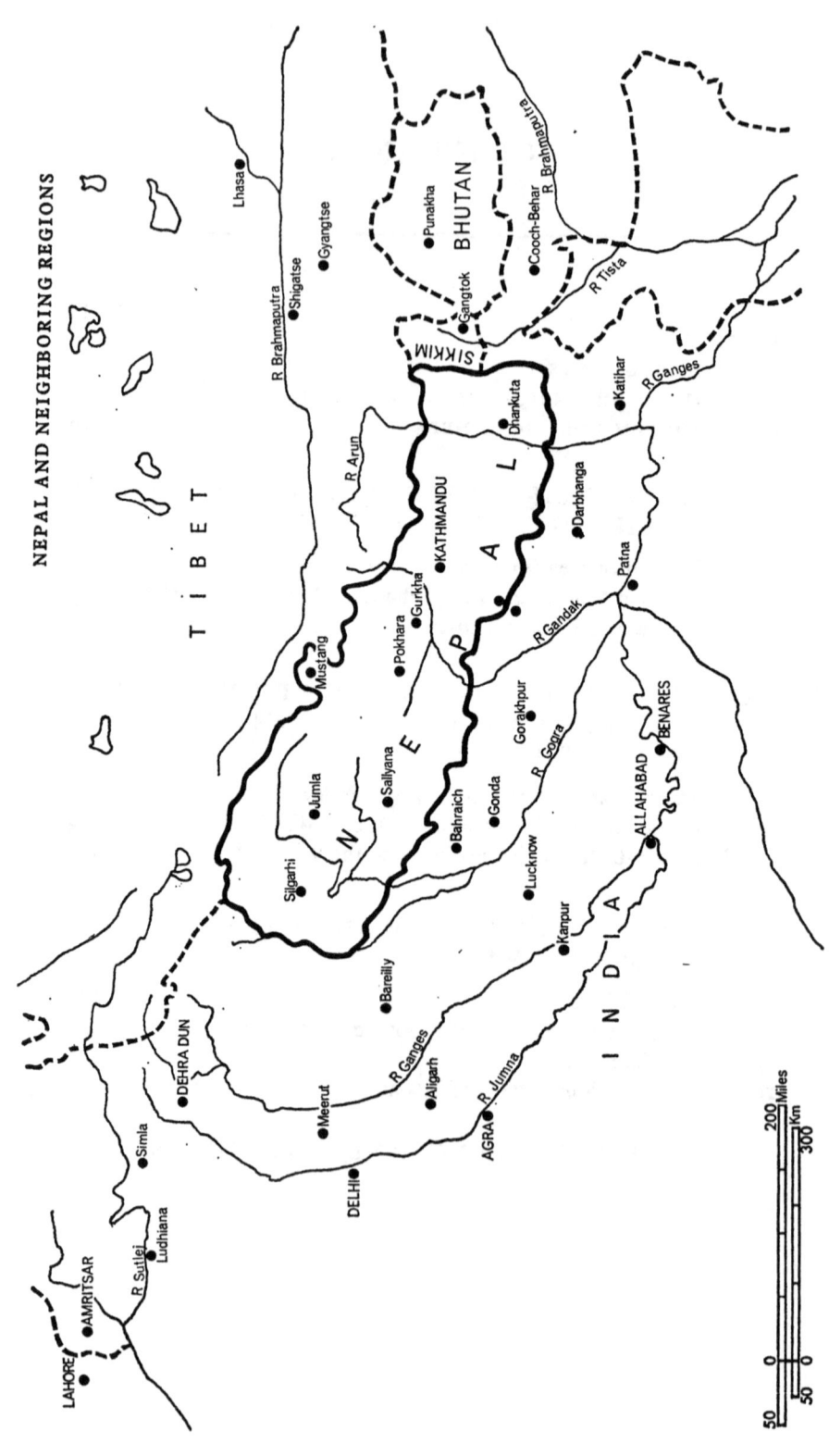

POLITICAL MAP OF MODERN NEPAL

PART I

BRITISH–NEPALESE RELATIONS TO THE END OF THE NINETEENTH CENTURY

CHAPTER 1
A GENERAL SURVEY
(TO 1857)

Nepal's relations with British India have always been an enigma. On the surface they were usually calm and harmonious, but underneath they were never free from turmoil. The natural desire of Nepal was to be completely free in her internal and external affairs. This ambition of hers did not suit the political strategy of the British Government, since Nepal, in order to maintain her freedom, would not submit to the dictation of the British. At the same time the Government of Nepal needed British support to maintain itself in power, and dared not openly oppose the British for fear of defeat. In the course of this study it will be shown how relations between the two nations were maintained.

Nepal lies along the northern border of India. On its north it skirts the southern range of the Himalayas beyond which lie China and Tibet; on the south it touches the borders of the Indian States of Uttar Pradesh, Bihar and West Bengal. From east to west, it extends from the Mechi (Mahanahde) River and Sikkim to the Sutleg River. Its maximum length is about 525 miles; its breadth varies from 90 to 140 miles.

Nepal is largest in size and population among the three Himalayan states (Nepal, Sikkim, and Bhutan). It has an area of 54,510 square miles and a population of 8,431,537 (1960), which makes it the most densely populated nation in South Asia. It has lofty mountain ranges which include some of the highest peaks of the world—Mount Everest and Kanchenjungha, about 29,000 and 28,000 feet respectively. Surrounded by these sky-high mountains, the valley of Kathmandu (the capital of Nepal) is situated between the Sapta-Gandak and Karnali river basins on the west and the Sapta-Kosi river basin in the east. The land is not only fertile for production of rice, wheat, millet, maize, potatoes and green vegetables for its people, but also abounds in natural beauty and picturesque scenery.

Nepal is divided into three geographical regions: A. The tropical region of the Terai which consists of a strip of land about twenty to thirty miles wide on the southern boundary of Nepal, including open flat country as well as dense forests at an altitude of up to 4,000 feet. B. The central regions, which include Kathmandu and which are the most densely populated and the most important part of the country. The altitude of this central region reaches to 10,000 feet. Kathmandu lies at an elevation of 4,700 feet and enjoys a generally temperate climate but with a rainy season lasting from June to October. In this region, a number of rivers and rivulets spring from the mountain-heads and flow into the valleys. C. The mountainous region, consisting of high mountain ranges of the Himalayas varying from 10,000 feet to over 29,000 feet.

Nepal is supposedly the only Hindu Kingdom on earth. But about one-eighth of its population are Buddhists. The races of Bhotias, Newars, Limbus, Kirantis and Lepchas are Buddhists while the races of Gurkhalese, Magars and Gurungs are Hindus. Also, there is a small Muslim population, approximately 800,000 in number, who emigrated from Kashmir and India and who now mostly reside in the Terai region. There are very few Christians in Nepal, the result of the banning of Christian missionaries in 1786. However, since 1951 a few Christian missionaries have been permitted to come into the country as educators and Christianity is now increasing slowly.

The races of Nepal have separate languages or dialects. The Gurkhali and the various Western races use Parbatia which, unlike the other dialects, is of Sanskrit origin. The Newars have their own separate language and alphabets. (Three of these alphabets are known to their priests although only one is in general use.) Their language, called Gubhajius, resembles Tibetan interspersed with many Sanskrit words. The Bhotias use the Tibetan language and alphabet.[1]

Nepal and the Suzerainty of India

The scope of this thesis does not include the question of whether Nepal was ever part of India or paid tribute to its great or small kings. There is no intention to take up this controversial issue here for lengthy discussion, but it would not be out of place just to mention the controversy. Most Indian historians and a few Europeans have accepted the theory that Nepal was under the suzerainty of Samudra-Gupta in

[1] Demographic information in Nepal taken from:
Chaudhuri, K. C., *Anglo-Nepalese Relations* (From the earliest times of the British rule in India till the Gurkha War), pp. 1-3, Calcutta: Modern Book Agency Private Ltd., 1960.
Baral, Isvar and Mazumdar, Debu, *Nepal: 1960-61. Trade and Information Directory*, p. 3. New Delhi: Nepal Trading Corp., n.d.
'Nepal', *Encyclopedia Britannica*, Vol. 16, p. 220. New York, 1957.
Karan, Pradyumna P., *Nepal, a Cultural and Physical Geography*, pp. 47 and 67. Lexington: University of Kentucky Press, 1960.

the fourth century AD. Dr R. C. Majumdar, one of India's most eminent historians, wrote that:[1]

'The date of Manadeva must be used as the sheet-anchor of Nepalese chronology for the present, as we know of no other dated event before his reign. As Manadeva was the 20th Lichchhavi king according to the Vamsavalis, we may place the foundation of the Lichchhavi kingdom in Nepal in the first or second century AD. The existence of the Lichchhavis as a political power, before the time of Manadeva, is known from the marriage of Chandra-Gupta I and a Lichchhavi princess, referred to above. Whether this Lichchhavi princess belonged to, or was connected in any way with, the ruling house of Nepal we cannot say. But it is certain that the Lichchhavis of Nepal had to acknowledge the suzerainty of Samudra-Gupta. The nature and duration of the Gupta suzerainty in Nepal cannot be exactly determined. But the fact the Lichchhavis of Nepal came into prominence only after the decline of the Gupta empire is not perhaps merely a coincidence. We may assume that they were subordinate to, or at least were kept in check by, the Gupta emperors, and the decline of the empire gave them the opportunity to rise to prominence and make themselves masters of nearly the whole of Nepal.'

Professor Sylvain Levi, in his book *Nepal*, discussed the above point in the following words:

'Nepal figures in authentic and positive history only from the IVth Century of the Christian era. The first dated document which mentions the name of Nepal is the panegyric of the Emperor Samudra-Gupta on the pillar of Allahabad; the inscription enumerates the tribes (or nations) subdued in the character of tributaries, vassals or direct subjects to the authority of the powerful sovereign who gave to India for a while the Imperial unity. The king of Nepal (Nepala-urpati) is mentioned in the inscription, but ranked second last among the princes who "paid the tribute, obeyed the orders and came to prostrate themselves to satisfy the haughty will of the master (or lord)"; he is placed between the prince of Kamarupa on the one hand and the prince of Kartrapura on the other. The name of Kartrapura has not yet been found elsewhere and remains enigmatic. The name of Kamarupa has lasted; it continues to officially designate the district to the North-West of Assam on the Southern frontier of Bhutan. The names of Nepal and Kamarupa are frequently compared in literature as they are on the pillar of Allahabad.'[2]

[1] Majumdar, R. C., *The History and Culture of the Indian People, The Classical Age*, Vol. III, pp. 83-4. Bombay: Bharatiya Vidya Bhavan, 1962.
[2] Levi, Sylvain, *Nepal*, English Translation, Vol. II, p. 67. New Delhi: Indian School of International Studies.

Some historians also claim that Harsha-Vardhane, who ruled India from AD 606 to 647, conquered Nepal although Dr Majumdar rejected this claim, finding no positive evidence in its favor.[1]

Dr D. R. Regmi, an eminent Nepalese historian, forthrightly challenged the theory that Nepal was ever a tributary state to India. In his book, *Ancient Nepal*, he wrote:

'The valley of Kathmandu was never regarded as outside India's sphere of influence; all forces, cultural or political, seem to have affected it. Geographically and economically the valley was inseparable from the Indo-Gangetic plain. There was no natural boundary to separate the sub-Himalayan tract where the valley was situated from the Gangetic plain. Kathmandu did not stand in splendid isolation and at every period of history its relation with India had been intimate. There is a legend that as early as the Mahabharata days, the ruler of Nepal figured in the great fight. Buddhism entered Kathmandu if not at its very birth surely long before the Christian era started. This may be dismissed as imaginative, but there cannot be any doubt that the Maurya Princes and the Lichhavis were at the head of administration. Temporarily even the Kushans and the Guptas held sway over the country. Then there is the fact of Indian dynasties ruling in the valley; all ruling dynasties of Nepal—the Mauryas, the Lichhavis, the Thakuris, the Karnatakas, the Mallas and the Shahs, were emigrants from the plains.

'This, however, should not be misconstrued as to mean domination from India. Nepal's autonomy is traditional; this autonomy was respected by external rulers, even by the Guptas, and was scrupulously maintained by the ruling dynasties with a feeling of complete identity with the ruled. There is no truth, therefore, in the statement that the valley was a Hindu colony, owing allegiance to the mother country. The intimate geographical, cultural and economic relations subsisting between Nepal and the Indo-Gangetic plain would not by any standard reduce Nepal to a colonial status *vis-à-vis* India under any circumstances.'[2]

Another claim sometimes made is that Asoka, the great Hindu (later Buddhist) king, visited Nepal and brought it under his suzerainty. Rejecting this idea, Dr Regmi wrote:

'The Ceylonese Pali chronicles, the Mahavamsa and Dipavamsa do

[1] Majumdar, R. C., *op. cit.*, p. 85.
[2] Regmi, D. R., *Ancient Nepal*, pp. 40–1. Calcutta: Firma K. L. Mukhopadhyay, 1960.

not at all mention Nepal while narrating the story of Asoka's life and career. Every detail of his pilgrimage is noted in either treatise. There is no reason for the omission of Nepal in these if he had ever gone there.'[1]

He concluded his arguments by saying:

'On any consideration it looks most unlikely that Asoka had at any time visited the Valley of Nepal and could impose his suzerainty over this country. Any suggestion leading to the acceptance of the old thesis will be absolutely imaginative.'[2]

Likewise, it does not appear that Nepal ever came under any of the Muslim rulers of India, including the Great Moguls. The only Muslim ruler who ever reached Kathmandu was Ilyas Shah of Bengal. Professor N. B. Ray gives the following account of Ilyas Shah's invasion of Nepal:

'The accession of Shams-ud-din Ilyas Shah to the throne of Lakhnawati opened a new chapter in the history of Bengal. He founded a dynasty of able and vigorous kings who won military glory and revived Bengal's contact with the outside world. He achieved the political unity of Bengal and carried his victorious arms far outside the boundaries of Bengal. He overran Tirhut and made a bold thrust across the inhospitable region of Terai into the fastness of Nepal, which was yet untrodden by Muslim soldiers. He advanced as far as the capital, Kathmandu, destroyed the holy temple of Svayambhunatha and returned with a rich booty. The Invasion, which was of the nature of a plundering raid, took place in AD 1350 and the Nepalis claim to have defeated the Muslim invader.'[3]

In any case, no permanent conquest resulted from Ilyas Shah's foray.

The discussion on the question of whether Nepal was ever under the suzerainty of India thus seems inconclusive. Both sides leave doubts about their arguments. Neither seems to have spoken the final word on this point. Perhaps it is better to leave the issue for discussion at some future date when definitive evidence may be discovered by some scholar.

The Early History of Nepal

The early history of Nepal is essentially the history of the Valley of

[1] Regmi, *op. cit.*, p. 205.
[2] Ibid.
[3] Ray, N. B., 'Bengal', *The History and Culture of the Indian People, The Delhi Sultanate*, Vol. VI, Chap. X-E, p. 197. Bombay: Bharatiya Vidya Bhavan, 1960.

Kathmandu (NOTE: The inhabitants generally call the Kathmandu valley the 'Nepal Valley' or 'Nepal' for short). Most of the accounts of this period were from Chinese and Indian pilgrims who visited Nepal. However, to the present day, no accurate chronological history of early Nepal has been written. Historians generally assume that the Kirantis dynasty ruled Nepal from about 700 BC until after AD 100.[1] During this period, Buddha was born (in 560 BC) and Buddhism was introduced into Nepal. After the rule of the Kirantis, the Maurya, Lichhavis, Thakuris, Karantakas, Mallas and Shah racial groups emerged. They were migrants from the plain.[2] Also during this period, the Nepalese enjoyed very good relations with China, Tibet and India, their relations with the latter being developed through marriages, trade and cultural intercourse.[3]

In the fourteenth century, the Mallas overthrew the Thakuris and organized the society of Nepal according to the severe orthodox caste laws of the Hindus. Jaksha Malla ruled for fifty years and extended his power far beyond the Nepal valley. In 1488, he divided the kingdom among his four heirs, and the resulting four small kingdoms (Kathmandu, Bhatgaon, Patan and Banepa) persisted until the Gurkha conquest of 1769.[4] About this period, Francis Hamilton wrote in his book, *An Account of the Kingdom of Nepal*:

'In particular, I obtained little or no information concerning the history of the princes who governed Nepal at the time of the conquest; except that the Newars had been long subject to a family of their own nation, all the members of which assumed the name of Mal, and, for some time previous to the conquest, had separated into three lordships, Kathmandu or Kathmaro, Lalita Patan and Bhatgang, which circumstance greatly facilitated the enterprise of the chief of Gorkha.'[5]

Chaudhuri confirms these historical points, writing:

'The Gurkhas inhabited the place of the same name, which was one of the four sovereign principalities into which Nepal then was divided. These were: Kathmandu, Patan or Lalita Patan, Bhatgang and Gurkha.'[6]

As mentioned earlier, the unification of Nepal was started by the

[1] Hagen, Toni, *Nepal, the Kingdom in the Himalayas*, p. 81. Berne: Kümmerly and Frey, 1961.
[2] Regmi, *op. cit.*, p. 40.
[3] Hagen, *op. cit.*, p. 83.
[4] *Ibid.*, p. 84.
[5] Hamilton, Francis, *An Account of the Kingdom of Nepal*, p. 186. Edinburgh: Archibald Constable and Co., 1819.
[6] Chaudhuri, *op. cit.*, p. 5.

small kingdom of Gurkha. The Gurkha rulers originally came from a few families of the Rajput Kshatriyas who were driven out of Chitor, India, in 1303 by Sultan Alou-d-din. These homeless warriors wandered about the Nuwakot, Kaski and Lamjang areas of Nepal until, in 1559, they settled in Gurkha after overthrowing the Khadga Raja, the then Gurkha ruler. In 1742, Prithvi Narayan became King of Gurkha. Narayan, an ambitious ruler who wanted to enlarge his kingdom, set out with his army to conquer the other small kingdoms of the area. Unable to develop any unity of opposition, the petty chiefs and rajahs of the Nepal area succumbed to Narayan in quick succession.[1] In further campaigns, he conquered parts of India (namely the Terai, Kumaon, Garhwal, Simla and Sikkim areas) and also large areas of the Tibet plateau and the valleys of the inner Himalayas.[2] When he conquered Mackwanpur, he aroused the hostility of the English East India Company (hereafter called the Company) and Nawab Mir Kasim of Bengal. Mir Kasim sent a force to help the Rajah of Mackwanpur but the force was repulsed by Narayan's troops and Mackwanpur was subsequently conquered.

The Rajah of Kathmandu was the only ruler to make a strong defense against Narayan. When his turn for conquest came, he requested the help of the Company. The English agreed to send aid, hoping to obtain 'the revival of Indo-Nepalese trade relations which had been disturbed recently by the Gurkha conquests'.[3] The English had the additional and humanitarian motive of attempting to save the people of Kathmandu from being massacred by the Gurkha forces. This danger was illustrated by the report of Father Giuseppe, Prefect of the Roman Mission, who wrote in part:

'... Pirt'hwi Narayan, who was at Navacuta (a long day's journey distant) issued an order to Suruparatna his brother to put to death some of the principal inhabitants of the town, and to cut off the noses and lips of everyone, even the infants, who were not in the arms of their mothers; ordering at the same time all the noses and lips which had been cut off, to be preserved, that he might ascertain how many souls there were, and to change the name of the town into Nakkatapur.'[4]

In 1767, the Company sent a Captain Kinloch with a small force to assist the Rajah of Kathmandu. Kinloch's force captured Sindhuli,

[1] Chaudhuri, *op. cit.*, p. 9 and Hagen, *op. cit.*, pp. 81–5.
[2] Hagen, *op. cit.*, p. 85.
[3] Chaudhuri, *op. cit.*, p. 20.
[4] Giuseppe, Father, 'An account of the Kingdom of Nepal', *Bengal Asiatic Research Society*. Communicated by John Shore, Esq. Typed copy in the British Embassy, Kathmandu, Nepal.

an important fort at the foot of the Nepal hills, but was unable to penetrate further into the mountains and subsequently returned to India with its mission not accomplished. Chaudhuri writes of the failure of the Kinloch expedition:

'(i) Heavy rain set in and lasted for many days. This rendered a river (Bagmati) impassable. Further, the roads were not so good as the Vakeels of the Nepal Raja Jayprakash Malla had given them out to be. (ii) Scarcity of grains began to be so severely felt that the troops were living on starvation scale provisions. Despite extreme scarcity of foodgrains the expedition would have certainly pushed on to Nepal but for the uncertainties of the hill rivers. (iii) Although the strongest assurances were given by the Rajah's men to provide grain for the detachment in large quantities once it reached Sindhuli, actually it did not come. (iv) The loss of Sindhuli dispirited the Gurkha troops and it was in fitness of things that Capt. Kinloch would try to push as quickly as possible to the relief of the Nepal Raja when chances of success against the Gurkhas seemed to be brighter. But the unlucky circumstances of bad weather, and the reluctance of the Bazar people to provide grains to the expeditionary troops made it impossible for Capt. Kinloch to reach Nepal. (v) The camp followers started deserting, particularly after some of the stragglers on the road were killed by the Gurkhas; this made the situation worse. (vi) All the above circumstances coupled with the bad behaviour of the sepoys made Capt. Kinloch decide not to run further risks but return to Janakpur.'[1]

After the return of Kinloch's expedition, Prithvi Narayan had no strong opponent to contend with. He overthrew the Rajah of Kathmandu in 1769. He then consolidated all the four kingdoms previously existing into a new 'Kingdom of Nepal' and became its king.

One cannot deny the spirit and zeal with which Prithvi Narayan made Nepal a united, strong, and independent country out of many smaller principalities. By the end of the eighteenth century, the Kingdom of Nepal was about twice as large as it is today, extending from Punjab to Sikkim.[2] In spite of his barbarous and ferocious nature, Prithvi Narayan gave Nepal the prestige of being a sovereign country, which it did not have prior to 1769. He established a centralized government and infused a feeling of nationalism into the minds and hearts of the Nepalese. Without any doubt, he should be called the 'founder and builder of Modern Nepal'.

[1] Chaudhuri, *op. cit.*, pp. 26–7.
[2] Hagen, *op. cit.*, p. 85.

A GENERAL SURVEY

Position of the East India Company in India

It would perhaps be useful at this point to review the early history of the East India Company in India. It will be recalled that Europe's first contacts with India were during the Mogul period[1] and were based on economic trade motives rather than political relations. In the year 1600, the East India Company obtained a royal charter giving it the exclusive right to trade in the East. Accordingly, the Company sent an envoy to the Mogul Emperor at Delhi to obtain permission to establish a trading post on the Indian coast. Sir Thomas Roe, the Company's first ambassador to the Mogul court, made it clear that the policy of the Company would be to promote trade and not to acquire territory. He declared the policy of the Company thus: 'Let this be received as a rule that, if you will profit, seek it at sea and in quiet trade.'[2] The Mogul Emperor accepted this declaration and for over a century the East India Company depended for its protection upon the power of the Great Moguls.

The decay of the Mogul Empire during the eighteenth century forced the abandonment of this policy. At the same time, the rivalry between Great Britain and France in Europe forced the hands of the British, compelling them to indulge in politics in India. The French ambition to destroy the influence of Britain in trade in India led to a serious armed conflict which started in 1746 and ended in 1760 with complete defeat of the French at Wandewash. Simultaneously, the collapse of the authority of the Great Mogul embroiled the Company with one of his successors, the Nawab of Bengal. The total defeat of the Nawab by Clive at the battle of Plassey in 1757 gave the Company control of Bengal. This was the first step in the creation of the British empire in India.

Because of these wars, the revenue and profits of the Company fell sharply. Widespread corruption and bribery developed among the Company's employees.[3] To check their misconduct and to provide help to the Indian people, the British Parliament passed the 'Act of 1774' which, with minor modifications, remained in operation as the governing instrument of British rule in India till 1858. Under this act, authority to appoint the Governor-General and other officials remained in the hands of the Company Directors, and the Company retained undisputed control of commerce in India. However, its political activities were supervised and placed under the final control of a British Cabinet minister, the President of the Board of Control. Later,

[1] Coupland, R., *Britain and India, 1600–1941*, p. 3. London: Longmans Green and Co., Ltd., n.d.
[2] *Ibid.*, p. 4.
[3] Coupland, *op. cit.*, pp. 6–17.

the Act of 1813 deprived the Company of its India trade monopoly and by the Act of 1833, it lost the monopoly of the trade with China and was asked to end all its commercial dealings. Until its final dissolution in 1858, it was no longer in any sense a body of merchants, but purely a political and administrative machine.[1] Its importance was shown by Sir Reginald Coupland who wrote that, '. . . by 1820, all India from Cape Comorin to the eastern margin of the Indus plain and the Punjab had been brought, directly or indirectly, under British rule'.[2]

Nepal's Relations with the East India Company

Relations between the East India Company and the four small kingdoms of Nepal were insignificant. Indeed, no significant trade or other relationships developed with a government in the Nepal region until after Prithvi Narayan united Nepal under his rule in 1769. From that time until the mid-nineteenth century, Nepalese–Company relations remained unsettled and often marred with misunderstandings, hostilities and enmity. Later discussion will show that both parties actually wanted to maintain peace but circumstances forced them into conflict with each other. And, in spite of these conflicts, continuing efforts were made by both parties to come to peaceful terms with each other.

The East India Company, as noted earlier, was mainly interested in trade with India. Yet, it could not avoid becoming involved in such political side-issues as the Nepalese–Tibetan conflict, Nepal's internal political crises and the expansionist tendencies of Prithvi Narayan and his successors. In 1770, following the failure of the Kinloch expedition, the Company made an attempt to improve trade relations with Nepal by sending James Logan to Nepal to sound out the Nepalese Government on the matter. Unfortunately, Logan became involved in internal Nepalese politics and took a position supporting ousted Malla king Jayprakash of Kathmandu against Prithvi Narayan. Long before Logan could succeed in his intrigues, Narayan had established himself in full control in Kathmandu.[3] Logan's trade mission was a complete failure and no further reference to Logan is found in available historical records.[4]

The failure of the Company to halt Prithvi Narayan's vigorous expansionist activities caused the British to become rather disturbed about the security of their border with Nepal. The Company exercised considerable caution in dealing with the Nepal Durbar, not wishing

[1] Coupland, *op. cit.*, pp. 21–2.
[2] *Ibid.*, p. 7.
[3] Chaudhuri, *op. cit.*, pp. 34–9.
[4] *Ibid.*, p. 28.

to incite bad feelings that might lead to war. But the credit for maintaining peace on the Nepal–India border goes to the British Governor-General, Warren Hastings, who, during the turbulent period of his Governor-Generalship from April 1772 to February 1785, successfully maintained a policy of tactful non-intervention with Prithvi Narayan, Pratap Singh and Rana Bahadur Shah, the rulers of Nepal during this period.

Hastings adopted his non-intervention policy because he was aware of the suspicion with which the 'hill people' (Nepalese) regarded the British. For their part, the Rajahs of Nepal sealed off the Nepalese border because they thought that trade would be followed by soldiers and political penetration. Yet Hastings' policy did exert an important influence on the Rajahs since, in spite of their suspicion, they did not want to antagonize the British to the extent of forcing recourse to arms. Thus, neither side wanted to go so far as to jeopardize the state of peace between them and each wished to retain the friendship of the other.

An example of this situation occurred when Rajah Chait Singh of the State of Bejaygarh revolted against the Company. Gurkha military aid was thought to be needed by the Company in order to crush the revolt. Prithvi Narayan readily came to the Company's aid, using this incident to impress on the British the fact that Nepal was friendly toward them and desired friendly official relations with the Company, while at the same time keeping them at arm's length. However, before the Nepalese help arrived, Bejaygarh was captured. Nonetheless, Governor-General Hastings remembered this incident with favor. In a letter written in 1784 to Rana Bahadur Shah (then King of Nepal), Hastings recalled the Bejaygarh incident, noting his previous friendly relations with Prithvi Narayan and expressing his desire for continued friendly relations between the two parties.[1]

Four successive Governors-General: Hastings, Cornwallis, Shore and Wellesley, worked to maintain peaceful relations with Nepal and to promote increased trade with the Company. Each of them sent friendly letters together with a mission to the King of Nepal. Nothing came of their efforts until 1787 when a rupture in Nepalese–Tibetan relations occurred over certain currency problems.[2] Soon afterward, China joined the conflict on the side of Tibet. At this time Rana Bahadur Shah wrote to the Company in India for help. Lord Cornwallis, then Governor-General, did not want to decline the request, nor did he want to bring on trouble with China by joining the Nepalese side. Hence, he decided to promote a settlement between the parties,

[1] Chaudhuri, *op. cit.*, pp. 53–9.
[2] Regmi, *Modern Nepal*, p. 169. Calcutta, 1961.

sending a mission headed by Col. Kirkpatrick. However, before the Kirkpatrick mission managed to reach Nepal, the Chinese had forced a humiliating treaty on the King of Nepal. He agreed to acknowledge Chinese suzerainty and to send a tributary mission to China every five years, with presents for the Chinese Emperor. After this treaty, the Nepalese were no longer enthusiastic about receiving the English representative. The only positive result to come from the Kirkpatrick mission was a commercial treaty signed in 1792 by Nepal and the East India Company.

In 1795, Governor-General Sir John Shore decided to send another embassy, headed by Maulvi Abdul Qadir, to Nepal. Shore selected Maulvi Saheb because he thought the Nepalese would be 'less apprehensive of an Indian Muslim (Maulvi Saheb) than of a Firanghee, (and probably also because the British did not feel they could trust an Indian Hindu to go to a Hindu state). Maulvi Saheb was, in addition, an experienced and trusted servant of the Company. His mission did not produce any new treaty as had the previous Cornwallis mission, but it did acquire some valuable information regarding trade possibilities. Maulvi suggested to the Government of India that the latter should open a factory or trading post in Nepal, but this was not done.

Prithvi Narayan died in 1775 and was succeeded by Pratap Singh who died in 1778. Rana Bahadur succeeded Pratap Singh in 1778, at the age of three and one-half years. His mother, Queen Rajendra Lakhshmi, was appointed Regent to look after the infant King and administer the country. During Rana Bahadur's minority, there was a struggle for power for the Regency between Rana Bahadur's mother and his uncle, Bahadur Shah. Finally, in 1794, when Rana Bahadur reached the age of twenty, he murdered his uncle and took the reins of government in his own hands. For five years, he carried on what could best be described as a 'reign of terror'.[1]

Like other previous rulers of Nepal, Rana Bahadur tried to show friendship toward the British. When in 1797 the Nawab Wazir of Oudh died, Wazir Ali who had hoped to succeed to the position was bypassed by his rival, Sa'adat Ali, with the help of the British. Wazir Ali, regarding the British as his enemies, killed several of them and fled into the hills of the Terai. As soon as Rana Bahadur learned of this, he wrote to the Governor-General of India offering full help in capturing Wazir Ali. This was considered by the British as a friendly

[1] Aitchison, C. U., *A Collection of Treaties, Engagements, Sunnuds, Relating to India and Neighboring Countries*, Vol. II, p. 188. Calcutta, Bengal Printing Co., Ltd., 1863.
Rose, Leo E. and Fisher, Margaret W., *England, India, Nepal, Tibet, China, 1765-1958*. Berkeley: University of California Press, 1959.
Chaudhuri, *op. cit.*, pp. 98-105.

act on the part of Rana Bahadur because he offered his assistance without any prior request from the Company.[1]

The British lost their 'friend' in 1799, when Rana Bahadur's ill temper and barbarous acts finally became too much to bear and he was forced by his Nepalese courtiers to abdicate in favor of his one-and-a-half-year-old son. He then retired to Banares. His departure brought the need for a regency in Nepal to look after the infant ruler. But this time, the regency was invested dually in the hands of Queen Raj Rajeshwari (one of Rana Bahadur's wives) and a joint council. Soon another queen, Subarna Prabha, overthrew the dual regency and took over as Regent of the child King. One of her acts was to appoint Damodar Pande as her chief administrator. This was a significant change since it was the first time that a chief administrator (or Prime Minister) had been appointed in Nepal.[2] Until that time, the country had been ruled directly by the King (or Rajah) or, when the king was a minor, by a regent.

After the exiled Rana Bahadur arrived in India, the Company decided that a fresh attempt should be made to bring about closer relations with Nepal and to press for full implementation of their commercial treaty of 1792 (the treaty concluded by the Kirkpatrick mission, noted earlier). Nepalese internal problems and intrigues were of such a nature that the treaty had not been implemented by the Nepal Government and the Company felt that greater Nepalese efforts to fulfil the treaty were desirable. The Company additionally wanted to make some arrangements for surrender of fugitive dacoits (robbers), a matter that was creating a problem on the border. At the same time, the Company attempted to keep Rana Bahadur in India by providing him with full honors and a handsome pension, thus hoping to please an old friend and also to win favor with the courtiers in Nepal by removing Rana Bahadur from Nepalese politics.

Moving to take advantage of this period of improved Nepalese relations, the Company deputed Captain Knox to negotiate in Nepal for a new treaty and to press for the establishment of a Residency in Kathmandu. After lengthy negotiations, a treaty of friendship was signed in October 1801. Relations with India were almost settled when Rana Bahadur's older Rani, who had gone with him to Banares, returned to Nepal and took the country into her own hands. Captain Knox, whose negotiations had been with the previous leaders, faced an impossible situation and finally in 1803 returned to India. In 1804, Lord Wellesley abrogated the treaty. Upon the dissolution of the treaty, the Company had no further obligation to keep Rana Bahadur in

[1] Chaudhuri, *ibid.*
[2] Rose and Fisher, *op. cit.*, p. 3.

India, so he returned to Nepal in 1804 and once again took control of the government—thus completing the circle.

In Nepal at that time, the Pandes and Thapas were the two major families outside the royal family. In the struggle for power in 1800, Queen Raj Rajeshwari was supported by the Pandes and appointed Damodar Pande as the chief administrator. But when Rana Bahadur returned to Kathmandu from exile, he overthrew Damodar Pande and himself became chief administrator. He soon banished his queen, Raj Rajeshwari, and became all powerful as Regent and chief administrator. After two years Rana Bahadur was killed and another of his queens, Tripura Sundari, became the Regent. In 1806, she appointed Bhim Sen Thapa (of the Thapa family) as the chief administrator. Bhim Sen Thapa remained in power continuously for thirty years.[1]

Administration of Bhim Sen Thapa

This period of thirty years (1806–36) was one of the most troublesome and irritating phases of British–Nepalese relations since their beginning in 1769. One major contributing factor was that there was no agreement to govern their relations except the Treaty of 1792, which remained a dead letter almost from the day it was signed. But the most important cause of hostility was Bhim Sen Thapa's policy of encroachment on British territory and expansion of Nepal to the Kashmir border and to the Sutleg River.[2] (His expansion beyond the Sutleg was frustrated by the signing of a treaty between Rajah Ranjit Singh and the Government of India in 1809.) In May 1810, the British Government once again tried by negotiations to improve the relations between themselves and the Nepalese, but affairs gradually went from bad to worse until they became unendurable.[3]

The War of 1814–16

'In May 1814 the Gurkhas suddenly raided three police posts in Butwal in the Gorkhpur District, killing its inhabitants. This incident served as the immediate *casus belli*.'[4] After this deliberate provocation, the British were left with no alternative but to declare war on Nepal, and so, they took this step on November 1, 1814. The military situation was relatively even. British military forces were commanded by four able and experienced generals: Marley, Wood, Gillespie and Ochterlony.

[1] Aitchison, *op. cit.*, p. 189.
[2] Chaudhuri, *op. cit.*, p. 145.
[3] Wright, Daniel, ed., *History of Nepal*, p. 31. Calcutta: Susil Gupta, 1958.
[4] Majumdar, Kanchanmoy, 'Indo-Nepalese Relations, 1837–1877'. Unpublished Ph.D. thesis, Indian School of International Studies, New Delhi, 1962, p. 26.

A GENERAL SURVEY

The Nepalese-Gurkhas, however, were in an advantageous position as they were fully aware of the military routes and the tactics best suited to a terrain consisting of mountains and jungles. Also, the Gurkhas were on the defensive and the British were forced to take the offensive against them, which is always a more difficult military role. This was the first time the British had come into direct combat with the Gurkha soldiers and they came to admire the Gurkhas for their loyalty, bravery and courage. This impression of the Gurkhas was a lasting one; later the idea of Gurkha recruitment for the British Army became a cardinal point of their policy toward Nepal.

The Nepalese campaign was a most arduous one, with both sides fighting bravely. In the beginning, the British suffered heavy losses; but gradually the tide of the campaign turned in their favor—though not without a considerable military effort on their part. General Gillespie, one of the main commanders, was killed and Generals Marley and Wood went through the most difficult campaign of their long careers. General Ochterlony was the most successful British field commander. He pushed a Gurkha army beyond the Kali River, forcing them to sue for peace; but this peace overture was short-lived because of the military successes the Gurkhas were having against the other British commanders. At this point, General Ochterlony was placed in supreme command of the British forces. Under his leadership, the British captured the strategic town of Mackwanpur. This success brought them within thirty miles of Kathmandu, the Nepalese capital city. The Gurkhas were now exhausted, their forces shattered and their morale very low. They capitulated and on December 2, 1815, signed a peace treaty dictated by the British.

But the military action was not yet over. The Gurkhas, wishfully thinking to defeat the British in a second encounter, backed down on the 1815 peace treaty and resumed the conflict. Finally they were defeated again and forced to sign a peace treaty at Segowlee in March 1816.[1]

The defeat of the Gurkha army made two things clear to the Nepalese: (1) the East India Company was a powerful force in India to reckon with, and (2) it was better for the Gurkhas not to come into direct armed conflict with it in the future. But a British defeat in the Gurkha War could have had a disastrous effect on their rule in India and other parts of Asia. Undoubtedly the history of India would have been considerably different, since in 1814 the Maratha confederacy was still a very formidable power. The Marathas and some of the other states of India were watching the war in Nepal with much interest; and it is obvious that they would have been encouraged to engage in hostilities

[1] Majumdar, K., *op. cit.*, pp. 27–37; Wright, *op. cit.*, p. 32.

against the British with more vigor and hope had the British been defeated by the Gurkhas.

All the hopes of the Marathas and the other Indian states were shattered with the signing of the peace treaty at Segowlee by the Gurkhas. Now, the British could turn their armies to the other rebellious areas and subdue them. The third Maratha War brought the complete defeat of the Marathas by the British in 1819, and British supremacy became generally accepted in India. The next major challenge to their authority would not come until the Mutiny of 1857.

Treaty of Segowlee

The treaty of Segowlee was completely different from the two earlier treaties the British had with Nepal. The Treaty of 1792 had been commercial in nature and the Treaty of 1801 was merely an acceptance of friendly relations between the two countries. But the Segowlee treaty had political overtones and was accepted as 'political' by both parties. In all, the treaty comprised nine articles. The first article stated that both countries should live in perpetual peace and friendship. Articles two to five dealt mostly with the cession of territory by Nepal. Ceded by Nepal was most of the Terai (or lowlands) west of the river Kali (this territory was subsequently handed back by the British to the Indian state of Oudh from which it had been taken earlier by the Gurkhas). Nepal also ceded the districts of Kumaon and Garhwal and all of the Terai land west of the Gandak River. The British government agreed to give Nepal two lakhs of rupees ($38,000) annually as pensions to Nepalese chiefs for their ceded territories, although this section was annulled in December 1816, when the British government returned the Terai land between the Raptee and the Koori to Nepal.

As to Sikkim, the Nepalese government agreed not to molest or disturb the Rajah of Sikkim and in all differences between these two states, British arbitration was accepted.

The article most disliked by Nepal in the entire treaty was Article Seven.[1] This article implemented Governor-General Wellesley's policy to prevent employment of French officers by the Nepalese. Article Seven read as follows:

'The Rajah of Nepal hereby engages never to take or retain in his service any British subject, nor the subject of any European or American state, without the consent of the British Government.'[2]

The reason for this prohibition came from British experience twenty years earlier with the Sultan of Mysore who had established diplomatic

---

[1] Aitchison, *op. cit.*, p. 207; Majumdar, K., *op. cit.*, pp. 27–31; Wright, *op. cit.*, pp. 31–2. [2] Aitchison, *op. cit.*, p. 207.

relations with the French Republic. His representative made plans with the French for an attack on the British by Mysore supported by a French army. Also, French officers had made the Maratha armies unpleasantly efficient. After these experiences, the British announced a policy of forbidding any Indian prince to hire any foreign nationals in their governmental services or armies without British permission. While Nepal in the past had not employed any non-Asian nationals in their government or army, the British used the 1816 treaty to impose the same restriction upon them as on the Indian princes.

In one important respect, however, Nepal had a position superior to the princely states of India. They were forbidden to have diplomatic relations with one another for fear they might form a military alliance directed against the East India Company. By contrast, no restrictions were placed on the right of Nepal to maintain diplomatic relations with foreign states and she continued to have such relations with China and Tibet. Nepal's position was also unique in that she alone had the right to maintain a diplomatic representative in Calcutta. In the Treaty of 1816, both governments agreed that an 'accredited "Minister" from each shall reside at the court of the other'.[1] This was a significant change from the Treaty of 1801 where both governments had only agreed to appoint a 'confidential person to each other, as Vakeil'.[2] Mr Gardiner was the first British Resident to be appointed under the 1816 Treaty and he proceeded to his post at Kathmandu in that same year.[3]

The Treaty of 1816 thus gave Nepal the status of an independent state as regards relations with the British Government in India, while also not prohibiting diplomatic relations with other Asian and European states. As such, it constituted significant recognition of Nepal's claims as a sovereign country.

Post-War Relations

Nepal had lost the war but Prime Minister Bhim Sen Thapa had not accepted the Treaty of 1816 as constituting the final word on British relations with Nepal. He used every possible method to avoid close relations with the British. He even tried to get help from China to expel the British Resident and if possible renew the war, but he was unsuccessful in this design.[4] The British government, however, wanted to follow a conciliatory policy towards Nepal. Gardiner, the new

[1] Aitchison, *op. cit.*, pp. 196 and 207.
[2] *Vakeil* is a Persian and Urdu word for the diplomatic representative of a government. Now obsolete and no longer used, it originally meant 'one who could argue the case of others, as an attorney'.
[3] Wright, *op. cit.*, p. 32.
[4] Ibid.

Resident, was told that he should try to remove 'all future causes of misunderstanding', and should maintain a friendly attitude towards the Nepalese Durbar (court) with the idea of strengthening the confidence of the Nepalese in the British government.[1] The British were aware of Nepal's intrigues with China against them, but nevertheless hoped to establish better relations with the Durbar. For their part, the British did not want to annex more territory, and they saw no gain in another war with first-class fighting men who had an understandable feeling of enmity and a strong patriotic determination to maintain their independence. An additional reason was that the final war against the Marathas was about to break out. So in a policy statement, the Resident was informed that:

'The Government have no motives for reducing the Nepal power and resources below the present state, when many powerful considerations suggest the expediency of avoiding a war with that people, however justly provoked.'[2]

This policy of conciliation and friendship was evident all through the British relations with the Nepalese from 1816 to 1947 when they left India. In the long run, this policy amply repaid the Government of India, as later chapters will show.

The last month of 1816 saw a new two-and-a-half year old king ascend the throne of Nepal. This came at the time just after the end of the war with the British and the signing of the Segowlee Treaty. With the King unable to rule, the entire power of government stayed in the hands of Bhim Sen Thapa, who governed Nepal with an iron hand.

From the time he came to power, Bhim Sen Thapa made it his policy to maintain cool and distant relations with the British. The conspiracies against the British did not diminish at any time; indeed, the Nepal Durbar tried to enlist support against the British from some of the Indian princes, but was unsuccessful. All attempts by the British to renew a commercial treaty or to establish close relations with the Nepal Government were frustrated. Fortunately, this policy of aloofness and isolation did not bring the Nepalese government back into armed hostility with the British. In part, this may have been due to the British realization that despite his anti-British policy, Bhim Sen was a strong and capable Prime Minister who succeeded in maintaining a stable government. B. H. Hodgson (Resident from 1833-43), in one of his reports, wrote:

[1] Majumdar, K., *op. cit.*, pp. 33–7.
[2] *Ibid.*

'If Bhim Sen continues to rule unchecked, his death or retirement would be followed by a civil war which would be detrimental to the peace and commerce of our two countries.'¹

Because of the power of Bhim Sen, the King became a political cipher. In 1833, only a year after the death of the Regent, Queen Tripura Sundari,² he made an attempt to free himself from the clutches of Bhim Sen but failed.

The Nepalese king was not the only one who was afraid of the power of Bhim Sen. Even the powerful Government of India was on the alert. Hodgson, while respecting the stability that Bhim Sen brought to the Nepalese government, nevertheless became very disturbed over Bhim Sen's growing military power. He felt that Bhim Sen posed a distinct threat to continued British domination of India. He wrote:

'... Upon the whole, then, Nepal is fully as formidable at this moment (1833) as she was before the war. She hangs like a thundercloud on the heart of our territory, and with the command of 30,000 soldiers as well armed and disciplined as our own, and vastly superior to ours in every moral respect, she has at this moment, no aim but war.'³

He compared Nepal to 'a thorn in the side of the growing British empire'. He suggested that either it must be 'uprooted or its edge had to be rounded'. Failing this, he thought there would be 'no security for British India'.⁴ Hodgson thus tried to convince his government that it must take a firm attitude toward the Nepalese. He went so far as to urge a change in the policy of non-intervention, but his arguments were not accepted.

One important decision taken by Bhim Sen Thapa during this period was helpful to the cause of peace. It was his agreement to the delimitation of the frontier between Nepal and the Indian state of Oudh. A commission was set up consisting of representatives of the Nepalese and Oudh governments and a British chairman. The commission completed its boundary demarcation work in 1833 and its recommendations were accepted by all parties. As Sir Francis Tuker stated, 'a

---
¹ Kumar, Satish, 'Political System of Nepal under the Ranas, 1845–1901'. Unpublished Ph.D. thesis, Indian School of International Studies, New Delhi, 1961.
² She was the last of the Regents (1806–32), wife of Rana Bahadur and grandmother of King Rajendra Vikram Shah (who succeeded to the throne of Nepal in December 1816 on the death of King Girvan Juddha Vikran Shah at the age of nineteen).
³ Majumdar, K., *op. cit.*, pp. 46–60.
⁴ *Ibid.*

common cause of friction and standing excuse for Gurkha aggression was at long last removed'.[1]

Bhim Sen Thapa ruled Nepal singlehanded for thirty years. For over a generation he held down his rivals, the Pandes, with an iron hand; he fought the intrigues of the king and the queen; he made the king his puppet; he built a strong army for Nepal; and he faced his most powerful neighbor, the British government, with his policy of isolation and strong government. In the secret communications of the Residents, he was appreciated, feared and admired. Bhim Sen had determination, conviction, courage, administrative ability and ambition. He was ruthless to his internal enemies, he was hungry for power, and he knew that his only alternative was utter ruin. But when the end arrived, it came too tragically for so great a man. Francis Tuker, in his book *Gorkha, The Story of the Gurkhas of Nepal*, described the fall of Bhim Sen Thapa in the following words:

'In 1837 Nepal was due to send to Peking the quinquennial Embassy and presents, under the terms of the treaty of 1792. It had been for Bhim Sen to choose the delegation, but this time the King insisted on his prerogative. Not daring to go so far as to insult his Prime Minister by appointing a Pande to lead it, he selected one of his own cousins, a Chauntriya. On this, the whole edifice of the Thapas began to crumble. The importunate Brahmans obtained for one of their men Raghunath Pandit, the appointment of Chief Justice; Ran Jang Pande received from the King the lands, goods and honours the family had lost to Bhim Sen; Mathbar Singh was dismissed from his post at the head of the Government of Gorkha and another son of Damodar Pande took his place. But Bhim Sen remained untouched.

'Then came the end. The Senior Queen of all people, his enemy, suddenly lost her young son. At once the Pande spread about the rumour that Bhim Sen had attempted to poison the Queen, but missed his mark. The court and administration at Kathmandu were plunged into confusion. Ran Jang Pande, at the King's ear, persuaded him to strike at once. Forthwith, the jealous prince seized Bhim Sen, degraded him and cast him in irons into prison. Mathbar was secured and thrown in to join his uncle. Ran Jang Pande seized supreme power, consumed with lust for vengeance. Evidence against the tyrant was needed. The Baids—the doctors—were put to the torture. Then one confessed, falsely, to having been ordered by the fallen chief to administer the poison. To seal his mouth, he was then either tortured till he died or, more mercifully, just crucified. Another was burned on

[1] Tuker, Sir Francis, *Gorkha, The Story of the Gurkhas of Nepal*, p. 101. London: Constable and Co., 1957.

the forehead with hot irons till the brain was exposed, and on the cheek till the bone was laid bare. Yet another, a Newar, was impaled and his heart cut out while he still lived, but no corroboration of the one poor confession could be obtained. The King was an enthralled spectator of these doings. Landon says that four years later the Pandes confessed that the whole charge was false.

'... The cowards did not, even then, dare to execute him. Ran Jang gave orders that by savage treatment he was to be brought to suicide. Beside him they placed a kukri, hoping. Bhim Sen held out against all they could do. Then they brought him news, true or false, that his wife had been compelled to walk naked in broad day-light through the streets of Kathmandu. With kukri so handy, he pierced his throat. For nine days he lingered, then ended his tragic life. The date is 29th July 1839.'[1]

Bhim Sen's Fall and Its Effects on Nepal's Politics

The death of the powerful Prime Minister was followed by bloodshed, disintegration of the administrative system, and a chaotic situation. Nepal once again became the scene of bitter internal intrigues by the King, the Queen and the various rival power seekers, all of whom killed their opponents without hesitation. The barbarity displayed became so distasteful to the British government that the Governor-General expressed his feelings of 'extreme disgust and abhorrence at the measures of indignity, insult and cruelty which the Government of Nepal has adopted towards the late and able minister of that State'.[2] The Government of India was also concerned because the fall of Bhim Sen did not improve British relations with Nepal. In fact, the 'war party' of Ran Jang Pande became an influential power in the state. Never in the affairs of the two states had tension become so strong, even surpassing the tension of 1814. Fortunately for the Nepalese, the British at that time were surrounded on all sides by problems. China and Burma were threatening, the condition on the northwest frontier was not under control, the invasion of Afghanistan was about to commence and above all, the military state of the Indian army was far from reassuring.[3]

The Queen and the Pandes, as the main architects of the anti-British policy, proceeded to build up pressure for war against the British. As part of this plot, the Nepalese soldiers were told that their pay was to be reduced, by order of the Government of India. The agitation was further inflamed when the King informed them that the

---

[1] Tuker, *op. cit.*, pp. 102–3.
[2] *Ibid.*, p. 105.
[3] Majumdar, K., *op. cit.*, pp. 62–102.

real reason for their pay cut was to provide Nepal with funds for the invasion of India.[1] The result of this announcement was that the soldiers, though they had seen little service since 1816, suddenly wanted to move to Lucknow and Patna and throw the British out of India—and an army of 30,000 well-trained and well-disciplined Gurkha soldiers was a serious matter! Hodgson's life was in danger and was only saved by his timely warning to the King that he had been aware of the whole plot and that word of it was, by now, far outside the confines of Nepal and speeding to Calcutta across the plains of India. This bombshell frustrated the plans of the conspirators and the entire conspiracy collapsed.[2] The death of the Queen in October 1841 finally ended the hopes of the 'war party' and the Pandes for enlistment of the support of the Maratha chieftains, the Sikhs, the Rajputs and the Amir of Afghanistan, with whom she had corresponded.[3]

During this entire period from 1837 to 1841, the British continued to maintain a conciliatory policy toward Nepal aimed at winning the friendship of the Nepal King. Auckland, then Governor-General of India, held to this policy believing that the Nepalese situation would improve, though gradually. Despite Hodgson's repeated warnings, Auckland did not change his mind. He wrote:

'A change in the military character and habits of the Nepal population would undoubtedly be most desirable. But we must not begin what it is hoped will be an approach to a better state of things by an appearance of thwarting or setting ourselves against the prevailing disposition of your nation of soldier-mountaineers.'[4]

In spite of the Governor-General's policy of forbearance and conciliation, his Council felt the need for formation of a pro-British Party in the Nepal Durbar. This party was to consist of the Junior Queen, the Thapas, the Guroos, the Chautarias and all other elements hostile to the Pandes,[5] even though its creation would involve British interference in Nepal's political affairs. In a parallel move, the Governor-General informed the Nepal government that if they did not withdraw their soldiers who had moved into Ramnager (in British territory), the British Government would force them out.

The combined effect of the British threat and the firm British attitude was that the Nepalese retired from Ramnager. This created

[1] Tuker, *op. cit.*, p. 106.
[2] *Ibid.;* Wright, *op. cit.*, p. 33; Kumar, *op. cit.*
[3] Tuker, *op. cit.*, p. 107.
[4] Mukerjee, K., *History of India* (Modern Period), Sixth Edition, p. 117. Calcutta: Mondal Brothers & Co., no date.
[5] *Ibid.*

dissension in the royal court. Hodgson, who had been instructed to see that the 'war party' was completely ousted from power, took full advantage of this crisis and publicly demanded the removal of Ran Jang Pande. His pressure was sufficient to force Ran Jang Pande's dismissal, after which the King presented the list of his proposed ministers to the Resident for approval. This act of the King led to the renewal of friendship between Nepal and India.[1]

As part of this renewed friendship, the Maharajah (King) of Nepal on November 6, 1839, signed an engagement under his Red Seal and sent it to the Resident. The Maharajah promised the cessation of all intrigues against the British, in or out of Nepal, and agreed to have no intercourse with the dependent allies of the Company except with the Resident's permission; British subjects would not be compelled to plead in civil suits in the courts of Nepal, and an authentic statement of all duties leviable in Nepal would be delivered to the Resident.[2]

The Governor-Generalship of Lord Auckland (1836-41) was a time of exceedingly serious problems in regard to Nepal. He had a Resident with whose policy he differed most of the time. But it was to the credit of both Lord Auckland and Hodgson that war with Nepal was avoided. Certainly, the procurement of the engagement from the Maharajah of Nepal in 1839 represented an important contribution by Hodgson to improved British-Nepalese relations.

Lord Ellenborough and the Retirement of Hodgson

It was at this time, with the 'war party' no longer in power, the Senior Queen dead (in 1841) and the anti-British Pandes ousted from all important government posts that Lord Ellenborough came to India as the new Governor-General. In Nepal, the previous era of hostilities had ended and a positive policy of friendship and co-operation was now in force. As an example of the 'new policy', the King of Nepal offered the services of the Royal Army of Nepal to the Indian Government to be used against the Afghans or against Burma.[3]

This new atmosphere of congeniality between Nepal and Britain was aided by Lord Ellenborough's firm policy of non-interference in the internal affairs of Nepal and the Indian princely states.[4] Lord Ellenborough felt that the Nepalese policy of his predecessor, Lord Auckland, had been a risky one; he also felt that those who had worked with Auckland were also responsible for his dangerous policy. He regarded Nepal as a 'foreign country' and believed that any overt

[1] Tuker, *op. cit.*, p. 107.
[2] Aitchison, *op. cit.*, pp. 212-13.
[3] Tuker, *op. cit.*, p. 109.
[4] Majumdar, K., *op. cit.*, pp. 221-2.

interference in the internal affairs of a foreign state was, in fact, a challenge to its dignity and independence. He disapproved of Hodgson's intriguing with the Nepalese political parties and with the King and Queen. He especially disapproved of Hodgson's (successful) efforts to act as 'kingmaker' in Nepal. His attitude of disapproval grew until finally he found it necessary to replace Hodgson as Resident and to assign Major H. Lawrence to the post.[1]

The retirement of Hodgson was felt in the Durbar. According to Tuker, 'the Raja burst into tears' and called him 'the Saviour of Nepal'.[2] Indeed, no one can doubt the ability, tact, judgment, loyalty and courage of Brian Hodgson, who was the British representative in Nepal for ten years. He was active not only as the British Resident but also as an astute politician, a 'kingmaker', and above all a scholar of the Himalayan regional languages, cultures, animal life, and people. But perhaps Hodgson's lasting monument is the thousands of manuscripts which he collected from Nepal and which are now kept in the India House Library in London.

Mathbar Singh's Prime Ministership

While Lord Ellenborough was engaged in modifying his government's foreign policy, a struggle for power was taking place in the Nepal Durbar. The major actors were the King, the Heir Apparent and the surviving Maharani (Queen) Lakhshmi Devi, with the King and the Heir Apparent openly fighting for control of the government. The Bahadurs (military leaders) and the influential civilian leaders of the government finally wearied of this quarrelling and forced the King to resign in favor of the Heir Apparent.

With this royal shakeup, Queen Lakhshmi Devi began to lose her grip on state affairs. She turned for help to Mathbar Singh, the nephew of Bhim Sen Thapa who was living in Simla supported by the British government's handsome (for that time) pension of one thousand rupees ($190.00) per month. Mathbar Singh had been closely following the intrigues and counter-intrigues developing in the royal capital. In fact, he later moved from Simla to Gorukpore, close to the border, in order to watch the situation from a better vantage point. A deputation of his well-wishers went to wait on him and bring him to Kathmandu. He arrived on April 17, 1843.[3] On the insistence of the Queen, Mathbar

---

[1] Tuker, *op. cit.*, p. 109; Majumdar, K., *op. cit.*, pp. 221-2.
[2] Tuker, *op. cit.*, p. 110.
[3] Nicholette, C. H., Assistant Resident, *Nepal Residency Records*, Serial No. 4, 1840-51.
Oldfield, in *Sketches from Nepal*, wrote that the deputation which went to escort Mathbar Singh to Kathmandu went there in February 1843, and escorted

Singh was restored to his family honors and property although he did not accept the prime ministership of Nepal immediately upon his return. However, he was subsequently appointed to the high offices of Prime Minister and Commander-in-Chief on December 26, 1843.[1] Once again, the Queen had succeeded in putting into office the man whom she wanted.

Mathbar was described by the new Resident, Sir Henry (then Major) Lawrence, as 'an intelligent young man, particularly expert in military matters but, though young in years, profoundly versed in intrigues'.[2] He was also to be remembered by the British as the first Nepalese Prime Minister to pay an official visit to the Governor-General.[3]

Immediately after assuming power, Mathbar took full revenge on the Pandes, killing them or exiling them from Nepal. This drastic but traditional act did not eliminate the court intrigue against him, however. The Queen found, to her great frustration, that Mathbar was not interested in setting aside the claim of the Heir Apparent in favor of her son. And from the beginning, the King was not happy with Mathbar because he was the Queen's nominee. A clever and devious

him back to Kathmandu on April 17th of the same year. Northey and Morris in *The Gurkhas*, gave the same date for the dispatch of the deputation. Nicholette, the Assistant Resident, gave the same date for Mathbar Singh's return to Kathmandu as Oldfield. Oldfield, H. A., *Sketches from Nepal*, Vol. I, p. 335. London: W. H. Allen & Co., 1880. Northey, W. Brook and Morris, C. J., *The Gurkhas, Their Manners, Customs and Country*, p. 53. London: John Lane, 1928.

[1] Nicholette, the Assistant Resident, wrote: 'On the 26th of December, Mathbar Singh was nominated to the Premiership, with full concurrence of all the Chiefs, including those of the late Ministry, thus nullifying the decree which was issued in 1839 to the effect that none of the Thappa clan should ever receive public employment for seven generations.' *Nepal Residency Records*, Serial No. 4, 1840–51. According to Oldfield, 'Mathbar remained out of office; he became the most influential person in the Darbar, and though the leaders of all sides paid court to him, he carefully held aloof, biding his time, and openly identified himself with none of the rival parties in the State.' He further writes, 'On the 25th of December, General Mathbar Singh was formally appointed Prime Minister and Commander-in-Chief.' Oldfield, *op. cit.*, p. 338.

Percival Landon, in his book *Nepal*, gives November 28, 1843, as the date when Mathbar became Prime Minister. (Landon, Percival, *Nepal*, Vol. I, p. 247. London: Constable and Co., 1928.)

Dr Leo Rose and Dr Margaret Fisher, however, hold that Mathbar Singh became Prime Minister in April 1843. *Nepal Residency Records* show that Mathbar became Prime Minister on December 26, 1843. These records are contemporary and completely reliable. Moreover, the *Residency Records* and Oldfield both state that Mathbar did not accept the office immediately after his return, so that it could be concluded that he became Prime Minister on December 26th, as stated in the *Nepal Residency Records*.

[2] Wright, *op. cit.*, p. 33.
[3] Foreign and Political Department, File No. 96 (4)-H 1934.

man, the King was careful not to let Mathbar know that he distrusted him. One example of this occurred during an annual function in the Durbar wherein the King named Mathbar as Prime Minister for life, 'for his services' and as a 'mark His of Highness's confidence in his future zeal'.[1] An appointment of this kind was unheard of in the history of Nepal. Yet at the same time, even though he elevated Mathbar with this extraordinary lifetime appointment, he was plotting with certain courtiers against Mathbar.

Events moved to a deadly climax. Several rivals, including Mathbar's nephew, Jung Bahadur, were gaining in favor with the various power groups in the royal court. Possessing a lifetime appointment as Prime Minister, Mathbar Singh blocked these other aspirants to the office. The inner circle of the King's advisers decided that Mathbar must be removed from office—permanently—and entered into intrigues aimed against Mathbar's life. At about the same time, the Queen came to the conclusion that Mathbar must be removed. She turned to Gagan Singh to organize a plot to eliminate Mathbar. Gagan Singh was the most influential minister in Mathbar Singh's cabinet and a major contender for the prime ministership. He was also the Queen's lover. It was his plot that won the race to assassinate the Prime Minister.

On May 17, 1845 (some scholars put the date at May 18, 1845), Mathbar Singh was summoned to the royal palace on the pretext that an accident had happened to the Queen. There are many differing accounts of what happened then, but it is enough to say that he came to the palace and was instantly shot. The King then informed the Governor-General of the assassination. In his letter, he accused Mathbar Singh of treason and other acts of disobedience, writing, 'therefore I put the said traitor Thappa to death with my own hands, killing him with gun and sword'. On this point, Sir Henry Lawrence (then Resident) stated, 'Gagan Singh and four or five others killed the Minister. The Maharaja may have mangled the corpse; but I must doubt His Highness having courage to fire a gun, much more to face his late Minister.'[2]

Despite Lawrence's statement, there remain several varied opinions as to who actually killed Mathbar Singh. Many scholars, among them Landon, Daniel Wright, Tuker and others, believe that Jung Bahadur was the actual assassin. Nicholette wrote in the *Nepal Residency Records* that Jung Bahadur had confessed to many people that he was the

---

[1] Nicholette, *op. cit.*; Oldfield, *op. cit.*, p. 342; Wheeler, James T., *India and the Frontier States of Afghanistan, Nepal and Burma*, p. 668. New York: Peter Fenelon Collier, 1899.

[2] Oldfield, *op. cit.*, p. 348.

murderer of his uncle. But other scholars, such as Oldfield and Northey,[1] put more blame for the murder on Gagan Singh and his friends. Of course, the king took the whole credit to himself when he wrote to the Governor-General. Realistically, it is impossible to determine who actually fired the gun that killed Mathbar Singh; the only certainty is that Gagan Singh was the plot ringleader.

Prime Ministership of Fatteh Jung

Once again the country was without a Prime Minister; again there was a crisis. Jung Bahadur was offered the prime ministership but declined it in favor of the post of Commander-in-Chief of the Army.[2] (He had come to realize that from this post he actually wielded more power than the Prime Minister.) The King then supported Fatteh Jung, a member of the Pande family who had fled to India during the purge of the Pandes by Mathbar Singh. The King reasoned that if Fatteh Jung rejected the prime ministership, he (the King) would take the post and put his son, the Heir Apparent, on the throne. Fatteh frustrated the King's plan by accepting the post and forming a coalition cabinet in May 1845. Gagan Singh stayed on as a member of Fatteh Jung's cabinet.

The new government professed friendly relations with the British, reflecting the prevalent Nepalese attitude that a confrontation with the British was to be avoided at almost any cost. In return, the British did all they could to reciprocate this friendship and to encourage its growth. In fact, relations became so cordial that the King rejected a request from the Sikh Government for military aid against the British and, instead, offered the Nepalese Army to the British to use against the Sikhs. Of course, the King's motives were not entirely pure; he hoped to profit from this cultivation of British goodwill. Indeed, after the British won their war against the Sikhs, the Nepal Durbar made the following request:

'that the British Government, in this day of its triumph, and augmented possessions, should give something out of its abundance to its poor friend of Nepal, which had been so staunch and offered her troops so often.'[3]

The Durbar hoped the British would give them the area of Kumaon or some other territory in the Terai.

[1] Landon, op. cit., p. 105. Wright, op. cit., p. 33. Northey, op. cit., p.54. Tuker, op. cit., p. 118.
[2] Nicholette, op. cit.
[3] Oldfield, op. cit., p. 352.

Through this period, Prime Minister Fatteh Jung was having great difficulty in the internal power struggle between the King and the Heir Apparent versus the Queen (Lakhshmi Devi) who was still manœuvering to get her son on the throne.[1] Fatteh Jung, who supported the King in this dispute, found himself continually opposed by Gagan Singh, who sided with the Queen (and who still hoped to become Prime Minister). Jung Bahadur, by his control of the Army, represented the real power in the government, but he ostensibly remained aloof although he favored the King while still managing to retain the friendship of the Queen.

The inevitable break in this unstable situation came on the night of September 14, 1846, when Gagan Singh was assassinated while praying in his private room. Here, too, considerable doubt exists as to who actually killed the Queen's lover. According to the *Nepal Residency Records*, the King asked his two sons to try to eliminate Gagan and thus to restore the honor of the royal family. It is also believed that Fatteh Jung was involved with the young princes and that they hired an assassin, Heera Lal Jha, for the act.[2]

Needless to say, when the news of Gagan Singh's murder reached the Queen, she became furious. Vowing to find the real culprit, she

---

[1] Dr Kanchanmoy Majumdar, in his unpublished thesis on 'Indo-Nepalese Relations, 1837–1877', discussed 'The Patna Conspiracy (1845–46)' which is presumed to have taken place during this period. He said that Babu Kunwar Singh and a Nawab of Patna named Khawaja Hussain Ali Khan went to Nepal, and that the king of Nepal assured them of military aid to 'erase the names and marks of Europeans from Hindoostan'. Dr Majumdar decided that the assumption of Nepalese complicity was baseless. Majumdar also quoted Colvin, the British Resident, who rejected the theory that Nepal had been contacted and had offered help. Dr K. K. Datta wrote, in the footnote of his book *Biography of Kunwar Singh and Amar Singh*, on page 66, 'The contents of these letters were given benefit of doubt in the absence of any other corroborative evidence.' Furthermore, during the period 1845–46 Nepal was itself passing through a serious power struggle. Each contestant needed British help and so, on this basis also, it cannot be accepted as reasonable that Nepal promised help to Babu Kunwar Singh. If we accept that Khawaja Hussain Ali was given asylum in Nepal, it cannot have been by the Nepal Durbar but only by local officers. It is reasonable to believe that when the conspiracy failed, many accomplices escaped to Nepal. But this 'escape' cannot be considered 'political asylum' given by the Nepal Durbar.

Foreign Secret Consultations, February 28, 1846, July 24 and 25, 1846, 144–5; *Bengal Government Judicial (Criminal) Proceedings*, January 14, 1846, 95–101; January 21, 1846, 40–51; January 28, 1846, 43–43U; April 1, 1846, 30–4. K. K. Datta, *Biography of Kunwar Singh and Amar Singh*, pp. 64–8, Patna, 1957. *Foreign Political Consultations*, February 28, 1846, 12–14; April 4, 1846, 3–4. *Important Judicial Bundles*, Alphabet M, No. 37, State Central Record Office, Bihar, Patna.

[2] Nicholette, *op. cit.*

called for all of the government ministers and sirdars (courtiers) to meet the next day at the royal palace. Suspecting nothing, all of the participants came without their supporting groups—except Jung Bahadur who came with three of his Army regiments. According to Jung Bahadur's report to the Resident, the meeting would have been a peaceful one had not Fatteh Jung's son attacked a member of the Royal Bodyguard.[1] What ensued then was the Kot (Palace) Massacre, one of the most barbarous and ghastly affairs in the history of Nepal. Fatteh Jung, according to reports, tried his best to avoid violence but the fury of the Queen was ungovernable. The Army regiments became involved and before the night ended, at least fifty-five of the most influential leaders of Nepal were dead, including Fatteh Jung and all the ministers of the court—except Jung Bahadur. Landon believes that this number does not represent even one-tenth of those who were killed.[2] In reporting the Kot Massacre, Jung Bahadur claimed:

'. . . that had he not restrained the Queen she would have put the heir apparent and his brother to death on the spot and would have imprisoned the Raja.'[3]

Jung Bahadur always maintained that it was the Queen who was entirely responsible for the whole affair because she held the supreme power at that time.

Emergence of Jung Bahadur and his First Term as Prime Minister

The Kot Massacre brought a drastic change to Nepalese politics. Jung Bahadur emerged as the only survivor with significant political power. The Queen and the King, recognizing this (in one of their rare moments of agreement), united to appoint Jung Bahadur to the post of Prime Minister, making the appointment while the bloodshed was still going on within the palace. Thus Jung Bahadur, after carefully nursing his ambitions for many years, reached the top position in the government of Nepal. As to the events of the previous years, the precise nature of his role is not known, but certainly he played a major role in the conspiracies and intrigues that preceded his rise to power.[4] His Prime Ministership inaugurated the domination of Nepalese politics by a new 'first family', the Rana family, founded by Jung Bahadur in 1846 and destined to rule Nepal for over 100 years.

Also inaugurated was a new era of co-operation in relations with

---

[1] Landon, *op. cit.*, p. 125.
[2] *Ibid.*, p. 124.
[3] Oldfield, *op. cit.*, Vol. I, p. 363.
[4] Landon, *op. cit.*, p. 127.

British India. Jung Bahadur lived to see the success of his policy which was based on firm friendship with the British and on isolation of Nepal from the outside world in order to maintain its independence. Symbolically, as captain of a small vessel in the great sea of British power, he managed to keep his ship floating until the time came when it no longer required help. He needed peace and tranquility at home and abroad in order to establish a strong administration to govern a country which for a decade had seen neither peace nor tranquility. He had to steer his course in accordance with this idea. He may be called greedy, ambitious, selfish, and ruthless but, equally, none can deny his energy, foresight, courage and diplomacy.

The first order of his benefactress, the Queen, was to eliminate the Heir Apparent in favor of her own son. When Jung Bahadur disobeyed, the Queen turned against him and started plotting against his life; but Jung was too shrewd for her. Her plot gave him a good excuse to prove his loyalty to the King who had granted him full powers of life and death over the enemies of the Heir Apparent, saying that 'the enemy of my beloved son is my enemy'.[1] Immediately the intriguing Queen and her two sons were ordered to leave the country. The King then decided to visit holy places in India, delegating all his powers to the Heir Apparent, who was a close friend of Jung Bahadur. The King did not return for a considerable time, so Jung Bahadur, with the help of sirdars and guroos (nobles and Hindu theologians), put the Heir Apparent on the throne and then informed the (former) King that he was always welcome in the country but only as an ex-king. Having full control over the internal affairs of the country, Jung Bahadur then cultivated the good will of his most powerful neighbor, British India. He agreed to a delimitation of the boundary between Nepal and India, sent some presents to India, and offered the services of Nepalese troops to the British in the second Sikh war. In spite of his offer of help against the Sikhs, he nevertheless gave asylum to the Queen of the late Sikh ruler, Ranjit Singh,[2] although her presence in Kathmandu was both unexpected and undesired.

Jung was very disappointed when Lord Dalhousie, then Governor-General, declined his offer of troops. Lord Dalhousie felt that it was not so much from friendship for the British that Jung had offered troops but to provide employment for the large and idle Nepalese army.[3] He remained suspicious of the Nepalese offer in spite of Resident Thoresby's assurance that it was symbolic of Jung Bahadur's sincere friendship.[4]

[1] Nicholette, *op. cit.*
[2] *Ibid.*
[3] Majumdar, K., *op. cit.*, pp. 282-3.
[4] *Ibid.*

A GENERAL SURVEY

Jung Bahadur's Visit to England

In the autumn of 1849, when Jung Bahadur felt secure in his position in Nepal, the Governor-General was approached on behalf of the King of Nepal who desired to send a complimentary mission to London to pay respect to the Queen of England. The King's request was immediately approved and Jung Bahadur, together with a large number of relatives and officers, was deputed for the mission. Jung engineered this visit because he wanted to see personally the power and grandeur of England. This was also Jung's first visit to India. On his way to England he stopped at Calcutta where the Governor-General, Lord Dalhousie, and his entire staff gave him an imposing reception. A nineteen-gun salute was fired in his honor. After a short visit, he sailed for England, reaching Southampton on May 25, 1850. He was received in the Throne Room by Her Majesty, Queen Victoria, and was given diplomatic precedence next after the Spanish Ambassador. The Nepalese party took six months for its trip. Jung Bahadur visited large factories, arsenals, and other important projects in London and returned to India via France and other places of interest.[1] Upon arrival in Nepal, Jung was given a warm reception by the King who accompanied the procession to receive the Kharieta (official letter) from Queen Victoria. As a result of this visit to England, Nepal, for the first time, honored an English monarch's birthday; a twenty-one gun salute was fired on May 24, 1851,[2] the birthday of Queen Victoria.

An important result of Jung Bahadur's visit was the series of reforms which he introduced in the penal code of Nepal. Among others, capital punishment was abolished except for murder, and mutilations as a punishment were forbidden. One unusual result of these reforms came up when conspirators against his own life were brought before Jung. These prisoners were under sentence of death imposed upon them by the King, but it was Jung himself who objected to the severity of the punishment; and with the help of the British government, Jung sent all of the conspirators to India to serve life imprisonment terms. This was a frequent matter since, during his first ten years in office, there were many plots against his life.

In his first term as Prime Minister, Jung also carried out many other public actions, including negotiations in 1855 of a treaty between the British and Nepalese governments for the extradition of criminals. This treaty was one of strict reciprocity[3] and was an important step in promoting friendly relations between the two countries.

[1] Foreign and Political Department, File No. 96 (4)-H, 1934. (N.A.I.)
[2] Nicholette, *op. cit.*
[3] Ramsay, G., *Nepal Residency Records*, Serial No. 4.

BRITISH INDIA'S RELATIONS WITH NEPAL

The Tibet-Nepal War of 1854-56

At the end of 1854, war started between Nepal and Tibet. For some time, Jung had been putting his army on a war footing on the pretext that he was invited to assist the Imperial Government of China against the Tai Ping rebels. But actually he was preparing forces against Tibet. There were causes for conflict such as the mistreatment of Nepalese merchants by the Tibetan authorities and the rejection of their appeals for justice. A number of small border skirmishes had taken place. Nepal's Vakil (representative) stationed at Lhasa had several times brought these issues to the attention of the Tibetan authorities but to no avail. Even letters sent from the Nepal Durbar had no effect. When all its efforts failed, Nepal felt it had no alternative but to go to war.

The war lasted for two years. It was a hard war for Nepal; there were many difficulties in sending food and reinforcements to the troops, especially with the Himalayan passes being open only for about five months of the year. However, Nepal's military success was such, that Tibet asked for peace. After lengthy negotiations, a treaty was finally signed on March 25, 1856. Its main points were that Tibet should pay 10,000 rupees ($2,000.00) annually to Nepal, Nepalese troops would leave Tibetan territories, and a Nepalese Vakil would continue to be stationed in Lhasa to look after the interests of Nepalese subjects and trade.[1]

Interestingly, this war had no effect on British–Nepalese relations. Resident Ramsay sided with Nepal, believing that the war was 'provoked in one way or other by the Chinese-Tibetan Government'.[2]

The two years of conflict with Tibet were barely over—the ink on the treaty was scarcely dry—when on August 1, 1856, Jung Bahadur resigned the Prime Ministership. His move caught everyone by surprise. Ramsay first learned of it when he was informed by the Orderly Officer that Jung had resigned and his brother Bum Bahadur had taken over the post of Prime Minister. Landon writes that soon after Jung's resignation, a deputation of influential people, sirdars and guroos 'offered the crown to him' but he did not accept, and that the King himself offered Jung the fiefs of Kaski and Lamjang with the hereditary title of Maharaja to pass from Prime Minister to Prime Minister and with the authority to overrule the King in these territories. Jung Bahadur then came to Ramsay saying that the King had taken a solemn oath to abdicate if Jung did not accept these honors.[3] Padma

---

[1] Ramsay, *op. cit.*; Oldfield, *op. cit.*, pp. 413–18; Wright, *op. cit.*, p. 39.
[2] Ramsay, *op. cit.*
[3] Landon, *op. cit.*, p. 149, from Ramsay, *op. cit.*; Ramsay, *op. cit.*: also noted in Tuker, *op. cit.*, p. 149.

Jung Rana, his son and official biographer, wrote that the people also appealed to Jung to accept these favors in lieu of the crown that had been offered to him earlier.[1] And true to form, Jung 'accepted the honors'; so that Ramsay was shortly able to report to his government that Jung had been formally invested with the title of Maharajah and had been presented with the sanads[2] (documents of sovereignty) of the provinces of Kaski and Lamjang, the perpetual sovereignty of which was bestowed upon him and his descendants.[3]

In reality, Jung had stage-managed this whole drama to make it appear that the King was so pleased with him that these favors were forced on him in spite of his refusal.[4] As a matter of fact, the King had very little choice in this entire situation except to act as he did and to agree with whatever Jung Bahadur advised. Ramsay wrote in a letter to his government:

'... the occurrences of the past few days can hardly have taken place as they have been reported to me and I have detailed them—but they have resulted from much previous consideration, consultation and arrangement; the Maharaja, whose dread and whose dislike of Jung Bahadur and his party is about equally balanced having acted throughout merely as he was bid.'[5]

Jung Bahadur emerged from this series of events with more power than ever before, even though he was no longer Prime Minister. As the 'power behind the throne', Jung freely manoeuvered the King for his own purposes. Comparing Jung and the King, Ramsay wrote in a demi-official letter to his government:

'In my opinion, Jung Bahadur is too greedy, selfish and ambitious to let matters rest as they now are. The King is a perfect non-entity, a mere tool in his hand, and being moreover almost an idiot, would be incapable of conducting the Government of the country were he to attempt to do so. . . .'[6]

[1] Kumar, *op. cit.*
[2] 'Sanad is the Persian word for written letter or declaration, which was used in India in regard to diplomatic exchanges between rulers. In common use it may denote any piece of writing, even a receipt for money. We use the word officially to denote a recognition of duty, an engagement of honour, or a grant of rights by Paramount Power, although Indians have never agreed that it denotes a grant of rights....' Nicholson, A. P., *Scraps of Paper, India's Broken Treaties, Her Princes, and the Problems*, pp. 330-1. London: Ernest Benn Ltd., 1930.
[3] Ramsay, *op. cit.*
[4] Kumar, *op. cit.*
[5] *Ibid.*
[6] *Ibid.*

As one example of Jung's power, he forced the King to proclaim that the prime ministership should henceforth be hereditary in the Rana family and should pass from brother to brother rather than in direct succession to the eldest son. Thus, he assured his return to the prime ministership in the future at his convenience.

One unforeseen difficulty developed with Jung's new situation. Now that he was out of office, the British government refused to recognize him as anything more than a respected citizen of Nepal. This became a sore point between Jung and Ramsay, and relations between the two remained strained during the remainder of Ramsay's tenure as Resident. But in spite of this interpersonal friction, relations between the two governments were friendly and uneventful until the death of Prime Minister Bum Bahadur in May 1857. Jung Bahadur's return to power and his second term as Prime Minister will be discussed in the next chapter.

In summary, the first part of Jung Bahadur's rule was characterized by smooth and peaceful relations with the British. Jung's trip to England was a master stroke; after the trip, he never questioned British power and gave his full friendship and support to the British Government in India. Within Nepal, Jung completely neutralized the King as a power-figure in Nepalese politics and gave Nepal an uninterrupted peaceful administration for his entire term, in place of the murders and *coups d'état* that had characterized previous administrations.

Hydarabad and Thailand: A Comparison with Nepal

The status of Nepal *vis-à-vis* the British Government in India was unique; Nepal had more independence than any of the princely states of India but had less than a completely sovereign Asian state. Nepal's status can perhaps best be illustrated by comparing it with Hydarabad, the major princely state of India, and Thailand, an independent state that maintained its sovereignty largely as a product of the colonial rivalry between France and Great Britain.

Hydarabad

The relationship of the princely states to the British Government in India needs clarification at this point. For its part, Britain unvaryingly refused to admit that these relations were governed by international law such as covered, for example, the alliance between Britain and Portugal. Britain's claim was that the princely states belonged to a special category of colonial dependent allies where the senior ally (Britain) had the right to interpret the alliance as she chose (the doctrine of 'paramountcy'). The late K. M. Panikkar describes these British government-princely state relations as follows:

A GENERAL SURVEY

'The internal states of India and their relations with the British Government afford no parallel or analogy to any institution known to history. The political system they represent is neither feudal nor federal, though in some aspects it shows similarities to both which have misguided alike the statesman and the political thinker. It is not an international system, though the principal states in India are bound to the British Government by solemn treaties and are spoken of in official documents as allies. Nor would it be correct to consider it a political confederacy in which the major partner has assumed special rights, because it is admitted by all parties that the Constituent States have no rights of secession.'[1]

Panikkar thus confirms that the princely states were not independent units, especially when Britain interpreted and enforced the meaning of the treaties.

Within this overall framework of British domination, the policy of the British government went through several changes. During the latter part of the eighteenth century, the East India Company followed a policy of non-interference in the affairs of the Indian states. Lord Wellesley, Governor-General from 1798 to 1804, changed this policy from non-interference to 'Subsidiary Alliance', stating:

'The fundamental principle of His Excellency the Governor-General's policy in establishing the subsidiary alliance is to place the states in such a degree of dependency on the British power as may deprive them of the means of prosecuting any measure hazardous to the security of the British Empire.'[2]

Hydarabad was the largest of the 562 Indian princely states, having a population of 18,655,108 and an area of 82,168 sq. miles. Lying south of the Vindhyas Mountains on the tableland of the Deccan, Hydarabad was the geographical link between north and south India. It had a special historical importance because here the French and British fought for supremacy of India and the British won the Battle of Wandewash in 1760, a defeat that sounded the death knell of French power in India.[3]

Treaty Relations

British treaty relations with Hydarabad followed the typical pattern of the princely states although the dominant position of Hydarabad among the princely states gave these relations a special importance. An

---
[1] Panikkar, K. M., *Indian States and the Government of India*, p. 9. London: Martin Hopkinson, Ltd., 1932.
[2] Panikkar, *Indian States*, p. 10. London: Oxford University Press, 1942.
[3] Mukerjee, *op. cit.*, pp. 31-2.

examination of the Treaty of 1798 between Lord Wellesley and the Nizam of Hydarabad shows the nature of the relationship between the two governments and the development of Wellesley's doctrine of 'Subsidiary Alliance'. Article Three of this treaty, for instance, clearly shows the effort by Wellesley to place the Nizam in a position of military reliance on the British:

'The proposed reinforcement of subsidiary troops[1] shall be in the pay of this state from the day of their crossing the boundaries. Satisfactory and effectual provision shall be made for the regular payment of this force, which including the present detachment, is to amount to six thousand sepoys with firelocks, with a due proportion of field pieces manned by Europeans, and at the monthly rate of Rupees, 201,425. The yearly amount of subsidiary for the aforesaid force of six thousand men, with guns, artillerymen, and other necessary appurtenances, is Rupees 24,17,100. The said sum shall be completely discharged in the course of the year, by four equal instalments; that is, at the expiration of every three English months, the sum of Rupees 6,04,275 in silver, of full currency, shall be issued, without hesitation, from His Highness's treasury, and should the aforesaid instalments happen to fall at any time the least in arrears, such arrears shall be deducted, notwithstanding objections thereto, from the current kist of peshcush (instalment in advance) payable to His Highness on account of the Northern Circars. Should it at any time so happen, moreover, that delay were to occur in the issue of the instalments aforesaid, in the stated periods, in such case assignments shall be granted on the collections of certain districts in the state, the real and actual revenue of which shall be adequate to the discharge of the yearly subsidy of the aforesaid force.'[2]

In contrast, Nepal was never required to make a similar commitment in any of the treaties signed between it and British India. The Nepalese Army was paid and controlled solely by the Government of Nepal. The only restriction was that Nepal must not employ any British, European, or American subject without the consent of the British government, but similar restrictions were also imposed on Hydarabad and the other princely states (the object here to prevent the employment of military mercenaries to improve the efficiency of their armies).

---

[1] This meant that the Nizam must rely for the defense of his state on the subsidiary troops controlled by the British. The Nizam was supposed to pay the entire cost of the maintenance of the troops and if he failed the British government could reimburse itself by taking over the revenue of a particular tract of land which was mortgaged or was given as security for the payment of troops.

[2] Aitchison, op. cit., Vol. V, p. 50.

A GENERAL SURVEY

The next treaty between Hydarabad and Britain was signed in 1800 and gave further evidence that the Nizam was gradually losing his power to the British government. Article Three of the Treaty of 1800 read in part.

'... so that the whole subsidiary force furnished by the Honourable East India Company to His Highness shall henceforward consist of eight battalions of sepoys (or eight thousand firelocks) and two regiments of cavalry (or one thousand horse), with their requisite complement of guns, European artillerymen, lascars, and pioneers, fully equipped with warlike stores and ammunition, which force is to be stationed in perpetuity in His Highness's territories.'[1]

In total, this treaty article gave the British government not only the right to station a larger army in the Nizam's dominions at the Nizam's expense, but also to station European officers for the training of the army personnel.

In Article Five of the Treaty, the Nizam ceded territory for the maintenance of the British army stationed in his dominion for his protection. This article read as follows:

'For the regular payment of the whole expenses of the said augmented subsidiary force (consisting of eight thousand infantry, one thousand cavalry, and their usual proportion of artillery) His Highness the Nawab Ausuph Jah hereby assigns and cedes to the Honorable East India Company in perpetuity all the territories acquired by His Highness, under the Treaty of Seringapatam on the 18th March, 1792, and also all the territories acquired by His Highness under the treaty of Mysore on the 22nd June 1799, according to the schedule annexed to this treaty.'[2]

Nepal, in contrast, was never asked to sign such a treaty even after its defeat in the War of 1814–16.

Article Seven of the Treaty of 1800 went further. It read:

'The territories to be assigned and ceded to the Honorable Company by the fifth Article, or in consequence of the exchange stipulated in the sixth Article, shall be subject to the exclusive management and authority of the said Company and of their officers.'[3]

On the principle that 'the man who pays the piper calls the tune', the

[1] Aitchison, *op. cit.*, Vol. V, p. 70.
[2] *Ibid.*, p. 71.
[3] *Ibid.*

Nizam thus lost all control over the army stationed in his own territories for his own protection. A similar limitation of sovereignty was never imposed on Nepal.

By Article Fifteen of the same treaty, the Nizam relinquished his control over external affairs to the East India Company. This article reads:

'As by the present treaty the union and friendship of the two states are so firmly cemented as that they may be considered as one and the same, His Highness the Nizam engages neither to commence nor to pursue in future any negotiations with any other power whatever without giving previous notice and entering into mutual consultation with the Honorable East India Company's Government; and the Honorable Company's Government on their part hereby declare that they have no manner of concern with any of His Highness's children, relations, subjects or servants, with respect to whom His Highness is absolute.'[1]

By contrast, Nepal maintained diplomatic relations with Tibet and China; and while the Government of India wanted to end Nepal's relations with China, it admitted that it had no legal right to do so and took no action in that direction. Nepal also retained the right to go to war, and exercised this right against Tibet in 1854.

The Treaty of 1800 left the Nizam almost powerless: he gave up all control of foreign affairs, his military was controlled entirely by the British but paid by the Nizam, and the British had full control of the payment. But this did not fully satisfy the British; consequently, in May 21, 1853, the Nizam signed a treaty that was even more restrictive than the earlier ones.[2]

Panikkar, writing about the Treaty of 1853, pointed out that it had three outstanding characteristics:

(1) It was indissoluble. After the signature of this treaty the Nizam was not free to pick and choose his friends. The state came to be in permanent alliance with the British.
(2) A British Army officered by Europeans but paid by the Nizam was established in his territory. This force was for the purpose of internal as well as external defense and it gave the company a handle wherewith to interfere in the internal affairs of the state.

[1] Aitchison, *op. cit.*, Vol. V, pp. 74–5.
[2] *Ibid.*, p. 103.

A GENERAL SURVEY

(3) The treaty stipulated that the foreign relations of the Nizam should be conducted exclusively through the company.[1]

According to Panikkar, the 1853 Hyderabad Treaty may therefore be regarded as the 'subsidiary alliance *par excellence*'.[2]

Foreign Relations

Hydarabad's observance of the treaty restrictions on her powers to conduct foreign relations was irreproachable. In fact, Hydarabad went beyond the spirit of the treaties and gave many indications of positive co-operation with the British Government in India to forward the latter's foreign policy aims. The Nizam offered his loyal co-operation to the British in their efforts in Egypt and Afghanistan; and in 1887, he suprised India and Europe with an offer of £600,000 and troops to aid the British in the defense of the North Western frontier. To this, the Nizam added an expression of his willingness to take to the field in person if the need arose.[3]

Domestic Relations—Indications of Hydarabad's Subordinate Status

In 1877, the Governor-General convened an Imperial Assembly at Delhi of all of the heads of the princely states. The occasion was the proclamation of Queen Victoria's new title of Kaisar-i-Hind, or Empress of India.[4] Charles Lewis Tupper, in his book *Our Indian Protectorate*, noted that 'according to Eastern ideas, to attend a formal gathering convened at the behest of a ruler is a customary mode of signifying homage'.[5] Some of the important rulers were not willing to attend the Assembly because they felt that it was beneath their dignity and lowered their prestige as independent rulers. Nonetheless all of them, including the most important, were present according to the wishes of the Governor-General. Panikkar, in his book *Indian States and the Government of India*, claims that all the Indian states were invited and in effect were forced to attend,[6] but in any case, the effect

---

[1] Panikkar, *Indian States*, pp. 9–10.
[2] *Ibid.*, p. 10.
[3] McAuliffe, Paton R., *The Nizam: the Origin and Future of the Hydarabad State*, p. 57. London: C. J. Clay and Sons, 1904.
[4] In 1876, Queen Victoria assumed the title of Kaisar-i-Hind, after the death of Bahadur Shah, the last Indian sovereign who sat on the throne of Delhi. To enforce the title of Kaisar-i-Hind on the Queen, a Durbar of all Indian states was called in Delhi.
[5] Tupper, Charles Lewis, *Our Indian Protectorate*, p. 125. London: Longmans, Green and Co., 1893.
[6] Panikkar, *Indian States and the Government of India*, p. 29.

was to place the princely state rulers in a subordinate position to the Queen of England.

In contrast, there was a subtle but significant difference in the action of Nepal. While Nepal was invited to the assembly, the King of Nepal did not attend the Assembly in person. Instead, Nepal was represented by General Dhere Shamsher as the ambassador of his sovereign to the Imperial Assembly, thus showing the difference between its status and the status of the princely states whose rulers attended in person.

On the question of royal honors, Sir William Lee-Warner wrote: 'The first of these obligations [of honors] arises from the prerogative of the crown to grant honours and decorations, and to settle precedence. From the fact that the King-Emperor of India exercises this power, two obligations follow: first, that the Viceroy's decision as to relative rank is authoritative; and secondly, that no honours can be received from other sources without His Majesty's sanction.'[1] The Nizam accepted honors from the British King, including the raising of his title from 'His Highness' to the high honor of 'His Exalted Highness'. By accepting these honors, he accepted a subordinate status to the British rulers.

The right of a ruler to appoint (and remove) his own cabinet members is a matter of internal affairs in an independent country. Here too, the situation in Hydarabad showed its subsidiary position to the British. There were many cases which show that the Nizam had no power even to appoint or dismiss his own chief minister. When Meer Alim died in 1808, the Nizam appointed Munier-u-Mulk as his minister, against the wishes of the East India Company. The result was that the minister was not permitted by the Governor-General to take an active part in the affairs of the state, the management being left to Chandoo Lall who was entirely dependent on British influence for his elevation to power.[2] Again on another occasion, when the Nizam removed his minister, Sir Salar Jung, from office in 1861, the remonstrances of the British Resident forced the Nizam to reconsider his decision with the result that Sir Salar Jung was retained in office.[3]

On the whole, however, the State of Hydarabad, owing to its size and importance, had a much greater degree of independence in domestic affairs than many other princely states. The Nizam maintained his own internal communication system through the Nizam State Railway and Deccan Airways; he was the only ruler in India who had his own gold currency and who printed a hundred-rupees note; he was the first ruler who had an information and broadcasting department, with a

---

[1] Lee-Warner, Sir William, *The Native States of India*, p. 318. London, n.d.
[2] Aitchison, *op. cit.*, Vol. V, pp. 6–7.
[3] *Ibid.*, p. 10.

radio station; and he also established the first university in which the Urdu language was the exclusive medium of instruction.[1]

After analyzing Hydarabad–British relationships, one reaches the inevitable conclusion that the 'subsidiary alliance' established by Lord Wellesley completely took away the power of the Nizam in the field of external affairs and placed some significant restrictions on his internal power as well. The Nizam became almost a prisoner, or puppet, in the hands of the British Resident.

Paramountcy of Britain

The 'paramount power' in India was unquestionably in the hands of the British. Panikkar has described this term, 'paramount power', as meaning:

'... the complex of Crown rights, both general and particular, which limit the sovereignty of the States. In its general aspects it applies equally to all States, from Hydarabad down to the smallest Jagir in Kathiawad. This is what may be called Basic Paramountcy and covers such prerogatives of the Crown as sanction of adoption, the decision of disputes between States, intervention in cases of gross misgovernment and conduct of relations with foreign States.'[2]

On the basis of Paramountcy, for example, the British government removed the rulers of the states of Baroda in 1873 and Manipur in 1891 because of misdeeds or misgovernment.[3] But the power of Paramountcy also imposed obligations upon the Crown. They were: '(1) Maintenance of the territorial integrity of the States; (2) Protection from outside aggression and internal commotion; (3) Maintenance of the dynasty and the continuation of the rights, privileges and izzat [prestige] of the Rulers.'[4]

While the doctrine of Paramountcy had its supporters among the British officialdom, it also had its critics. One such writer was A. P. Nicholson who, in his book, *Scraps of Paper*, was quite critical of the British government's attitude towards the princely states. He cited many instances of intervention in the internal affairs of a princely state, some of which incidents have been quoted in this chapter. Nicholson supported his arguments by quoting part of the Harcourt Butler Committee's[5] report which acknowledged the British govern-

[1] Urdu is now listed in the Indian constitution as one of the fourteen official Indian languages. It is also the national language of Pakistan.
[2] Panikkar, *Indian States*, p. 21.
[3] Nicholson, *op. cit.*, p. 52.
[4] Panikkar, *Indian States*, p. 22.
[5] The ruling princes had asked the Viceroy for an impartial tribunal before

ment's frequent intervention in the internal affairs of princely states.[1]

The right of Paramountcy was neither claimed nor exercised over Nepal. The Nepal Army was not controlled by the British government, nor did the British force the hands of the King to choose his Prime Minister according to their wishes. Even in its external affairs, Nepal was free to make war and sign a peace treaty with Asian states, i.e. Tibet and China. The only unwritten agreement between the British and the Nepalese was that the Government of Nepal would not establish relations with any European powers.

The question was often raised why Nepal was not treated like the Indian princely states. The answer to this question could be the following: first, from the outset, Nepal was always regarded as an independent state and was treated accordingly; second, to conquer Nepal by force would have been a very difficult military operation because of lack of roads and the mountainous terrain; third, the War of 1814–16 gave the British great respect for the fighting quality and determination of the Gurkha soldier; fourth, during the nineteenth century—and the first half of the twentieth—Tibet and China were not the danger to the security of the British Indian Empire that they have become since 1950 and hence there was no need to control Nepal; and last, the British wanted peace and friendly relations on their northern border. Actually their policy of friendly relations with Nepal paid in the end since Nepal supported the British cause in India from the time when the Rana family came to power until the British left India in 1947.

Thailand

A comparison can also be made between the status of Nepal and that of Thailand, a weak but legally a completely independent state and the only state in Southeast Asia that did not become a dependency of one or another of the European colonial powers (in spite of the fact that it was a coastal country and was coveted by powerful European nations such as Portugal, Holland, Great Britain, and France). Its area is 200,148 square miles, with a population of 25,000,000. It is bounded on the north by Burma and Indo-China; on the east by Indo-China; on the south by Indo-China, the gulf of Siam and Malaya; and on the west by the Bay of Bengal and Burma.[2]

Thailand's first contact with the European powers came when the Dutch opened factories in 1602 at Patani and in 1608, at Ayut'ia. This

which they might bring evidence of their broken treaties, and their request led to the appointment of the Indian States Committee presided over by Sir Spencer Harcourt Butler.

[1] Nicholson, op. cit., p. 188.
[2] The Encyclopedia Americana, Vol. 26, p. 486. New York, 1957.

was followed by an embassy sent by the King of Thailand to the Hague in 1609. In 1612, a letter from King James I of England to the King of Thailand[1] opened up trade between Britain and Thailand. Both the Dutch and the British maintained factories or trading posts in Thailand but eventually closed them because the Thais were very suspicious and hostile toward Europeans. Moreover, the products of Thailand were not good enough to win markets in Europe. Also, the Thais were jealous of their independence and were willing to fight to maintain it. For the Dutch and the British, a war of conquest would have been expensive and not worth the trouble.

After a lapse of more than a century, the English East India Company in 1822 decided to send an embassy to Thailand to negotiate a treaty. John Crawford was deputed as the representative of the Governor-General of India. But Crawford was absolutely forbidden to ask for any of the privileges which had formed so important a part of the commercial treaties of the sixteenth through the eighteenth centuries, such as the erection of forts or factories, extraterritorial jurisdiction, monopolies, etc.[2] Even on the important question of restoration of the Sultan of Kedah to his throne, an issue which closely affected the interests of the British settlement at Penang, Crawford was not given any clear-cut advice by the British Government of India; and it was 'left entirely to Crawford's discretion as to whether the subject should be mentioned at all'.[3] The major interest of the Crawford mission was in expanding British trade with Thailand;[4] and it was agreed that the Company would not enter into armed conflict with the Thai government even though the Thai army was weak and could have been defeated by a small Indian force.

Crawford's mission failed—for many reasons. Among the most important were the fear and suspicion felt toward the British by a powerful court faction led by Prince Kromchiat, plus the fact that Crawford had nothing to offer in return for Thai concessions.[5] The principal result of Crawford's mission was the valuable information which he collected about the geography, population and resources of Thailand, the character of the government, and the weakness of its power.[6]

[1] Hall, D. G. E., *A History of South-East Asia*, pp. 297-9. London: Macmillan and Co., Ltd., 1960.
[2] Mills, Lennox A., 'British Malay, 1824-1867', *Journal of the Malayan Branch of the Royal Asiatic Society*, Vol. III, Pt. II, p. 131. Singapore, November, 1925.
[3] *Ibid.*, p. 132.
[4] *Ibid.*, p. 131.
[5] *Ibid.*, pp. 131-5.
[6] *Ibid.*, p. 133.

In 1825, the British government sent Captain Henry Burney to Bangkok to make another try at negotiating a treaty with the Thai government. Burney was more successful than his predecessor, Crawford. In June 1826, he concluded a treaty with Thailand which opened limited British–Thai relations.

In the negotiations, Burney (like Crawford) was placed in a very disadvantageous position by his government since he too was not permitted to make any concessions to the Thais and had to rely entirely on his gifts of persuasion. Burney skilfully played on the fears of the Thai court about British power, the result of which was that he gained a few trade concessions. But he failed to persuade Thailand to abandon its claims of domination over the Malay states of Kelantan and Trengganu and was forced to agree to some major concessions. Article Five of the treaty, which stated that 'English subjects who visited a Siamese country must conduct themselves according to the established law of the Siamese in every particular',[1] was especially disliked by the British because it put them at the mercy of the Thai law. According to Mills, the fact that Burney achieved even partial success was due to the 'timidity of the Siamese', and the 'recent British victories in Burma'.[2]

Not much change took place in British relations with Thailand until Mongkuk became King in 1854. Mongkuk, who tried to modernize Thailand, abandoned the policies of isolation and of suspicion toward foreigners. He was the first king to realize that to allow Europeans to trade freely need not lead to the loss of independence. By signing the Treaty of Friendship and Commerce with Britain in 1855, he opened the door of Thailand to Europeans.[3]

The Treaty of 1855 made many important concessions to the British. Article Ten of this treaty, for example, extended to the British the same concessions that might be given to other European powers but also granted them the same rights and privileges which the Chinese alone had enjoyed previously. The article read:

'The British Government and its subjects will be allowed free equal participation in any privileges that may have been, or may hereafter be granted by the Siamese Government to the Government or subjects of any other nations.'[4]

---

[1] Aitchison, op. cit., Vol. I, p. 319.
[2] Mills, op. cit., p. 146.
[3] Hall, op. cit., p. 579.
[4] Bowring, Sir John, *The Kingdom and People of Siam*, Vol. I, p. 221. London, 1857.

A GENERAL SURVEY

In the long history of British–Nepalese relations, one cannot find similar privileges given by the Nepalese to the British in any of their treaties. The British had the right to trade in Nepal but British merchants and subjects, including the Residents, were not permitted to go where they chose.

Another important concession granted by Mongkuk to the British was the establishment of extraterritorial rights;[1] Nepal never granted this right to the British.

Later, the ambitious activities of Napoleon III made Mongkuk uneasy to such an extent that he sought closer co-operation with the British.[2] As British-French rivalry grew more intense, Thailand took full advantage of it. Recognizing this, in 1889, the French Ambassador in London suggested to British Prime Minister, Lord Salisbury, that it would be 'to the advantage of both countries to declare Siam a buffer state between their respective empires'.[3] In fact, France signed a treaty with Thailand in 1896 which preserved Thailand's independence although she was shorn of some of her outlying provinces. Thus, Thailand maintained her independence throughout this period, despite her weakness, because the interests of the great powers were best served in this way.

The Entente Cordiale of 1904 finally ended the Franco–British controversy over Thailand and left both sides free to come to terms separately with the Thai Government.[4] In 1907, Thailand and France buried their differences and France abandoned all claim to jurisdiction over Asian subjects in return for cessions of territory.[5] In the same year, Britain and Thailand also came to terms. By the Treaty of 1907, Britain surrendered all her extraterritorial rights over the Malay states of Kelantan, Trengganu, Kedah and Perlis.[6]

As can be seen, Thailand's guiding principle in foreign policy was one of opportunism; she was on the side of whatever power would best promote her interests. During World War II, Thailand again followed the same policy. In December 1940 she abruptly changed from the side of Great Britain to the side of Japan and declared war against Britain and the United States on January 25, 1942.[7] As a reward, she received part of French Indochina, Malaya, and Burma. But when the Thai government decided that Japan was losing the war, the pro-Japanese government resigned and Thailand acquired a new

[1] Hall, op. cit., p. 581.
[2] Ibid., p. 582.
[3] Ibid., p. 601.
[4] Ibid., p. 582.
[5] Ibid., p. 612.
[6] Ibid.
[7] Ibid., p. 682.

leader, Pridi Banomyong, who was the head of the Free Thai movement and was held in high regard in Washington. Now Thailand joined hands with the United States and became an American ally.

Legally, Thailand has always been an independent and sovereign country—more so than Nepal. Practically, Thailand has managed to remain independent because she has cleverly taken advantage of rivalries between foreign powers, and has opportunistically shifted from one side to the other. Her guiding policy has always been—how best to preserve Thai independence. On the other hand, Nepal was never in the same fortunate position as Thailand of being able to play one great power against another. Nepal maintained her independence by a policy of loyalty to her stronger neighbor, Britain. Even when she did get the chance to change sides against the British, she did not do so, because she feared that if her side lost, Nepal would be merged into India like the Indian princely states.

Many conclusions can be drawn from a comparison of the relations between Britain and Nepal and between Britain and Thailand. They sum up to the general observation that although Thailand was legally more independent than Nepal, Nepal was also very close to *de facto* complete independence.

CHAPTER 2

THE INDIAN MUTINY AND JUNG BAHADUR'S PRIME MINISTERSHIP

At the beginning of 1857, General Bum Bahadur was the Prime Minister of Nepal, having been installed after the resignation of Jung Bahadur in August 1856. Prime Minister Bum Bahadur's tenure in office was a short one. He died on May 24, 1857, after serving less than one year. His term was unique in two respects: he was the first Prime Minister in the history of Nepal to die peacefully in office; and his actions in office gave evidence of an attitude of greater co-operation and friendship with the British than any of his predecessors, including Jung Bahadur. As one indication of this attitude, he allowed British (Indian) troops and police to cross the Nepalese frontier north of Oudh in pursuit of a notorious freebooter, Fuzl Ali.[1] Previously, British troops had been strictly prohibited from entering Nepal, during peacetime, for any reason whatever.

Another indication of Bum Bahadur's attitude of friendship toward the British was his admission of Mr Herman Schlagintivet, a Swiss member of the Magnetic Survey of India, for whom the British had requested permission to conduct a scientific mission at Kathmandu. Mr Schlagintivet was interested in determining heights (by triangulation) of the mountains in the Kathmandu area. His permission to enter Nepal was given contrary to Jung Bahadur's expressed wishes.[2]

Bum Bahadur's death created a problem regarding a replacement in the office of Prime Minister. The answer came easily: Jung Bahadur was anxious to re-assume the office. As noted earlier, during the prime ministership of Bum Bahadur, the British Government in India extended no official recognition to Jung Bahadur, treating him only as

[1] Ramsay, G. *Nepal Residency Records Serial No. 4 Events 1840–61.*
[2] Oldfield, H. A., *Sketches from Nepal*, Vol. II, p. 19, *op. cit.*; Landon, Perceval, *Nepal*, Vol. I, p. 148, *op. cit.*

a respected and important citizen of Nepal. This attitude deeply wounded his feelings because he always felt that he was of greater importance than anyone in the country. He also complained that he had gotten completely out of touch with the Resident and with the day-to-day workings of the Nepal Government. His decision to regain the power and prestige of the prime ministership was a natural consequence of his unhappy situation while out of office—and of the political power he wielded, even while out of office.

The question has been raised as to when Jung Bahadur became Prime Minister for the second time? Drs Margaret Fisher and Leo Rose have maintained that Jung became Prime Minister in May 1857, immediately after the death of Bum Bahadur.[1] This date is also accepted by Perceval Landon.[2] But a different date is given in British and Nepalese government records. The *Nepal Residency Records* show that, following the Nepalese custom of not making a permanent appointment to the office for forty-five days after the death of an incumbent officeholder, the prime ministership was given temporarily to General Krishna Bahadur.[3] Ramsay, the British Resident, wrote a letter to Edmonstone, the Government of India Foreign Secretary, informing him that a session of the Nepal Durbar was held in Kathmandu on June 19, 1857, and that the Orderly Officer[4] in attendance at the Residency brought 'the following message from the officiating Minister and from Maharajah Jung Bahadur'.[5] This wording shows that Jung Bahadur was not Prime Minister before June 20, 1857, at the earliest. According to a Lall Mohar (King's Red Seal document), Jung Bahadur was appointed Prime Minister on June 28, 1857.[6]

While accepting the prime ministership for the second time, Jung Bahadur engaged in some rather unusual tactics. Jung's objective was to impress the British Government with his friendship for them and at the same time, to show his countrymen that the prime ministership of Nepal was not a matter of great importance to him and that he accepted it only on the advice of the Governor-General of India.

[1] Fisher, Margaret W., and Rose, Leo E., *England, India, Nepal, Tibet, China—1765–1958*, p. 8.
[2] Landon, op. cit., Vol. I, p. 148.
[3] Ramsay, *Nepal Residency Records*, Serial No. 4.
[4] Orderly Officer—the duty of this person is to be with the Resident, representing the Durbar at the Residency. He was always a Nepalese and would give information from the Prime Minister (both official and unofficial information) to the Resident and vice-versa.
[5] Ramsay to Edmonstone. Dated June 20, 1857, No. 41 of 1857, *Foreign Secret Proceedings*, Part II, November 27, 1857. (N.A.I.)
[6] Abstract translation of a Lall Mohar from His Highness, the Maharajah of Nepal to Maharajah Jung Bahadur Ranajie corresponding to June 28, 1857, *Foreign Department Secret Consultation*, September 25, 1857, No. 473.

Ramsay's aforementioned letter to Edmonstone describes Jung's maneuvers as follows:

'... that the Orderly Officer in attendance at the Residency, came to see me late last night, after I had retired to rest and brought the following message from the officiating Minister and from Maharajah Jung Bahadur, viz.

1. That a Durbar had been held that day at which the Maharajah, and his father (the ex-King) joined by many influential Sirdars (officers) and by Maharajah Jung Bahadur's own brothers, had requested Jung Bahadur to resume the Prime Ministership of this state, but that he had refused to do so, and had declared, that he only consents to accept the office, upon the advice of His Lordship, the Governor-General of India.

2. ... that the Maharajah wished to depute Jung Bahadur to the Residency, as a special ambassador, to consult with His Lordship, as to whether he might or might not resume the Prime Ministership, and also to His Lordship's advice on many points connected with the future government of this State.

3. He said, provided I would assent to it, Maharajah would march down *immediately* to Patna, escorted by 2,000 men, and proceed thruee (sic), either in a steamer or by Dak (mail) accompanied by only a few (20 or 30) followers. The Maharajah proposed to write me a 'Yaddasht' upon this subject, and also that I should forward a 'Khureeta' from himself to the Governor General, requesting His Lordship to receive Maharajah Jung Bahadur and to advise him upon several points which he would bring to His Lordship's attention, connected with the future Government of this State.'[1]

In replying to Jung's message, the Resident made it clear that the Government of India had no wish to intervene in the domestic affairs of Nepal, as follows: (continuation of the message, above)

'4. In reply to this message, I observed that the British Government acknowledged the independence of Nepal, and had no desire whatever, to meddle in matters connected with her internal administration; that we looked upon her as a friend and as an ally and would be most unwilling to risk any interruption to the good feelings [sic] that has [sic] gradually sprung up between the two States and which has been so steadily increasing up to the present moment, by taking any part

---

[1] Major G. Ramsay, Resident at Nepal to G. F. Edmonstone, Secretary to the Government of India in the Foreign Department, Ft. William, dated Nepal Residency June 20, 1857. *Foreign Secret Proceedings*, Part II, November 27, 1857, No. 414. (N.A.I.)

in her internal affairs—a cause which may thereafter lead to misunderstanding and mischief, and I said that it was contrary to the rule of the Governor General and the Supreme Government of India, to hold direct communication on Political matters, with any officers, however high their rank might be that might be deputed to the seat of Government by the Rulers of the Native States . . .'[1]

Edmonstone, in his answer to Ramsay's letter, concurred with Ramsay's position:

'. . . the language then held by you has been entirely approved; that it is a rule of the British Government in India as in England to abstain scrupulously from interference in the affairs of other independent states, that the rule is one to which the Governor General in Council will at all times adhere; and that he is satisfied that a departure from it is never without risk of ultimate injury to the good understanding which should bind neighboring and friendly States together however disinterestedly the interference may be exercised'.[2]

The whole episode raises the question of why Jung Bahadur made so unusual a request to the Indian Government. Part of the reason could be that Jung had presented himself to the Nepalese people as a man who was more important than the Prime Minister and even sometimes equal to the King of Nepal. By accepting the prime ministership, he would be lowering himself in the eyes of the people. His thought might have been that if the Governor-General of India requested or advised him to take the office, then the importance of the position would be enhanced in the public view. It is also possible that he actually wanted to please the British Government in India because he understood British strength after his visit to England in 1850 and thought it would be wise to have the support of a powerful neighbor. Whatever his motives, it must be said that he used a very undignified method to achieve his goal.

The Indian Mutiny and the Role of Nepal

Even before Jung Bahadur began his second term as Prime Minister, he had noticed discontentment among the princes of India and the Indian Army soldiers. On his own initiative, Jung called a meeting of influential Sirdars and other important leaders of Nepal on February 27, 1857, to discuss the possibility of helping the British Government

[1] See note 1, p. 71.
[2] G. F. Edmonstone, Secretary to the Government of India, in the Foreign Department, to Major G. Ramsay, Resident in Nepal. Dated Ft. William, November 18, 1857. *Foreign Department Secret No. 415.* (N.A.I.)

in India should the need arise. Ramsay in a despatch to Edmonstone, dated February 29, 1857, reported the meeting as follows:

'... that Maharajah Jung Bahadur assembled his brothers and leading Sirdars of this Durbar inclusive of those of the rank of Lieutenant Colonel at a grand Council on the 27th instant, laid before them his plans with reference to our government observing that he was fully acquainted with our vast power and resources, and desired to offer to us all the assistance which his nation can afford in our present temporary difficulties, believing that, not only will the act redound to his own credit and good name but that it may hereafter be extremely beneficial to his own country and materially increase the friendship and good feeling now subsisting between the two States which he considered it was specially to the interest of the Goorkhas to promote. He desired the Sirdars to give him their advice and opinion upon the point to speak openly and undisguisedly without fear of giving him offence and to remember that if they coincided in his views, and promised him the support they must not hereafter blame him, if the troops suffered hardships and meet with heavy losses or matters turn out to their mutual disadvantages.'[1]

Ramsay went on to report that the Sirdars and others at the meeting unanimously accepted Jung Bahadur's policy recommendations in favor of Nepalese aid to the British.[2] On the strength of this backing, Jung offered six regiments of the Gurkha (Royal Nepal) Army.

Oldfield writes that Jung Bahadur gave three reasons for offering assistance to the British, showing Jung's real foresight as to the needs of his future relations with the British. The three reasons were:

'1st. To show that the Gorkhas possess fidelity, and will pour out their blood in defense of those who treat them with honour and repose confidence in them.
2nd. That I know the power of the British Government, and that were I to take part against it, my country would afterwards be ruined and the Gorkha dynasty annihilated.
3rd. That I know that upon the success of British arms and reestablishment of the British power in India its government will be stronger than ever, and that I and my brothers will then benefit by our alliance with you, as your remembrance of our past services will render our present friendship lasting and will prevent ever molesting us.'[3]

Ramsay, receiving Jung's offer of troops, accepted it. However, he

[1] Ramsay to Edmonstone. Dated February 29, 1857, No. 64 of 1857. *Foreign Despatch Secret Proceedings*, Ft. William, November 27, 1857. (N.A.I.)
[2] Ramsay to Edmonstone, February 29, 1857, *op. cit.*
[3] Oldfield, *op. cit.*, pp. 29–30.

acted without prior consultation with the Government of India. Lord Canning, then Governor-General of India, reversed Ramsay and politely rejected Jung's offer; and the Court of Directors subsequently censured Ramsay for his action.[1] Edmonstone wrote to Ramsay that the Governor-General in Council was 'unwilling to accept it (the Nepalese offer) until the head of the rebellion should be crushed by the triumph of our own arms and the effect of that triumph should become manifest'.[2]

In spite of this rejection, Jung Bahadur did not give up hope of helping the British in the Mutiny. When he learned of their defeat at Cawnpore, the rumour of the death of General Wheeler and the rebellion of Nana Saheb, he immediately offered help in greater amount. Ramsay wrote that Jung Bahadur offered three divisions of Gurkha Sepahees, each division to consist of five regiments of 550 men, for a total of 2,750 men per division. Jung offered to take personal command of the entire force although he would keep his brothers and other trusted associates to help him. Jung told the Resident that he wished to show 'that he was a real friend of the British'. He said, 'If all the Princes of Hindoostan were to rise against us, the Nepalese will take our side against them, believing that by so doing they would thereby strengthen the friendship between the two countries, which would ultimately lead to the advantage of the Nepalese State'.[3] These offers were conveyed to the Resident through Kurbeer Khurtree, the Orderly Officer, who also told the Resident that in return for these services, Jung Bahadur wished that the Government of India would 'bestow upon him a tract of Country elsewhere, or recognize him as an independent Prince in Nepal'.[4] Ramsay rejected these rewards asked by Jung; and soon afterward was informed that Jung had removed these conditions altogether, and that the troops were offered with no strings attached.

[1] 'To the Honourable, the Secret Committee of the Honourable the Court of Directors.
Honourable Sirs,
We have the honour to acknowledge the receipt, on the 11 instant, of the following despatches from your Hon'ble Committee:—
No. 130, dated 8 August—Acknowledging receipt of despatches dated 19 June last, and entirely agreeing in the censure passed on Major Ramsay for accepting and pressing for the fulfilment of the offer made by General Jung Bahadur to lend troops to aid in suppressing the Mutiny in the Bengal Army.'
Foreign Department Secret Consultation. Despatch to Secretary, September 22, 1857. (N.A.I.)

[2] Edmonstone to Ramsay, dated November 18, 1857. No. 353 *Foreign Department Secret*, No. 425. November 27, 1857. Part II. (N.A.I.)

[3] Ramsay to Edmonstone. Dated Nepal Residency, July 17, 1858. *Foreign Dept. (Secret)* No. 423. (N.A.I.)

[4] *Ibid.*, paragraph 9.

THE INDIAN MUTINY

After the defeat of the rebels in Delhi and elsewhere, Lord Canning decided to accept Jung Bahadur's offer of Gurkha troops. The Gurkhas were wanted to act as auxiliaries to a British Army commanded by Sir Colin Campbell and assigned the mission to recapture Lucknow.[1] Canning's acceptance was written as follows:

'With the view then of relieving the people of the disturbed Districts, as soon as possible from the oppression under which they are now suffering and with a desire to reciprocate the feeling of friendship and confidence which the Nepal Durbar has so unequivocally expressed, the Governor General in Council accepts the services of the three Divisions of Goorkha troops, with guns equipped and commanded in the manner proposed and he desires that you will at once communicate this resolution to Raja Jung Bahadur, explaining to him the grounds on which the Government has proceeded in this matter.'[2]

Lord Canning's acceptance of the use of Nepalese troops was done with extreme caution, and some reluctance. From the beginning, the Government of India had been hesitant in this matter, and the reasons for its position are evident. If the Gurkha troops had gone to India in the early stages of the revolt, they might possibly have been persuaded by the rebels to join the rebel cause since it looked for a time as if the British would be defeated. The Government of India also knew that Jung Bahadur's forceful determination had persuaded the Bahadurs, Sirdars and many other influential Nepalese to side with the British but that there remained a fairly large group still working against his policy. This opposition was headed by no less a person than the Raj Guroo (state chief priest) and included other members of the Great Council of the Nepal Government.

A further factor contributing to the Government of India's hesitation to accept Jung Bahadur's offer was the discovery of a plot described as 'an attempt at mutiny of a regiment of the Nepalese troops and to murder Maharajah Jung Bahadur'.[3] According to the plot, Jung's assassination was to be carried out in June 1857 by a Gurkha officer. The existence of the plot clearly indicated that at least some of the Gurkha regiments had been successfully infiltrated by the rebels.

[1] Majumdar, K., *op. cit.*; Ramsay, *Nepal Residency Records* No. 4, *op. cit.* (N.A.I.)
[2] Edmonstone to Ramsay, dated November 18, 1857, *op. cit.*
[3] Secret Despatch to Secretary of State. *Foreign Department Secret Consultation* No. 33, June 19, 1857. (N.A.I.) Ramsay, *Nepal Residency Records*, No. 4, *op. cit.*

Jung's reaction to the plot against his life was to order the annihilation of the entire regiment to which the Gurkha officer-assassin was assigned, which would have meant the death of more than 1700 men if Ramsay had not induced him to change his mind. Ramsay was well aware of the possible disastrous effect on British–Nepalese relations that could have come from Jung's order.[1] And now, Ramsay and Lord Canning were alerted to the fact that Jung had powerful enemies opposing his pro-British policy within his own Army.

There was still another factor to be considered by Lord Canning. This was the danger that some Raja or Nawab of India might successfully induce Jung Bahadur to help him against the British. Ramsay had already informed Edmonstone about a letter sent to Jung by the rebel King of Oudh asking for help. Ramsay wrote that:

'In the letter from the rebel King, he simply observed that the inhabitants of the Gorukpore District having been dissatisfied with the Government of the Kaffirs,[2] he had appointed Mohamed Hoossein Khan Bahadoor to the charge of that District who had fought with and beaten the Kaffirs on several occasions, who had consequently fled from the place, but that they were making preparations to return there to attack him, he (the King) therefore hoped that in consideration of the friendship that had so long existed between the Governments of Oudh and Nepal, Jung Bahadoor would give orders to his subordinate authorities, to afford every assistance in time of need, in expelling the Kaffirs from the Country—which, should the two States combine in this cause would soon be thoroughly effected.'[3]

Considering all the various risks involved in accepting the Nepalese offer, Lord Canning was right in accepting Jung Bahadur's offer only when he felt the course of the war had turned clearly toward the British side.

Immediately upon the receipt of the letter from Lord Canning accepting his offer of Nepalese troops, Jung Bahadur mobilized his army and began to move the selected troops on to aid the British. Three thousand Nepalese soldiers under the command of Colonel Pulwan Sing Bushmat were ordered to the Nepal border to rendezvous with a British officer. Another detachment under Lieutenant Heera Sing was despatched from Palpa to the relief of Gorukpore which

---

[1] Ramsay, *Nepal Residency Records* No. 4, *op. cit.*
[2] Kaffirs—those who do not believe in God.
[3] Ramsay to Edmonstone, dated Nepal Residency, October 29, 1857. *Foreign Department Secret Consultation*, No. *440*, November 27, 1857 (No. 87 of 1857). (N.A.I.)

was seriously threatened.¹ Later, these troops moved to Azamgarh and Jaunpore and during the four months of their campaign, won many small battles against the rebels. Jung Bahadur meanwhile hurried to the help of the British with a force of 8,000 men, which was later increased to 14,000 men (a very large force for Nepal). First, he restored the authority of the British in Gorukpore by overthrowing the Nazim (Magistrate) of that District, Mohammed Hoosein. By January 1858 he had shattered the military strength and prestige of the rebels in the area.²

Jung Bahadur then met with Sir Colin Campbell and went over the military strategy to be employed for the capture of Lucknow. In several days of action, Jung's Gurkha forces captured the famous Chattar Manzil and the Moti Mahal. Finally, the Gurkha assault on the Kaisar Bagh completed the relief operation at Lucknow. The Gurkhas, true to ancient military custom, looted the fallen city and thus completed their work.³

Meanwhile, in December 1857, a detachment of 290 Gurkhas were sent to Kumaon where the Commissioner of Kumaon had asked for help to defend that area. The Gurkhas had several successful battles with the rebels and showed their gallantry, winning the praise of the Commissioner.⁴

The services of Maharajah Jung Bahadur and the Nepalese army to the British during the dark days of the Mutiny were warmly acknowledged by the British Secretary of State in a secret despatch (dated March 17, 1858) to the Governor-General. This despatch is quoted here in its entirety because of its special importance as a statement of the British Government's acknowledgement of the value of the Nepalese military services and of the territorial reward authorized for these services.⁵

[1] Ramsay, *Nepal Residency Records*, No. 4, *op. cit.*; Landon, *op. cit.*; p. 149.
[2] Majumdar, K., *op. cit.*; Landon, *op. cit.*, p. 149; Ramsay, *Nepal Residency Reports*, No. 4.
[3] Ramsay, *Nepal Residency Records*, No. 4, *op. cit.*; Landon, *op. cit.*
[4] Ramsay, *Nepal Residency Records*, No. 4, *op. cit.*; Majumdar, K., *op. cit.*
[5] No. 1933 (Copy) *Secret*.
To
 the Right Hon'ble
 The Governor General Of India in Council

1. The Maharaja Jung Bahadoor offered at the commencement of our difficulties to give our Government the efficient aid of Nepalese Troops. Toward the end of July, this aid having been accepted, a body of 3,000 Nepalese troops entered our Territory and moved upon Segowly.

2. The troops were followed by others, and ultimately the Maharaja himself at the head we believe of from 14 to 20 Battalions, followed his advanced guard, recovered Goruckpore for us, and thence marched upon Fyzabad, while,

The victories of the Gurkhas at Bihar, Gorukpore, Azamgarh, Jaunpore, Allahabad and Oudh made them quite proud of their help to the British. All of those who had seen the Gurkhas fight had nothing but praise for their gallantry. They proved again that they were first-class fighting men.[1]

by means of the Nepaulese Troops first sent to our relief he has protected our Districts of Azamgarh and Jounpore, and Banaras itself.

3. These were great services rendered to us in our utmost need.

4. We are unwilling to imagine the position in which we should now have been without this aid from the Maharajah—and still less of the course which events must have taken had the Maharajah taken advantage of our distresses, and directed against us the force he has employed in our defense.

5. The Maharaja may possibly have thought that the example of a successful revolt of our troops against us might lead to a similar revolt of the Nepaulese Troops against the Government he administered—and that it was in the common interest of all constituted authorities to suppress a mutinous Soldiery, but he must also have had in view the obtaining from us of some substantial mark of our gratitude, which might make his name famous amongst his countrymen.

6. There could be no reward so grateful to His Highness as the restoration of the Districts which lie between the frontier of Nepaul and that of Oude, and which were ceded to us in 1816, and by us made over to Oude.

7. We must admit that the acquisition of these Districts is a legitimate object of Nepaulese ambition, and we cannot hesitate to authorise you to acquaint the Maharajah that, in consideration of the great service he has rendered to us, you will forthwith appoint officers to mark out the future line of frontier between the Nepaulese dominions and ours, from our districts of Goruckpore to Rohilcund, in such a manner as to afford to Nepaul a belt of Terraie and of plain along the whole line, similar to that which intervenes between the Mountains of Nepaul and our District of Goruckpore.

8. According to our map, there is a road or way which leaves the left bank of the Gogra soon after that River enters the Terraie, and passing below Muhoumes goes, by Gooluree and Dhumgurkee, to a stream which runs into the Kurnalli.

9. This road till it reaches the stream and thence the stream itself, would seem to be, so far a convenient boundary.

10. We do not desire that the Nepaulese frontier should actually touch the Gogra; and, therefore, it would be better that, from the point where the stream we have mentioned enteres the Kurnalli, a line should be drawn from the Kurnalli, across the other two streams which seem to flow parallel nearby to it, to a point on the left bank of the farthest of these two streams, near the Road from Bharatpoor and along that Road, to the line to be drawn according to the instructions given before, till it reaches our District of Goruckpore.

11. We hope the Maharajah will be satisfied with this cession. It is better that we should frankly offer it than that His Highness should ask for it.

East India House,   We are etc.
17th March 1858   sd/-Ross D. Mangles
(True Copy)   G. F. Edmonstone, Secretary to Government of India with the Governor General.

Mangles to Canning, *Foreign Department, Secret Despatch from Secretary of State*, 1858. No. 1933 (N.A.I.)

[1] Ramsay, *Nepal Residency Records*, No. 4, op. cit.

After the victory at Lucknow, Jung Bahadur along with British Army Brigadier MacGregor, started his return journey to Nepal going by way of Allahabad, Benares, and Gorukpore. This route was selected so that Jung could meet with the Governor-General who was then campaigning at Allahabad. At this meeting, Lord Canning announced the decision of the Government of India to grant a large tract of territory (see footnote 5, p. 77) to Nepal in consideration of the services rendered to the British Government during the Mutiny.[1] Needless to say, Jung accepted the territorial award.

According to Landon, Padma Jung (Jung Bahadur's son, who wrote a biography of his father) wrote that Jung Bahadur felt his days of service during the Mutiny were the most important of his life.[2] Jung's objectives were to prove his loyalty to the British, to secure the permanency of the governmental power in the hands of his family and to save his country from future molestation by the powerful British Government, and all of these goals were ultimately fulfilled.

The Role of Jung Bahadur and the British
Maharajah Jung Bahadur returned to Nepal with enormous wealth which he and his troops took in the sack of Lucknow. Ramsay, the Resident, described the march of the Gurkhas back to Nepal as 'more like that of a rabble than an armed force'.[3] On the journey home, the thoughts of the Gurkha troops, and of Jung Bahadur, likely dwelt on the many tempting offers he had received from the rebel leaders while he moved with his forces to the plains of India to assist the British. Jung admitted that he was in constant touch with the rebel leaders, who offered to make him the King of Oudh if he joined them.[4] However, he had no intentions of alienating the British; hence, he disregarded the rebel offers. But nevertheless, he felt a certain sympathy with his enemy. The offers made to him also had some effect on the Gurkha soldiery, 'many of whom openly gave out that they would return to the plains during the next cold season, to annex certain of our districts to their own country'.[5] This talk was not taken seriously by Ramsay, who expressed his opinion that:

'... This (Lucknow) expedition strengthens our prestige immensely throughout the Nepalese Dominions, and that the Goorkhas have a

---
[1] Ramsay, *Nepal Residency Records*, No. 4, *op. cit.*; Landon, *op. cit.*, p. 149; Tuker, *op. cit.*, p. 157.
[2] Landon, *op. cit.*, p. 149.
[3] Ramsay, *Nepal Residency Records*, No. 4, 1858, *op. cit.*
[4] *Ibid.*
[5] *Ibid.*

far higher appreciation of, and respect for our power *now*, than they ever entertained before.'[1]

Regarding these rebel offers, Jung Bahadur tried to follow a policy of pleasing both the British and the rebels insofar as he could. To please the British, Jung sent the letters received by him from the rebel leaders to the Resident with the request that they should be transmitted to the Governor-General for his inspection. These rebel letters asked the Maharajah of Nepal, in the name of religion, to refrain from helping the British.[2]

Jung's position in these matters was indicated by the Assistant Resident, Captain Byers, who wrote:

'... If his lordship should be of opinion that the communication (from the rebels) should be treated with contempt, and receive no reply, the Maharaja will remain silent; if however, His Lordship approves of the proposed reply, or any portion of it, His Excellency will send it to the ambassador at Toolseepore.

He also desires me to say that the letter to the address of the Maharaja of Nepal, has not been shown to His Highness, and will receive no reply from him, as it is unusual for His Highness to correspond directly with anyone except the Right Honourable the Governor General, but through him (the Maharajah Jung Bahadoor, his Prime Minister).'[3]

In a similar way, a letter received from the Rajah of Gonda was sent by Jung Bahadur to the Resident for inspection. The letter read:

... I hear a rumour that your Highness will come down to the aid of the Begum—when great men are in trouble, they ask protection from great men, and they assist each other—It is my earnest request that your Highness must do so. The country is losing its faith (dharum) through the oppression of the English, and without your Highness's aid it will be impossible for it to preserve its religion—do as you think best.'[4]

[1] Ramsay, *Nepal Residency Records*, No. 4, 1858, *op. cit.*
[2] Captain C. H. Byers, Assistant Resident, Nepal. In charge of the Residency to G. F. Edmonstone, Esquire, Secretary to the Government of India, in the Foreign Department, with the Governor-General, Allahabad. Dated: Nepal Residency, June 10, 1858. *Foreign Department Secret Consultation*, August 27, 1858, Nos. 97–108, No. 32 of 1858. (N.A.I.)
[3] *Ibid.*
[4] Captain C. H. Byers, Assistant Resident at Nepal ... to G. F. Edmonstone, ... Dated: Nepal Residency, October 23, 1858. *Foreign Political Department*, November 19, 1858, Nos. 75–77. (N.A.I.)

THE INDIAN MUTINY

In his replies, Jung Bahadur wrote to the rebel leaders that if they had not murdered any British lady or child, they should immediately ask for pardon from the British Government. Praising the British, he wrote in one letter to certain rebel leaders:

'... since the star of faith and integrity, sincerity in words, as well as in acts; and the wisdom and comprehension of the British are shining as bright as the sun in every quarter of the globe, be assured that my Government will never disunite itself from the friendship of the exalted British Government, or be instigated to join, with any Monarch against it, be he as high as heaven—What grounds then have we for connecting ourselves with the Hindoos, and Mohamedans of Hindoostan...'[1]

It is interesting to note that the answers sent by Jung Bahadur were exactly what was approved by the Governor-General of India.

Jung Bahadur and the Rebel Fugitives

Many of the Mutiny rebel leaders and their supporters attempted to escape the wrath of the British by fleeing to Nepal. Aware of this, the British requested Jung Bahadur to check the influx of rebels into Nepalese territory and not to offer asylum to them.

Jung Bahadur, however, conspired with the important rebels, allowing them to enter Nepalese territory with the help and co-operation of the Nepalese officers on the border.[2] Regarding one rebel group, Colonel Kelly wrote to the Resident on April 2, 1859, that 'On the morning of the 28th *ultimo* (March), they (the rebels) were in such a state of distress for want of food that Mohamed Hoosein and other rebel leaders, who had given themselves up, assured me that their whole force must have surrendered through fear of starvation in a day or two had they not received from the Gurkhas supply of rice on the 29th *ultimo*'.[3]

At the same time, Colonel Kelly reported to the Resident a very interesting piece of information which threw light on Jung Bahadur's

---

[1] The Secretary to the Government of India with the Governor General to Captain C. H. Byers, Assistant Resident at Nepal. In charge of the Residency. Dated: Allahabad, June 28, 1858. *Foreign Department Secret Consultations*, August 27, 1858, Nos. 97–108. (No. 1881.) (N.A.I.) See Appendix III. Letter from Jung Bahadur to Munnos Khan, the Nana Rao and the Raja Benee Madao Buccus, dated September 1859.

[2] Ramsay, *Nepal Residency Records*, No. 4, 1859; Majumdar, K., *op. cit.*, pp. 324–7.

[3] Ramsay, *Nepal Residency Records*, No. 4, 1859, *op. cit.*

relations with the rebel leaders and why they were expecting assistance from Nepal. Kelly's memorandum read, as follows:

'Mohamed Hoosein says that after the battle of the 25th *ultimo* while he was with the rebels at Mahpore about 2 coss West of Nyahkote, Brigadier Pulwan Sing and another Goorkha Captain had come to Balo Rao and demanded one crore of Rupees. If this sum will be paid to them in ten days, they will assist them with troops to fight against the English Government—on their return to Bootwul, the Nana, Bala Rao and Munno Khan, told to all the rebel Chiefs about the promise of assistance by the Goorkha Chiefs on being paid the above sum. Mohamed also says that he had seen a letter from Jung Bahadur to Bala Rao saying that he does not want the valuable stones or money in papers, but he wanted money in cash.'[1]

On November 1, 1858, the Governor-General of India proclaimed a general amnesty to include those rebels who were in the Terai in 1859.[2] Very few of the latter took advantage of this offer. The reason probably was that the principal rebel leaders like Nana Saheb, Bala Rao, the Begum of Oudh, Benee Madho, the Rajah of Gondah Munnoo Khan were hoping to organize an army, with promises of help from Jung Bahadur.[3] They raised the morale of their supporters by telling them that when the rains were over, the Gurkhas would move down to their assistance. Without their knowing it, Jung Bahadur decided to use his army to oust them from the Terai.

In November 1859, Jung Bahadur went to the Terai with 10,000 soldiers. In the Butwal District, the rebels were anxiously waiting for help from the Nepal Durbar; when they saw Jung Bahadur approach with his big army, they flocked to him from all sides confident that he had come to help them. Too late, they realized their error. Jung Bahadur proceeded to throw the rebels out of the Terai and to turn them over to the British. Brigadier Holdich, in his report to Sir William Mansfield, the British Chief of Staff, wrote:

'The Nepalese authorities have delivered up nearly every rebel leader remaining alive, whilst the death of others (among them Nana Rao and Bala Rao and Azimoollah) had been most satisfactorily accounted for.'[4]

[1] Colonel Kelly to G. Ramsay, the Resident. Dated Camp Raxaul, April 5, 1859. *Foreign Political Dept.*, May 20, 1859, No. 264.
[2] Ramsay, *Nepal Residency Records*, No. 4, op. cit.
[3] Majumdar, K., op. cit., pp. 324–7.
[4] Brief memo of the political relations between Her Majesty's India Government and the State of Nepal, continued from April 30, 1854, to October 31,

The Brigadier did not believe that an armed rebel remained in the Terai. (Later on, the Indian Government learned that Brigadier Holdich had been overly optimistic.)

In reality, this expedition by Jung Bahadur was against the rank and file of the rebels and the minor leaders. It soon became clear to the British that Jung was protecting a few leaders who were Brahmins or of royal descent. Among them were Nana Saheb, Bala Rao, the Begum of Oudh and her son, Birjis Qadar. These leaders were in friendly communication with influential Nepalese leaders like Jay Kishen Pure and Badri Nar Singh[1] who had enough power in the Durbar to ensure that their rebel friends would not be handed over to the British.[2] While writing to Colonel Kelly, Ramsay observed:

'The more I hear and see what is passing at this Durbar, the more convinced am I that the sympathy of the Sardars and of the Army are with the rebels rather than with us.'[3]

The double game played by Jung Bahadur regarding these important rebel leaders made the British suspicious of him. Knowing his power in Nepal, it was hard to believe that anything could be done against his wishes. The obvious conclusion was that he had ceased to co-operate with the British Government in so far as their desire to capture these key rebel leaders was concerned.[4]

Above all, Jung Bahadur was unwilling to surrender Nana Saheb whom the British were particularly anxious to capture since he had been responsible for the massacre at Cawnpore.[5] But Jung could not bring himself to hand over a Brahmin to be executed. His feelings about Nana Saheb were disclosed in remarks made by the Orderly Officer to Dr Oldfield. The Orderly Officer said that Jung felt himself to be in a very difficult situation with respect to the Nana. Jung felt sure that when he went to the Terai, the Nana would seek an interview with him. If the Nana 'throws himself down at his (Jung's) feet and claims his protection as a Brahmin, what could he do?'[6] 'From the

---

1861, as called for in circular from the Foreign Secretary to the Government of India. No. 4790 of August 23, 1861. *Nepal Residency Records*, No. 4, *op. cit.*

[1] Majumdar, K., *op. cit.*, pp. 324-7.
[2] *Ibid.*
[3] *Ibid.*
[4] *Ibid.*
[5] *Ibid.* 'I am convinced', wrote Ramsay, 'that he (Jung Bahadur) knows more of their (rebels) plans and movements than he chooses to admit.'
[6] Lord Canning to Sir Charles Wood, Secretary of State for India, *Foreign Department*, Ft. William, October 8, 1860, No. 144. (N.A.I.)

very first day, he (Jung) made up his mind to shield Nana', so Lord Canning informed the Secretary of State, in London.[1]

Percival Landon is considered to have more definite information than any other writer regarding Jung Bahadur's attitude toward the principal rebel leaders and particularly the Nana. According to Landon, the Nana and his party were received at the border by Kedar Nar Singh, a Nepalese general who had been specially assigned for this task by Jung Bahadur.[2] At the beginning, Jung Bahadur was not very favorable to the Nana and his party, and he informed them that he would not protect them at the expense of injuring his relations with the British. He agreed, however, to grant asylum to the females of the Nana's party.[3] Quoting the Calcutta Records, Landon wrote that the Nana consented to leave the females of his party under the protection of Jung Bahadur provided that he himself was not molested.[4] This became a sort of 'gentlemen's agreement' between the Nana and Jung.

On this point of asylum for the rebel leaders, Kanchanmoy Majumdar quotes a source which stated that, '... in addition, the Begum of Oudh and her minor son, Birjis Kader, the two wives of Baji Rao II, the ex-Peshwa, and the wives of Bala Rao and Nana Saheb were given asylum by Jung Bahadur. They lived at Kathmandu on a monthly subsidy of Rs. 400 ($78.00) granted by the Nepal Government.'[5] R. C. Majumdar also believed that both Nana Saheb and Bala Saheb lived and died in Nepal, and that the Nana could not have wandered around there without the active or at least indirect support of Jung Bahadur.[6]

In order to relieve British pressure, Jung Bahadur reported the deaths of Bala Saheb and Nana Saheb to the Resident. The former, according to Jung, died on June 30, 1860. The death of the Nana was reported to Ramsay in a very casual way by Jung as having taken place on September 24, 1860.[7] From that time onward, Ramsay did not trust any information from Jung regarding the Nana's death. Also sceptical, the Indian Government requested the Nepal Durbar to furnish more specific information regarding the Nana's supposed death. To convince the British, Siddhiman Singh produced what he said was the frontal bone of the Nana. (According to Hindu custom,

---

[1] Lord Canning to Sir Charles Wood, *op. cit.*
[2] Landon, *op. cit.*, p. 158.
[3] *Ibid.*
[4] *Ibid.*
[5] Majumdar, K., *op. cit.*, pp. 324-7.
[6] Majumdar, R. C., *The History and Culture of the Indian People, British Paramountcy and Indian Renaissance*, Vol. IX, Part I, p. 588.
[7] Memo of the Political Relations between Her Majesty's Indian Government and the State of Nepal. *Nepal Residency Records*, No. 4, *op. cit.*

the frontal bone of a Brahmin should be sent to Benares, the holy place.)[1] At the same time, the Nana's mother was insisting that both of her sons were dead.

The British Government continued to be sceptical, and Jung Bahadur developed great reluctance to discuss this issue with the Resident. In July 1861 the Resident wrote to Mr E. C. Baley, 'if the Nana be still alive, the secret is buried in the breast of Jung Bahadur...'[2] The Resident reported that Jung offered, 'If you believe the Nana to be alive, you may send persons into Nepal to search for him, who shall be attended by several Nepalese officers to assist them in procuring supplies and to protect them from insult or injury. If they succeed in finding the Nana, I will seize him and give him up to you, but before they cross the frontier, a formal written engagement must be made to this effect between the two governments, with a proviso that, if you do not find the Nana within a reasonable time, the British Government shall cede to Nepal the tract of territory that has lately been refused me, viz. the low lands now comprising the British Teraie, north of the eastern portion of Oude, which lie between the Arrah Nuddee and Bhugora-tal.'[3]

Jung Bahadur knew perfectly well that the Government of India would never accept this proposal. They realized that it would have been impossible for British forces, operating in an unfamiliar land, to search successfully for the Nana under the guidance of Nepalese officers. All that would have come from acceptance of Jung's offer would be the loss of some British territory to Nepal. This impossible proposal added to the already strong suspicion that the Nana was still alive in Nepal. Lord Canning wrote to the British Secretary of State that Jung Bahadur had no serious intention of turning over the Nana. According to Canning, Jung said that he could catch the Nana any time he pleased, 'and it could easily be done by treachery; but that he would do nothing that was dishonourable'.[4] Hoping to bribe Jung by appealing to his well known weakness for money, the British Government had announced a reward of one lakh of rupees ($19,000) for capturing Nana Saheb but even this bait was not effective with Jung. Landon collected several interesting versions of how he died. All of them have been documented and have some evidence to support them.[5] Finally the British decided not to search for the Nana any more. The Government of India felt certain that he lived in Nepal

[1] Landon, *op. cit.*, Vol. II, p. 161.
[2] *Ibid.*, p. 162.
[3] *Ibid*, p. 162.
[4] Lord Canning to Sir Charles Wood, Secretary of State, *Foreign Department*, October 8, 1960, No. 144.
[5] See Landon's *Nepal*, Vol. II, Chapter IX on 'Nana Saheb', pp. 156–70.

with the full knowledge and protection of Jung Bahadur, and that he would never be caught owing to the Prime Minister's refusal to hand him over.[1] Most of the scholars who have written about Nepal came to the conclusion that the Nana lived in Nepal and died there. Unfortunately the correct story of the Nana's death remains unknown until this day. On this issue scholars have to wait until some fresh evidence is found.

Jung Bahadur was very helpful in searching out some English ladies who were Christians and were held as hostages in the camp of Nana Saheb. The Nana had assured Jung Bahadur that two Christian women and one English lady had been sent back to India. The British authorities reported that these ladies did not reach the plains of India. Landon claimed that this could have been a mistake as 'Bala Rao showed Siddhiman Singh a receipt for the safe arrival of ladies at Gorukhpur signed by Mr Burns'.[2] On suspicion Bala Rao's place of residence in Nepal was searched but no women were found. However, through the active support of Jung Bahadur most of the English hostages with Nana were recovered.

It seems probable that Jung Bahadur helped the rebel leaders partly because of their immense wealth which they brought from India. Landon wrote that Jung bought the jewels of Nana and of the Begum Huzrat Mahal of Lucknow for a very small sum. Landon also stated that Jung Bahadur had passed an order forbidding any private person to buy the jewels of Nana Saheb.[3] Most of the jewels of the rebel leaders were bought by Jung Bahadur directly or indirectly. Landon further claimed that a 'certain number of these jewels were offered as bribes to Siddhiman Singh or to Jung Bahadur'[4] by the rebels, and that the Resident, Colonel Ramsay, reported that Jung Bahadur sold an estate in Butwal for Rs. 36,000 ($7,000) to the Nana family.[5] It would be unjust, however, if it were accepted that Jung Bahadur protected the rebel leaders from the British simply because of their wealth. In fact, in some cases he helped them by granting them land in his own territory without payment. Colonel Lawrence, the Resident, reported that the Nepal Durbar had conferred a Jagheer (landed property) on Surfraz Ali Khan, who was a rebel. Jung Bahadur denied this and stated that it was given to him by some influential Mohammedans who lived in the Terai. However, according to Jung Bahadur, Surfraz Ali Khan's son, was given employment in the Durbar with pay of Rs. 200

[1] Majumdar, K., *op. cit.*, pp. 324–7; Majumdar, R. C., *op. cit.*, p. 588; Landon, *op. cit.*, Vol. II, p. 162.
[2] Landon, *op. cit.*, p. 160, *Nepal Residency Records*, No. 4, 1859, *op. cit.*
[3] *Ibid.*, p. 163.
[4] *Ibid.*, p. 160.
[5] *Ibid.*, p. 162. .

($38.00) a year.¹ This could only have been done with Jung Bahadur's consent. When Bala Rao, the brother of Nana Saheb, asserted that he and his brother belonged to the priestly (Brahmin) caste and for that reason claimed the obedience of Jung Bahadur, the latter informed him that the English were his friends but that he would do whatever he could provided it did not hurt his friendship with the British.² Jung Bahadur earlier said that when the Nana claimed his protection as a Brahmin, 'what can he do'.³ The facts seem to show that Jung Bahadur gave sanctuary to rebel leaders who could afford to pay for it, but that in addition to this he protected Brahmin leaders because he was himself a Hindu and also because he was the Prime Minister of a purely Hindu state.

The Quarrel with Colonel Ramsay

The demand for the removal of the Resident Colonel G. Ramsay was first made when Jung Bahadur was returning after his victory in the Mutiny and halted at Allahabad to have a personal interview with Lord Canning, the Governor–General of India, in March 1858. At this meeting he brought some sixteen charges against the Resident and made a written request for his removal. Among the major charges against Colonel Ramsay the Maharajah Dhiraj accused him 'of kicking of our subjects, and, above all, that of desecrating the first of our Hindoo temples in Nepal or the Pussputtee Nath by violating those precincts into which none but Hindoo can be admitted; into which no former Residents or any other European Gentlemen ever before attempted to force themselves; took place whilst the Maharajah was absent from Nepal'.⁴ Ramsay was summoned by the Governor-General to Allahabad in the month of May to answer the charges. After full deliberation the British Government sent a Yaddasht (official Reminder) to Jung Bahadur announcing that Colonel Ramsay 'will shortly resume his functions, as representative of the British Government at the Court of the Maharajah of Nepal, and that he be supported in the discharge of his duties, by the full and unshaken confidence of the Right Honour-

---

¹ Colonel R. C. Lawrence, Resident in Nepal to C. U. Aitchison, Officiating Secretary to Government of India, Foreign Department, with the Governor General. No. 14, dated July 10, 1868 (Confidential). *Foreign Political Department*, July 1868, Nos. 375–6. (N.A.I.)

² Landon, *op. cit.*, p. 160.

³ Lord Canning to Sir Charles Wood, *Foreign Department*, October 8, 1860.

⁴ Yaddasht sent by His Highness the Maharajah Dhiraj of Nepal to Captain C. H. Byers, in charge of the Residency, this day twenty-fifth of June, one thousand eight hundred and fifty-eight of the Christian era. *Foreign Department Secret*, July 30, 1858, Nos. 120–39 and K. W. paragraph 10. (N.A.I.) *Nepal Residency Records*, No. 4, 1858, *op. cit.*

able the Governor-General....'¹ This Yaddasht angered Jung Bahadur. He immediately discussed the matter with Captain Byers, the Assistant Resident, and asserted that the Governor-General had promised him at Allahabad that he would remove 'Colonel Ramsay and appoint Colonel C. Mackenzie or some other officer, in his place'.² Jung Bahadur quoted General MacGregor who according to him also knew about the Governor-General's promise. The Prime Minister went on to remind Captain Byers of the help he gave to the British during the Mutiny. In view of this he hoped that his request would be accepted.³ Jung Bahadur accused the Governor-General of breaking his promise and said that he felt that he had lost his honor in the eyes of his countrymen. He asserted 'that Lieutenant-Colonel Ramsay's return here is only the first step towards the British picking a quarrel with the Nepalese in order to take their country'.⁴ The Prime Minister strongly refused to accept Ramsay as Resident and even threatened that if he should receive any personal injuries or insult in Nepal he would not be responsible. The Durbar would never recognize Ramsay as Resident until he received a satisfactory reply from the Governor-General in reply to his charges. He asked Captain Byers,

'Why should your Government put me into such a dilemma? If I recognize him (Lieutenant-Colonel Ramsay) as Resident, I shall stultify my own assertions, and prove that what I have given out, on the repeated assurances of your own Government officers, is utterly false—or on the other hand, if I do not recognize him as Resident, your Government will take the matter up as an insult to themselves. If Lieutenant-Colonel Ramsay returns, my honor is gone in the eyes of my Countrymen—that gone, I am desperate: of what value is my life? Either his or mine must be sacrificed.'⁵

To reinforce this threat he even asked the Maharajah Dhiraj of Nepal to write a Yaddasht on this point to the acting Resident. In his Yaddasht the Maharajah Dhiraj bluntly asked, 'How happens it, then that after

---

¹ Abstract translation of a Yaddasht from Captain C. H. Byers, Assistant Resident in charge of the Residency, to the address of His Excellency Maharajah Jung Bahadur, Prime Minister and Commander in Chief of Nepal, dated June 24, 1858. *Foreign Department Secret*, July 30, 1858, Nos. 120–39 and K. W. (N.A.I.)
² Captain Byers to Edmonstone, Nepal, June 26, 1858 (Duplicate), *Foreign Department Secret*, July 30, 1858, Nos. 120–39 and K.W. (N.A.I.)
³ Byers to Edmonstone, Nepal, June 26, 1858. No. 56 of 1858, *op. cit.*
⁴ *Ibid.*
⁵ Captain Byers to Edmonstone, Nepal, June 26, 1858. No. 56 of 1858 (Duplicate), *op. cit.*

the short period of two months, every promise made by His Lordship should be retracted. . . .'¹ The Maharajah Dhiraj dealt with the issue at length and finally ended with this threat

'In conclusion, should all I have said be again overlooked by the Right Honourable Governor General, and should Lieutenant-Colonel Ramsay be forced upon me, as the Resident of Nepaul: in such a case, do I say I am fully resolved to quit Kathmandoo, and to fix my residence in some distant and solitary hills, where Maharajah Bahadur shall follow me.'²

The Governor-General took strong exception to the statement that 'the Governor-General had retracted on his promise', and completely ignored the threat of the king to leave Kathmandu with his Prime Minister. The final result of all this correspondence was that the Maharajah Dhiraj as well as Jung Bahadur accepted Ramsay as the Resident. In another Yaddasht the Maharajah Dhiraj was apologetic about his accusation of the Governor-General's breach of faith and explained that

'. . . the reason was that what I said in my Goorkha dialect was translated into oordo, which was again rendered into the English language, and in this process my meaning was altered. However in future His Lordship's instructions will be attended to'.³

While agreeing to receive Ramsay as Resident the Maharajah wrote:

'Agreeably with the orders which His Lordship has been pleased to issue in vindication of the honor of the British Government, and the fulfilment of the wishes of that of mine, we consent to receive Lieutenant-Colonel Ramsay, as Resident, and on his return to Nepal to pay him all the honor and respect, which the Durbar has shown to Residents in former years.'⁴

---

[1] Yaddasht sent by His Highness the Maharajah Dhiraj of Nepaul, to Captain C. H. Byers, in Charge of the Residency, this day the twenty-fifth of June, one thousand eight hundred and fifty-eight of the Christian era. (Red Seal of His Highness the Maharajah of Nepal.) *op. cit.*

[2] *Ibid.*

[3] Abstract Translation of a Lall Mohree Yaddasht from His Highness the Maharajah Dhiraj to the address of Captain C. H. Byers. Assistant Resident in charge of the Nepal Residency, dated the 28 of Assadh Sumbut 1915, corresponding with July 23, 1858. *Foreign Department Secret*, August 27, 1858, Nos. 93–5 and K.W. (N.A.I.)

[4] *Ibid.*

In another despatch he wrote:

'The Nepal State is ready to obey the order of His Lordship, with eyes and head (with honor) with the hope that after the order issued by His Lordship has been obeyed, His Lordship will do them the great favor of making a change in the person of the Resident.'[1]

Maharajah Jung Bahadur wrote to Captain Byers in connection with Ramsay's return to Kathmandu,

'... that I have always obeyed the orders of His Lordship the Governor General; I obey them on the present occasion, and will also do so for the future.'[2]

In one of his interviews with Captain Byers, Jung Bahadur said,

'... that he looked up to the Governor General as to a father and as an obedient son, bows in submission to His Lordship's direction.'[3]

Captain Byers in his reply wrote to Jung Bahadur as follows:

'... the Governor General entertains the hope, that both His Highness the Maharajah Dhiraj and Your Excellency, may meanwhile reflect on what has passed, and satisfy yourselves that, in relegating Lieutenant Colonel Ramsay to Nepal, His Lordship has no other wish or design, than to vindicate the honor of the Government, and to give to the character of its representative, the protection, which common justice demands.'[4]

When Ramsay resumed his appointment as Resident Jung Bahadur paid him a visit to smooth relations between the two. Ramsay wrote to Simson that in his interview with the prime minister

[1] Yaddasht from Maharajah Dhiraj to Captain Byers, July 1858, op. cit.
[2] Abstract Translation of a Yaddasht from His Excellency Maharajah Jung Bahadoor Ranajee, Prime Minister and Commander in Chief of Nepal to the address of Captain C. H. Byers, Assistant Resident in Charge of the Nepal Residency, dated the 28th of Assadh Sumbut 1915, corresponding with July 23, 1858, op. cit.
[3] Captain Byers to Edmonstone. Dated Nepal Residency, July 22, 1858. (Duplicate) No. 47 of 1858. *Foreign Department Secret*, August 27, 1858, No. 92. (N.A.I.)
[4] Abstract Translation of a Yaddasht from Captain C. H. Byers, Assistant Resident in Charge of the Nepal Residency, to His Excellency Maharajah Jung Bahadoor Ranajee, Prime Minister and Commander in Chief of Nepal, dated July 21, 1858. *Foreign Department Secret*, August 27, 1858, Nos. 90–1. (N.A.I.)

'... he desired that all that has passed between us may be forgotten and forgiven upon both sides, and said that, if in any coming discussions between the two States he should ever allow himself to be influenced by personal feelings towards me or refer to what has lately taken place, might it be considered as a stain upon his own honor and upon the honor of his family....'[1]

Outwardly the Ramsay affair was finally settled amicably but it left a feeling of resentment in the mind of Jung Bahadur for some time. Gradually he and his successors forgot the differences of the past and this incident did not affect the relations of the two states. In a memorandum which was prepared by Ramsay himself for the record of the Residency, he wrote that

'Maharajah Jung Bahadur now made no secret that the paper of complaints that he had handed to the Governor-General at Allahabad was mere blind, and that his one grievance for which he had vowed that he would cause the Resident's removal, was, the latter's having refused to permit him to interfere between the Minister General Bum Bahadoor and himself.'[2]

It was true that Ramsay did not recognize Jung Bahadur as more than a respected and influential Nepalese citizen while Bum Bahadur was prime minister of Nepal from August 1856 to May 1857. Jung Bahadur resented and probably disliked Ramsay from that time. How far this is correct it is hard to say. It appears probable that Jung Bahadur had some kind of personal grudge against the Resident although the exact nature of it is not known. For a moment this issue caused strained relations between the two Governments, but the firm attitude of the Governor-General ended the crisis. Undoubtedly this incident hurt the prestige of the Nepal Government and also that of Jung Bahadur in the eyes of the British.

Extradition Between Nepal and British India

British India and Nepal had a common frontier and had to live side by side despite the differences in religions, customs, culture, occupations and languages. With the growth of friendly relations between them it became a practical necessity for them to negotiate some sort of agreement to regulate their day to day raids, robberies, killings and other

[1] Ramsay to Simson, Under-Secretary to Government of India. Dated Nepal Residency, February 23, 1859. No. 30 of 1859. *Foreign Department Secret*, December 30, 1859, No. 603. (N.A.I.)
[2] Ramsay, *Nepal Residency Records*, No. 4, 1859.

intercourse. Under the circumstances such an agreement should have been reached much earlier, but this was prevented by the strong anti-British feeling of the previous rulers of Nepal. They did not want to have any kind of legal relations with their powerful neighbor. Probably they felt the force of the principle expressed by Machiavelli:

'A Prince ought to take care never to make an alliance with one more powerful than himself for the purpose of attacking others, because if he conquers, you are at his discretion.'

When Jung Bahadur found himself fully in control of power in Nepal after being almost ten years in office, he signed the first extradition treaty with the British Government on February 10, 1855. The Treaty of 1855, which was signed on a reciprocal basis stated in Articles 2, 3, and 4 that the Nepal Government was bound to deliver up to the British Government all those persons who were British subjects charged with murder or attempted murder, if the British authorities demanded them with full requisition, provided the evidence were sufficient to justify their apprehension according to the laws of the country in which the said criminals might be found.[1]

After a lapse of ten years the two states found it was necessary to bind themselves more closely on the issue of extradition. It was agreed that the new treaty would be just a supplement to the earlier treaty. Ramsay wrote to the Secretary of the Government of India that Maharajah Jung Bahadur was especially anxious that embezzlement by public officers or other persons might be added to the list of offences specified in the 4th Article of the existing Extradition Treaty, for which surrenders were to be mutually made by either Government.[2] This issue had also been raised in 1855 by the prime minister of Nepal. The omission of this crime and of cattle-stealing from the Treaty of 1855 was ordered by the Court of Directors in spite of the Governor-General's advocacy of their inclusion. This action almost brought the negotiation to the breaking point. By 1866 the Durbar felt,

'that and the crime of cattle-stealing has now been assented to, and as both that offence and embezzlement by public officers or other

---

[1] *Foreign Department A. Consultation.* February 1863, Nos. 85/87. (N.A.I.) Sir W. Muir, Secretary to the Government of India, Foreign Department. to the Resident in Nepal. No. 915, dated Simla, September 12, 1867.
Judicial Department, Patna Commissioner's Office. No. 38, 1863-84 (B.C.R.O. Patna).

[2] 'On the Extradition Treaty with Nepal'. From Colonel G. Ramsay, Resident at Nepal, to the Secretary to the Government of India, in the Foreign Department, Fort William, No. 9, dated March 23, 1866. *Foreign Department Political,* June 1866, No. 34. (N.A.I.)

persons are included in the Treaty with Bhootan, which the Maharajah has lately seen in the public papers, there will be no objection to their both being added to the Treaty with Goorkha Government'.[1]

Ramsay forcefully supported Jung Bahadur's insistence upon the inclusion of 'embezzlement by public officers' only, and not including the crimes of 'cattle-stealing', and 'serious theft'. The Government of India agreed to its inclusion in the treaty of the '23rd of July 1866, supplemental to the Treaty with the State of Nepal of the 10th of February 1855, for the mutual surrender of heinous criminals, adding to the 4th Article of the said Treaty. . . .'[2] The Durbar agreed that the phrase 'or other persons', should be excluded and the British Government accepted the rest of the request of the Durbar. It was a happy ending to a small but critical negotiation. It was also agreed between the two parties that this agreement should not have any retrospective effect.[3]

The conclusion of this agreement gave the Nepal Durbar great satisfaction. On many occasions it had been put in an embarrassing position because several of its officers, after collecting lakhs (hundred thousand) of rupees from the revenue, absconded into British territory, and there was no way that the Durbar could get them back. But in spite of the Extradition Treaty the problem of stealing, dacoity (gang robbery), murder, and other crimes on the border remained a problem for both governments. The treaties made it easier to deal with these crimes since they authorized both sides to punish offenders if they were caught by the authorities. Moreover, the treaties opened the door for co-operation of the two governments in other fields in the future.

Commercial Policy of Jung Bahadur

In many fields Jung Bahadur adopted a liberal attitude after his return from England, but on the question of commerce and trade he believed in the misunderstood phrase: 'With the Bible comes the banner, and with the merchant comes the musket.' In spite of his friendly and co-operative policy during the Indian Mutiny and the rest of his prime ministership, he kept a vigilant eye on the trade of the country. The earlier relations between the British and the Nepal governments were

---

[1] 'On the Extradition Treaty with Nepal'. *Foreign Department Political*, June 1866. No. 34, *op. cit.*

[2] Notification, Foreign Department, No. 834, dated Simla, August 14, 1866. *Foreign Department Political*, August 1866, No. 102. (N.A.I.)

[3] From Colonel G. Ramsay, Resident at Nepal, to the Secretary to the Government of India, in the Foreign Department, with the Governor General, Simla, No. 24, dated July 25, 1866. *Foreign Department Political*, August 1866, No. 100. (N.A.I.)

mainly of a commercial nature, and with this in view a Treaty of Commerce had been signed by the East India Company and the Government of Nepal in 1792.[1] Article 7 of this treaty reads,

'This Treaty shall be of full force and validity in respect to the present and future rulers of both governments, and being considered on both sides as a Commercial Treaty and a basis of concord between the two States, is to be, at all times, observed and acted upon in times to come, for the public advantage and the increase of friendship.'[2]

As this treaty did not have much effect on the commercial relations between the two states, a new engagement was signed between the Government of India and Nepal on November 6, 1839.[3] The fifth paragraph of this engagement reads,

'The Nipal Government engages that an authentic statement of all the duties leviable in Nipal shall be delivered to the Resident, and that hereafter unauthorized imports not entered in this list shall not be levied on British subjects.'[4]

In the year 1875, Mr C. E. R. Girdlestone, the British Resident, wrote that 'The commercial relations between British India and Nipal are regulated by an engagement dated November the 6th, 1839, which has the force of treaty'.[5]

In the month of July 1858, Jung Bahadur had asked for an undertaking from the Iraqi merchants of Nepal which read as follows.

'We the undersigned Irakees do herein write that we will not sell any merchandise on credit from the date of this agreement. We will sell our goods for cash only. If we sell upon credit, we will not come forward to complain against any one, saying that such and such has not paid us. If we do come to complain, do not cause the money to be paid to us. We will make no excuses. We have written this paper willingly and of our own accord in the Suddur Jungee Kotwalee Cutcherry at the Indra Chowk.'[6]

---

[1] See Appendix I. Treaty of Commerce with Nepaul, March 1, 1792.
[2] Aitchison, C. U., Treaties, *op. cit.*, Vol. II, p. 197.
[3] See Appendix IV, for the Engagement between British India and Nepal, dated November 6, 1839.
[4] Aitchison, *op. cit.*, Vol. II, pp. 212-13.
[5] C. E. R. Girdlestone, Resident to H. Lepoer Wynne, Official Secretary in the Government of India Foreign Department. Dated Nipal Residency, June 9, 1874. *Foreign Department Political—A*, February 1875. Nos. 24-37 A. (N.A.I.)
[6] Translation of Mochulka signed by the Irakees Merchants of Nepal,

Ramsay wrote in his report to Cecil Beadon, Secretary to the Government of India, that, 'similar Mochulkas[1] were taken from other merchants, including those from Benares, Bettiah, the Kulwars, Marwarees, and from all the other classes of British merchants who had establishments in the city, and who had for years past been in the habit of trading with this country upon the same footing as other merchants, subjects of this state'.[2] It is interesting to note that these Mochulkas stated that they were signed 'willingly' and 'of their own accord'. The truth was that the merchants signed the Mochulkas because it was the order of the prime minister, and if they had refused they would have been expelled from the country, and thereby have lost outstanding debts of several lakhs of rupees which were owed to them by the Nepalese. These merchants were willing to leave the country provided they recovered their outstanding debts.[3]

The reason for this drastic action taken against British merchants was said to be that influential Sirdars and Jung Bahadur's own brothers and relatives were active in business, acting through third persons as their agents. They owed money to foreign merchants. No one could compete with the Sirdars, who could take the law into their own hands. All the complaints made by the merchants fell on deaf ears. The Mochulkas greatly handicapped the foreign businessmen so that henceforward they could not do business whereas the Sirdars and Jung's relatives could do so. Actually, the latter wanted the British merchants to abandon their debts and leave the country at once to the great profit of their rivals. When the Resident inquired from Jung Bahadur as to the cause of this injustice, the prime minister evaded a direct answer by saying that the Iraqis were suspicious people and that they could have transmitted false stories and news from Nepal to British India during the Mutiny. Later he changed his own statement by saying that the Iraqis were making numerous claims of outstanding debts in the court, and that sometimes the individual against whom the case was brought had no means of payment. So he thought that it would be better for them to sell in cash instead of on credit.[4]

Ramsay reported that the prime minister and his relatives had not the least interest in the country's prosperity, and that the measure they had taken could ruin the whole trade of Nepal. They had the monopoly of oil, and now they wanted the monopoly of the sale of wood. By Sumbut 1915 corresponding with July 17, 1868. *Foreign Department Political*, August 26, 1859, No. 213. (N.A.I.)

[1] Mochulka means undertaking.
[2] Ramsay to Beadon, Nepal Residency, August 6, 1859. No. 100 of 1859 (Copy). *Foreign Department Political*, August 26, 1859, Nos. 211–14. (N.A.I.)
[3] *Ibid.*
[4] *Ibid.*

monopolizing these articles they could double the price. This would only affect the poorer class. The Resident gave an interesting story about Jung Bahadur's brother, Krishna Bahadur. He wanted the Resident to write letters as the British representative to Indian merchants in Patna and other places to buy opium worth 300,000 rupees at double the price and also to arrange that it should not be tested at the border so that he could earn a handsome profit.[1] There were many other instances of discrimination on the part of the Durbar in connection with trade. Nepal was the only country of Southern Asia which Europeans were not allowed to enter for trade. A Mr Norris, desirous of carrying on a timber business with Nepal, approached Jung Bahadur in Allahabad and thought that permission was granted. But later he was quoted such a high price that he decided not to enter into business with Nepal. This was the method used by Jung Bahadur to discourage British merchants.[2]

The Governor-General expressed his regret over the Mochulkas to the Nepal Durbar. He further said that in European states the restriction which had been placed on British subjects would have been considered as an act of 'undisguised ill-will'. He felt that Nepal was not influenced by feelings of 'unfriendliness', and stated that he 'assumed no right to interfere with, or even to advise upon the commercial policy of Nepal'.[3] He regretfully suggested that if the Durbar wanted to exclude British subjects from trading in Nepal, it should do it directly instead of indirectly. He, however, reminded the Nepal Government that the policy of isolation had been abandoned even by China and Japan.[4]

This demonstration of strength and politeness by the Government of India had a good effect. The prime minister informed the Resident that the Mochulkas were 'torn up', and Iraqis were allowed to carry on their business as they had been accustomed to do in former days. He promised that they would receive the same treatment and justice in the Nepalese courts as Nepalese subjects.[5] Jung Bahadur, however, did not make any concession to European businessmen. But apart from that the trade relations between the Nepal Durbar and British

[1] Ramsay to Beadon, No. 100 of 1859, *op. cit.*
[2] *Ibid.*
[3] Copy of an English Draft of a Yaddasht from Lieutenant-Colonel G. Ramsay, Resident to Maharajah Jung Bahadoor Ranajee, Prime Minister and Commander in Chief of Nepal, dated September 12, 1859. *Foreign Department Political*, October 14, 1859, No. 168. (N.A.I.)
[4] Ramsay to Beadon, No. 100 of 1859, *op. cit.*
[5] Abstract translation of a Yaddasht from Maharajah Jung Bahadoor Ranajee, Prime Minister and Commander in Chief of Nepal to the address of Lieutenant-Colonel George Ramsay, Resident, dated 10th of Koonwar (Thursday) Sumbut 1916, corresponding with September 22, 1859. *Foreign Department Political*, October 14, 1859, No. 170. (N.A.I.)

subjects became normal when Jung Bahadur agreed, in September 1859, to abide by the engagement of 1839.

Nepal being a hilly country, its roads and trade routes were very primitive and naturally under these conditions any great increase in trade from British India or from any other place was not practicable. Transport was by carts, coolies and in some cases by river boats of which there were too few. And the level of trade was too slight to necessitate the improvement of the roads in Nepal. Most of the routes which were in good condition in British territory became cart tracks across the border. Most of the border roads had custom-houses to check the export and import of goods. Nepal had been exporting spices, opium, rice, forest products, chemicals and medicines, hides, furs, sandalwood, timber and many other articles; and its imports had been clothes of all kinds, shoes, sporting rifles, guns and gunpowder, pottery, fruits, salt, oil, dry fruits, woollen clothes, shawls, rugs, flannel, silks, silk thread, brocade, embroidery both Indian and European, and besides them many other items of daily use.[1] These imported goods were mostly used by those who had money, and some of the commodities were exclusively consumed by the prime minister and the royal family. The British subjects who were engaged in trade with Nepal were mostly Brahmins, Khatris and Bunyas of the Agrawal caste. Iraqis and Kalwars and Telis were engaged in trade near the British districts of Bustee and Gorukpore.[2] The barter system was prevalent, and British Rupees and Nepalese Mohurs[3] were commonly used side by side.[4]

Girdlestone the Resident, reported in 1876 that there was no evasion in the courts of Kathmandu of the engagement of 1839, by which the Nepalese Government engaged that 'British subjects shall hereafter be regarded as her own subjects in regard to access to the Courts of Law, and that the causes of the former shall be heard and decided without denial or delay, according to the usages of Nepal'.[5] The Resident had received no complaint against the Durbar and the courts of Nepal were just and fair in their judgments. In cases which were rather intricate and expensive, the Durbar had ordered special courts composed of some of the highest officers in the country to do justice. But Jung Bahadur did not move from his old position of not allowing Europeans

[1] C. E. R. Girdlestone, Resident to T. H. Thornton, Official Secretary to the Government of India, Foreign Department, No. 15 P, dated Kathmandoo, September 19, 1876. *Foreign Department Revenue A*, August 1877, No. 22. (N.A.I.)
[2] *Ibid.*
[3] Nepalese currency was gold Mohurs.
[4] *Ibid.*
[5] Girdlestone to Thornton, No. 15, September 19, 1876, *op. cit.*

to trade in Nepal. Girdlestone reported a story similar to the one a former Resident had reported in 1859 about Mr Norris, an Englishman. Girdlestone wrote that two European planters met Jung Bahadur in 1872–73 and told him of their desire to carry on business in timber. Jung Bahadur asked such a heavy price that both decided to avoid doing business in Nepal.[1] Girdlestone did not see any decline in trade and took an optimistic view about it.

In the last days of Jung Bahadur's prime ministership Girdlestone defended the trade policy of the Nepal Durbar by writing:

'We do not appreciate the protective tendencies of American and Australian colonies, but neither do we interfere with them, and I do not see that we have any right to interfere with Nepal which like ourselves imposes and maintains duties, not in order to protect a branch of industry, but for revenue purposes only.'[2]

During the entire period of his rule Jung Bahadur maintained a protective trade policy with firm opposition to the entry of Europeans into Nepal for trade. After the abrogation of the Mochulkas he tried to do justice and to avoid any friction with the British Government on the issue of trade. After 1859 he maintained smooth relations with the British Government with the hope that they would not force him to admit European businessmen. In this he succeeded.

Effects of Jung Bahadur's Policy on British–Nepalese Relations

Jung Bahadur was a keen observer of the Nepal Durbar's internal politics. He was a shrewd man with high ambition and adventurous ideas. He had weighed the influence and strength of British power in India and neighbouring countries like Thailand, Burma and China. He had noticed the influence of the former Resident Hodgson in the Durbar. He remembered the Ikrarnamah[3] signed by ninety-four chiefs of Nepal on January 2, 1841, to support the British–Nepal alliance and to ensure that the British Resident 'should ever and always be treated in an honourable and friendly manner. . . .'[4] Jung Bahadur convinced himself that no government in Nepal could survive without the support of the British Government. His visit to England in 1850 brought him back more convinced than before of British strength and power. While out of office for a short period, he found himself weak in his own country against the power of the British Resident. No one can deny his desire

[1] Girdlestone to Thornton, No. 15, September 19, 1876, *op. cit.*
[2] *Ibid.* Extra Supplement to Gazette of India, August 14, 1875, p. 2.
[3] Pledge of Acceptance. See Appendix V, 'Ickrah Nameh'.
[4] Aitchison, *op. cit.*, p. 220.

for an independent Nepal under his direct rule, but he knew that he could not weaken the influence of the British; and above all he cherished his own prestige, power, and influence. He wanted to maintain a balance between British influence and the independence of Nepal, and at the same time to keep himself and his family in power in perpetuity. He was watching for an opportunity, and that opportunity came to him in the shape of the Indian Mutiny.

Jung Bahadur promptly seized this opportunity. Knowing that the British were in sore trouble, he tried to dictate his terms by asking them to 'bestow upon him a tract of country elsewhere in India as a reward for his services or recognize him as an independent Prince in Nepal'.[1] When he failed to secure anything personally for himself, he asked something for his country, '... by giving his Government a small strip of territory, say a piece of the Tulseepur district in Oudh....'[2] He was so anxious that his offer should be accepted that he even offered his wives and son as hostages.[3] He reminded the British of all the Sirdars and influential people in the Durbar who were his enemies and who always thought that he was betraying the country for his own personal ends. To face their criticism he asked his powerful ally for prestige, 'Give me *Izzut* (prestige) in the eyes of my own country and of the world.... I ask nothing for myself individually, but I desire that it should be handed down to posterity that during my Ministership I obtained for my country, from the British Government, an extension of her dominions, however trifling that may be. This will silence all my enemies now and will give me a great name hereafter.'[4] Jung Bahadur did not hide his feeling about British power. He saw that his strength and the strength of his government could be strengthened through the power and prestige of the British. His own name and reputation and the prestige of the Gurkha soldiers depended on the greatness of the British.[5] Time and again he reminded the Resident that the success of the British in India during the Mutiny would make them far stronger than ever. In consequence of this his alliance with them would help his brothers and his country in the future because his services would be a reminder to the British not to molest his country.[6]

All this combined flattery and friendliness towards the British was intended to forward the attainment of Jung Bahadur's ambition to obtain the throne of Nepal or to be recognized by the British as the

[1] Ramsay to Edmonstone, July 17, 1858, *op. cit.*
[2] Majumdar, K., *op. cit.*
[3] Ramsay to Edmonstone, July 17, 1858, *op. cit.*
[4] Majumdar, K., *op. cit.*
[5] *Ibid.*
[6] *Ibid.*

sovereign of some other state elsewhere. The major obstacles to the achievement of this cherished goal were the British Government and veneration of the Nepalese for the supposedly god-king of Nepal. This was so strong that Jung Bahadur could not dethrone him and take his place unless he had the firm support of the Government of India. In 1856 Jung Bahadur received the title of Maharajah because the king of Nepal bestowed on him the sovereignty of Lamjang and Kaski. But at that time the British Resident declared that the British Government of India recognized only one Mararajah in Nepal and that was the Maharajah of Nepal. This seems to be one of the reasons why he resigned the prime ministership of Nepal. When he failed in his ambition he tried to please the British by requesting the Governor-General to give him permission to accept the prime ministership of Nepal in 1857, and also by offering help to the British during the Mutiny. He tried to dictate the terms for his assistance but failed. He could have murdered the Maharajah of Nepal had he not known the result of a rumor that Bhim Sen Thapa had tried to poison the Senior Queen but missed his mark and poisoned her youngest son, who died.[1] The result of this rumor was that the strong man of Nepal, Bhim Sen, was thrown into prison. 'Landon says that four years later his enemies, the Pandes, confessed that the whole charge was false.'[2] Jung Bahadur had also many enemies among the Sirdars of Nepal, and therefore he could not take the chance of killing the Maharajah of Nepal unless he was sure of British support. Killing the Maharajah was a sin against God, and no one would have tolerated this crime. When he saw that this plan had failed, Jung Bahadur tried to gain territory, honor, prestige and respect from the British Government, so that his own people would ultimately realize his services to the country, his greatness and his strength and would offer him the kingship in place of the Maharajah of Nepal, whom he had already pronounced an insignificant, useless, and characterless person. He wanted to make himself the hero of the nation like Julius Caesar whose victory and fame forced the Romans to accept him as their dictator. In practice Jung Bahadur enjoyed the *de facto* powers of the Maharajah and he needed just a little help from the British to become the real Maharajah.

All his attempts to secure the support of the Government of India by flattery and friendliness failed to win its aid for the removal of the king or to make him the Maharajah of some other state. Probably the Government of India was getting all it wanted from him and was afraid that overthrowing the king would create a more serious problem for itself in Nepal.

[1] Tuker, *op. cit.*, p. 102.
[2] *Ibid.*

Jung used every possible method to enlist British support. He informed the Resident about the misconduct of the Maharajah Dhiraj. He answered him that the king was 'vomiting unnatural crime' with three Syces (horse-keepers). He reminded Ramsay that the king was 'an eccentric and of cruel disposition', that in his youth he sometimes even sacrificed human lives for his pleasure. Because Jung Bahadur as prime minister had ordered those Syces not to go to the king's inner apartment, the king according to him had tried to commit suicide twice in one day.[1] Ramsay wrote to Durand that Jung Bahadur anxiously asked 'what am I to do'. He even told Ramsay that the king wanted to abdicate. He stressed that he was at his wit's end and could find no solution to the problem.

'... I never was placed in such a position before. The Maharanees asked me to interfere and to prevent the King's going on as he had been doing, and now I have kept the Syces from him, and he has been trying to kill himself; they want me to yield and to suffer him to disgrace himself and become an outcast. If he kills himself owing to my restraining him, the people and the Sirdars will all call out that I have killed him; if I allow him to do as he pleases, they will say that it is my fault, and that it is owing to me that the King has become an outcast, and that this disgrace has happened to the country. Everybody all over India will hear of it, and will talk of it, and will blame me for allowing it.'[2]

Ramsay, a clever and experienced Resident, immediately grasped the position in his mind. He knew that Jung Bahadur was preparing to eliminate the king, and before doing so wanted to judge the reaction of the British. So Ramsay administered a polite but firm rebuff and explained the policy of his Government as follows:

'... that the matter was of a purely domestic nature concerning the Goorkhas only, and having no direct political bearing upon the relations between the two States, and that I believed my Government would object to my offering any more definite advice than I was about to give him. I said that I believe His Excellency the Viceroy would disapprove my taking upon myself a responsibility of this nature, and giving advice which might or might not lead to measures of coercion against the sovereign, which I had no right to suggest. I told him that, with reference to the abominable crime to which he had referred, I thought

---

[1] 'Alleged misconduct of the Maharajah Dheeraj'. Colonel Ramsay, Resident at Nipal, to Colonel H. M. Durand, CB, Secretary Government of India, Foreign Department (No. 34, dated November 1, 1864). Foreign Department Political, November 1864, Nos. 52–8. (N.A.I.)

[2] *Ibid.*

that not only the members in general of the King's family, but the Sirdars and the people would approve of his taking such steps as would prevent its occurrence; but that he should remember that although he is the minister of Nipal, he is also a subject, and that he ought to be very careful not to interfere with his sovereign's authority more than is absolutely called for by the peculiar circumstances of the case.'[1]

The answer given by Ramsay was in keeping with his earlier conclusions. As far back as 1856, he wrote to the then Secretary Edmonstone about the designs of Jung Bahadur on the throne of Nepal. Ramsay believed that some day Jung intended to make himself Regent after putting aside the existing ruler. His sons were minors, and Jung Bahadur would start his own hereditary dynasty.[2] On the same issue, Lord Dalhousie once wrote that if any one believed that Jung was doing all that he was doing for love, he was completely mistaken. When the time became opportune Jung Bahadur, who was the ruler for all practical purposes, would become king because the Rajah would have some kind of accident which would remove the last obstacle to his prime minister's ambition. When this took place he would expect the British Government to recognize him for his services in the Indian Mutiny.[3]

When it became clear to Jung Bahadur that the Government of India would not help him in his ambition to become king of Nepal he decided to secure the right to the hereditary prime ministership for his family. To achieve this he was even prepared to remove the restrictions on the movements of the Resident which had been imposed from the first day of British diplomatic representation in Nepal.[4] In any action Jung Bahadur had to take either to become king of Nepal or make his family hereditary prime minister of Nepal, he needed British help for two reasons. Firstly, he was not very sure about his own power, and secondly, British power carried great weight in Nepal. The factions agreed that to retain power in Nepal one must have the support of the British. It is not known if the British approved of Jung's idea of hereditary prime ministership but it is clear that they did not oppose Jung Bahadur in this move.

In his relations with the princely states of India, Jung Bahadur's actions were indirectly controlled by the Resident. None of the treaties signed between the Nepal Durbar and the Government of India made any mention of the relations between Nepal and the princely states.

[1] Ramsay to Durand, No. 34, dated November 1, 1864, *op. cit.*
[2] Majumdar, K., *op. cit.*, pp. 375–6.
[3] *Ibid.*, p. 337.
[4] *Ibid.*, pp. 275–6.

But it was understood that Nepal would not have direct relations with them. In many cases, even if the Resident did not use pressure, Jung Bahadur asked for permission simply to please the British Government. When he received letters from the Rajahs of Bhutan and Bulrampur, he immediately reported the matter to the Resident. By doing so he lost nothing and proved himself a loyal ally. The answers sent by him were approved by the Governor-General of India. The Rajah of Bhutan had asked for military help against the British, and Jung recommended him '. . . to go and supplicate for mercy and concede whatever the paramount power may demand'.[1] And to the Rajah of Bulrampur who wrote just a friendly and complimentary letter he replied politely, and in conclusion wrote, '. . . and continue your correspondence with me'. The Resident requested that he erase the final words of his letter in which he invited the Rajah of Bulrampur '. . . to continue the correspondence'.[2] When the Maharajah of Betiah invited Jung Bahadur and the staff of the Residency to attend the ceremony of investiture of his son with the Brahminical thread, the Resident informed the Bettiah Rajah that the 'Nepal Durbar does not hold any communications with the Rajahs and Chiefs of the plains of India, without the permission of the Government of India'.[3] The Government of India never allowed Indian princely states to have communications with one another and still less with an independent state like Nepal. In practice, Jung Bahadur took indirect action with princely states, but always through the Indian Foreign Office. The Maharajah of Nepal wrote to the Governor-General of India doubtless

---

[1] Correspondence between Maharajah Jung Bahadur and Deva Dhurma Rajah (Chief of Bhootan). Lieutenant-Colonel C. R. Lawrence, CB, Officiating Resident, Nipal, to Colonel H. M. Durand, CB, Secretary to Governemnt of India in the Foreign Department, Fort William, dated March 18, 1865. Abstract translation of the substance of a letter from the Deva Dhurma Rajah, to the address of Maharajah Jung Bahadoor. Abstract translation of a reply from Maharajah Jung Bahadoor, to the Deva Dhurma Rajah, dated, *Foreign Department Political*, March 1865, Nos. 244–8. (N.A.I.)

[2] 'Receipt of a letter by Sir Jung Bahadoor from the Rajah of Bulrampore'. From Lieutenant-Colonel R. C. Lawrence, CB, Officiating Resident at Nipal, to the Secretary to the Government of India, in the Foreign Department, at Fort William, No. 18, dated November 16, 1865. Translation of a letter from Maharajah Digbijay Sing, of Bulrampore, to Maharajah Jung Bahadoor, dated October 10, 1865, corresponding with the 6th of Kartick Budee 1273 Fuslee. Translation of a draft of a letter from Maharajah Jung Bahadoor, to Maharajah Digbijay Sing, of Bulrampore. *Foreign Department Political*, December 1865, Nos. 118–21. (N.A.I.)

[3] C. U. Aitchison, Under-Secretary to the Government of India, Foreign Department, with the Governor-General, to the Resident at Nipal (No. 192, dated Simla, April 21, 1863). Political Department Proceedings, May 1863. (B.C.R.O.)

at the dictation of Jung Bahadur, that '... I truly consider the British Government as my protector', and asked his permission to send the prime minister of Nepal to pay his respects to the Governor-General and to the Queen in London, to thank Her Majesty for the title of knighthood conferred upon the prime minister.[1] In another request Jung Bahadur asked for permission to marry his son to the daughter of Rajah Rundhoje Sahai and later asked for permission to carry on correspondence with this Rajah.[2] Indian princes did ask permission for the marriages of their children if it concerned their relations with another prince and if the British Government's interests were involved. On one occasion Jung Bahadur was refused permission for himself and his armed followers to bathe in the Ganges at Allahabad, which was sacred to Hindus, but when he asked permission for the second time it was granted.[3]

Jung Bahadur wished to revisit England in 1862. He also wanted to take his children and his brother's children to England for their education and to leave them under the protection of Her Majesty the Queen. He also wished to visit other European countries, not through the British Government but independently as an ambassador of his king. To have direct contact with any European power was forbidden by the treaty of 1816. Jung dropped his entire scheme when it was disapproved by the Governor-General on the ostensible ground that his absence from his country for such a long period might be injurious to Nepal. Actually the British Government did not want him to have direct contact with European countries. This principle was laid down by Governor-General Wellesley. Maharajah Jung Bahadur made another attempt to go to England to pay his respects to the Queen, and take his and his brother's children to England for education in 1874. This time he had no intention of visiting other European capitals as the representative of the Maharajah of Nepal. On this occasion his wish was granted but he was requested not to take the children for

[1] Translation of a letter from the Maharajah of Nipal to the Governor-General of India, dated September 26, 1874. *Foreign Department Political—A*, October 1874, No. 69. (N.A.I.)

[2] 'Permitting Maharajah Jung Bahadoor to correspond with the Rajah Rundhoje Sahai.' Lawrence to Durand, Fort William, No. 5, dated March 21, 1865. *Foreign Department Political—A. Consultations*, March 1865, No. 291. (N.A.I.)

[3] Jung Bahadur to Colonel Jung Bahadoor, 39 Park Street, Calcutta. 'Ask permission from Viceroy to bathe at Allahabad with 70 soldiers armed' (Service Telegram), Byculla, February 10, 1875. Viceroy's reply to Jung Bahadur, 'Inform Sir Jung Bahadoor there is no objection to his bathing at Allahabad or his being attended by seventy armed soldiers'. Fort William, February 12, 1875. Telegram No. 5249. *Foreign Department Political—B. Proceedings*, March 1875, Nos. 145-6. (N.A.I.)

education along with him. He left for Bombay on December 17, 1874, *en route* to Europe, but the plan had to be abandoned owing to an accident with which Sir Jung met at Bombay on February 1, 1875.[1]

Sir Jung Bahadur tried sincerely to win the confidence of the British Government, and on many issues he succeeded. When there was a rumor that he had evil designs on Bhutan in 1861, Ramsay, the Resident, wrote to Mr A. Campbell, the Superintendent of Darjeeling, that if the Maharajah had any design upon Bhutan, or any thought of extending the Nepalese territory in this direction it was not likely that he would practice such deception upon them. The Resident could not conceive of Sir Jung's 'breaking faith with us'. The Resident very strongly emphasized that Jung 'never had the remotest intention of deceiving me to acquiesce in his setting foot within that province'. Ramsay vigorously objected that Jung's loyalty should have been suspected in this area of British territory. He saw no reason for such distrust, and he called it 'equally imprudent and impolite to betray' the feeling of trust of Sir Jung Bahadur on the part of the British.[2] Even in 1858, when there was a suspicion that he had ambitious designs on British terri-

[1] Lieutenant-Colonel G. Ramsay, Resident at Nepal, to Colonel H. M. Durand, CB, Secretary to the Government of India, with the Foreign Department, Fort William. Dated Nepal Residency, April 21, 1862. No. 10 of 1862. *Foreign Department Political*, May 1862, Nos. 23–4. 'Maharajah Jung Bahadoor's desire to visit England'. From Lieutenant-Colonel R. C. Lawrence, CB, Officiating Resident at Nipal, to the Honorable W. Muir, CS, Secretary to Government of India, Foreign Department with the Governor–General, Confidential, No. 16, dated Nipal Residency, October 7, 1865. Muir to Officiating Resident, Confidential, No. 886, Simla, October 19, 1865. *Foreign Department Political*, October 1865, Nos. 79–80. Lawrence to Secretary, Government of India, Confidential, No. 17, Kathmandoo, October 30, 1865. Lawrence to the Viceroy and Governor-General of India, dated November 1, 1865. Copy of a Memorandum by Colonel R. Lawrence, dated November 1, 1865. Memorandum Maharajah Sir Jung Bahadoor, *Foreign Department Political*, November 1865, Nos. 91–4, 'Maharajah Sir Jung Bahadur's contemplated second visit to Europe in 1875'. *Foreign and Political Department Secret*. File No. 96 (4)—H. 1934. 'Visit of Maharajah Sir Jung Bahadur, Prime Minister of Nepal to England.' Girdlestone to Aitchison. *Foreign Department Political—B*, October 1874, Nos. 85–105. Abstract translation of a Yaddasht from Maharajah Sir Jung Bahadur Rana to Lieutenant-Colonel Lawrence, Officiating Resident at Nipal, dated November 23, 1865. 'My friend since in the opinion of His Excellency the Viceroy and Governor-General, my journey to England would not be advantageous for me, I beg to express the satisfaction I feel in acquiescing in His Excellency's views, and to inform you that I am glad and contented (Razi and Khooshi) to relinquish my proposed visit to England.' *Foreign Department Political—A*. December 1865, Nos. 53–4. (N.A.I.)

[2] Ramsay to A. Campbell, Superintendent of Darjeeling, No. 76, dated December 19, 1860. *Proceedings of the Lieutenant Governor of Bengal, Political Department*, January 1861, No. 20. (B.C.R.O.)

tories, Jung Bahadur informed Captain Byers, the acting Resident, that 'his army should never be employed against the British Government but on the contrary should always be at our service'. Byers told Brigadier Wroughton that 'any hostility on the part of the Nepalese is highly improbable so long as Jung Bahadoor lives'.[1]

In spite of the confidence shown in Jung Bahadur by successive Residents, the Government of India remained cautious about the grant of arms in any form to the Nepal Durbar. It was also quite reluctant to allow the employment of Europeans of any nationality in the service of the Durbar. This was done according to Article VII of the Treaty of 1815–16. In the one exception when the Governor-General verbally gave permission to Jung Bahadur to employ a European as a tutor, the Maharajah even had to inform the Residency officially about it according to Article VII of the treaty of 1815–16.[2] In the case of arms importations into Nepal the British Government had stringent restrictions. In 1868, the Governor-General approved a list of arms which Jung Bahadur wished to import 'as a matter of favour to Maharajah Jung Bahadur'. But he laid down the principle that in the future the Nepal Durbar must apply in advance for permission 'as the Government of India controls the importation of fire-arms, great and small. . . .' The Secretary cautioned the Resident on this issue.[3] In 1872, the Government of India refused a request from Bubbur Jung the son of Jung, Bahadur, to import a 'mountain battery'.[4] In 1868, when Jung Bahadur wished to establish depots for the sale of timber in Calcutta, Patna, Gorukpore, and Buhram Ghat, and sought permission for the officers and men who would be employed there to 'carry arms', the request was denied by the Governor-General on the ground that it was against the policy of the Government to give such permission to ordinary persons.[5]

---

[1] Byers to E. A. Samuells, October 25th. *Foreign Department Political, External Affairs—A. Consultations.* December 31, 1858. Nos. 2532-4 (Copy). (N.A.I.)

[2] (Signature Illegible) Fort William, April 6, 1872. *Foreign Department Political—B*, April 1872, Letter No. 845-P. (N.A.I.)

[3] 'Fire-arms and casting gear for Jung Bahadoor.' Secretary to Resident. No. 340, dated April 3, 1868 (Confidential). *Foreign Department Political*, April 1868, Nos. 225-31. (N.A.I.)

[4] Secretary to Resident, September 7, 1872. *Foreign Political—B. Proceedings*, December 1872, Nos. 18-24 (No. 4-P Confidential of 1872). (N.A.I.)

[5] Memorandum from A. Mackenzie, Under Secretary to the Government of Bengal (No. 2881, dated Fort William, June 10, 1868. Forwarded to the Judicial Department of this office for information. From Sir R. Temple, Secretary to the Government of India, Foreign Department, to Lieutenant-Colonel R. C. Lawrence, Resident in Nipal (No. 613, dated Fort William, April 3, 1868. (B.C.R.O.)

The appeasement policy of Jung Bahadur gave him many set-backs and frustrations on issues like the importation of arms and ammunition, requests to revisit England, and the assertion of a little more independence in foreign affairs by visiting other European capitals as an ambassador of his own sovereign. It is clear that he had failed to win the complete and unshaken confidence of the British Government in India. But his pro-British policy was far from a complete failure: it also brought him some notable success.

The Success and Achievements of Jung Bahadur's Policy of Friendly Co-operation with the British

When the Nepalese faced a scarcity of food in their country the British Government immediately came to their rescue, as any state will aid another country. The Government of India in a statement made it quite clear that it concurred with the Lieutenant-Governor of Bengal and with Sir Richard Temple that 'no distinction should be made between British subjects and subjects of Nepal if the latter should apply for relief in British territory, and that we should do what we can to assist the distressed people beyond our border with supplies'.[1] This was the standard policy of the British in times of need and distress in Nepal.

On the question of entry of British European subjects into Nepalese territory, Jung Bahadur tactfully succeeded in keeping them out, and so saved his country from their influence. In the first analysis, however, one can say that this did not prove entirely beneficial to the Nepalese since they were deprived of the benefits of modern civilization, which they could have gained through direct contact with the English. Lawrence wrote to Girdlestone in 1868 on this issue:

'The orders of the Nepal Government against the admission into the country of any European who had not been furnished with a "pass" either by the Durbar or by the British Resident are so stringent, and are so scrupulously enforced, that it would be almost impossible for a European of the above named class to penetrate the interior of the country.'[2]

---

[1] Letter No. 572 of the 11th instant, with enclosed minute from Sir Richard Temple, regarding the threatened scarcity in that portion of Nepal territory which borders on Tirhoot and Chumparun, from the Officiating Secretary to the Government of Bengal. In the Statistical Department. To the Deputy Secretary to the Government of India, Department of Agriculture, Revenue, and Commerce, Calcutta, dated February 10th, issued February 1874. Minute of the Honourable Sir Richard Temple, KCSI, No. 11, dated Motiharee, February 5, 1874. *Foreign Department General—B*, February 1874, Nos. 98–101. (N.A.I.)

[2] Lawrence to Girdlestone, Officiating Under Secretary to the Government

When the extradition treaty of 1855 was drawn up Jung Bahadur tactfully and politely managed to insert into it the offenses of 'embezzlement by officers' and 'cattle-lifting'.

The crowning result of his policy was the return of some of the territory Nepal had lost after her defeat in 1815–16. By the Treaty of 1860, Nepal received back from the British Government 'the whole of the lowlands between the River Kali and Raptee, and the whole of the lowlands lying between the River Raptee and the District of Goruckpore, which were in the possession of the Nipal State in the year 1815, and were ceded to the British Government by Article III of the Treaty concluded at Segowlee on the 2nd of December in that year'.[1] This territory was returned to Nepal 'in consideration of the great service he has rendered to us. . . .'[2] During his prime ministership, Jung Bahadur succeeded in having the boundary between the two states demarcated. He was of the opinion that uncertainty regarding the line of demarcation might at some future period lead to difficulties, and so he suggested that 'two intermediate marks or small pillars may be erected between every two pillars. . . .' This was accepted in principle.[3] When he complained about crimes committed on the border, the British Government of India appointed Mr J. D. Gordon to conduct an enquiry. The twenty-nine page report submitted by Gordon discussed the entire issues of border crimes and other problems, and because of it the situation was better controlled on the border.[4] In his lifetime he settled all the problems affecting the boundary between Nepal and India, because he was apprehensive that in the future they might lead to friction between the two states.

Sir Jung Bahadur was very particular about the ceremonials and the salute accorded to him and to the representatives of the state whenever

of India. Foreign Department with the Governor-General, No. 10, dated October 23, 1868. *Foreign Department General—B*, January 1869, Nos. 1–3 (N.A.I.)

[1] Aitchison, *op. cit.*, Vol. II, p. 224. Landon, *op. cit.*, p. 150. Ross D. Magles to the Governor-General of India in Council, *Secret Despatch from Secretary of State. Foreign Department*, 1858, No. 1933. Jung Bahadur to Lord Canning, *Foreign Department Secret*, August 27, 1858, Nos. 109–27 and K.W., Secret Despatch from the Secretary of State to the Governor-General, dated February 9, 1858, No. 1924,

[2] Secret Despatch from Secretary of State, 1858. No. 1933. *Ibid.* India Office Library.

[3] Lawrence to the Commissioner of Patna Division, dated Nepal Residency, December 11, 1869. Government of Bengal, Judicial Department, 1869. (B.C.R.O.)

[4] J. D. Gordon, Magistrate, on Special Duty to the Secretary to the Government of Bengal, Fort William, April 11, 1865. No. 2. Copy of *A Proceedings* for July 1865, from Government. *Political Department, Police Branch*. (B.C.R.O.)

they visited India. He himself visited India at least four times and on all occasions was received cordially and with dignity by the Governor-General of India. He was granted a salute of nineteen guns as a mark of personal distinction, but his representative Dhere Shamsher in 1860 received a salute of fifteen guns only.[1] His one weakness was his interest in the honors and titles conferred on him by the British Government. These included, among many, the honour of knighthood and his reception by Queen Victoria in 1850 when he visited London.

Jung Bahadur died on February 25, 1877. In concluding this account of his long tenure of power, an appraisal should be made of his success and his failures. As with all governments the record is mixed, but on balance his achievements outweighed his defeats.

When Jung Bahadur accepted the prime ministership for the second time in 1857, he had four purposes in mind, viz. to keep Nepal independent from the complete domination of the British; secondly, to make himself and his descendants the real rulers of the country; thirdly, to overthrow the nominal rulers, the reigning dynasty, and become the Rajah of Nepal; and lastly, to keep the British Government on his side by whatever means were necessary, as the surest method of achieving his other objectives. He succeeded in three of his aims, but failed to obtain the throne because the British were scrupulously honest in refusing to intervene in Nepal's domestic affairs by assisting him in overthrowing the Maharajah Dhiraj.

He maintained friendly and co-operative but not close relations with the British Government of India. Whenever necessary he yielded even to the extent of accepting insult, but he never allowed the door of Nepal to be opened to Europeans in any field whether commercial, social, or political. His keen and watchful eyes had seen the changed condition of the princely states in India, whose independence even in domestic affairs had gradually diminished from what they had been when they originally signed their treaties of alliance with the Government of India. He told Ramsay in 1853,

'What fools the Kings of Oude have always been. If they had acted as we have done, and refused to mix themselves up with you in any way, you would not have had any excuse for taking their country. . . . All the other native States have either fallen entirely under your rule, or you interfere with their management; that would soon happen here.'[2]

---

[1] *Foreign and Political Department Secret.* File No. 96 (4)-H, *op. cit.*, 'Salutes to Native Princes and Chiefs, *Foreign Department Political*, November 1865, Nos. 179–92. Memorandum from C. E. R. Girdlestone to the Government of Bengal (No. 101, dated Fort William, January 18, 1869). (B.C.R.O.)

[2] Majumdar, K., *op. cit.*

He was convinced that if he relaxed the restrictions imposed on Europeans and his policy of isolation, he was bound to meet the same fate as the other princely states of India. He was very proud of his policy of friendly co-operation and isolation towards his powerful ally, and was convinced that it was because of his policy that Nepal remained independent. He told the Resident during one of his bitter moods:

'You may say that we are independent; the British Government tells us that it has no desire to interfere with us or to meddle with our internal affairs; nor even to advise us respecting them. We attribute that independence solely to our own peculiar policy (you can call it selfish if you like, but we can not alter it to please you). We know you are a stronger power; you are like a lion, we are like a cat; the cat will scratch if it is driven to a corner, but the lion will soon kill the cat. You can force us to change our policy; you can take our country, if it pleases you to do so. But we will make no changes in that policy, by strict observance of which, we believe, that we preserved our independence as a nation to the present time, unless you *compel* us to do so.'[1]

One should not overlook the position of the British Government in connection with Nepal's remaining independent. The Maharajah Dhiraj, in his Khureeta to the Governor-General, on December 16, 1874, had reminded the Governor-General about the assurance given by Lord Northbrook when he wrote, '. . . the British Government will never dispossess the Nipal State of a single strip of land. . . .'[2] On another occasion Colonel Anderson, a surveyor, in answering a question from Colonel Siddhiman Singh said that 'the British Government had desire whatever to annex any territory belonging to Nepal. . . .'[3] These statements of the British officials were made in public, but even in private and secret discussions which were known to the officials or to the Governor-General alone they concurred with the above statements. In connection with an extradition case, the notation on the file to be put before the Governor-General, which was signed 'C.U.A.' on April 22, 1875, reads:

'His Excellency.
As Nipal is an independent and not a feudatory State, and we have no

---

[1] Majumdar, K., *op. cit.*, pp. 396–7.
[2] Abstract translation of a Khureeta from Maharajah Dhiraj to Lord Northbrook, Viceroy and Governor-General of India, dated 23rd Ughun, Sumbut 1931 (December 16, 1874). No. 285. *Foreign Department Political—A.* January 1875. (N.A.I.)
[3] Resident to Secretary to the Government of India, No. 2—A, dated Camp Semra, Bustee District, March 16, 1874. *Foreign Department Political—A.* April 1874, No. 260. (N.A.I.)

Treaty ground to make the demand, I am not in favour of making it. . . .'[1]

The British Government of India never wanted to reduce Nepal to the status of a princely state. The war of 1815–16 had given it great respect for the fighting qualities of the Nepalese. They would defend their independence fiercely. Nepal was a mountain country with few and poor roads. British invasion meant a long war with many casualties and heavy expenditure. Indian revenue was small, and the Indian treasury strongly opposed any war because of the great difficulty of paying for it. Economically Nepal had nothing that would repay the cost of conquest. Strategically conquest was unnecessary to control Himalayan frontiers. The British knew that Nepal would resist, e.g. a Chinese invasion. Also, Tibet and China were too weak to be any threat during the British regime in India. After 1857–58, it had become clear to the British that Jung Bahadur would not invade India nor help any other state to do so. Therefore, the British were content that Nepal should be a friendly and largely independent state. Even so they took precautions, e.g. they were reluctant to allow Nepal to import arms, and they forbade diplomatic relations with Indian princely and European states. In view of the above restrictions and statements Nepal was largely but not entirely an independent state.

The credit for giving a stable government to Nepal during and after his prime ministership must go to Jung Bahadur. Under the circumstances, he could not have done better than he did for Nepal. Considering also the political condition of the country, probably the only course left for him was the one which he actually adopted. It cannot be denied that his own power and the benefit of his family were uppermost in his mind when he made his family the real rulers and reduced the Maharajah and his successors to the status of permanent puppets of their hereditary prime ministers. His reorganization of the government was nothing more than the exaltation of the power of his family and for this any condemnation by his countrymen is understandable and excusable.

[1] Noting on the file for the Governor-General, by C. U. A., April 22, 1875 *Foreign Department Political—A.* October 1875, Nos. 85–93. (N.A.I.)

CHAPTER 3
FRUSTRATION AND COMPROMISE

The sudden death of Maharajah Jung Bahadur on February 25, 1877, at the age of 61, ended thirty years of rule by one strong man.[1] He was immediately succeeded by his brother Sir Ranodip Singh, who was next in line according to the roll of succession prepared by Jung Bahadur himself. Sir Ranodip Singh was described by the British as a 'weak man'.[2] Fortunately for him, Jung Bahadur had already firmly established a strong foreign policy based on 'isolation, friendly co-operation and a firm attitude on certain issues toward the British Government'. All Ranodip Singh had to do was to continue the policies originated by his predecessor.

Although the succession was smooth, the internal political situation held the promise of trouble for Ranodip Singh. This was because in addition to the prime ministership, Ranodip also adopted the title of Maharajah by taking over the estates of Kaski and Lamjang. According to Juggut Jung, a son of Jung Bahadur, these properties had been given to his father and after him, to his descendants. Girdlestone, the Resident wrote to Mr A. C. Lyall, upholding the view of Juggut Jung: 'The original Parbatyia copy is before me now, and the expression is *santan dar santan samma rajai bhog garo*—that is literally, enjoy the kingdom up to offspring upon offspring.'[3] Naturally Juggut Jung felt strongly against his uncle and started conspiring to overthrow him. Juggut Jung was well liked throughout the kingdom since he was the oldest son of Jung Bahadur and also because of his own personal influence. Sir Ranodip Singh felt insecure in his high position and to win support, he gave a

---

[1] Secretary of State for India to Government of India, No. 38, dated India Office, London, April 26th. *Foreign Department Political—A Proceedings*, August 1877, No. 51. (N.A.I.)

[2] 'State of Parties in Nepal.' Report by Under-secretary, Government of India, July 14, 1881. *Foreign Political—A*, February 1882, Nos. 283–304. K. W. of Nos. 285–99. (N.A.I.)

[3] C. Girdlestone to A. C. Lyall, *Foreign Department Political—A Proceedings*, September 1879. Nos. 386–90. K. W. No. 1. (N.A.I.)

FRUSTRATION AND COMPROMISE

state banquet to the principal servants of the Nepal Government. On the same day he issued a manifesto to all of them. This was a remarkable document consisting mainly of exhortations to unity.[1] His insistence on this unity shows that there existed some discord in the ruling family.[2]

At the same time that a new administration took office in Nepal, British India received a new Governor-General in 1876. He appointed Mr F. Henvey in 1877 as the new Resident in Nepal. Henvey subsequently complained to the Government of India about the policy of the Nepal Government toward the British. He objected to the restrictions placed on the movements of the Resident in Nepal, and he complained about the espionage system of the Durbar, by which the Resident and the Residency were surrounded. He also took exception to the social isolation in which the Resident was kept because the Durbar did not want him to learn about Nepal independently. Lastly, he felt that the native states of India regarded Nepal with respect and wished they dared to imitate its attitude towards the Government of India. This must be regarded as the correct policy for an orthodox Hindu state which had kept itself free from the control of the British. The independence which had been maintained by Nepal because of the generous forbearance of the Indian Government, and the willingness to go to war was attributed by the Hindu princes of India to the peculiar system adopted by Bhim Sen Thapa and earnestly and accurately followed by the late Sir Jung Bahadur.[3] Henvey shut his eyes to several other factors which have been discussed in an earlier chapter, such as economic backwardness (not strategically important in those days) and the determination of the Gurkhas to resist if attacked by the British.

Henvey did not receive any answer from the government about his complaints against the Durbar's attitude. This probably meant that the British Government did not approve of his ideas. In addition to the issue of the free movement of the Resident, the major conflicts between the two states were the questions of recruitment of Gurkhas for the Indian Army, and the denial of permission for Europeans to enter the Kingdom of Nepal. Other problems in which the Indian and Nepalese Governments did not see eye to eye concerned trade, the abolition of slavery and Suttee (burning the widow on the pyre of her husband) and the importation of arms and ammunition and their manufacture in Nepal.

[1] See Appendix IV.
[2] F. Henvey, Resident in Nepal to C. U. Aitchison, Secretary to the Government of India, Foreign Department No. 59 P, dated Nepal Residency, December 3, 1877 (Confidential). *Foreign Secret Proceedings*, December 1877, No. 93–4. (N.A.I.)
[3] Henvey to Thornton, No. 30P, dated Nipal, June 22, 1877. 'Sub: Position of the Resident at Kathmandu.' *Foreign Department Secret Proceedings*. December 1877, Nos. 104–33, pages with notes. (N.A.I.)

When Sir Ranodip became Prime Minister, he felt it necessary to declare his policy towards the British Government. Ranodip told the Resident that his policy was going to be the same as that of Sir Jung Bahadur. He said that 'he had been entirely in the confidence of the late Sir Jung Bahadur, who had exhorted and instructed him to pursue the same course of steady and undeviating friendship towards the British Government'.[1] The statement of the new Prime Minister made it very clear that while he would follow a policy of friendly cooperation, he was opposed to any change in the *status quo*. The frustration of the Resident is evident from this statement:

'I do not suppose that this plain speaking will have endeared me to the Prime Minister; still less that, though the bee of persuasion had sat upon my tongue, I could not in a century of talking have induced them to alter a policy which began with Knox in 1802, revived with Boileau and Gardner in 1816 and has been maintained ever since throughout all the vicissitudes of internal strife and revolution.'[2]

When the Maharajah learned through a newspaper about the possibility of a war between Russia and England in 1878, he lost no time in offering assistance, as he put it 'because of my friendship for the British Government'.[3] The Maharajah even sent his representatives through the interior of the state to investigate the possibility of recruiting soldiers for the Indian army. Impey, the acting Resident at that time, warned his Government to keep a cautious eye on these offers. The British felt that this activity would give the Nepal Durbar an excuse for increasing its forces at the expense of the British and for exciting the already war-like and restless spirit of its ruler and people, to the possible future embarrassment of the Indian Government. The offer of assistance was politely refused by the Viceroy, who added that 'His Excellency does not the less appreciate the friendly intentions and overtures of the prime minister . . . .'[4] When Sir Ranodip was asked to relax the restrictions on the movements of the Resident, he declared

[1] Henvey to Thornton, No. 13P, dated Nipal March 27, 1877. (Confidential.) *Foreign Department Secret Proceedings*, December 1877, No. 104. (N.A.I.)

[2] Henvey to Thornton, dated Nipal, April 29, 1877. *Foreign Department Secret Proceedings*, December 1877, No. 106. (N.A.I.)

[3] Surgeon J. Scully, Officiating Resident to A. C. Lyall, Secretary to Government of India, Foreign Department, No. 111, dated Nepal Residency, April 19, 1878. (Confidential.) *Foreign Department Secret*, May 1878. No. 76. (N.A.I.)

[4] E. C. Impey, Officiating Resident, Nepal to A. C. Lyall, Secretary to Government of India, Foreign Department. No. 14P, dated Katmandoo, April 30, 1878. (Confidential.) No. 77. Lyall to Impey No. 1027P, dated Simla, May 18, 1878. No. 78. *Foreign Department Secret Proceedings*, May 1878, Nos. 76–9. (N.A.I.)

frankly and strongly, his inability to alter in any particular the restrictive policy of his predecessors.[1] These few episodes showed the dual policy of the Nepal Durbar towards the British Government in India. Internally, Ranodip was not strong enough to change the old policy. He had to please his younger brothers and also the sons of Jung Bahadur. In 1879, Ranodip, in order to keep his younger and powerful brother, General Dhere Shamsher in good humor, suggested to Maharajah Dhiraj that Dhere be sent on a complimentary mission to India to present the thanks of the Durbar to its mighty neighbour. Generally the prime ministers of Nepal did not miss any chance to show their friendliness to the Viceroy.[2] Soon after this decision, the Commander-in-Chief, General Juggut Shamsher died. A bitter internal power struggle between the nephew and the uncle started. Juggut Jung, son of the late Jung Bahadur, hoped to seize the prime ministership whenever his uncle Ranodip Singh would die. However, Dhere Shamsher, the brother of Ranodip Singh, had the same ambition. The problem for the prime minister was to keep both of them contented and friendly to himself. The Resident reported that Dhere Shamsher offered the post of Commander-in-Chief to Juggut Jung, but that he did not accept it on the plea that unless Dhere should resign his claim to the prime ministership, it had no value. Dhere Shamsher refused this demand. Finally, the matter was settled: Dhere Shamsher became Commander-in-Chief and Juggut was given the command of the Western Forces. The important point was that the commander of the Western forces had more influence in the army than the Commander-in-Chief.[3] The matter did not end there. There was a plot against the life of Sir Ranodip Singh in 1882, in which Juggut Jung was implicated, although at the time of the conspiracy he was in India. Fortunately for Sir Ranodip, it was detected and the plot was defeated. Juggut Jung stayed in India until 1885,[4] and denied all the charges made against him. The Secretary

[1] T. H. Thornton to F. Henvey. No. 1724P, dated Simla, July 19, 1877, *Foreign Department Secret Proceedings*, December 1877, Nos. 104–33. (N.A.I.)
[2] Abstract translation of a Kharieta from His Highness Maharajah Adhiraj Surendra Vikram Shah Bahadoor Shamshere Jung of Nepal to the address of His Excellency the Right Honorable Lord Lytton, G.M.S.I., Viceroy and Governor-General of India, dated 2nd Poos Sambat 1935 (December 11, 1878) *Foreign Department Political—B*, 1879. No. 102–12. (N.A.I.)
[3] 'Death of General Juggut Shamsher, Commander-in-Chief, Nipal Army.' *Foreign Department Political—A Proceedings*. September 1879, Nos. 386–90. K. W. No. 1. (Correspondence between the Resident and the Secretary, Government of India, and other office notes.) (N.A.I.)
[4] 'Proposal to increase the allowances granted to General Juggut Jung.' *Foreign Department Political—A*, June 1884, Nos. 259–64. K. W. (Mostly office notes from officials of the Foreign office to the Secretary and to the Governor-General.) (N.A.I.)

of the Government of India felt that one day Juggut Jung might become the prime minister of Nepal and advised his government in his memorandum on the question of how to treat Juggut Jung that 'it seems wise not to estrange the future ruler of Nepal'.[1] The proposal made by Maharajah of Holkar to the British for the increase in the allowance of Juggut Jung from Rs. 2,500 ($450.00) to Rs. 3,000 ($580,00) was not appreciated by the Governor-General. Holkar's plea was politely refused, because the Government of India did not welcome an Indian Prince interfering in the relations of the Government of India with Nepal. The Governor-General wrote, 'It would be certainly dangerous to give the Maharajah an opening for interfering between us and other native states; for there is no knowing how far he might not go if he could once establish himself in the character of mediator'.[2]

The Resident in Nepal favoured the return of Juggut Jung to Nepal. As soon as Juggut Jung returned, he and his uncle, Sir Ranodip Singh, became reconciled and worked closely together. This was suspected by the ambitious family of Dhere Shamsher. The result was a brutal conspiracy against the prime minister and Juggut Jung, which was carried out on November 22, 1885. Maharajah Sir Ranodip Singh, and many others who were close relatives and might possibly succeed him were murdered.[3]

So the rule of Sir Ranodip Singh ended in tragedy. He was a weak man and from the beginning of his rule he was opposed by his own nephews and other followers of the late Sir Jung Bahadur. In the short period of eight years, two conspiracies against him were formed. Because of Ranodip Singh's ill health and weakness, Dhere Shamsher, who became the Commander-in-Chief in 1879, after the death of General Juggut Shamsher, controlled the real power until his death in 1884. Sir Ranodip's policy towards the British Government was badly managed because of Dhere Shamsher. It could be said that during the prime ministership of Sir Ranodip Singh most of the matters in dispute between the British and Nepalese were discussed superficially but that very little was done to settle them.

Sir Ranodip's Policy Towards the British and Girdlestone's Suspicious Attitude

There were many problems which created strained relations between

[1] From Government of India to the Secretary of State for India. No. 6 (Secret), dated Fort William, January 9, 1883. *Foreign Department Secret—E,* January 1883, Nos. 407-9. *Foreign Department Political—A,* June 1884, Nos. 259-64. (N.A.I.)

[2] *Ibid.*

[3] 'Note by Colonel J. A. Berkeley, late officiating Resident in Nepal' (Confidential). *Foreign Secret—E,* February 1887, No. 406. (N.A.I.)

the British, Indian and Nepalese governments, particularly the restrictions on the movements of the British Resident. Mr Girdlestone and other Residents had been of a strong attitude towards the Durbar on the question of relaxation on the movement of the Resident in the kingdom of Nepal as a whole. As long as Jung Bahadur was prime minister, this matter did not lead to a serious conflict. But during the rule of Ranodip, Girdlestone and Impey, the officiating Resident, both strongly recommended their government to force Nepal to change its policy. Impey suggested to Dhere Shamsher that there should be a gradual change in the old policy of treating the Resident like a prisoner. Dhere Shamsher replied that the reasons for not opening the door to the Europeans were that the Nepalese were pledged by tradition not to allow any except co-religionists in Nepal; that the people, the army and the Gurkhas would throw the minister from power if he relaxed the rule; and lastly, that the people were ignorant and would not allow the Europeans near their temples and their Gods.[1] Girdlestone dismissed this explanation as merely a pretext. He believed that the real reasons for not opening the kingdom to the Residents and other Europeans were first, that the nobles did not want to disclose the real character of Nepal to Europeans and secondly, that they had impressed on their subjects that the Durbar was more powerful than the British Government of India, and also that the British were too afraid of the Durbar to insist on the right of entry. They also feared that relaxation might lead to annexation.[2] The Secretary of the Indian Foreign Office, however, felt quite differently. He did not like the idea of forcing the Durbar to make concessions, although he believed that the Durbar, under the pressure, would collapse like a house of cards. He also considered that unless it were really necessary the Government of India should not take any action which would destroy friendly relations.[3] In 1882, when Sir Ranodip Singh was anxiously waiting for the recognition of the new Maharajah Dhiraj, Prithvi Bir Vikram Sah (who was accepted as the King of Nepal in 1881 by the Nepal Government) the Resident asked 'whether advantage should not be taken of the occasion to press for relaxation on behalf of the Residency, for obtaining which

[1] Impey to Lyall, dated Patna, February 14, 1879. (Confidential) 'Hindrance placed by Nipalese Officials in way of Resident, in Nipal while on tour in Deokur and Dhang Valleys (2). Proposed improvement on Resident's position and the admission of Europeans in Nipal.' *Foreign Department Political—A Proceedings*, October 1879. Nos. 49–54. (N.A.I.)
[2] Girdlestone to Lyall. Doondwagaon, Dhang Valley, dated February 19, 1879. (Demi-Official.) *Foreign Department Political—A Proceedings*, October 1876, K. W. 2. Nos. 49–54. (N.A.I.)
[3] Office Note signed by H.M.D. and T.C.P. September 5, 1879, and November 5, 1879. *Foreign Department Political—A Proceeding. Ibid.*

the recognition of the present Maharajah Dhiraj might serve as a useful lever.'[1] The Secretary of the Government of India wrote a marginal note on the file for the Governor-General which made the attitude of the Government very clear:

'... I am not sure that our own security demands an alteration of the Resident's position, and, failing, it is, I think, open to question whether we have a right to exact from an independent state concessions to which its rules, and perhaps its people, are strongly opposed ... the Durbar is not bound, being independent, and outside the recognized circle of our Indian feudatories, to give him the right of free movement within its territories, and free communication with its subjects...'[2]

On the question of entry of Europeans into Nepal, an issue which was strongly supported by Resident Girdlestone, the Secretary advised Girdlestone

'... that the Governor-General in Council does not consider it expedient at present to put authoritative pressure upon the Nipalese Durbar for the admission of Europeans into the country'.[3]

In spite of this clear and forthright rejection of Girdlestone's proposals, he continued obstinately to pursue the same policy during Sir Ranodip Singh's tenure of power. Girdlestone even advocated that, first of all, the British Government of India should block the import of foreign goods, and if this did not succeed, then the Resident should be withdrawn from the country. In short, he advocated a policy of creating as many difficulties as possible for the prime minister and his followers until they yielded. He was a firm believer in a show of strength. According to him, the entire history of British relations with Nepal showed that 'plain speaking' did not work, while in the few instances in which the Government of India had taken a strong attitude and had shown its strength, the Durbar had given way.[4] Finally he wrote, 'My advice is

---

[1] Report of the Under-Secretary, *Foreign Political—A*, February 1882 Nos. 283–304. (N.A.I.)

[2] Secretary notes on file. 'Nipal Affairs', Foreign Secret, K. W. No. 1 (Ripon Papers Volume 86). (B.M.M.M. Catalogue-Add. 43576.)

[3] Ibid.

[4] Report of the Under-Secretary, *Foreign Political—A*, K. W. of Nos. 285–99, *op. cit.*, Girdlestone to H. M. Durand, dated the Residency, Nepal, December 19, 1884. (Demi-Officials.) *Foreign Secret—F. Department.* April 1885, No. 72, Girdlestone to Secretary, Government of Bengal and the Revenue Department, Darjeeling. No. 173, dated Nipal Residency, July 16, 1881. *Foreign Secret,* April 1882. (N.A.I.)

that freedom for the Resident should be an integral part of the new policy'.[1] Girdlestone's ideas were much like those of Brian Hodgson, the former Resident. In both cases, the Government of India rejected the proposals of its representatives. The Governor-General and other officials agreed that the policy of the Nepal Durbar to keep the Resident in complete isolation was wrong, and they did not approve of it; but at the same time they did not have any inclination to force the hands of the Nepalese rulers. They did not want to have an open rupture with the Durbar on this question. The Government of India was more eager to have increased numbers of Gurkha recruits from the Nepalese rulers instead.[2] They did not feel it was prudent to start a serious conflict with a Durbar which was obstinate, unpredictable, and dangerous. The Secretary wrote:

'... I regard Nipal, with its large and eager army, as an element of the gravest political danger. In the event, never a very improbable event, of serious disturbance in India, that army must be regarded as more likely to act against us than with us....'[3]

Although the Nepal Durbar, since the time of Jung Bahadur, had tried to be friendly and co-operative with the British, nonetheless they feared that if an opportunity arose through which Nepal could gain, the Nepalese would not hesitate to oppose them. These were the reasons which prevented the Indian Government from taking any strong action against the Durbar on the question of entry of Europeans and the movement of its Resident inside the Kingdom of Nepal. This issue remained a bone of contention between Nepal and the British, and it was not solved during the prime ministership of Sir Ranodip Singh.

The Question of Trade During Sir Ranodip Singh's Prime Ministership
Trade between the two countries remained in a state of uncertainty and flux. Nepal's trade was carried on mostly with two countries: Tibet on the north and British India on the south.[4] Mr E. Buck, Director of Agriculture and Commerce, wrote,

'The conditions of trade with Nipal differ from those of trade with Tibet, for the simple reason that in the case of Tibet our boundary runs

[1] *Foreign Secret Department—F*, April 1885, No. 72. *Ibid.*
[2] The question of recruiting will be discussed in a separate chapter.
[3] *Foreign Secret.* February 1882. K.W. No. 1. (N.A.I.)
[4] Digby, William. *Nipal and India, 1857-1887*, p. 21, 1890. London, Political Agency, 25 Craven Street, Charing Cross.

along the summit of the snowy range, and in the case of Nipal along the strip of forest and jungle which lies at the foot of the Himalayas.[1]

The basic obstacles to free and increased trade between India and Nepal were four. The antiquated system of communication, that is to say, few and poor roads, none of which were worthy of the name. Main lines of roads such as civilization knows were not to be found beyond the British frontier. Naturally, it was difficult to have more trade. Secondly, the Durbar established bazaars on the border of India and Nepal and ordered merchants to conduct their trade at these points. The result was that freedom of trade was hampered, because British merchants had to cross the Nepalese border with their merchandise, sell the merchandise only at the bazaars, and then return with what they could not sell. This practice affected exports and imports, since those articles which were returned unsold were listed both as exports and imports. Thirdly, the merchants of British India had no knowledge as to what should be the valuation of goods in Nepal. The Durbar never supplied any correct price estimates. Lastly, came the un-co-operative attitude of the Durbar on the question of hiring foreigners to help modernize the communication system and its refusal to repair or build new roads owing to the fear that the Government of India had designs on Nepal's independence.[2]

Girdlestone decided in 1879 to take up the issue of trade with Sir Ranodip Singh and to suggest the ways by which all hindrance to its expansion could be removed. Girdlestone was a strong supporter and advocate of increased trade with the kingdom of Nepal, and thought that direct measures should be adopted for its extension but was pessimistic of success. In the field of agriculture, he felt that trade could only be expanded by increasing the population of the Terai and the lower valleys.[3] Unfortunately, there had been no definite estimate of the exact population of Nepal. The British thought it was two million, whereas the Nepalese claimed that it was five million in 1879.[4] Girdlestone also believed there must be hidden mineral wealth in the country, but its exploitation and export for refining would cost more than it was worth. Also, the number of the upper or higher classes was small and their life was not very luxurious, so that the demand for goods of high

[1] Buck, E., Director of Agriculture and Commerce, North West Provinces and Oudh, to C. Robertson, Secretary to Government of India. North Western Provinces and Oudh. No. T-187C, dated Allahabad, December 1877, No. 2. (N.A.I.)
[2] Buck. *Foreign Department Revenue—A Proceedings*. December 1877, No. 2. (N.A.I.)
[3] Girdlestone to Lyall, No. 22P, dated Nepal, June 30, 1879, *Foreign Department Political—A*, October 1879, No. 134. (N.A.I.)
[4] *Ibid*.

quality was very small. Finally, the Durbar had carefully provided enough food, drink and clothing produced by home industries for the poorer classes so that they lived in complete ignorance of the benefits of modern civilization and of the outside world.[1]

The British Government had always been very careful not to interfere in internal affairs. In pursuance of this policy, in 1859, during the rule of Jung Bahadur, its Resident informed the Durbar that the Governor-General in Council assumes no right to interfere with or even to advise upon the commercial policy of Nepal'.[2] So in 1879, Girdlestone was afraid that when he made suggestions for the improvement of trade the Durbar would quote the solemn pledge given by his government in 1859. Nonetheless he went forward and submitted a memorandum to the prime minister of Nepal on July 18, 1879, in which he suggested ways and means of improving the trade of Nepal. He advised first, the improvement of the road track on the Nepalese side so that they would connect the Indian roads with Nepal's business center; secondly, a greater freedom for the merchants of both countries to meet freely, and if possible the abolition of bazaars so that Indian merchants could visit the interior of Nepal; thirdly, the methods of farming and the collection of revenue from the farmers should be improved and the duties and customs levied by the Nepal government should be made known to the Resident; and lastly, Girdlestone requested detailed information about the timber trade.[3] The result of this memorandum was not completely negative, but neither were the suggestions heartily embraced. The prime minister, Sir Ranodip, evaded all the proposals. Later on, however, the Nepal Durbar began to build and repair the roads. British Indian merchants no longer were compelled to take shops in the bazaar except for certain centers and they were allowed, as earlier, to go inside the country to sell their goods. The Durbar became alive to the shortcomings of the farming system and tried to improve it. The Durbar agreed to supply a list of the customs and duties levied by it on imports and it also showed interest in supplying the prices and names of depots of timber.

Sir Ranodip agreed about the handicaps to trade put before him by Girdlestone and at the same time made excuses for not doing anything.[4]

[1] Girdlestone to Lyall, *Foreign Department Political—A*, October 1879, No. 134. (N.A.I.)   [2] *Ibid.*

[3] 'Memorandum of verbal representation, now put in writing at the request of the Prime Minister', by Mr Girdlestone, on July 18, 1879, *Foreign Department Political—A*, October 1897, No. 136. (N.A.I.)

[4] Report by Shew Shanker Sing, Mir Munshi of Nipal Residency of a conversation between the prime minister of Nipal and the Resident, on August 7, 1879; Girdlestone to Lyall, No. 37P, dated Nipal, August 13, 1879; *Foreign Department Political—A*, October 1879, Nos. 137 and 135, respectively. (N.A.I.)

This shows that in spite of pressure from the Resident, the prime minister would not do much directly to improve trade facilities between the two countries but he did gradually make small concessions which led to some minor improvement. The total registered trade between India and Nepal in 1877–78 was $4,720,800, and in 1882–83 $6,093,536.[1] These figures showed the improvement and increase in the amount of trade due to the Resident's suggestions and also to the reforms introduced by the Durbar. This was a welcome change for both sides.

The Question of Arms, Ammunition and Extradition

The question of arms and ammunition was hardly raised during the prime ministership of Maharajah Jung Bahadur. But his successor, Sir Ranodip, actively engaged in collecting war materials. It was known to the Government of India that a Snider cartridge factory had been established in Nepal, and various articles which might be used for warlike purposes had been imported. It was also alleged that when Maharajah Ranodip Singh visited India in 1880, he and his followers on their return journey smuggled a very large quantity of percussion caps and other munitions into Nepal.[2] This, needless to say, agitated the Indian Government.

When Dhere Shamsher became Commander-in-Chief he steadily tried to increase the strength of the Nepalese army. He was essentially a militarist, and was considered to have anti-British views.[3] It was reported by the Commissioner of the Patna Division that 'large quantities of sheet copper were being taken to Nepal for the manufacture of percussion caps and perhaps of cartridge cases'.[4] It was also suspected that a machine for making Snider cartridges was smuggled through Patna into Nepalese territory.[5] The Government of India became quite active and tried to prevent the smuggling of arms and other materials to Nepal. The Lieutenant-Governor of Bengal felt that it was important to have restrictions placed on the importation of sheet copper to Nepal. A suggestion was made to the Governor-General to the effect that

---

[1] Digby, *op. cit.*, pp. 21–2.

[2] Report by Under-Secretary, Government of India. *Foreign Political—A*, February 1882, Nos. 283–304, *op. cit.* Memorandum from His Excellency Maharajah Sir Ranodip Singh, Rana Shadur, KCSI, *Foreign Department Secret—E*, February 1884. No. 63. (N.A.I.)

[3] Horace A. Cockerell, Secretary to the Government of Bengal, Judicial, Political, and Appointment Department to the Secretary to the Government of India, Foreign Department; dated Darjeeling, June 12, 1880 (Confidential), No. 720T. *Foreign Department Political—B*, April 1881, Nos. 401–6; Girdlestone to Cockerell, The Residency Nepal, May 22, 1880. (N.A.I.)

[4] *Ibid.*

[5] *Ibid.*

'under section 4 of the Indian Arms Act XI of 1878 the prohibitions and provisions regarding military stores in sections 6 and 19(c) of that Act be extended to sheet Copper in the Districts bordering Nepal'.[1] It was believed that Nepal had succeeded in privately and secretly importing a rolling-machine, and therefore it was assumed that probably copper was being rolled in Nepal.[2] At the same time a Mr R. N. Mathewson was supposed to be helping the Nepal Durbar to procure arms and ammunition secretly from England. The Deputy Commissioner of Police of Calcutta had received information from several sources that Mr Mathewson had been engaged by the Nepal Government for buying and delivering on the Nepal frontier a large quantity of breech-loading rifles and machinery for making cartridges.[3] The Government of India took all precautions to check the smuggling, and the office of the Secretary of State for India in London was alerted to keeping watch on Mr Mathewson's movements. In making this request to the India Office in London, the Secretary of the Government of India observed that,

'I doubt whether we shall long be able to prevent the states outside our Indian frontier from equipping their troops with arms of precision; but the more we can put off the time when Nipal, Burmah and Afghanistan shall possess organized forces with European arms, the better for our own army estimates.'[4]

In the same period, the Nepal Durbar requested the Resident to ask the Government of India permission to purchase military rifles and ammunition. The Resident recommended to his Government to give arms and ammunition to Nepal as a free gift, provided the Durbar would agree to improve facilities for trade, give greater freedom of movement to the Resident, and grant full freedom to the British for obtaining recruits for their army. This gift should be made annually because only then would the Durbar keep its promise. However, the Resident contradicted himself by also advising that the arms gift should not be given to the prime minister (Sir Ranodip), using the excuse that the prime minister might go to war with Tibet.[5] The hands of the Government

[1] Cockerell to the Secretary, *Foreign Department Political—B*, April 1881, Nos. 401-6. (N.A.I.)
[2] Cockerell to Secretary, No. 3668 (Confidential), *Ibid.*
[3] J. Lambert, Deputy Commissioner of Police, Calcutta to Cockerell: Memorandum No. 1P, dated June 29, 1881 (Confidential), *Foreign Secret*, September 1882, No. 234. (N.A.I.)
[4] Sir A. C. Lyall to Colonel Sir O. T. Burne, dated Foreign Office Simla, July, 8 1881, (Demi-Official), *Foreign Secret*, September 1882, No. 235. (N.A.I.)
[5] C. E. R. Girdlestone to H. M. Durand, dated the Residency, Nipal, December 19, 1884 (Demi-Official.) *Foreign Secret—F*, April 1885, No. 72-101. (N.A.I.)

were strengthened when the Secretary of State for India approved the recommendation to grant a limited supply of arms of precision, and also to allow the Durbar to periodically purchase rifles in the future in return for concessions in the field of recruiting, liberation of trade, free movement for the Resident, and permission for Europeans to enter the country.[1] Thus, the Government of India offered a small concession on condition that the Durbar agreed to all its demands. The Secretary wrote, 'We must secure the most satisfactory guarantees before we commit ourselves'.[2]

In spite of these concessions from the Government of India, Sir Ranodip tried his best not to concede any of the Indian demands. However, the new Governor-General, Lord Dufferin, approved the policy of Girdlestone for the improvement of the relations between the Government of India and Nepal by means of mutual concessions. Following the inauguration of this new policy the successive Residents worked faithfully to promote it but no agreement was reached during the remainder of Ranodip Singh's rule.

The extradition of accused and of criminals had been solved by the provisions of the treaty of 1855, and by the supplementary memorandum of 1866. A further supplementary agreement was needed for the purpose of covering those who escaped from custody while undergoing punishment. On the request of Sir Ranodip a supplement was signed between the Nepalese and British Governments on June 24, 1881, which read as follows:

'That the offence of escaping from custody whilst undergoing punishment after conviction of any of the offences specified in the fourth Article of the aforesaid treaty, or in the aforesaid memorandum, shall be deemed to be added to the list of offences specified in the fourth Article of the aforesaid treaty.'[3]

Problem of Extradiction Between Indian Princely States and Nepal

The extradition treaties between Nepal and India (cited earlier) applied only to Nepal and the Indian provinces under direct British rule. They did not cover the subjects of the Indian Princely States. In the year 1884, two men of Rampur State committed murder in Rampur and then

---

[1] 'Proposed improvement of the relations between the Government of India and Nepal by means of mutual concessions.' From Secretary of State, No. 15, dated July 18, 1884. *Foreign Department Secret—F*, November 1884, No. 234. K.W. No. 1. (N.A.I.)

[2] Notes on the file by the Secretary. *Ibid.*

[3] 'The Extradition Agreement with Nepal.' From the Resident, Nipal, No. 42P, dated June 28, 1891. *Foreign Department Political—A*, March 1882. K.W. Nos. 111-17. (N.A.I.)

escaped into Nepal. Considering the seriousness of the crime, Rampur State requested the British Government to demand from the Nepal Durbar the extradition of these men. Nepal and Rampur had no direct treaty, and Rampur subjects were not British subjects. The Extradition Treaty of 1855 between India and Nepal contained no provision by which either state could demand the extradition of a subject of any third state. This issue became an interesting subject for discussion in the Foreign Office of the Government of India. There was no precedent for such a situation but this fact was not very unusual. There have been a number of examples of voluntary extradition by states without treaties. In fact, there have been court decisions upholding an obligation under general international law to extradite, although this view no longer is taken by courts.[1] The Secretary of the Government of India felt that the only alternatives were to ask for extradition 'as a favour or

[1] Cases of voluntary extradition by nations in the absence of any specific extradition treaties occurred mostly in Europe. 'International Cooperation in the Administration of Justice', *Cases and Other Materials on International Law*, Chapter 9, pp. 936–40, given as an insurance which took place in the United States.

IN RE DANIEL WASHBURN
United States, Court of Chancery of New York, 1819.
4 John. Ch. 106, 8 Am. Dec. 548.

Daniel Washburn was brought before the Chancellor upon *habeas corpus*, allowed and directed to the sheriff of Rensselaer county. It appeared by the return, that he was detained in custody by virtue of a *mittimus* from the recorder of Troy, under a charge of having in his possession 170 bills of the Bank of Montreal, of the denomination and value of five dollars each, which had been feloniously taken from some person unknown, and that he had received and secreted the bills, knowing them to be so stolen. The prisoner was being held for surrender to Canada, but it does not appear from the report that his surrender had been sought by Canada. . . .

CHANCELLOR KENT. 'It is the law and usage of nations, resting on the plainest principles of justice and public utility, to deliver up offenders charged with felony and other high crimes, and fleeing from the country in which the crime was committed, into a foreign and friendly jurisdiction. When a case of this kind occurs, it becomes the duty of the civil magistrate, on due proof of the fact, to commit the fugitive, to the end that a reasonable time may be afforded for the government here to deliver him up for the foreign government to make the requisite application to the proper authorities here, for his surrender. Who are the proper authorities in this case, whether it be the executive of the state, or, as the rule is international, the executive authority of the United States, the only regular organ of communication with foreign powers, it is not now the occasion to discuss. It is sufficient to observe, that if no such application be made, and duly recognized, within a reasonable time, the prisoner will then be entitled to his discharge upon *habeas corpus*. If the judicial authority has afforded sufficient means and opportunity for the exercise of this act of commutative justice, it has done its duty. Whether such offender be a subject

comity', or else to modify Article 2 of the Treaty of 1855 (between Nepal and India) in such a way as to treat the subjects of the feudatory states as if they had the status of British subjects. However, the British Government in India was not anxious to take up the issue because there was every possibility that Nepal would ask for a separate treaty to deal with subjects of Indian states. The British Government of India wanted to avoid making a new treaty with Nepal which might have to accept openly Nepal's independent status. Some of the British officials were even hoping that the Durbar would not look too closely into the matter since the legal case for demanding the extradition of the Rampur criminals was weak. In the case of the Indian princely states, the procedure of extradition had been regulated by express agreements negotiated with the consent of the British Government of India as the paramount power. The Rampur case, however, was unique since one state, Rampur, was a protected state while Nepal was a virtually independent state. Such a situation had never arisen previously for the British Government in India. There was the further possibility that at some future time a Nepalese criminal might escape to the territory of a feudatory state. In such a case the question would arise how Nepal

of this country, would make no difference in the application of the principle; though, if the prisoner, as in this case, be a subject of the foreign country, the interference might meet with less repugnance.'

This doctrine is supported equally by reason and authority. Kent also cited Vattel, Martens, Grotius and Heineccius in support of his argument.

The view of Chancellor Kent has not been adopted in the practice of the United States. Beginning with the provisions in a treaty of 1842 with Great Britain, the United States has concluded extradition treaties with most of the states of the world, and in practice extradition is confined within the limits of treaty provisions. Thus, 'extradition will be asked only from a government with which the United States has an extradition treaty, and only for an offense specified in the treaty'. Department of State Memorandum on Applications for the Extradition from Foreign Countries of Fugitives from Justice (September 1921). Nor, under the statutes may a person be extradited by the United States at the request of another state apart from treaty provision; the surrender of Arguelles to Spain in 1864 when no extradition treaty had been concluded with Spain (see 2 Wharton's Digest of International Law, p. 746 *et seq.*) may be viewed as exceptional. (This does not apply, however, to the surrender of persons in the Canal Zone to Panama.) The British attitude is similar. 'The common law prevents the Crown from surrendering to another state fugitive criminals who have committed crimes abroad and escaped to Great Britain and this common-law right is enforceable by writ of *habeas corpus*. Therefore, if the Crown wishes to bind itself by treaty to extradite fugitive criminals, it must secure the necessary legislation by Parliament, and any attempt at extradition which falls within the scope of a treaty and of the Extradition Acts, 1870 to 1906, can be defeated by writ of *habeas corpus*.' Arnold D. McNair, in 9 British Yearbook of International Law 1928), p. 60.

could claim the extradition of its subject.[1] After protracted arguments and discussions among the officials of the Foreign Office, the following conclusions were reached: (a) the British Government should treat the subjects of the Native (Princely) States as British subjects when dealing with an outside power; (b) in this case it should be impressed on the Nepalese Government that the subjects of Rampur State were quasi-British subjects and on that basis their surrender could be demanded; (c) the Durbar should be discouraged from demanding any new treaty on this subject through which Nepal might formally assert her independence and thus indirectly show the protected states the way in which they might assert their independence.[2] So the Government of India finally decided that the subjects of Rampur and Sikkim should be treated as British subjects only for the purposes of extradition from Nepal. These two states bordered on Nepal and there was the likelihood of a similar problem arising four or five times a year. When negotiations began, the Durbar tried to get a new treaty on this issue, but eventually it agreed to surrender the two criminals from Rampur to the British authorities.[3] Because of the peculiar status of Nepal with regard to the British Government, the matter became decidedly complicated, but the Nepal Durbar did not try to force a new treaty on this issue, and the problem was solved amicably.

Ranodip's Prime Ministership and its Results: A Summary

During the eight years of Maharajah Sir Ranodip Singh's prime ministership, he tried his best to be a loyal ally of the British in external affairs. There are many examples to illustrate his friendly attitude. In 1880, he showed his concern when the British Resident was murdered in Kabul and expressed his hope for a British victory in the Afghan war. On hearing a rumor that there might be war between the British Government and Russia, he went further than a formal 'expression of concern' and actually offered military assistance similar to Jung Bahadur's offer during the Indian Mutiny in 1857. He sent good wishes and congratulations to the English on their victory in Egypt in 1882. He did all this to 'increase the existing friendship' between the two governments. British officials, however, described him as a 'weak and obsti-

---

[1] 'Extradition of two Rampur subjects from Nipal.' From the Government of the North-Western Provinces and Oudh, No. 671-VI-364-2, dated June 24, 1884: 'Forwards, for consideration, copy of a letter from the Agent to the Lieutenant Governor for Rampur regarding the extradition of two Rampur subjects from Nipal.' Notes on files by Secretary and other Officials. *Foreign Internal—A*, September 1884, Nos. 14-18. K.W. (N.A.I.)

[2] *Foreign Department Internal—A*, September 1884. Nos. 14-18, K.W. (N.A.I.)

[3] *Ibid.*

nate' prime minister, and regarded his overtures as a 'cheap' method of showing friendship and loyalty. The British Government also felt that these signs of good will were made to gain favours of titles, and to strengthen his own army and his own position in the kingdom. However, on the questions of recruitment, entry of Europeans, improvements in trade relations, and relaxation of restrictions on the Resident's movements, Ranodip Singh conceded very little.[1] On the recommendation of the Resident, he was invited to India in 1880 and was received cordially wherever he went.[2] Near the end of his life he submitted a memorandum to the Governor-General of India concerning certain of his grievances against the Resident, Girdlestone, and also attempting to vindicate his past conduct. He accused the Resident of distrusting him and threatening and insulting him on many occasions. This statement was somewhat similar to one which Sir Jung Bahadur had made verbally to Lord Canning, the then Governor-General of India, against the then Resident, Ramsay. The difference between the two was that Jung Bahadur demanded the removal of Ramsay, whereas Sir Ranodip wrote to Lord Dufferin as follows:

'Lastly, I beg leave to state that I have no other object in laying these matters before you, but simply to vindicate my conduct and to prove that I am innocent. I am greatly pained at being so groundlessly accused; but I assure you that I have no intention to refer to this subject any more, or to disturb the existing friendship between Mr. Girdlestone and myself. I shall be very glad to forget all after the case has been once laid before you.'[3]

The memorandum was not even placed before Lord Dufferin and was returned to the prime minister after a thorough discussion among high officials of the Indian Foreign Office. They described it as a 'treacherous attack on the Viceroy's representative'. At the same time they did not instruct the Resident to ask for an explanation from the prime minister,

---

[1] Girdlestone to Grant, Secretary to the Government of India, No. 89P, dated Nepal Residency, September 21, 1882. *Foreign Political—A*, 1882, Nos. 142–86; Girdlestone to Lyall, No. 42P, dated Nipal, September 24, 1879, *Foreign Department Political—A*, November 1879, Nos. 577–9; E. C. Impey to Lyall, No. 16P, dated Kathmandoo, June 4, 1878 (Confidential) *Foreign Secret*, July 1878, Nos. 1–2; Surgeon J. Scully, Officiating Resident to Lyall, No. 11P, dated Nepal Residency, April 10, 1878 (Confidential) *Foreign Department Secret*, May 1878, Nos. 76–9; *Foreign Political—A*, February 1882, Nos. 283–304, op. cit., *Foreign Secret—F*, April 1885, Nos. 72–101. (N.A.I.)

[2] *Foreign and Political Department.* File No. 96(4)-H, 1934.

[3] 'Memorandum from His Excellency Maharajah Sir Ranodip Singh, Rana Bahadur, KCSI' *Foreign Secret—E*, 1884, No. 63. (N.A.I.)

due to the fear of 'a diplomatic rupture'.[1] The entire matter was laid to rest and no further communication took place on this subject between the two governments.

The prime ministership of Maharajah Sir Ranodip Singh could be described as a period of frustration for both governments, with little substantial accomplishment. Outwardly there was cordial friendship, but under the surface the long standing tensions continued between the two countries.

Bir Shamsher and the Policy of Compromise

Before the emergence of Jung Bahadur as prime minister in 1846, the king had the power to appoint his own minister. Jung Bahadur changed this rule by making a 'roll of succession' by which the prime ministership of Nepal would remain in his family. The King retained only nominal power of appointing the prime minister from the roll of succession prepared by the prime minister, and as noted earlier, Sir Ranodip Singh succeeded Jung Bahadur, according to the rule that he laid down in the roll of succession. The weakness of the arrangement was that it made no allowance for the frustrated ambition of certain members of the Rana family, nor for the fact that *coups d'état* and bloodshed to gain power were not uncommon in the history of Nepal. A classic example of this flaw took place with the coming to power of Bir Shamsher in 1885.

Bir Shamsher was the nephew of Sir Ranodip Singh and the son of Dhere Shamsher. According to Jung Bahadur's list, Bir Shamsher would have had to wait for the prime ministership for a long time, since he was seventh on the succession list. Most probably he would never have succeeded to the high office which he coveted. So in 1885, he decided to force his way and become prime minister. On November 22, 1885, he led a successful *coup d'état* against the government. Sir Ranodip Singh was murdered and most of the remaining leaders who had a claim to the prime ministership were either murdered or fled to the Residency. Bir Shamsher and his followers, not overlooking any possible rivals, also killed Juggut Jung, oldest son of Jung Bahadur, and most of his brothers. Thus, they eliminated almost all the possible contenders for the office of prime minister. Those who were left alive were exiled to India. Bir Shamsher came to power after successfully

[1] 'Prime Minister of Nepal's Grievances against Girdlestone. From Lieutenant General Khudga Shamshere Jang of Nepal. Nil. Expresses Sir Ranodip Singh's thanks for the kindness shown to him by His Excellency the Viceroy in certain matters which were discussed two or three years ago in respect to the interchange of courtesies, etc. Submits a memorandum on the subject of certain grievances which the prime minister has against Mr Girdlestone.' *Foreign Secret—E*, February 1884, Nos. 62–6. K.W. No. 1. (N.A.I.)

arranging the *coup d'état*. However, he had so many enemies that he had to wait to receive the recognition of the British Government of India. Bir's anxiety over the recognition of his government was based on his fear of the influence of Jung Bahadur's relatives on the Government of India. On the other hand, the British had considerable difficulty finding a solution for the problems created by this *coup d'état*. Their major problem was how to handle the refugees who had fled from Nepal or those who had been exiled by Bir's government. In the first place the Resident was instructed to see that the remaining family of the late Sir Jung Bahadur was protected and if possible sent to India. But as the large number of refugees increased, the responsibility of the Government of India also increased. The refugees had to be given large enough allowances so that they could live in India; they also had to be prevented from using India as a secure base from which to plot the forcible overthrow of the Bir government. Although they were under British protection, they could not be allowed to abuse this hospitality by conspiring against the government of a British ally.

At the same time, the Government of India did not want to intervene in the domestic affairs of Nepal. The Nepal refugees, of course, tried to obtain arms, financial and moral support from the British to overthrow the Bir government. Under these circumstances, the Government of India could have dictated its own terms for helping the refugees. The British could have demanded that in return for helping Jung Bahadur's relatives they would promise to abolish the restrictions imposed by the Nepal government on the British Resident and to grant the other demands which had been requested for years past. Jit Jung, the son of Jung Bahadur, put the refugees' case before Lord Dufferin in the following emotional words:

'... that he had come to Calcutta in accordance with the advice which his father, Sir Jung Bahadur, had always given his children, that in all their troubles and difficulties they should look for help to the British Government, which Sir Jung Bahadur had most loyally served, and which he firmly believed would never allow his name or family to be dishonored or forgotten.'[1]

General Jit Jung further assured the Governor-General that:

[1] Private interview granted to Jit Jung Bahadur Rana, late Commander-in-Chief of the Nipal Army by His Excellency the Viceroy, on Thursday, January 28, 1886, at the Government House, Calcutta. The General also presented a memorandum to the Viceroy. The visit was of an entirely unofficial nature The General was conducted to His Excellency's room by Lieutenant Evans-Gordon, Attache, Foreign Department, who acted as interpreter. *Foreign Secret—E*, February 1886. Nos. 248–52. (N.A.I.)

FRUSTRATION AND COMPROMISE

'... if the Viceroy of India would signify by the slightest sign his approval of the aspirations of Jung Bahadur's children, the entire army would at once desert the traitors whose deposition would be as speedily effected as their usurpation.'[1]

The Governor-General categorically refused to interfere in the internal affairs of Nepal. He said that this was not the first time that such a barbarous act had taken place there. He strongly deplored the use of violence in taking over power. Nevertheless he adhered absolutely to his government's traditional policy of non-intervention and reminded the son of Jung Bahadur that any interference would have been strongly opposed by Jung Bahadur himself. He pointed out that it would also be contrary to the treaty between the Nepal Durbar and the British Government of India. The Viceroy made the point to General Jit Jung that the government had at no time guaranteed the continuance of Jung Bahadur's dynasty. He also reminded Jit Jung of the help rendered to his brother, General Juggut Jung, when he was implicated in the conspiracy against Sir Ranodip in 1882. The reader will recall that Juggut Jung and several close relatives were involved in a conspiracy, but before the plot succeeded it was discovered. The British Government intervened so that most of the conspirators were exiled in India. The British Government also persuaded the Nepal Durbar to give Juggut Jung, who was in India at the time, a substantial allowance, which the Government of India supplemented by Rs.800 ($160,00) from the Indian treasury.[2] Upon hearing the Viceroy's statement and his refusal to help the refugees to recover their position in Nepal, Jit Jung offered his own services to the British Government. The Viceroy told Evans-Gordon, the interpreter, to inform the Foreign Secretary of this offer. He said that he saw no reason 'why some advantage should not be taken of Jit Jung's offer', but told Evans-Gordon not to translate his comment to Jit Jung.[3] There is no document available to show whether the Government of India ever used Jit Jung's offer to serve the British.

The Nepal refugees left no stone unturned in trying to change the policy of the Indian Government in their favor, but without success. Just a month after Jung's interview with the Viceroy, the British Government informed Jit Jung that it had recognized the new regime and warned him that the refugees would not be assisted to overthrow

---

[1] *Foreign Secret—E*, February, 1886 Nos., 248–52.
[2] From the Government of India to the Secretary of State for India, No. 6 (Secret), dated Fort William, January 9, 1883. *Foreign Secret—E*, January 1883, Nos. 407–9; *Foreign Secret—E*, February 1886, Nos. 248–52. (N.A.I.)
[3] *Foreign Secret—E*, February 1886, Nos. 248–52. (N.A.I.)

Bir Shamsher.[1] From that time onward, British India had to deal with a prime minister whose father (Dhere Shamsher) had an anti-British feeling. Only after discussing the entire period of Bir Shamsher's rule can one reach any conclusion as to the wisdom of the Viceroy's decision to recognize him and to reject the request of the refugees for aid in overthrowing him.

The relations between the governments of India and Nepal had historically depended upon the relations between the Resident and the prime minister. Their attitude towards one another had often been a determining factor in the formation of official policy. The advice of the Residents had weighed heavily with the Government of India in deciding its policy. The officials in Calcutta had no first-hand knowledge of Nepal, and the opinions of the Residents had very considerable influence since they were the men on the scene.

When Bir Shamsher came to power, Girdlestone was the Resident in Kathmandu. He was an official of long experience who had been a strong advocate of a firm policy towards the Durbar. During his tenure of office, he had encountered many difficulties with Ranodip Singh. Girdlestone was on leave during the *coup d'état* of 1885 and also at the time when the Government of India recognized Bir Shamsher's government. Probably if he had been on the spot he would have asked for acceptance of all the British demands before giving recognition to Bir's government. But Colonel J. C. Berkeley, the acting Resident in Kathmadu, played an important part in the recognition of the Bir regime. In his confidential report to the Secretary he wrote that 'Jung Bahadur was steeped in blood'. He further added that 'the present minister and his family are as bad as they can be; but they had already rendered us service, and it is conceivable that they might be able to do as much for us as Jung Bahadur did'.[2] He frankly advised recognition of Bir Shamsher in the following words:

'Unless we mean to change our whole policy towards Nepal, and to abandon strict neutrality for active interference, it seems to me that it does not matter to us which set of cut-throats has the upper hand.'[3]

Berkeley felt that the immediate effect of the *coup d'état* on the relations between the Government of India and the Durbar was favourable to

---

[1] W. J. Cuningham, Secretary to Government of India, Foreign Department to General Jit Jung Rana Bahadur, No. 563-E, dated Fort William, March 29, 1886. *Foreign Secret—E*, May 1886. No. 53. (N.A.I.)

[2] Berkeley to Cuningham, dated Residency Baroda, January 4, 1887. (Confidential) Demi-Official. *Foreign Secret—E*, February 1887, No. 504. (N.A.I.)

[3] Berkeley to Cuningham. *Foreign Secret—E*, February 1887, No. 405. (N.A.I.)

the British. For the first time in Nepalese history, a ruthless government which had always opposed any intervention by the Indian government in its affairs waited anxiously for the Governor-General to decide whether he would recognize them.

The manner in which the Resident and the Government of India solved the refugee problem by placing the refugees in different places in India and arranging handsome allowances for them made a strong impression on the Nepalese government and the people alike. It was reported that the major question which was asked by the Nepalese was, 'What will the English Sarkar do?'[1] On this regard, the Shamshers, just after they seized power, tried to win the favour of the Indian Government by facilitating its most important object, the recruitment of Gurkhas for the Indian army. The anxiety for British recognition, however, did not mean that Bir Shamsher was pro-British, or that there would be any fundamental change in the Durbar's policy toward India. The Shamsher family had had the reputation of being hostile to the British. It was known that the father of Bir Shamsher was anti-British, and that he had opposed strongly Jung Bahadur's support of the British during the Indian Mutiny. After his recognition by the Government of India, Bir Shamsher returned to the traditional policy of isolation although he claimed that he continued to help the British in the matter of recruitment.

The end of Girdlestone's tenure of office and the period of service of Major Durand, who succeeded him in 1888 as Resident, were not a very happy time. Just before Girdlestone's retirement from Nepal, he took the obstinate Maharajah Bir Shamsher to task for his 'examining British merchants' letters before despatch.'[2] Bir Shamsher used to open and read the letters addressed to British merchants in Kathmandu before delivering them. Girdlestone reported this practice to the Secretary of the Government of India. This led to Bir Shamsher's censure by the British Government.[3]

Major Durand, during his period as Resident, formed a very bad opinion of Bir Shamsher's rule. Durand complained especially that the restrictions on his freedom of movement had the result that 'now the position of the Resident in Nepal is not such that any accurate information as to the course of affairs in Nepal would be communicated to

---

[1] 'Note by Colonel J. C. Berkeley, late Officiating Resident in Nepal.' Dated January 4, 1887. (Confidential) *Foreign Secret—E*, February 1887, No. 406. (N.A.I.)

[2] Girdlestone to the Officiating Secretary, Foreign Department, No. 78–C, dated Camp Segowlie, January 22, 1888. *Foreign Secret—E*, March 1888, No. 165. (N.A.I.)

[3] *Ibid.*

him by the Durbar'.[1] Durand wrote that the rulers of Nepal were playing China against India and quoted General Chandra Shamsher as saying 'that Nepal is subordinate to China, and in no way so to the Government of India'.[2] It was true that Nepal was tributary to China but the state tribute was only a nominal one. It was ridiculous on the part of Chandra Shamsher to use the words 'Nepal tributary to China'. Nepal certainly did not intend to allow China to control it. What it wanted was to ensure its independence from Indian control.

In spite of Chandra Shamsher's utterances, the Bir Shamsher government offered to help the British against Russia if there should be a war. Durand, however, greatly distrusted the Nepalese and regarded this offer as just another trick by which the Durbar hoped to obtain a reward. In his opinion, 'if words are allowed to count, the Minister would do anything that the British Government desired'.[3] Durand believed that Bir Shamsher was steadily opposed to any rapprochement with India, and that he would not open the country to the British, although he knew well that if the Indian Government should treat the Nepalese in the same way that they treated the British 'and close India to the Nepalese, his position would be a very unpleasant one'.[4]

During the British–Tibetan dispute in 1888, Bir Shamsher wrote to the four Kazis of Lhasa that:[5]

'The British Government is great and enlightened, such a Government, I do not apprehend, will do an injustice to any one. Everyone I should say must accede what is just and proper.'[6]

Further, to put more confidence in the minds of the Kazis he wrote:

'... I write this to remove your doubts that we have been dealing with the British for the last hundred years, and during which time we have always found them just, kind and straight forward in all their dealings to us.'[7]

It is an illustration of the distrust which influenced relations between

---

[1] Report by Major Durand, Resident. *Foreign Secret—E*, October 1890, Nos. 88-9. (N.A.I.)
[2] *Ibid.*
[3] *Ibid.*
[4] *Foreign Secret—E*, October 1890. Nos. 88-9. (N.A.I.)
[5] Kazi means judge.
[6] 'Abstract translation of a letter from His Excellency the Maharajah to the four Kazis of Lhasa, dated Baisakh, Sudi Sumbut, 1945.' *Foreign Secret—E*, June 1888, No. 308. (N.A.I.)
[7] *Ibid.*

the two governments that this manifestation of friendship by Bir Shamsher was looked upon by Durand and others as nothing more than empty words.

Both Girdlestone and Durand were dissatisfied with the attitude of Bir Shamsher. It seems that neither of them trusted him. It was Girdlestone who by reporting against Bir Shamsher's practice of opening the letters of British merchants brought 'censure' upon him, while Durand suspected even Bir's offer of help to the British against Russia if there should be a war. Both men were strong advocates of a strong policy in dealing with Nepal. Possibly their pride was hurt when they saw that a backward state presumed to limit trade, ban Europeans, restrict the Residents' movements and even complain to the Governor-General of their conduct. However, in the field of diplomacy one has to subordinate pride to gain the main purpose of creating better and friendly relations even with a state small in size but proud and determined to protect and defend its freedom. Only then can both parties win respect for each other. It can be said, then, that the mutual distrust that developed between Girdlestone and Durand, on the one hand, and Bir Shamsher on the other, was not to the advantage of either India or Nepal.

Residentship of Colonel H. Wylie and the Policy of Conciliation

In 1891, Major Durand was succeeded as Resident by Colonel Wylie who believed in a policy of conciliation and compromise instead of the previous 'strong policy' which had engendered so much suspicion and hostility. He hoped for mutual understanding and started his work on these lines, writing to the Secretary to the Government of India thus:

'The position of affairs when I first went to Kathmandu in 1891 may be described as one of grave mutual distrust between our Government and that of Nepal, and knowing how perfectly sincere we were in our desire to be on friendly terms with that State, and also that we had no ulterior designs upon it, I believed it to be my duty to endeavour to bring about a better understanding between ourselves and the Durbar.'[1]

Colonel Wylie regularly submitted a 'brief report on the progress of Nepal from 1891 to 1899', which gave a clear picture of the country's internal as well as external affairs. The questions of boundary demarcation or crime committed near the boundary and other small matters were handled in a friendly and accommodating manner. The Durbar had been assisting the British officials in suppressing frontier crimes,

[1] Wylie to Sir Mortimer Duran, dated Camp Via Segowlie, December 14, 1893. (Confidential) *Foreign Secret—E*, November 1896, Nos. 127-62. (N.A.I.)

arresting and surrendering even those people to whom the Extradition Treaty did not apply. The Rajah of Sikkim himself was handed over to the Indian government when he was captured while endeavoring to escape from his state to Tibet through Nepal. There were no serious boundary disputes and most of the boundary issues were settled peacefully. Wylie reported that there appeared to be an increasing trade between the two countries. The statistics of exports and imports which were compiled by the Government of India were as follows:

Year	Exports Rupees	Dollars (million)	Imports Rupees	Dollars[1] (million)
1895–96	1,83,36,959	$2\frac{1}{2}$	1,36,23,888	$2\frac{1}{4}$
1896–97	1,89,30,554	$2\frac{3}{8}$	1,53,67,519	$2\frac{1}{3}$
1897–98	2,05,65,292	4	1,82,88,103	$2\frac{1}{2}$
1898–00	2,14,09,805	$4\frac{1}{8}$	1,60,63,496	$2\frac{1}{3}$
1899–1900 (for eleven months period)	2,09,34,021	4	1,37,44,745	$2\frac{1}{4}$[2]

The Secretary of State, as well as the Government of India, laid down four major British objectives in Nepal. They were:

1. Increased facilities for raising Gurkha recruits.
2. Liberation of trade.
3. Removal of restrictions now placed on the movement of the British Resident in Nepal.
4. Access to the country for Europeans.[3]

It was agreed that the first of these demands was the most important.

---

[1] The present exchange rate (1969) between rupees and dollars is Rs. 7.50 equals one dollar. The exchange rate of the rupee has varied from time to time. The above figures are only an approximate estimate.

[2] 'Reports on the events of the past year, and on the normal and material progress of Nepal', by H. Wylie (1895–99) and Loch to the Secretary, Government of India, Foreign Department. No. 41P–73027, Nepal. Residency, June 25th: No. 36–P/8–302, May 24, 1892; No. 35–P–9–3027, May 27, 1893; (Demi-Official) October 24, 1894: No. 32P–123027, May 23, 1896 (Confidential), No. 44P–14–3027, June 17, 1898 (Confidential) No. 50P–15–3027, June 17, 1899, No. 1 A–16–3027, June 11, 1900 (Confidential) July 1895, Nos. 473–4; June 1892, Nos. 136–7, June 1893, Nos. 389–93; March 1895, Nos. 69–70; June 1896, Nos. 283–5; August 1898, Nos. 238–40; August 1899, Nos. 95–6; July 1900, Nos. 284–5. *Foreign Secret—E.* (N.A.I.)

[3] 'Note on our position with regard to Nepal', by Colonel Wylie, March 19, 1894. *Foreign Secret—E*, November 1894, Nos. 127–62. (N.A.I.)

FRUSTRATION AND COMPROMISE

These were the same concessions for which the Government of India had been asking for years, but with very little success. Colonel Wylie while agreeing with his government's objectives, suggested that 'mutual concessions might lead to a better understanding between the Nepalese and ourselves'.[1] On the suggestion of Wylie, Bir Shamsher invited Lord Roberts, the Commander-in-Chief in India, to visit Nepal in 1892. Wylie secured an invitation for Roberts because he had observed that 'Sir Frederick (Lord Roberts) had a wonderful power of attaching natives to himself'. This was an unprecedented suggestion because never before had a British officer of such high rank been invited to visit Nepal. During his visit Lord Roberts saw the parade of some 18,000 Nepalese soldiers at Kathmandu in his honor. In summing up his impression abour Nepal Lord Roberts wrote:

'Notwithstanding the occasional differences which have occurred between our Government and the Nepal Durbar, I believe that, ever since 1817, (1815–16) when the Nepal war was brought to a successful conclusion by Sir David Ochterlony, the Gurkhas have had a great respect and liking for us; but they are in perpetual dread of our taking their country, and they think the only way to prevent this is not to allow anyone to enter it except by invitation, and to insist upon the few thus favoured travelling by the difficult route that we traversed. Nepal can never be required by us for defensive purposes, and as we get our best class of Native soldiers thence, everything should, I think, be done to show our confidence in the Nepalese alliance, and convince them that we have no ulterior designs on the independence of their kingdom.'[2]

Wylie also took other steps in his pursuance of his policy of conciliation. He asked that the title of Knight Commander of the Star of India be conferred on Bir Shamsher, and this recommendation was accepted. Wylie also encouraged Bir Shamsher to accept Lord Roberts's invitation to visit India, a visit which Bir made in 1893.[3]

In earlier years, because of the smuggling of arms and ammunition into Nepal, the Indian Government had set up inspection posts on the frontier between the two states. However, experience showed that these posts did not help in stopping the smuggling and only succeeded in adding an extra burden on the Indian treasury. Both Girdlestone and Durand had opposed their abolition. Durand had further opposed the grant of any concession to the Durbar on the importation of arms and

---

[1] 'Note on our position with regard to Nepal', by Colonel Wylie, March 19, 1894, *Foreign Secret—E*, November 1894, Nos. 127–62. (N.A.I.)

[2] Lord Roberts of Kandahar, Field Marshal, *Forty-One Years in India*, Volume II, p. 452, London: Richard Bentley and Son, 1897.

[3] *Foreign and Political Department Secret*, File No. 96(4)-H, 1934. (N.A.I.)

ammunition in order to gain more army recruits, because he thought he could get the recruits without making any concessions.[1] Wylie suggested the abolition of the border inspection posts because he thought due to this restriction the Durbar had started the practice of smuggling and had actually bought a large quantity of arms and machinery. He argued that the abolition of the border inspection posts would give the Nepalese confidence in themselves and in the sincerity and friendship of the British Government. Colonel Wylie frankly admitted that the Nepalese did not trust the British motives in Nepal. With the same astuteness, he remarked that the British had been equally suspicious of the Nepalese.

To check the growth of mutual suspicion and distrust, Wylie advised the Government of India to grant permission to the Nepalese to buy arms and ammunition on the basis of 'mutual concession'. He wrote, 'I think, in Nepal, our fault has been a want of recognition of Bir Shamsher's acts of friendliness, which have been very real'.[2] He pointed out that the principal object of the British had been to obtain more recruits from Nepal. In this regard, the Durbar has shown so much co-operation that not only had the army received the required number of recruits, 'but commanding officers have been able to select men of the particular classes which they fancy'. The credit for this success in recruitment, he noted, must go to Bir Shamsher because never before under any previous prime minister had Gurkhas been so freely recruited for the British army. Lord Lansdowne, the Governor-General, accepted Wylie's arguments, so that when Bir Shamsher visited Lansdowne at Calcutta in February 1893 he was given proof of British friendliness in the form of permission to purchase arms and ammunition on the open market. Bir Shamsher then requested Wylie to supply him with a price list for arms and machinery, informing him that the Government of Nepal was ready to spend in one year eighteen lakhs of rupees (six hundred thousand dollars). Later, Bir submitted an enormously large list of arms and ammunition to be purchased, together with another list of the machinery needed for manufacturing military equipment in Nepal. The immediate reaction of Wylie to the list submitted to him was, 'If the war material mentioned in the list to which I refer is purchased, Nepal will be better armed in some important respects than we ourselves in India'.

[1] 'Searching posts of the Nepal border to prevent the illicit importation of arms', 'Home Department office notes. Demi-Official from H. Luson, Under-Secretary to the Government of Bengal, dated the 20th May 1891.' Notes on office files, *Foreign Secret—E*, October 1891, Nos. 159–61. Also *Foreign Secret*, October 1887, Nos. 37–61 (File No. 42). *Foreign Secret*, June 1884, Nos. 438–62; *Foreign Secret*, September 1888, Nos. 4–13. (N.A.I.)

[2] For citation of this quote and subsequent quotes in this section see footnote on pp. 140–41.

While favoring improved Indian–Nepal relations, Colonel Wylie was rather disappointed at the way Lord Lansdowne gave a blank check to Maharajah Bir Shamsher. In his disappointment, Wylie said, 'I have been the great advocate for concession, but throughout I have urged that a firmer and more open line should be taken with the Durbar, and I think it is unfortunate that we have not done this'. The Resident was disturbed that the only stipulation which Lord Lansdowne made was 'that the Resident's position in Nepal should be treated with courtesy'. Wylie noted that Lord Lansdowne's solitary stipulation had not been complied with by the Durbar, nor did compliance seem forthcoming in the near future.

The Government of India's officials, upon seeing Nepal's arms requests, expressed the fear that Nepal would like to attack British India. Wylie, however, thought that the Nepalese wanted arms to make the country safe against any attack from India, and to increase Nepal's political value in the eyes of Hindustan, Tibet, China, and perhaps eventually in those of Russia. Wylie displayed his diplomatic ability by persuading Bir Shamsher that the quantity of arms he wanted to buy was excessive. So effective was Wylie's persuasion that the prime minister assured him that Nepal would accept whatever quantity of arms the Government of India might decide was proper. Bir Shamsher even went further and said that 'we were the donors and Nepal the recipient in this transaction, and he would be grateful for whatever we allowed him to have'. He was so grateful for the British concession that he even showed Colonel Wylie the Nakhu Arsenal of Nepal. This mark of confidence enabled the Resident for the first time to make an estimate of the quantity of arms possessed by the Durbar, and how much machinery was available for the manufacture of ammunition.

Colonel Wylie reported the result of his negotiations to the Foreign Office in India. The officials of the Foreign Office and of the Military Department, and the entire Council of the Governor-General discussed the report thoroughly and reached the following conclusions:

1. The British Government would comply with the Durbar's requisitions;
2. A favourable reply should be sent to the Durbar immediately;
3. It remained only for the two governments to settle in friendly communication the quantity and description of arms and stores which would comply with the condition of 'reasonable indents';
4. The prime minister should consult Colonel Wylie in order to arrive at a clear and amicable understanding of what constituted Nepal's reasonable requirements for future deliveries of arms and

stores, so that the demand which would be made from time to time could be met promptly and without dispute;
5. Colonel Wylie should be instructed to make it clear that machinery was excluded from the negotiations; and that the measure of the reasonable requirements for arms and stores should be the quantity needed for an Army of 20,000 or at the utmost 25,000.

The purpose of this point was to make certain that the number of Nepal soldiers with modern equipment should not become too large. The same principle was used with Indian princes by restricting the number of Imperial Service Troops. Refusal of machinery made it almost impossible for Nepal to enlarge its army beyond 25,000. It was Wylie's astuteness, skill in diplomacy, and sincerity of purpose which enabled his Government to come to a final solution of this contentious problem without endangering its own security, and at the same time to win the confidence of a suspicious and not overly friendly neighbor.

Lord Elgin replaced Lord Lansdowne as Governor-General in 1894. When he finally presented Lord Elgin's Kharieta to Bir Shamsher, Wylie did not hesitate to express his government's disappointment and his personal disappointment, at the Durbar's failure to make any concession in return for the arms agreement. He said he hoped that in the future, Bir Shamsher would reciprocate by showing the same feeling of sincerity, friendliness and confidence which the Government of India had shown towards Nepal. Wylie summed up his disappointment in an interview with Bir Shamsher, as follows:

'We have done a great deal for Nepal which owes everything to Great Britain; and this concession about arms and ammunition is, you must admit, a wonderful concession. I can't conceal from you that my Government are disappointed at the way you have treated this concession. So am I . . . *and you have made no sign that you appreciate what we have done for you, Lord Lansdowne showed you how you could give proof of friendship and good feeling. He showed that you could do so in treating the Resident less LIKE A PRISONER AND MORE LIKE a trusted friend. If you want to show friendship then fall in with the Viceroy's wishes, and thus show that you respect them.*'[1]

[1] For discussion on pages 138 to 141 see the following notes: Foreign and Military Department, Government of India. Demi-Official from Colonel H. Wylie to Sir M. Durand, dated Camp Via Segowlee, December 14, 1893: (Confidential). Demi-Official letter from Colonel J. C. Ardagh to Sir H. M. Durand, 'The enclosed was with me by Colonel Wylie'. 'Note on our position with regard to Nepal', by Wylie, March 19, 1894, K.W. No. 4; 'Abstract translation of a copy of a letter Sri (5) Maharajah Dhiraj Prithvi Bir Bikram Jang Bahadur Shamsher Jang, to His Excellency the most Honorable Henry Charles Ketth Petty Fitz Maurice, Marquis of Lansdowne, Viceroy and

This remonstrance opened a new chapter of real friendship between the Governments of British India and Nepal.

In retrospect, the policy followed by Colonel Wylie for almost a decade proved to be moderately successful. He inaugurated the changes by which suspicion lessened and friendship grew between the two nations. This is evident from the following passage from a report by his successor, Lieutenant-Colonel W. Loch, in 1900.

'. . . I believe the Darbar is inclined to relax its policy of mistrust, certainly the Resident is not dogged about by spies to the extent complained of formerly, and a certain amount of latitude is extended to me in allowing me to visit parts of the country off the beaten track of visitors for the purpose of fishing. I am inclined to follow my predecessor's plan which was to work patiently to win the Darbar's confidence, rely on it for information and refrain from trying to obtain information through channels of my own.'[1]

An Examination of William Digby's Criticisms of British Policy

Before closing this chapter, it seems relevant to discuss William Digby's strong criticism of Lord Dufferin, Colonel Berkeley, and the British Government's policy towards the *coup d'état* in Nepal in 1885. In his book, *India and Nepal, A Friend in Need: A Friendship Forgotten*,[2] Digby briefly discussed British–Nepalese relations from the time of the help given by the late Sir Jung Bahadur to the British during the

Governor-General of India, 27th Kuar, Samvat 1950 (October 22, 1903); From Viceroy to the Secretary of State, No. 4 of 1894, Fort William, January 3, 1894; Kharieta from the Viceroy and Governor-General to His Highness the Maharajah Dhiraj of Nepal, Simla, May 15, 1894; Wylie to the Secretary, No. 42-P-4041, Kathmandu June 13, 1894 (Confidential); from Viceroy to Secretary of State, No. 189 of 1894, Simla, October 17, 1894; Discussion notes from the files of Military and Foreign Department, pp. 11-19, K.W. No. 1; Demi-Official from H. J. S. Cotton, Chief Secretary, Bengal Government to the Secretary, dated March 15, 1894 (with full discussion in the Council of the Governor-General of India). *Foreign Secret—E*, November 1894, Nos. 127-62; 'Reports on the events of the past year, and on the moral and material progress of Nepal', from 1891 to 1894, 96, 98, and 1899, *Foreign Secret—E, op. cit.*, 'Maharajah Sir Bir Shamsher Jung Bahadur Rana who was invited by Lord Roberts to attend a Camp of Exercise in Northern India in January 1893, wishes to pay a visit to His Excellency the Viceroy Lord Lansdowne at Calcutta in December before visiting the Commander-in-Chief at the Camp. *Foreign and Political Department*, File No. 96(4)-H, 1934, *op. cit.* (N.A.I.)

[1] 'Reports on the events of the past official year, and on the moral and material progress of Nepal', No. 1-A-16-3027, Nepal, June 11, 1900. From Lieutenant-Colonel W. Loch, Resident in Nepal, to the Secretary to the Government of India, Foreign Department. *Foreign Department Secret—E*, July 1900, Nos. 284-5. (N.A.I.)

[2] Digby, William, *op. cit.*

Indian Mutiny to the *coup d'état* of 1885 when the prime minister of Nepal, Sir Ranodip Singh, the brother of Sir Jung Bahadur, was murdered by the Shamsher branch of his family. Digby argued that Lord Dufferin should have helped the sons, daughters and relatives of Sir Jung Bahadur, who were refugees from Nepal, to throw out Bir Shamsher's government. Digby also criticized the Resident, Berkeley, for not supporting those who took refuge in the Residency. He quoted at length from the statement of General Dhoje Nursing, the adopted son of Sir Ranodip Singh to prove the error made by Berkeley. General Nursing wrote:

'... Generals Puddum Jung and Ranabir, and several of the refugees, were in manner turned out of the place. Had they been allowed to stop a few days longer, there was every hope of the army being undeceived, and the revolution suppressed before it had made much headway.'[1]

The General further wrote that, 'The King's uncle, Norendro Bikram Shah, sought protection at the Residency and was, contrary to all British traditions, refused shelter, and was handed over to his enemies'.[2] On the basis of this and many other similar statements from the refugees, Digby concluded thus:

'The audience asked for was never given, as will appear in succeeding chapters. Lord Dufferin, apparently, knew nothing of the services so frequently eulogised by his predecessors, or of the claim which the royal and noble Nepalese had upon his best efforts. The Foreign Office, which knew all about it, and which should have been quick to enable the Viceroy to show that it was a wise and prudent thing on the part of Asiatic notabilities to display friendship towards the Indian Government, apparently refrained from telling Lord Dufferin what he did not know. On no other hypothesis is the ex-Viceroy's conduct to be understood or explained.'[3]

If Digby had read carefully the full statement of the same General Dhoje Nursing, he would have found the following statement:

'How I escaped is still a wonder to me. It could only be providential: and, next to my God, I am thankful to the officers and men of the Residency for saving my life from the blood-hounds that were in pursuit after me.'[4]

---

[1] Digby, William, *op. cit.*
[2] Ibid.
[3] Ibid., p. 97.
[4] Ibid., pp. 94-5.

This contradicts the assertion that Berkeley gave no assistance to the refugees. Digby would not have blamed the Viceroy and the Resident for not helping Jung Bahadur's relatives if he had consulted the Government of India official records.

Digby also claimed that the relatives of Jung Bahadur were not given audience with the Viceroy. Again, before making this claim, he should have checked the Government of India official records. These records show that General Jit Jung, one of Jung Bahadur's sons and the former Commander-in-Chief of the Nepal Army, was received by the Viceroy at a private interview at Government House, Calcutta, on Thursday, January 28, 1886. At this interview the Viceroy reminded General Jit Jung that,

'Jit Jung should not forget how, when news of the recent murders in Nipal reached the Government, our Agent at Kathmandu had been instructed to ensure the safety of Jang Bahadur's jamily and to impress upon the Darbar the necessity of allowing those who wished to proceed unmolested to British territory.'[1]

At the same interview the Viceroy told the Nepalese General that

'... he entertained the warmest feelings of friendship for the sons of so distinguished a father and loyal ally, but that his personal feelings must not be confused with the wider political considerations which were associated with his office.'[2]

In addition to the interview with Jit Jung, Lady Dufferin granted an interview to the Queen Dowager of Nepal (the daughter of Jung Bahadur) on February 1, 1886. In her petition the Queen Dowager wrote:

'It is entirely owing to the kindness of His Excellency Lord Dufferin that I have been rescued from the clutches of the rebels, and I consider myself fortunate so far that I have got this opportunity of seeing your Ladyship.'[3]

Also, it should be noted that the Foreign Secretary of the Government of India agreed to meet General Kedar Nursing and General Dhoje Nursing to listen to their complaints.[4] Berkeley summarized the situation in one of his notes to the Indian Foreign Office in which he wrote:

---

[1] Memorandum: *Foreign Secret—E*, February 1896, Nos. 248–52.
[2] *Foreign Secret—E*, February 1886, *op. cit.*, Nos. 248–52. (N.A.I.)
[3] *Ibid.*, No. 253.
[4] *Ibid.*, No. 257.

'In regard to his claim upon the Government, no doubt they were great; for Jung Bahadur was a loyal and valuable ally; but his services were amply recognized in his lifetime; and the protection and support afforded to his family on the occasion of the late revolution were no small matters.'[1]

In his criticisms, Digby was apparently carried away by the emotional appeals of the sons, daughter and relatives of Sir Jung Bahadur and by the memory of the latter's services during the Mutiny. He also seems to have forgotten the treaty obligations of the British Government of India, which gave it no right to intervene in the domestic affairs of Nepal. In actuality, Jung Bahadur also came into power by murdering his own uncle and at that time the British Government likewise recognized the Government of Jung Bahadur and did not intervene in the domestic affairs of Nepal. The Viceroy reminded Jit Jung, that 'our interference in Nepal was expressly distasteful to Jung Bahadur himself...',[2] and that there was no obligation on the part of the British Government to guarantee the continuance in power of Jung Bahadur's family. The Viceroy knew that Nepal was still very suspicious that the British wanted to destroy her independence. Thus, if the Viceroy had used Indian soldiers to restore Jung Bahadur's family to power, he might have united the Nepalese in support of Bir Shamsher, and so involved himself in a war he did not want. The British would have then confronted the same problem as when they tried to restore Shah Shuja to his throne in the first Afghan war. Lord Dufferin was right when he said that his Government condemned the brutality of the murders but at the same time did not want to help create a 'Civil War in Nepal'.[3]

Berkeley knew that his government did not wish to be involved in war with Nepal. Like the Governor-General, he felt that he could not take sides in a domestic quarrel. Acting on the Viceroy's instructions, Berkeley did all that was permissible in the way of protecting the fugitives who took refuge in the Residency and sending them in safety to India. Digby's charge of harsh treatment is based on the statement of the refugees. These same refugees in many of their statements agreed that their lives were saved because of the officials of the Residency. This fact is substantiated by Berkeley's report in which he wrote that 'the fact of unquestioned protection and safe conduct being insured to the refugees by the influence of the Resident made a deep impression, not only on the ruling class, but on the people'.[4]

---

[1] *Foreign Secret—E*, February 1887, Nos. 405–6.
[2] *Foreign Secret—E*, February 1886, Nos. 248–52. (N.A.I.)
[3] *Ibid.*
[4] *Foreign Secret—E*, February 1887, No. 406. (N.A.I.)

The Viceroy also instructed Berkeley that 'you should endeavour to prevent any unnecessary bloodshed.'[1] It should be noted that even if the Viceroy had decided to help Jit Jung to overthrow the newly established government of Nepal, he would have run the risk of supporting the losing side. Even if Jung Bahadur's family fought their way back to power, there was no certainty they could retain it. So if Jung Bahadur's family regained control with Indian help, the final result might be the triumph of the Shamsher family who would naturally look upon the Government of India as their enemies. This would ruin India's policy of friendly alliance with Nepal.[2] Digby was, therefore, unjust where he accused Berkeley of 'making Bir Shamsher's treachery and ferocity respectable by ensuring its success'.[3] Berkeley condemned Bir Shamsher's *coup d'état*, but had no illusions about the governing class. His actions were based solely on what was best for British interests in India when dealing with a state whose code of political morality was similar to that of medieval Europe. The light-hearted way in which Nepal nobles murdered one another reminds one of England and Europe in the fifteenth and sixteenth centuries. At that time it was standard practice to remove political rivals by assassination, e.g. the Duke of Burgundy in France about 1418, the Kings Richard II, Henry VI and Edward V and his brother in England, and a large number of nobles in Italy. So nineteenth-century Nepal was merely old-fashioned in its methods.

Berkeley summed up his opinions as follows:

'My view is that there is little to choose between the "ins" and the "outs"; and that, though the value of Jung Bahadur's services to us was great, it is possible to exaggerate it. When all is said we cannot forget that Jung Bahadur was steeped in blood. And no one in Nepal doubts that if Juggut Jung had come to power there would have been a terrible reckoning with his enemies. The present Minister and his family are as bad as they can be; but they have already rendered us service, and it is conceivable that they might be able to do as much for us as Jung Bahadur did.'[4]

Lord Dufferin, the Viceroy, shared Berkeley's point of view and his policy was justified by events. A few years after the *coup d'état*, Wylie's

---

[1] G. S. Forbes, Junior Under-Secretary to Girdlestone, No. 1945E, Simla, July 20, 1887. (Confidential) *Foreign Department Secret—E Proceedings*, August 1887, No. 144. (N.A.I.)
[2] *Foreign Secret—E*, February 1886, Nos. 248-52. (N.A.I.)
[3] Digby, William, *op. cit.*, p. 96.
[4] *Foreign Service—E*, February 1887, No. 405. (N.A.I.)

combination of conciliation, shrewdness, and frankness ushered in a new era in the relations between the Nepal Durbar and the British Government of India and resulted in the establishment of good and durable relations.

ANGLO-NEPALESE RELATIONS IN THE FIRST HALF OF THE TWENTIETH CENTURY

PART II

CHAPTER 4
CHANDRA SHAMSHER AND HIS FOREIGN POLICY

The turn of the century found the relations between Nepal and British India on a more friendly footing than they had been in the past. About the same time, three events occurred which affected relations between the two countries. They were: the death of the Prime Minister in 1901; the departure of the Resident, Colonel Wylie; and the assumption of office by a new Viceroy, Lord Curzon, in 1899. Sir Bir Shamsher died suddenly on March 5, 1901 and was succeeded by Deb Shamsher, who was ousted by Chandra Shamsher within three months, in a bloodless *coup d'état* in June of the same year.[1] Chandra was the ruler of his country for the next twenty-eight years. He was the same man who, during the prime ministership of his brother, Sir Bir Shamsher, used to boast that 'Nepal was under the suzerainity of China, and was not on the same footing with the British'. It was only natural for British officials to expect some worsening of their relations with Nepal, a relationship which had existed for more than a century. But the policy begun by Colonel Wylie in the last decade of the previous century, which was based on 'mutual understanding' and mutual concession, continued to flourish. The reasons assigned for the downfall of Deb Shamsher were that he was progressive in his views on education, the liberation of slaves, and the starting of a newspaper; that he showed too much haste in trying to improve the condition of the country; and that he was too ambitious and over-confident. Yet another cause, and by no means the least important, was the ambition of Chandra Shamsher, who always thought himself to be more intelligent and more capable of running the government than his brother.[2] Chandra had ambition and

[1] Lt.-Colonel T. C. Pears, officiating Resident in Nepal to the Secretary to the Government of India, in the Foreign Department, No. 34–P–17–3027, dated Nepal, June 1, 1901. (Confidential) *Foreign Department Secret—E Proceedings.* July 1901, No. 79. (N.A.I.)

[2] Pears to Barnes, Secretary to the Government of India in the Foreign

strength of character, and adopted an energetic and, at the same time, co-operative attitude in his foreign policy. He clearly outlined the policy which he intended to follow towards the Government of India in the following letter to the Viceroy:

'I shall take this opportunity of assuring your Excellency's Government that I shall always deem it a sacred duty and valued privilege, not only to cultivate and continue unimpaired the friendly relations subsisting between the governments of India and Nepal, but to strengthen and improve them, so that we may realize all those expectations which the association with such a power like that of England naturally raises in our mind. I am fully conscious that our interests can best be served by the continuance of friendly relations between India and Nepal.'[1]

This statement of Chandra was scrupulously maintained by him throughout his prime ministership. Evidently, he buried his old tactics of trying to play off India against China, to maintain Nepal's independence.

Chandra Shamsher came to power at the time when the British Government of India's relations with Tibet were becoming increasingly strained to the point where an Indian army invaded Tibet in 1903. The Government of India believed that the Dalai Lama was making a secret treaty with Russia against the British. At the same time, he refused to allow a British diplomatic mission under the leadership of Colonel Younghusband to enter Tibet in order to counteract Russian influence. The outcome was that an Indian army invaded Tibet in 1903, and imposed a treaty upon the Dalai Lama. Russia was interested in Nepal, and most probably Chandra was aware of this through a letter written by General W. W. Sheppards. The letter has no date on it, but it is addressed to Sir Bir Shamsher. It could have been written sometime between 1886 and 1900.[2] During this period, Chandra Shamsher was in some high office of the state. When Sir Bir came into power, his name was seventh on the roll of succession and Chandra was in the fourteenth

Department, dated Nepal, June 27, 1901, *Foreign Department Secret—E Proceedings*, August 1901, Nos. 231–8; Lt. Colonel C. W. Ravenshaw, officiating Resident in Nepal to the Secretary to the Government of India in the Foreign Department, No. 35-P-18-3027, dated Nepal, June 20, 1902. (Confidential) *Foreign Department Secret*, August 1902, No. 107. (N.A.I.)

[1] Landon, *op. cit.*, Vol. II, p. 108.
[2] See Appendix VII. General W. W. Sheppards, officially known in India as Dr W. W. Sheppard of the Russian Imperial Staff, Commanding the Baskir Dinercan His Imperial Highness the Grand Duke Mehails. Army of Asia. (No date on the letter.)
On His Imperial Majesty the Czar of Russia and Asia Service, to Bir Shamsher Bahodour Rana, one of the nephews of the late Sir Jung Bahadur Rana General. *Foreign Department External—B*, February 1901, Nos. 327–8. (N.A.I.)

place. Under Bir Shamsher, Chandra was third in line to succeed. The letter of the Russian general was addressed to Bir Shamsher, but it must have passed through the hands of Chandra. It was in support of the refugee General Padma Jung Rana, a son of Sir Jung Bahadur. In the letter, the Russian general threatened the prime minister of Nepal that if Bir Shamsher did not vacate his office in favour of Jung Bahadur's son, the Russian army would conquer Nepal and punish Bir Shamsher. General Sheppard's letter shows that when the sons of Jung Bahadur failed to persuade the British Government to support them against Bir Shamsher, they approached the Russians. It is not clear whether the government of Nepal was aware of this threat or whether the Shamshers kept it to themselves. Certainly no mention of the letter has been found in any correspondence or conversation between the two governments. It could also be possible that the letter was intercepted by the Indian Government and never reached the Durbar, but it could equally be presumed that the letter came to the Nepal Government and was never shown to anyone else. The official records of both the governments of Nepal and India show no mention of sending any answer to this letter. No scholar on Nepal has ever mentioned it in his writings. No action was ever taken by any party connected by this letter.

Chandra Shamsher visited India to attend the Imperial Durbar in Delhi in 1903, on the invitation of the Viceroy, Lord Curzon. (At this point, it is interesting to note that the late Sardar Panikkar, in his book, *Indian States and the Government of India*, wrote that in 1877, the Amir of Afghanistan and the Prime Minister of Nepal were invited to the Durbar, and both politely declined the invitation.'[1] Regrettably, however, Panikkar failed to mention that General Dhir Shamsher, the younger brother of Sir Jung Bahadur and the father of Chandra Shamsher, was sent to the Durbar by the Maharajah Dhiraj as an ambassador to represent Nepal in 1877.[2] Panikkar also did not mention the Imperial Durbar in Delhi in 1903, and that Chandra Shamsher attended it, so that he gave a wrong impression that Nepal boycotted the Durbars of 1877 and 1903.) Nepal was represented in both Durbars held by the British Government in India. When he accepted the invitation, Chandra Shamsher once again demonstrated his feeling of friendship for the British Government in India in the following words:

'Nepal, as the Government of India well knows, is ever ready with her sword and all available military resources to face the enemies of the

[1] Panikkar, *op. cit.*, p. 32.
[2] *Foreign and Political Department Secret*, File No. 96(4)–H, 1934, *op. cit.;* (N.A.I.). Letter from Chandra to Ravenshaw, Nepal, June 7, 1902. Basta No. 47, *Nepal Foreign Office Papers; Political and External Files, India Secret Proceedings,* 1902. Vol. 225. (I.O.L.), London.

Government of India when occasion calls, and though she may do little, yet services should not be judged by their magnitude, but according to their promptitude and motives.'[1]

The sincere statements of Chandra Shamsher were a clear indication that in any eventuality, the Nepal Durbar would side with the British Government.

Anglo-Tibetan Conflict and Chandra's Role

When India and Tibet came into conflict, the position of Nepal became quite delicate. According to the treaty of 1856 between Nepal and Tibet, Nepal was required to come to the aid of Tibet if it were unjustly attacked from any quarter. Chandra Shamsher had no intention of fulfilling this treaty obligation. A further complication was that one of his diplomatic aims was to make sure that China would not give military assistance to Tibet, which was legally a Chinese dependency. Chandra Shamsher was greatly concerned over the reports in the newspapers that the Dalai Lama had sent a mission to the Tsar of Russia. The Nepalese representative failed to obtain any confirmation of the report from the Tibetan officials. In fact, they denied that any mission had been sent.[2] The Resident, Ravenshaw, reported about Chandra Shamsher that:

'Personally, he is a very agreeable and courteous man, and the good understanding between the British government and the Durbar seems likely to be maintained during his *regime*, but I do not think he will take any steps to remove the barrier of reserve and formality which hedge around the intercourse of the Resident with the Nepalese.'[3]

Soon after this report, the Resident sent another report in which he wrote:

'He (Chandra Shamsher) was somewhat disturbed at the newspaper reports that the Russian Minister in China had suggested to Prince Ching that China should grant independence to Tibet; he asked me if the Government of India or myself knew of the truth of the report; he

---

[1] Chandra Shamsher to Ravenshaw, *Basta No. 47*, June 7, 1902, *op. cit.* (N.F.O.K.)
[2] Ravenshaw, Resident to the Secretary to the Government of India, in the Foreign Department, No. 35P-18-3027, Nepal, June 20, 1902 (Confidential). *Foreign Department Secret Proceedings—E*, August 1902, No. 107. (N.A.I.)
[3] *Ibid.*

feared that independent Tibet meant Russia as next-door neighbour. Can you tell me if there is any truth in the report?'[1]

The principal consideration in Chandra Shamsher's mind was that a very cordial and friendly relation had existed for a decade between Nepal and the Government of India, and he had no desire to destroy a situation that was advantageous to him. He did not want to lose the friendly co-operation and sympathy of the British for the sake of any other country. His mind was set on this point. He was naturally worried over the information received from his representative in Tibet about Russian interest in that country. The British Resident apparently thought that Chandra Shamsher was afraid that if Russia managed to emancipate Tibet completely from China, 'Nepal would fall into our arms when we might be able to do something to improve communications and gain access to the country'.[2] But shortly afterwards, the Resident reported that

'The attitude of the Durbar towards us has been one of exclusion, that is, while treating the Resident with all respect and politeness, and always professing the greatest friendship, there has existed no real cordiality between the Minister and other high officers of the State and the Resident. Chandra Shamsher maintains this policy.'[3]

The Government of India was not at this moment contemplating any request to the Durbar to alter its regulations. Its principal preoccupation was to make sure of Chandra Shamsher's support against Tibet if war were to break out. Nepal was supplying all the information it could to Calcutta on Russian intrigues in Tibet and about the attitude of the government of the Dalai Lama towards the British.

At this time of crisis, Chandra Shamsher visited India, and had a very important personal interview with the Viceroy, Lord Curzon, on December 31, 1902, at 12 noon, in Delhi.[4] This interview was mostly concerned with the policy of Tibet, Russia, and the position of British India and Nepal. Chandra Shamsher was aware of the danger if the

[1] Ravenshaw to the Secretary to the Government of India, April 29, 1902. *Foreign Secret—E Proceedings*, September 1902, No. 128. (N.A.I.)
[2] Ravenshaw to the Secretary of the Government of India, June 28, 1902 (Confidential). *Foreign Department Secret—E Proceedings*, September 1902, No. 130. (N.A.I.)
[3] Ravenshaw to the Secretary of the Government of India, *Foreign Department Secret—E Proceedings*, August 1902, No. 107. (N.A.I.)
[4] See Appendix VIII. 'Conversation Between H.E. the Maharajah and His Excellency the Viceroy in 1902'. *Basta No. 47* (N.F.O.K.). This is the verbatim report of the conversation between the Maharajah and the Viceroy.

Tibetans should escape from the overlordship of China and accept protection from Russia. He felt that the first thing the Tibetan government would do would be to wipe out its defeat in the last war between Nepal and Tibet. Chandra Shamsher's fear was strengthened because he believed that the Tibetans were getting arms as well as machines for manufacturing arms from Russia, and that an arsenal and workshop were being fitted up in Lhasa. He told the Viceroy very frankly 'that he regarded the interests of Nepal as entirely bound with the British government in India, and that his government would be prepared to endorse and actively support any action which the British government might consider necessary for the protection of their interest.'[1] The Maharajah was convinced that if Russian intrigues did not cease in Tibet, then Nepal, for the sake of her own interests, would support whatever action the Indian Government might consider necessary.[2] Chandra was determined to make an end of Russian–Tibetan schemes while they were still in the formative stage. The Viceroy was extremely happy to find the Nepalese prime minister on his side, and because of the forthright assurances of the Maharajah, he immediately informed the Government of Great Britain that his previous report on Chandra Shamsher's policy had been entirely mistaken. In this report, dated August 16, 1901, Lord Curzon had written 'that strong measures on the part of the government of India would be viewed with much disquietude and suspicion by the government of Nepal....' He now corrected this by writing that 'So far from believing this to be true, we have the best of reasons for believing the very opposite to be the case'.[3] As a result of his interview, the Viceroy decided that it would serve the interests of both Nepal and India to work in complete union, and he even felt that the Nepalese Government could be invited to take part with the British Mission to Lhasa. 'If serious opposition were threatened, we think that they might be encouraged to send a separate column accompanied by British Officers, by an independent route to Tibet'.[4] There was no doubt that Nepal was as much afraid of a Russian protectorate over

---

[1] 'Note of an interview between His Excellency the Viceroy and His Excellency the Prime Minister of Nepal at Delhi.' *Foreign Department Secret—E Proceedings*, February 1903, Nos. 1-88, pp. 83-4. (N.A.I.)

[2] *Ibid.*

[3] Letter from the Viceroy's Council to the Right Honorable Lord George Hamilton, His Majesty's Secretary of State for India Camp Delhi, January 8, 1903, No. 4c of 1903, Government of India, Foreign Department, Secret/External. *Foreign Department Secret Proceedings*, February 1903. Nos. 1-88, p. 93. (N.A.I.)

[4] Viceroy's Council to the Secretary of State, January 8, 1903, No. 4-c of 1903, *Foreign Department Secret—E Proceedings*, February 1903. Nos. 1-88. (N.A.I.)

Tibet as the British were.[1] So it became the mutual purpose and interest of both governments to oppose Russian intrigues there. For that reason, Nepal was committed to help the British Mission to Lhasa.[2]

The policy of Chandra Shamsher might be described as one of non-belligerency. He sold supplies to both sides, but with bias in favor of the British. His support of the Indian Government was dictated by self-defense and self-interest. A strong Tibet would be naturally a serious danger to the existence of Nepal and especially if it were controlled by a great power like Russia. Nepal's 1856 treaty with Tibet (mentioned on page 152, previously) seems to have been ignored by all. In spite of its treaty relations with Tibet, Nepal steadily helped the British with moral as well as material support, such as coolies and yaks for transport with the Younghusband mission. At the same time, the prime minister of Nepal also sent suggestions and advice to the Dalai Lama, and tried to influence him to accept the British mission. The prime minister cited the example of his own country's relations with the Indian government.

The Government of India for its part was seriously discussing what should be done if Nepal should attack Tibet as the result of some serious misunderstanding. This discussion started because there was some tension between Nepal and Tibet, and the British were afraid that armed conflict might take place. If this happened, could the British intervene in the conflict? Would it injure British interests to allow Nepal to give military aid in case of opposition from Tibet to the British mission?[3] The answers to these questions were not simple. On two previous occasions (1792 and 1854), Nepal and Tibet actually fought, and on at least three other occasions (1873, 1880, and 1883), they created serious tension. In 1792, the East India Company sent help to Nepal against Tibet, but before the British soldiers could arrive, the war was over. On the other occasions, the British Government of India had not intervened because at the time, it was the policy of the Government to treat Nepal as an independent state and not as an ally. In the early twentieth century, the position was different; Nepal had become almost an ally. However, in spite of the British policy of non-intervention, every time there were strained relations, the Government of India used its good offices, although indirectly, on Nepal not to go to war. This pressure in no way violated the treaty obligation. It could be said that it was an instance of the dominant power putting

[1] *Foreign Department Secret—E Proceedings*, February 1903, Nos. 1–88.
[2] Ibid.
[3] 'Question whether the government of India could, on the occurence of certain eventualities, object to Nepal taking military action in Tibet to vindicate her rights.' Foreign Department Notes. Secret E, August 1904. *Foreign Department Secret—E Proceedings*, August 1904, 160–1. (N.A.I.)

pressure on a state too weak to oppose. But in 1854, Nepal did not pay any attention to the British Government in India's 'gentle pressure' in its conflict with Tibet. Eventually, in August of 1904, after Younghusband's expedition had fought its way to Lhasa, the Government of India reached the following decisions: (a) It was in the interests of the British not to allow Nepal to carry out any military intervention in Tibet, (b) The Government of India should not accept further military aid from Nepal, (c) The alliance with Nepal should not be on the basis of equal partnership, but it should be called a 'subordinate alliance', (d) It was also thought that once the British had won influence in Tibet, its relations with Nepal would improve.[1]

When all the advice and suggestions sent by Maharajah Chandra Shamsher to the Dalai Lama through his representative, Sir Jit Bahadur, in Lhasa, failed to have any effect, he wrote directly to the four Kazis (Magistrates) of Lhasa. Bahadur had already received instructions to help the Tibetans as well as Younghusband's mission. In his letter to the four Kazis the Maharajah told them to accept the British demands and assured them that if they disliked any of the terms, they could always lay their grievances before the British Government, which would be generous to them.[2] Finally, with the help of the Nepalese representative, a treaty was signed. Colonel Younghusband, in his official report, praised the sincere assistance given by the Nepalese envoy. This was followed by expressions of gratitude from the Government of India and from Lord Curzon. Colonel Younghusband suggested that 'a valuable Khillat (gift) together with a letter of thanks be presented to him (Jit Bahdur) by the Government of India through the Nepalese Durbar'.[3] Maharajah Chandra Shamsher visited India (Calcutta) in January, 1904, as the guest of the Government of India.[4] During his stay in Calcutta, he had two important interviews with the Viceroy concerning Tibetan affairs. The Viceroy thanked the Prime Minister for keeping the British Government informed about all the maneuvers in Tibet and for the friendly help extended to the British by the Nepalese representative in Lhasa and through secret information.

---

[1] *Foreign Department Secret—E Proceedings*, August 1904, Nos. 160–1. (N.A.I.)

[2] Chandra Shamsher to the four Kazis of Lhasa, dated Sunday the 6th Mangsir, 1961 (corresponding with November 28, 1904) (Translation). *Foreign Department Secret—E Proceedings*, March 1905, No. 475. (N.A.I.)

[3] Col. F. E. Younghusband to Dane, Secretary to the Government of India Foreign Office, Simla, November 3, 1904, *Foreign Office External—B Proceedings*, June 1905, Nos. 132–43. (N.A.I.); Landon, *op. cit.* Vol. II, pp. 110–12.

[4] 'Visit of Chandra Shamsher to Viceroy in India.' January 23, 1904. Basta No. 42–B (N.F.O.); *Foreign Political Department*, File No. 96(4)–H, 1934. (N.A.I.)

But, he politely shelved the request of the Prime Minister for machine-guns for his personal guard. He agreed, however, to supply other types of weapons and expressed his hope that the Nepal Government would continue to be as friendly as it was at the time to the Government of India. The Maharajah gave his permission, at the request of the Viceroy, that the secret information supplied by him on Tibetan affairs could be disclosed to the Parliament in London, but requested that it should not be given out to the public. The Maharajah was afraid that the Tibetans would take revenge on Nepal if they should learn who supplied the information. At the same time, the prime minister of Nepal politely but firmly said 'No' to the Viceroy's request that he might visit Nepal in the near future. He made the same old excuse that his people were ignorant, and would not know how to receive a guest as important as the Viceroy. He also pleaded that if the Viceroy visited Kathmandu, his own position would be weakened.[1] The real reason supposedly was the traditional policy of keeping British contact to the minimum. He cited the precedent of his brother, Sir Bir Shamsher, who successfully requested the Viceroy to abandon his idea of visiting Kathmandu.[2]

The Anglo-Tibetan affair was Chandra Shamsher's first essay in diplomacy, and it must be said to his credit that he managed it well. His astuteness and balanced diplomacy brought praise from both sides. There was no doubt that throughout the entire affair, his position often became difficult, but like an experienced captain of a ship, Chandra Shamsher managed to get out of the storm. He dealt skillfully with his two neighbors, one being powerful and the other obstinate and suspicious. Nonetheless, both accepted his suggestions, advice, and help when they were negotiating the treaty. By his policy, he brought strengths and safeguards for his country. When he helped to prevent Russia from gaining influence in Tibet, he also minimized China's influence there and strengthened the hands of his friends, the British. After this diplomatic victory, his natural aim was to achieve more and more freedom for his country. He gained the confidence of his most powerful neighbor, and on the basis of the help which he had given, he placed his country in a better bargaining position with the British Government of India to obtain more arms and more independence.

During the rest of his prime ministership, Chandra Shamsher did not press the Indian Government on the issues of extradition, boundaries, and trade. At the same time, he did not make any noticeable concess-

[1] See Appendix IX. 'Visit of Chandra Shamsher to Viceroy in India, 1904, 23rd January.' *Basta No. 42-B* (N.F.O.); *Foreign Political Department*, File 96(4)–H, 1934. (N.A.I.)
[2] 'Conversation Between the Resident and Sir Bir Shamsher Regarding the Viceroy's Visit to Kathmandu.' 1899, *Basta No. 42-B.* (N.F.O.K.).

ions to the British on the old issues. He knew that these matters were too unimportant to damage British–Nepalese relations. The Government of India on its side was not anxious to broach such questions as greater freedom of movement of the Resident in Nepal since it would, by doing so, embarrass its friendly neighbor. What was really important for the British was more Gurkhas for the army and a friendly attitude on the part of Nepal. Nepal wanted more independence and arms and ammunition to maintain that independence. Both governments concentrated on their principal objectives, and relegated to the background minor aims which could embarrass good relations. A later chapter will discuss the failures and successes of their respective policies.

Encouraged by his diplomatic success, Maharajah Chandra Shamsher invited the Commander-in-Chief of India, Lord Kitchener, to visit Kathmandu. Kitchener became the first Commander-in-Chief since Lord Roberts to visit the isolated and suspicious valley of Kathmandu. It would have been only natural for the Resident to think of some honor which could be conferred upon the Prime Minister and Commander-in-Chief of Nepal at the time of this visit, so that they should not feel that the concession which they had made in inviting Lord Kitchener was not appreciated in India. The Resident suggested merely the rank of Knight Commander of the Star of India for the Commander-in-Chief of the Nepal Army; however he did not recommend any honor for Chandra Shamsher.[1] Sir Louis Dane, the Secretary of the Government of India, while approving the idea of the Resident for the K.C.S.I. for the Commander-in-Chief, for the information of the Viceroy, wrote in his file,

'I see every advantage in associating the Minister Chandra Shamsher with one or other of the Gurkha Regiments or even in making him Colonel-in-Chief of them all. The question of giving 5,000 Martini-Henri rifles (this was proposed by the Resident on the request of Chandra Shamsher) or of improving the Nepal army and lending them British instructors is a very large one and will require most careful consideration. At any rate, it should be carefully excluded from discussion at any visit that may take place.'[2]

The Viceroy, in his note, concurred with his Secretary's point of view.

[1] J. Manner-Smith, Resident to Sir Louis Dane. Foreign Department, Simla, Demi-Official letter, No. 119, dated Kathmandu, the 11th (received 16th) July, 1906; Letter from the Resident in Nepal, No. 104, dated the 1st (received 7th) July, 1906. *Foreign Department Secret—E Proceedings*, February 1907, Nos. 575–87. (N.A.I.)

[2] File notes on Foreign Office discussion by Sir Louis Dane, *Foreign Department Secret—E Proceedings*, February 1907, Nos. 575–87. (N.A.I.)

So Lord Kitchener during his visit, honored the prime minister by conferring on him the rank of General in the British army and appointed him Honorary Colonel of the 4th Gurkha Rifles.[1] It is apparent that the prime minister actually felt honored by Lord Kitchener's accepting the invitation and by receiving honorary ranks in the army.[2] The Nepalese loved honors, British titles, and friendly expressions from the Viceroy, and the British Viceroys had always been generous with these, since they did not cost them a penny.

Chandra Shamsher's Visit to England
Since the visit of Jung Bahadur to England in 1850, no other prime minister of Nepal had boarded ship for the Western world. Bir Shamsher had been anxious to do so during the latter part of his rule, but the plan fell through because of the delay on the part of the British Government of India in sanctioning the trip. The official reason was given that because of the tension on the border of Tibet and Nepal, the prime minister did not want to leave the country. Chandra's position was decidedly different from that of any other prime minister of Nepal. Through his magnetic personality, clever diplomacy, and cordiality towards the British, he was in the good graces of the Viceroy. The British Government was more than inclined to see that he should travel to Europe. The Resident, Manner-Smith, urged that his visit should be placed on the same footing as that of Sardar Nasirullah Khan's, the prime minister of Afghanistan, and not that of any ordinary Indian prince.[3] In answer to the Resident's request, the Secretary's minutes read as follows:

'... It should be pointed out that this has certainly not been done of recent years, and it is most undesirable to give cause to the Durbar to think that Nepal would be treated as Afghanistan, but the question of the exact status of the State is one that should not be raised in correspondence or when Mr. Hobhouse visits Kathmandu in January. I am afraid that the Resident is suffering from megalomania about Nepal and may cause trouble.'[4]

[1] Note of Additions for the Brief History of Nepal. File No. 4385, 1907, Serial No. 615. Embassy to Nepal. (Nepal Residency Paper.)
[2] Manner-Smith to Dane, Nepal (received 22nd), November 16, 1906. *Foreign Department External Proceedings—A*, May 1907, Nos. 54–72. (N.A.I.)
[3] Manner-Smith to the Secretary to the Government of India, in the Foreign Department; No. 232, dated the Residency, Nepal December 26, 1907, (received January 2, 1908), para 3, p. 2, *Foreign Department External*, August 1908, No. 72. (I.O.L.)
[4] Extract from a note by Secretary, dated January 4, 1908. *Foreign Department Secret—E Proceedings*, September 1908, Nos. 457–9. pp. 12–13. (N.A.I.)

The political aide-de-camp wrote in a memorandum about Chandra Shamsher:

'The good will of Nepal is of the utmost value to India as a large number of our best soldiers (the Gurkhas) are recruited hence. Nepal is also closely connected with Tibet, and gave valuable assistance to the government of India in connection with the recent expedition to Lhasa. In Nepal, the Maharajah Dhiraj occupies much the same position as the Mikado in Japan before the Revolution: all power is vested in the Prime Minister, who is an absolute autocrat, politically, therefore, he is a person of great importance, and it is desirable that he should be treated in England with marked distinction.'[1]

The proposed visit of Chandra Shamsher kept both the India Office in London and the Indian Government in Calcutta very busy writing minutes and counter-minutes on innumerable questions about how to deal with him when he came to England. What status should he be given; how important was his country; what matters should be discussed with him; and what was the actual purpose of his journey?

Chandra Shamsher had many ideas which he wanted to discuss with the British Government in London, but the foremost was the actual status of Nepal. In his own mind, it was clear that Nepal was an absolutely independent and sovereign state. Secondly, he was very anxious to arrange for more arms and ammunition for his army; and lastly, he was interested in obtaining the right of free importation of industrial, agricultural, and scientific machinery.[2] The official letter from Manner-Smith to the Secretary to the Government of India contradicted the statement of Landon about the purpose of Chandra's visit to England which was given above. Manner-Smith wrote:

'The Prime Minister's object in undertaking this journey to England is mainly to show his loyalty to the British alliance, and to have an opportunity of paying his respects to His Majesty the King Emperor. While it is the desire of the Nepal Durbar that he should be received in England as the Representative of the Nepal government, and be given the same treatment as regards precedence, honors, and salutes, as was accorded to the late Sir Jung Bahadur in 1850; the Prime Minister clearly understands that it will not be open to him to discuss

---

[1] Memorandum by the Political A.D.C. W.H.L. Wylie (Confidential), File 520, 'Nepal Presents'. *Political Department*, April 1, 1908 (I.O.L. Microfilm).

[2] Landon, *op. cit.*, Vol. II, p. 120.

affairs of State in England, and that his dealings in all such matters rest with the government of India.'[1]

The Kharieta (letter) which was sent through Maharajah Chandar Shamsher by the Maharajah Dhiraj of Nepal to the King-Emperor of England and the personal interviews which the prime minister of Nepal had with the King, the Secretary of State for India, the Prime Minister, and others prove that they did not discuss with him any subject of importance.[2]

When Sir Jung Bahadur visited England in 1850, his stay in London was not well covered by the English newspapers. Chandra Shamsher's visit was reported by seventy-three newspapers, British and foreign. The foreign newspapers included the *Gazette De France*, the *New York Herald*, the *St Louis Post*, and the *Buffalo Times*. Invariably, all these newspapers omitted discussion of the political relations between the British and Nepalese. There were also some interesting letters to the editor. Some of the newspapers commented editorially on the visit, and photographs were generously used. Some of the headlines read as follows: The *Leeds Mercury* had a one-column headline, 'The King and Dewan, Nepalese Ruler's Visit to Buckingham Palace', 'Strange Laws of Caste'. The *New York Herald* had a one-column headline, 'Indian Ruler at Court in London, Dewan of Nepal and Suite Lend Greater Brilliancy to the Royal Reception'. The *Westminster Gazette* had a two-column lead, 'Dewan of Nepal's Visit', 'Chat with an Ex-Official'. The London *Times* published an account of Chandra in the 'Court Circular', and in a one-column story entitled 'The Prime Minister of Nepal, Reception by the King'. Most of the newspapers stressed his jewels and head dress and his glittering attire, but none of them discussed the political importance of the Himalayan Kingdom vis-à-vis India. Judging by the content of the news items, the editors considered that what would most interest their readers about Chandra Shamsher was the unusual and exotic. The newspapers actually reflected the feeling of the people of England in considering him a picturesque and unusual curiosity. However, Chandra Shamsher himself enjoyed the treatment given him by the government officials, the newspapers, the king and the queen, and also the people of England.[3]

[1] Manner-Smith to the Secretary to the Government of India, in the Foreign Department, 'Sub: Nepal: Visit of Prime Minister to England'. *Political and Secret Department*, File 3955, 1908 (I.O.L. Microfilm).

[2] See Appendix X. Verbatim notes on the interview of the Prime Minister of Nepal with British leaders including the King-Emperor. There are seven interviews. Also included in Appendix X is the translation of the petition from Maharajah Dhiraj to the King-Emperor and a Kharieta from Lord Minto, Viceroy of India, to the Maharajah Dhiraj, *Basta No. 45*. (N.F.O.K.)

[3] *Leeds Mercury*, May 12, 1908; the *New York Herald*, May 6, 1908; the

Upon his return to Nepal, Maharajah Chandra Shamsher was given an imposing reception by the government and the people of Nepal. His brother, the Commander-in-Chief and acting prime minister, praised him in the open Durbar on his achievements at home and abroad. The acting prime minister eulogized his brother's character and courage in dealing with the state administration. This speech by the Commander-in-Chief of Nepal could be described as a short history of the country, both internal and external, with major emphasis on the period of Chandra Shamsher. At one point, he quoted a passage from the history of the Delhi Coronation Durbar held in 1903. It runs thus:

'The British government first entered into relations with Nepal as early as 1767, and the relations have never been more cordial and satisfactory than they are at the present, a result which is due in no small measure to the diplomacy and ability of the enlightened minister who came to Delhi.'[1]

In the same Durbar at Kathmandu, Maharajah Chandra Shamsher presented a signed letter from King Edward VII to the Maharajah Dhiraj. The letter was published in full in the London *Times* of Wednesday, September 30, 1908. In his letter, the King wrote that 'It is my most earnest wish that Nepal may ever increase in prosperity and that the friendly relations which have so long existed between my country and your Highness's State may be confirmed and strengthened. . . .'[2]

It was obvious from the speech of Sir Chandra, which he made in reply to the address, that he had returned from England well satisfied as regards the attitude of the British Government towards his country. He said in his speech,

'. . . I am exceedingly happy to be able to say that the relations of the two governments which were of the friendliest and closest character have been drawn still closer and made still friendlier by this visit. I feel perfectly assured that there is not the least desire anywhere to impair our autonomy or to interfere with the administration of this

---

Westminster Gazette, March 21, 1908; the London *Times*, May 12, 1908 (B.E.K.)
[1] Translation of an address delivered by His Excellency the Commander-in-Chief of Nepal in a Durbar held to celebrate the return of Chandra Shamsher from England in 1908. *Foreign Department Secret—E Proceedings*, September 1908, Nos. 539–74, Enclosure 2. Proceedings No. 573A. (N.A.I.)
[2] 'Great Britain and Nepal.' 'Letter from the King', *The Times*, Wednesday, September 30, 1908. (I.O.L.)

government. This is what I have gathered from what I have recently seen and heard.'¹

It appeared from the entire report of Chandra Shamsher on his visit to England that the King and the Prime Minister of Great Britain, the Secretary for the State of India and other officials of the British government discussed no political issues with Chandra Shamsher, but were very cordial to him and paid him high honor. Before he left Nepal, it was almost understood that he would not discuss political issues in London, in spite of the fact that he would have liked greatly to do that. So for this reason, he was not seriously disappointed. The main result of his visit to England was that he saw with his own eyes the strength and grandeur of Britain, its factories, its industrial development, the strength of its army and navy, and, above all, a completely new type of civilization which was entirely different from his own. All that he saw in England and later in other countries of Europe greatly impressed him. In one of his speeches, as reported by Landon, he said:

'Wherever we have gone, we have found everyone anxious to make us feel that we were friends. I have been able today to personally thank their Majesties, the King and Queen; and I want to, and do, thank the British people for all their kindness and friendship. Yours is a great country. I have seen with admiration your splendid fleet, and am proud that it is the fleet of our ally. But to me, the greatness of your country is best seen in the good it has done for our great neighbour, India; in the peace, security, justice, and numerous other benefits it has given to that country.'²

Every word of the above passage gives evidence of the impression that Britain and the British had made on him. The Resident at Kathmandu confirmed that good feeling between Nepal and Britain had been further strengthened by the visit.³ The feeling which the Maharajah brought back from this visit was to be reflected throughout the future relations between the two countries.

When Chandra Shamsher made his visit to England, he left behind

[1] Speech delivered by Sir Chandra Shamsher, Prime Minister of Nepal, in the public Durbar held to celebrate his return from England. *Foreign Department Secret—E Proceedings*, September 1908, Nos. 539–74. Enclosure 3 Proceedings. No. 573A. (N.A.I.)
[2] Landon, *op. cit.*, Vol. II, p. 125.
[3] Annual Report on Nepal for 1908–9 by J. Manner-Smith, Resident to the Secretary to the Government of India. No. 128, Nepal August 10, 1909 (received 16th), *Foreign Department Secret—E Proceedings*, December 1909, Nos. 431–4. (N.A.I.)

him many unsolved problems. Ever since he had become prime minister, he had wished to obtain British recognition of a definite status for his country. He wanted also to make its defenses stronger by securing more arms and more ammunition. The perennial question of his country's relations with China and Tibet had become more intricate.[1] Last, but by no means least, he wished to strengthen his own power in his kingdom. Although some reference will be made from time to time to the actual status of Nepal, the subject is so important that it seems best to reserve a full discussion of it to the final chapter after the account of the relations between India and Nepal has been concluded.

Some time before, Chandra Shamsher actually sailed for England, he proposed to the Resident that under certain circumstances he was prepared to make a definite agreement with the Government of India regarding political subordination in dealings with China, on the lines of Article 6 of the Treaty of 1815 relating to Nepal.[2] Article 6 of the Treaty of 1815 made it incumbent on Nepal to come to the British Government for arbitration in its dispute with Sikkim, and bound Nepal to abide by the British decision. The Treaty of 1801 did not specifically state the role of the British Government toward Nepalese external and internal affairs. The Resident thought that the meaning of the Prime Minister's proposal was that if Nepal placed its diplomatic relations with China under control of the Government of India, he would like to have 'some condition which would emphasize the right of Nepal to pursue her own policy in internal matters undisturbed'.[3] But the fact was that the British officials, including the Viceroy and the Secretary of State, were not very clear about its actual position. Nepal wanted strong support from the British in the eventuality of a conflict with China. Chandra Shamsher genuinely wanted to make a fresh treaty with the Government of India which would establish clearly the relationship between the two countries. Butler, of the Indian Foreign Office, wrote to the Resident, Manner-Smith, that in September of 1908, he told Macdonald, the acting Resident, that he expected the British to support Nepal against China in case the latter made an attack. It was certain that he would be willing to conclude a treaty on this question.[4] The attitude of the Indian Foreign Office was that

[1] Chapter 9 deals with the relations of Nepal with Tibet and China.
[2] Manner-Smith to Secretary Dane, *Foreign Department Secret—E Proceedings*, September 1908. Nos. 457–9, pp. 1, 3, 5, 6 and 7, April 8, 1909 (Very Confidential). *Foreign Department Secret External*, File 324, 1911. (I.L.O.)
[3] Manner-Smith to Dane, *Foreign Department Secret Proceedings*, September 1908, Nos. 457–9. (N.A.I.)
[4] Butler to Manner-Smith, Simla, April 8, 1909. *Foreign Department Secret External*, File 324, 1911 (I.O.L.)

'China is nothing to us',[1] and it was not interested in concluding a treaty which would merely obligate the Government of India to support Nepal against China. As to the question of non-interference in internal administration autonomy, the British government had no objection to grant this to Nepal, although a definite pledge to this effect was given in Lord Elgin's Kharieta of May 15, 1894 to the Maharajah Dhiraj of Nepal.[2] Therefore, the Resident was instructed not to encourage the Maharajah to ask for a new treaty.[3]

The Government of India did not wish to have further discussions about China and Tibet with Nepal because of the Anglo–Russian Convention of August 31, 1907. The arrangement concerning Tibet in this treaty read:

'The governments of Great Britain and Russia, recognizing the suzerain rights of China in Tibet, and considering the fact that Great Britain, by reason of her geographic position, has a special interest in the maintainance of the *status quo* in the external relations of Tibet, have made the following arrangements.

'The two high contracting parties engage to respect the territorial integrity of Tibet and to abstain from all interference in its internal administration.'[4]

The gist of this arrangement was that Russia promised to abandon any attempt to establish her control over Tibet, and recognized that Great Britain had a special interest there. The British had no desire to annex Tibet, and the exclusion of Russian influence gave them all that they wanted. China exercized a weak suzerainty over Tibet, but the Manchu Empire was so feeble that India felt no concern on that score. It was therefore not in British interest to make a treaty which might involve the Government of India in a possible Nepalese quarrel with Tibet or China. A further consideration was that the Anglo–Russian Convention assigned to Great Britain a special interest in the maintenance of the *status quo* in Tibet's external relations. War between Nepal and Tibet would lead to complications that were thoroughly undesirable.

The Resident in Nepal was therefore instructed to explain to the

[1] Butler to Manner-Smith, *Foreign Department Secret* Simla, April 8, 1909. *External*, File 324, 1911, (I.O.L.)
[2] Manner-Smith to Dane, *Foreign Department Secret—E Proceedings*, File 324, 1908, Nos. 457–9. (N.A.I.)
[3] *Foreign Department Secret External*, File 324, 1911.
[4] Convention signed on August 31, 1907, between Great Britain and Russia, containing arrangements on the subject of Persia, Afghanistan, and Tibet, September 1907. 'Subject: Anglo–Russian Convention, 1907.' *Political and Secret Department*, p. 3082, 1907; Russia No. 1. (I.O.L.)

Maharajah the obligation of the British in the case of Tibet because of the agreement with Russia. If the Maharajah raised the question of Chinese aggression against Nepal, the Resident should assure him 'that our influence at Peking is strong enough to prevent China from making any serious movement against Nepal'.[1]

The Indian Government became distinctly cautious in its relations with Nepal. It was not interested in any concessions the Maharajah might offer because he would want a *quid pro quo* for anything he might give. It was emphasized that the Resident must not even ask for permission to go beyond the limits which had been fixed for his movements within the valley in which Kathmandu was situated. At the moment, the British wanted no change in Nepal's *status quo*.[2]

The result of these negotiations and of the tactful persuasions of the Resident was that Nepal, as a loyal but weak friend, agreed to act in accordance with British wishes. Chandra Shamsher was far from pleased with the result of his negotiations. In spite of his displeasure, he assured the Resident 'that it was very far from his intention to appear to be taking an unfriendly line of action . . .'. Chandra Shamsher also told the Resident that 'at the same time, it could not be denied that with the increase of good understanding and some intimate dealing had come a tightening of political control and a number of restrictions of old rights and privileges'.[3] The Resident further stated that:

'He said he was quite ready to act on my advice and treat the question of Nepal's position toward China as distinct from that of her relations to Britain.'[4]

Indirectly, the Nepal Durbar had repudiated its normal allegiance to China. The Prime Minister had agreed to consult the Government of India before committing himself to any new action, and at the same time, he agreed to keep the Government of India informed of any important transaction of any kind between his government and that of China.[5] It seems certain that Chandra Shamsher intended to honor his promises. His action was in accord with his policy of cultivating

---

[1] Butler to Manner-Smith, *Foreign Department Secret External*, File 324, 1911, *op. cit.* (I.O.L.)

[2] *Ibid.*

[3] Manner-Smith to the Secretary to the Government of India, Foreign Department No. 163, Nepal Residency, November 29 (received December 2), 1910. (Confidential) *Foreign and Political Department Secret—E*, July 1911. Nos. 693–703 (N.A.I.). *Foreign Department Secret External*. No. 11, February 2, 1911, File 324, Enclosure No. 1 (I.O.L.)

[4] *Ibid.*

[5] Manner-Smith to the Secretary to the Government of India, *Foreign and Political Department Secret External*, No. 11, February 2, 1911. (N.A.I.)

the friendship of the Government of India so that gradually Nepal could obtain more arms and ammunition and also a full recognition of her independent status. While the negotiations with Chandra Shamsher were in progress, the Indian Government took steps to guard the integrity of Tibet and Nepal from any possible attempt of aggression from China. After the Anglo-Russian Convention in 1907, the British Government sent a strong note of warning to the Chinese government in April 1910, saying that

'His Majesty's Government can not allow any administrative changes in Tibet to affect or prejudice the integrity of Nepal or of the two smaller States of Bhutan and Sikkim, and that they are prepared if necessary to protect the interests and rights of these three States.'[1]

This strong note of warning was answered by Prince Ch'ing as follows:

'As for the Nepalese, they are properly (or originally) feudatories of China, and Bhutan and Sikkim are both States in friendly relations with China. In the event of steps being taken in the future for the reorganization of the internal government of Tibet, such would have no other object than the advancement of progress and order in Tibetan territory, and should not affect those States in any way.'[2]

The Japanese and Russian ambassadors in China were kept informed about the correspondence between Max Muller and Prince Ch'ing in connection with the British position about Tibet.

Immediately after the overthrow of the Manchu Dynasty, the Republic of China went through a period of strained relations with Tibet. In the summer of 1912, the government of Szechuan Province dispatched a force to Tibet. The British had already protested against a large number of Chinese troops being stationed in Tibet. When the Chinese forces moved into Tibet and disorders occurred, war broke out between the two countries.[3] During this conflict, Nepal played the role of a neutral nation. The Nepalese representative in Lhasa played an important role as an intermediary between the belligerent Chinese and Tibetans. At this time, the Nepalese representative was the only impartial person in Lhasa. It was due to his efforts that both parties

---

[1] Max Muller to Prince Ch'ing, Peking, April 11, 1910, Enclosure 1 in No. 1 (Tibet Confidential) *India Secret Proceedings*, Vol. 225. Political and External Files. Title of Documents: J.O.L.M. 3/463 (I.O.L. Microfilm).

[2] Prince Ch'ing to Max Muller, April 18, 1910. Enclosure 2 in No. 1, *India Secret Proceedings*, Vol. 225. (I.O.L.)

[3] Mitter, J. P., *The Truth About McMahon Line*, p. 7 (n.d.)

agreed to a peace treaty. He negotiated the terms of the treaty which was signed on August 12, 1912. Secondly, when hostilities again broke out in the following September, he arranged for the safe withdrawal of General Chung, the Chinese Resident at Lhasa, and also managed the safe return of the Chinese garrison from Lhasa in December 1912. Lastly, he took the responsibility of guarding the surrendered Chinese arms.[1] This friendly gesture of Nepal greatly strengthened its position with Tibet, China, and British India. It also helped Nepal to obtain assurances from Tibet for the safety of Nepalese subjects in Lhasa as well as for their trade throughout the country. In spite of all this, the Chinese tried by indirect methods to bring Nepal under their control. General Chung wrote from Yatung in February 1913, to the Nepalese and suggested 'a union with five affiliated races of China'.[2] Chandra Shamsher characterized the proposal as 'absurd', and replied that it was impossible for Nepal 'to entertain the idea of a union with the five Affiliated Races said to constitute the Republic of China'.[3] From that time on, Nepal became more and more aloof from China.

The strained relations between China and Tibet, the continuous risk of war, and disorder on India's northern border, and the equivocal reply by Prince Ch'ing to Max Muller's letter of April 1910 led to an effort by the Government of India to improve the situation. It was not prepared to sit and watch the peace of its northern border breaking down, so it called a tripartite conference of Great Britain, China, and Tibet to settle the Sino-Tibetan boundary dispute. The Chinese plenipotentiary, Ivan Chen, came to India on October 6, 1913. Tibet was represented by a leading Tibet anminister, Lönchen Shatra, and British India, the host country, was represented by Sir Henry McMahon, the Foreign Secretary of the Government of India.[4] These three constituted the Simla Conference which met in Simla in 1914. After six months of protracted discussion and arguments, the draft treaty was agreed upon. The major provisions were as follows:

(1) Tibet was divided into two zones: Outer Tibet and Inner Tibet;
(2) Nominal Chinese suzerainty was recognized (over Tibet). China engaged not to convert Tibet into a Chinese province;
(3) Great Britain agreed not to annex any portion of Tibet;

---

[1] Annual report of events in Nepal submitted by H. L. Showers, Officiating Resident in Nepal to the Government of India, *Foreign Department Secret—E Proceedings*, September 1913, Nos. 272-4. (N.A.I.)
[2] *Foreign Department Secret—E Proceedings*, September 1913, Nos. 272-4. (N.A.I.)
[3] *Ibid.*
[4] Mitter, *op. cit.*, p. 7.

(4) China agreed to abstain from interfering in the administration of Tibet. She agreed also to abstain from sending troops to Tibet. She promised not to establish Chinese colonies there;
(5) By Article IX (of the draft convention) the proposed boundary between Tibet and China was drawn on a map which was initialled by all three plenipotentiaries.[1]

Nepal was not invited to take part in the Simla Conference.[2] For this reason, she felt uneasy because she was afraid that the existing arrangements between Nepal and Tibet might be disturbed as the result of the tripartite conference. To make the position clear to the Durbar, the Resident was asked by his government to talk to the Maharajah. The Resident reported that:

'After the failure of the Tibetan negotiations at Simla in July owing to the obstructive attitude taken by the Chinese government and their refusal to recognize the initialling of the Convention by their representative at the tripartite conference, I was authorized by the Government of India to communicate unofficially and very confidentially to the Prime Minister of Nepal the purpose of the Convention signed by the government representatives, British and Tibetan plenipotentiaries, and to explain the position to him. . . .'

The Resident was further instructed to give assurances to the Prime Minister

'. . . that nothing in the convention is intended or will be allowed to affect existing agreements or arrangements between Nepal and Tibet. It was added that in the event of the convention coming into force, the government of India will be prepared to give Nepal Durbar an official assurance that the existing agreements referred to are not affected and that they will do their utmost to secure that the interests of Nepal arising from these agreements are in no way prejudiced by the operation of the convention.'[3]

The reason given by the Chinese for their refusal to recognize the initialling of the Convention was the 'inacceptability of the provisions

---

[1] Mitter, *op. cit.*, pp. 8–9.
[2] Nepal's relations with Tibet and China will be briefly touched upon in this chapter, but more extensively discussed in Chapter 9.
[3] Manner-Smith to the Secretary to the Government of India in the Foreign and Political Department, Simla, No. 75C, dated Nepal Residency, 26th (received 31st) August 1915. *Foreign and Political Secret Internal*, October 1915. Nos. 1–3. (N.A.I.)

regarding the Sino-Tibetan frontier'.[1] The promise given by the British Government of India to the Prime Minister satisfied the Durbar, so no complications arose.

British Policy of Control of Arms to Nepal

An embargo on the control over the quantity of the supply of arms and ammunition to Nepal was one of the cardinal policies of the British Government of India. From the beginning of their relations, it was considered that the Nepal Durbar should not be allowed to import arms without the permission of the Government of India. Especially after the war of 1814–16, the supreme power became very cautious in this respect, and strictly limited the quantity of imports. The campaigns had given it very great respect for the military qualities of the Gurkhas. The underlying motive of the policy was to make Nepal dependent upon the British for arms, and also to make it impossible for its warlike people and government to attack British territory. Actually, it was a double policy, to keep Nepal dependent and keep India safe from any attack by their northern neighbor. The Gurkhas, who loved fighting, never acquiesced in this most unwelcome restriction. Whatever limited stock of weapons they were able to obtain, they used freely against the Tibetans, and often, also, against one another in a *coup d'état*, the way in which most prime ministers rose to power until 1901. These coup d'états did not last more than a day or two, but nonetheless, whoever had the larger stock of contemporary weapons stood the better chance of eliminating his rival. As the nineteenth century advanced and rifles, for example, replaced muskets, they felt the need of more modern weapons, but they could not obtain them without the permission of the British. Because of the geographic difficulties of transportation plus their state of backwardness, the Nepalese found it impossible to import arms from Tibet and China; therefore, the arms must come from India or from nowhere. Nepal was a land-locked state which meant that all imports had to go through India. Whenever they requested arms and ammunition, the Government of India questioned as to whom the weapons might be used against. For a long time they could think of only one country, and that was Tibet, but later they added China. In reality, Nepal itself was in little danger because the British would defend it, if not for its own sake then because it was part of India's defense against an invasion from the north. The Himalayas formed part of India's frontier defense, and the Government of India would not allow any outside power to establish itself in a kingdom which was on the southern slope of the mountains and extended to the edge of the

[1] Mitter, *op. cit.*, p. 9.

Indian plain. The Government of India felt, therefore, that any large stock of modern arms was unnecessary and might be dangerous. If any fighting had to be done, the government army would do it. The same policy was followed concerning the princely states. There was no objection to their having war elephants and men in fighting armor—purely ceremonial soldiers similar to the yeomen of the guards in London—but when it came to soldiers being armed and trained like the Government's own army, only a few of the leading princes were allowed to maintain such a number of modern soldiers, as the supply given to Nepal was strictly rationed.

Very gradually, the Government of India changed its policy toward Nepal to a moderate extent. A somewhat more liberal attitude was adopted in the 1890s when Wylie was Resident. He persuaded the Governor-General, Lord Lansdowne, to liberalize the policy toward Nepal concerning the purchase of arms and ammunition. After this, a letter was sent to Maharajah Bir Shamsher from Lord Lansdowne. In reply, Maharajah Dhiraj wrote thanking the Governor-General. His reply revealed the extent of the concession he received from the British Government of India on the import of arms. The letter in part read as follows:

'I have received, through my kind friend, Lieutenant Colonel H. Wylie, C.S.I., Resident at my court, Your Excellency's kind letter, dated 11th October, 1893, informing me that permission will be granted to purchase military stores and arms required for my state, and that no objection of any sort will be placed thereon, but that, on the other hand, assistance will be given, and that also if the arms required are supplied from the arsenals of the British government, they will be given at their cost price, and that all arms and stores purchased by me in Europe or India, according to the regulations and arrangements made by Your Excellency, will be exempt from customs duty;...'[1]

When Lord Elgin took over the Governor-Generalship of India, he wrote another letter to Bir Shamsher in which he explained to the Maharajah why Lord Lansdowne's letter of October 11, 1893, had been careful to preserve Indian control over the quantity of arms imported. He explained that

'... Lord Lansdowne's Kharieta of the 11th October, 1893, was not written without a reference to limits which, in the interests of the

[1] Letter from Maharajah Dhiraj to Lord Lansdowne, Governor-General of India, dated 27th Kuar Samvat, 1950 (October 22, 1893). *Foreign Secret—E Proceedings*, November 1894, No. 128. (N.A.I.)

peace and safety of India, Nepal's nearest and most important neighbor, it must clearly be incumbent on the government of India to prescribe in respect to the import of munitions of war by your Durbar.'[1]

Bir Shamsher later, in another interview with Wylie, agreed to the proposal of Lord Elgin.[2]

Except for the import of machinery for arms manufacturing, the British tried not to put too many restrictions on the Durbar's arms requisition. It was also decided by the British Government to seize arms, warlike machinery, and ammunition being clandestinely imported into Nepal, and immediately stop all aid to Nepal in this connection.[3]

When Maharajah Chandra Shamsher assumed the office of prime minister, he showed the usual keen desire to arm his army with modern weapons. He asked also to be allowed to import larger, in fact much larger, quantities than had been allowed to Bir Shamsher. In support of his request, he wrote:

'... I may assure you that the increased military efficiency of Nepal represents so much addition to the military resources of the government of India. But facts and figures will show that the country has not made any substantial addition to its military resources beyond the addition of 8,000 Martini-Henry rifles with 200 rounds of ammunition per rifle, six per guns of 200th with 1,000 rounds of shell, and the material for the manufacture of empty brass cartridges lately ordered from England....'[4]

In answer to his request and argument for more guns, Chandra Shamsher was told by the Resident that Bir Shamsher had not kept his promise 'by maintaining two arsenals at Nakhu and Sundri Jal for manufacturing not only rifles and cartridges but also guns, and the government of India has little or no knowledge of the extent to which these arsenals are used'.[5] The Resident also told Chandra Shamsher that the Government of India did know that the Durbar manufactured Maxims.

---

[1] Lord Elgin to Bir Shamsher, May 15, 1894; No. 146.
[2] Wylie to the Secretary of the Government of India, No. 42-P, 4041, dated Kathmandu, June 13, 1894. No. 149. (N.A.I.)
[3] File Notes. Discussion. K.W. No. 1. For the entire discussion on arms, see file *Foreign Secret—E*, November 1894. No. 127-62. (N.A.I.)
[4] Maharajah Chandra Shamsher to the Resident, *Foreign Department Secret—E Proceedings*, November 1902, Nos. 212-26, p. 326. (N.A.I.)
[5] Memorandum for transmission to the Minister of Nepal by the Resident. (pp. 16-17). *Foreign Department Secret—E Proceedings*, November 1902, Nos. 212-26. Enclosure to Proceedings No. 211. (N.A.I.)

CHANDRA SHAMSHER AND HIS FOREIGN POLICY

Chandra Shamsher agreed that it was a fact that during the regime of Bir Shamsher, the Nepalese had begun the manufacture of Maxims.[1] Owing to this breach of promise by the Durbar, the British Government of India declined to listen to the request for more arms for Chandra Shamsher. The Resident asked him the same old question, 'Against whom are they (the arms) to be employed?'[2] Chandra Shamsher made the same reply, skilfully brought up to date:

'Of late, I am inclined to think that our neighbours, the Tibetans, are far better off than ourselves in this matter. Their sources of supply are numerous, and with the recent arrangements by which Russia and China agree to erect Tibet into an independent state ... add to our anxiety and render our unpreparedness a matter of deep concern.'[3]

In support of his argument, Chandra Shamsher put forth an additional and pertinent argument:

'I venture to say that if His Excellency, the Viceroy, were as free and generous in the matter of armament to us as His Excellency has been to Afghanistan, I am sure that the services which Nepal could render in time of need, at much less cost and with absolute certainty, would compare very favorably with that of the Amirs. And I think the proposed erection of Tibet into an independent country, if true, suggests the advisability of a fresh discussion on the question of the arming of Nepal with modern arms of precision.'[4]

Chandra Shamsher added that he was quite appreciative of what the British had done for Nepal in the past by allowing it to import arms and ammunition. In his opinion, however, times had changed, and, in consequence, the need of the Durbar was greater than formerly. For this reason, he requested permission for the purchase of a machine for the manufacture of caps for Martini-Henry cartridges and machinery for the manufacture of gunpowder. His arguments were strong, but the British Government of India was, as always, reluctant to grant permission to import machinery for the manufacturing of armaments in Nepal. It pointed out that the Durbar was allowed to import arms through India without difficulty provided the Government of India considered that the demand was reasonable.

[1] Proceedings No. 212.
[2] Ibid.
[3] Chandra to Ravenshaw, Resident, dated October 6, 1902, *Foreign Department Secret—E Proceedings*, November 1902. Nos. 212–26. Proceedings No. 223. (N.A.I.)
[4] Ibid.

handra Shamsher was not a man who gave way easily. He looked for opportunity to press his demands over and over again. After giving help to Younghusband's mission to Tibet, he again pressed the right to import machinery. The Resident supported the demand and said that 'in order to remove the feeling in Nepal of distrust against us, the request for machinery asked for may be sanctioned without incurring any danger'.[1] This led to a free and frank discussion between the foreign office and the military department of the Government of India. Some of the officials advised giving full permission to import machinery, but others argued that after the peaceful settlement with Tibet, Nepal did not need machinery to manufacture armaments. However, most of the officials agreed that Nepal should be allowed to purchase arms with the help of the British government. Lord Curzon, the Viceroy, concluded this important discussion by putting himself on record by agreeing with his Secretary, who probably advised that Nepal should not be allowed to import machinery.[2] Lord Curzon wrote in his memorandum,

'I think on the whole that the Secretary is right. My reasons are twofold.

'In the first place, Nepal is not an independent State. The degree of its incorporation in the Indian Empire and subordination to the British crown is somewhat indeterminate. But it is, in any case, in a wholly different position from Afghanistan, and we certainly do not want to increase the evidence or symbols of independence.

'Secondly, there is no need for a well-armed Nepalese army, for there is no enemy for it to fight. War between Nepal and Tibet is now almost inconceivable. The Russians are hardly likely to be seen in this direction. There is, therefore, no case for modern scientific armaments. There is a further and vital differentiation from Afghanistan.

'I hope that our relations with Nepal may continue on the present ascending plane of harmony and confidence. I cannot conceive of our doing anything to interrupt it. But similar reliance cannot invariably, in the passage of time, be placed upon the friendships of Durbars and Chiefs, and it is at least not incredible that a Manipur[3] incident might one day take place in Nepal.

[1] Resident reports his interview with Maharajah Chandra Shamsher Jang in connection with the above subject. No. 107. Dated 19th (received the 24th) July, 1905. With Discussion. *Foreign Department Secret—E Proceedings*, December 1905. Nos. 225–59. (N.A.I.)

[2] The Secretary's advice was not found, but after Curzon's notes, it becomes evident what the Secretary had written in his memorandum.

[3] Lord Curzon had referred to the incident which took place in Manipur in 1891. The government of India had desposed the Senapatri, or commander-in-chief of the local state forces. He was the brother of the Rajah who was deposed. The Senapatri refused to obey the order of the representative of the

CHANDRA SHAMSHER AND HIS FOREIGN POLICY

'At Manipur we suffered terribly for the guns which we had foolishly given as a compliment to the Raja. That precedent has always made me cautious and apprehensive.'[1]

Although the prime minister of Nepal was not fully aware of the attitude of Lord Curzon, it was a great disappointment for him to see that his request was met only in part. Undoubtedly, he felt that the British Government of India did not trust Nepal. There was a mutual distrust of one another. The British feared that the Indian Nationalists might induce the soldiers or inhabitants of Nepal to help Indian agitators against the British in India.[2] On the other hand, Nepal was afraid that the British might reduce it to the status of a princely state. It was true that the British did allow the purchase of arms and ammunition in strictly limited quantities. The grievance of Nepal was that she was not permitted to buy machinery and that old arms could not be repaired. Just before Chandra Shamsher visited London, Lord Morley, the Secretary of State for India, was informed by the Indian Government of the controversy about the supply of arms and machinery to the Durbar. The Government of India emphasized that it was most desirable that the Nepal government should get its supply of arms through the British, and that Chandra Shamsher should not deal directly with arms factories in the United Kingdom or elsewhere while he was in Europe.[3]

Chandra Shamsher was preparing to go to England and at the same time, he was trying to get permission to buy machinery in London. The Indian government would not grant this permission to him. He then pressed his demand for more arms. This time the Military Department in India strongly supported the demand on account of the past services of the Durbar in many fields, and, in particular, because

Governor-General, and then offered armed resistance. He treacherously attacked the British representative and others of his party, and finally they were beheaded by the public executioner. The soldiers of the deposed Rajah retired toward Kachar (a town near Assam) with arms mostly supplied by the British government. At the end of April, the outrage was punished by the British government. The Senapatri and his accomplices were hanged. Manipur was a small hill principality situated on the border of Assam in India. (See *Oxford History of India*, V. A. Smith, pp. 765–6. Oxford Press, 1923.)

[1] 'Discussion notes on the file of the foreign office papers.' *Foreign Department Secret—E Proceedings*, December 1905. Nos. 225–59. (N.A.I.)

[2] See *Foreign Department External—B Proceedings*, September 1907, Nos. 101–9. (N.A.I.)

[3] To John Morley, His Majesty's Secretary of State for India from the Government of India, Foreign Department, No. 51, 1908, File No. 624/08. Letter to His Majesty's Secretary of State for India. 'Status of Nepal and Her Relations with the British Government.' Fort William, *Foreign Department Secret External*. No. 324, 1911. (I.O.L. Microfilm).

it had facilitated the recruitment of Gurkhas for the Indian army. The Military Department felt that the policy of the Indian government was impolitic.[1]

On the strong recommendation of the Resident, the Foreign Office allowed the Durbar to import arms and ammunition free of duty. This concession was granted because 'in view of the special services rendered by and expected from Nepal, it should be treated exceptionally in such matters'.[2] The finance department was not in favor of this concession since, in its opinion, it might become a very dangerous precedent because it could be claimed by other friendly countries as well. The finance department sent a strong note in support of its opinion. It argued that,

'... In any case, if government sanctions the present proposal, they cannot, without laying themselves open to the charge of making invidious distinctions, refuse similar claims from other friendly states on the frontier, such as Afghanistan and Bhutan; and it may not perhaps be impossible to refuse similar concessions to the Imperial

---

[1] 'Larger issues seem to me to be involved in this question than are apparent from the correspondence, and I think it is a pity the Government of India, ignoring these issues, should haggle with the Nepal Durbar about such a trifling matter. Our great dependence upon the Nepalese for recruiting and mobilizing facilities does not seem to be realized.

'In July, the Durbar asked for 5,000 old pattern rifles, discarded from our native army, and it was given 2,500; now, when a larger request (10,000) is made, the Government of India gives, two years after the original request was made, the remaining 2500.

'In my opinion, it is extremely impolitic to appear to behave ungenerously and with suspicion towards an independent state which is in time of emergency a factor of our Salvation. I would go further and dub as dangerously short-sighted a policy which permits us to trifle with Nepal's good will—a policy which can only be occasioned by ignorance of the importance to us of good relations with Nepal.

'... It will thus be seen that the difficulties in regard to the recruiting of our Nepalese soldiers and in connection with their service in our ranks are already sufficiently numerous. It would be most unpolitic to aggravate the Durbar to create additional hindrances and it is, therefore, undesirable by any action of ours to arouse in it feelings of disappointment or resentment. Appreciating to the full the military importance of this matter, I sincerely trust the Durbar's latest request will be met promptly and completely. The possession by Nepal of these additional rifles would constitute no danger; by improving the efficiency of the Nepalese army, it would sharpen a magnificent weapon which we may one day wish to use. It would also lessen the danger of a clandestine trade in arms from Chinese territory where anything that is paid for can be bought.'

'Military Department's opinion on the question of arms supply to Nepal.' *Foreign Department Secret External*, No. 324; 1911 (I.O.L. Microfilm).

[2] Note on file in the finance department. *Foreign Department External—A*, April 1908, No. 65–6. (N.A.I.)

Service Troops [the modern soldiers maintained by some of the Indian princes] if it is accorded to the armies of the above states.'[1]

The argument put forward by the finance department reflected its responsibilities, but on the other hand, the reason for allowing the concession were also cogent.

In the end, the finance department gave way reluctantly. The Durbar finally realized that without the help and the good will of the Indian Government, it would not be possible for the Gurkhas to be well equipped. Chandra Shamsher, in one of his interviews with the Resident in August 1907, told Manner-Smith that to obtain arms by surreptitious methods meant seriously taxing the Nepal treasury. Moreover, it would also increase the suspicion of the Government of India. He was frank in his discussion with the Resident, and told him that he also abandoned the idea of importing machinery because that process would be very costly and the result might be very unsatisfactory because of the lack of skilled craftsmen to operate the machines. But the Maharajah was not willing to close the existing arms factory in Nepal because 'public opinion' would not support such an idea. By this he meant the influential nobles and Sardars of the army would oppose the idea. He agreed however, to limit the production of arms in the state factories provided the Indian Government would guarantee to supply him with enough modern rifles to meet the requirements of the Nepal army.[2] Chandra Shamsher even went further and offered not to manufacture arms in the state arsenal if the necessary requirements for modern guns and other arms were met by the Government of India. To keep the weapons in good condition, however, he argued that some new machinery would be needed in the factories. The Resident, Manner-Smith, supported the requests of the Durbar because of these assurances, and suggested that

'... I would go as far as possible without prejudice to our rights of suzerainty, in the direction of treating Nepal as a friendly independent State whose interests are wrapped up in our own rather than as a subordinate feudatory whose actions must be watched.'[3]

J. Manner-Smith summed up his opinion as follows:

[1] *Foreign Department External—A*, April 1908, Nos. 65-6. (N.A.I.)
[2] Manner-Smith to the Secretary to the Government of India, *Foreign Department Secret External*, 1911. No. 324 (I.O.L. Microfilm).
[3] Manner-Smith to the Secretary of the Government of India, Foreign Department, No. 169, Nepal, September 26-27 (received October 2), 1907. No. 51 of 1908. *Foreign Department Secret External*, 1911, No. 324. (I.O.L. Microfilm).

'So long as the Durbar acts up to these terms, I think it would be wise to yield to their susceptibilities and their desire to improve their machinery to a moderate extent. The idea of aggressive action by the Nepalese against us in India under any circumstances may, I believe, be entirely set aside, and, as we have no intention of aggression ourselves, it is not a very serious matter if the State should become, to some extent, over-armed for her external needs, as no doubt she will desire to be until she learns that her safety no longer demands these precautions.'[1]

These arguments by the Resident had their effect on the British Government of India. The parties reached a reasonable and honorable compromise. The Durbar agreed to give up its demands for arms manufacturing machinery, and the Government of India decided to be generous and liberal in granting Nepal's request for the import of arms through the Indian government. This arrangement was agreed upon even before Chandra left for England in 1908. The result of this 'gentlemen's agreement' was that both parties became more friendly to each other. There remained very little room for suspicion on either side concerning this matter. On the return from England of the prime minister, the Government of India presented the Durbar with 7,500 Martini-Henry rifles from their arsenals in India.[2] Besides this gift of arms, the Government of India presented as a gift to the Durbar additional arms for the use of Durbar soldiers. The Durbar was obtaining enough arms for its soldiers without much difficulty. The Resident supplied detailed information on the purchase of arms by the Durbar with the full knowledge of the Nepalese Government.[3]

---

[1] No. 51 of 1908. *Foreign Department Secret External*, 1911, No. 324. (N.A.I.)

[2] Manner-Smith to S. H. Butler, Foreign Secretary, Government of India, No. 128, dated Nepal, 10th (received 16th) August 1909. *Foreign Department Secret External*, December 1909. Nos. 431–4. (N.A.I.)

[3] 'The troops are constantly at work and the best trained of them, like the rifle regiment, carry out attack of a position on the parade with perfect correctness. I am doubtful, however, if there is much, if any, training under Field Service conditions.

'With the object of improving the efficiency of their higher grade officers, the Durbar, with the previous sanction of the Government of India, imported from England 100 revolvers (Colts' New Service taking English 450–455 cartridges) and 10,000 cartridges for the same.

'During the year, 7,600 rounds of Martini-Henry ball ammunition were purchased by the Durbar for the annual musketry training of their troops. The Durbar also returned 3,569 empty Lee-Metford cartridge cases and received in exchange, on payment, an equivalent number of loaded cartridges.

'Another seven-pound breech-loading gun of local manufacture was added to their artillery armament, which now stands at 188 serviceable and 140 unserviceable guns.' Annual report of the events in Nepal by Lt.-Col. H. L.

CHANDRA SHAMSHER AND HIS FOREIGN POLICY

The information supplied by the Resident is typical in form on arms and ammunition. This agreement remained in practice even after World War I. No serious dispute arose between the two governments over this issue. This arrangement for arms and ammunition for Nepal's army was based on mutual trust and understanding of each other's needs.

When in 1914 the British Government presented some 5,000 old Lee-Metford rifles and 500,000 rounds of ammunition to the Tibetan plenipotentiary who came to attend the Simla Conference, the Prime Minister of Nepal immediately requested that he be given detailed information about this gift. The British Government of India took pains to satisfy the Nepal Durbar in assuring the Nepalese that the gift was in no way aimed against Nepal.[1] Nepal accepted the assurance and no rupture took place in the relations between Nepal and Tibet. Moreover, the gift of arms did not create misunderstanding between India and Nepal. This arrangement continued for as long as the British stayed in India. Chandra Shamsher was a shrewd politician. He handled the intricate problems which arose with the British Government of India with more ability than many of his predecessors in the same office.

Agitation in India and Nepal's Concern

Maharajah Chandra Shamsher showed his loyalty to the British Government in many ways before World War I. One of these was when he tried to check the entrance of seditious newspapers into Nepal from India. Upon receiving information from the Resident concerning the agitation and how the Indian vernacular newspapers were taking part in the movement against British rule in India, he immediately forbade all Nepalese from reading them. He probably also felt that seditious writing against India might incite Nepal's small but influential group against him and against his rule in Nepal. These newspapers included three from Calcutta, *Bande Mataram*, *Jugantar*, and *Sandhva*, as well as *India* from Lahore.[2] Soon afterwards, the Government of India sent another list of newspapers which were characterized as

Showers, Officiating Resident in Nepal. *Foreign Secret Department*, September 1913. Nos. 272–4. (N.A.I.)

[1] Report on the course of events in Nepal during the year 1914–15, by the Resident, J. Manner-Smith No. 75c, dated Nepal (received 31st) August 26, 1915. *Foreign and Political Department Secret Internal*, October 1915. Nos 1–3. (N.A.I.)

[2] J. Manner-Smith to L. W. Dane, Foreign Secretary, Government of India, Nepal, July 17, 1907. No. 104 (Confidential) *Foreign Department Secret External B Proceedings*, September 1907, Nos. 101–9. (N.A.I.)

seditious: *The Punjabee, New India, United Burma, Sultan, Navasakti, Mihir-O-Sudhaker, Charu Mihir,* and *Howrah Hitaishi*.[1] These newspapers did not include any published in Urdu, Maharathi, and Gujrati, as it was believed that none written in these languages were in circulation in Nepal.

Chandra Shamsher was very much disturbed when the Resident informed him that a Nepalese named Pirthimon Thapa was among the speakers at a meeting attacking British rule, and that he and his associates wanted to start a newspaper in India which would also be sent to Nepal. The speeches made by Thapa and N. L. Ghose, an Indian Christian, are worth noting here as reported by the Commissioner of Police in Calcutta. They clearly show dangerous signs of discontent with the British in India. When they spoke about distributing the newspaper among the Gurkha soldiers to explain the situation and their duty to the motherland, Chandra Shamsher interpreted this as a veiled criticism of the prime minister of Nepal.[2]

Chandra Shamsher wrote to the Resident that 'in order to put a timely and efficient check to Pirthimon Thapa's mischievious proceedings, I would at once ask our representative in Calcutta to try to seek him out and warn him . . .'. The Maharajah was prepared to take full action against this man if he had any property in Nepal. It was unbelievable to him that any of his subjects would act so wrongly, knowing the loyalty of the Durbar to the British government.[3] He wrote,

'I have a strong aversion against the very name of "Gurkha" being associated with anything disloyal towards the British government; should it be hereafter necessary, I will, with the greatest pleasure, agree to any feasible scheme that may strike you to put a stop to proceed-

---

[1] R. E. Holland, Assistant Secretary, Government of India, to Manner-Smith, September 4, 1907, No. 174-E-E.C., *Foreign Department External—B Proceedings,* September 1907, Nos. 101-9. (N.A.I.)

[2] 'A Nepalese, Pirthimon Thapa, addressed a meeting at College Square, 27th evening; about 200 present. Advocated publishing monthly newspaper for distribution among Gurkha soldiers to explain situation and their duty to the motherland; cause of poverty in India and true connection between Gurkhas and Bengalese and English; said unfortunately, Nepalese gentlemen visiting Calcutta found difficulty in mixing with Bengalis, not knowing Bengali; he will strive to bring Bengalis and Nepalese together. N. L. Ghose, Native Christian, said if Gurkhas, Bhutanese, and other tribes of north and east could be brought on their side, they would form a mighty nation.' Copy of a telegram from the Commissioner of Police in Calcutta to Director of Criminal Intelligence, dated May 28, 1907, *Foreign Department External—B Proceedings,* September 1907, Nos. 101-9. (N.A.I.)

[3] Chandra Shamsher to Manner-Smith, June 13, 1907. *Foreign Department External Proceedings,* September 1907. No. 101-9. (N.A.I.)

ings that are likely to affect prejudicially the spirit of loyalty of the British regiments.'[1]

The Resident inquired whether,

'the Nepalese Durbar would be willing to take steps to prevent the return to India of any Gurkha subjects whom it might be necessary to send back to Nepal on account of their connection with the agitators.'[2]

Maharajah Chandra Shamsher asked the Resident to inform the Lieutenant-Governor of Bengal that

'the Nepal Durbar would be quite willing to take steps to prevent the return of Pirthimon Thapa to India if the Bengal government would think it necessary to send him to Nepal and this notwithstanding his doubtful character as a true Gurkha subject.'[3]

At the same time, the Durbar tried to keep the British government informed of any word it received concerning the agitation in India. Following this practice, the Maharajah informed the Resident of a letter from one of the correspondents in India who wrote to congratulate him on his action against the Indian newspapers. The correspondent was to some extent dependent upon the Nepal government. He informed the Maharajah that the Maharajah of Durbhanga was secretly in communication with the Nationalists and was running a great risk by constantly having secret interviews with and receiving at his home the leaders of the agitation.[4] Chandra Shamsher also received a petition from Pirthimon Thapa in which Thapa informed the prime minister through his private secretary his idea of publishing a newspaper in the 'Khas language' which would be called 'Gurkha-Sathee'. Pirthimon Thapa explained the object of the newspaper as follows:

'The object of the paper is national love amongst the Gurkhas and love for the mother country (Nepal); it has nothing to do with the present Swadeshi movement and political agitation, as will be seen, if perchance anything improper should appear in the paper, and for that he was

---

[1] Chandra Shamsher to Manner-Smith, June 14, 1907, *op. cit.*
[2] E. A. Gait, Chief Secretary to the Government of Bengal, to Manner-Smith, June 7, 1907 (demi-official). *Foreign Department External—B Proceedings*, September 1907, Nos. 101-9. (N.A.I.)
[3] Chandra Shamsher to Manner-Smith, June 14, 1907, *op. cit.*
[4] Manner-Smith to Louis Dane, Nepal, August 5, 1907, *Foreign Department External—B Proceedings*, August 1907, Nos. 101-9. (N.A.I.)

ordered by the Sarkar to discontinue the paper, he would do so at once.'[1]

The Maharajah lost no time in informing the Resident about the petition. Chandra Shamsher's actions made it clear to the British that they could depend on him if there should be any agitation against them in India.

[1] Translation of a petition dated July 31, 1907, from Pirthimon Thapa of No. 5 Machua Bazer Street, Calcutta, to Sardar Marichman Singh, Private Secretary to His Excellency the Prime Minister of Nepal. *Foreign Department External—B Proceedings*, September 1907, Nos. 101–9. (N.A.I.)

CHAPTER 5
NEPALESE–BRITISH CO-OPERATION IN WORLD WAR I

The Great War of 1914 brought to the battlefield soldiers of many races whose existence was almost unknown outside their own countries. Nepal was one of them: until the Gurkha battalions arrived in France, few had ever heard of them outside the Indian army, of which they had formed a part since before the outbreak of the Indian Mutiny.[1] As soon as the World War broke out, Nepal decided to send help to its ally, as it had done in 1857. The Gurkhas rarely went outside their Himalayan kingdom; but thousands of them crossed the ocean and landed in France, a country completely unfamiliar to their customs, religion, language and way of life. The assistance was entirely voluntary: Chandra Shamsher said with truth that 'compulsion has no part in all the measures that I had taken in this connection'.[2] Nepal's assistance to the British Government at this critical hour surpassed all the hopes and expectations of the Government of India. The aid started even before the British Government was actually involved in the conflict and lasted to its last minute and even beyond. Maharajah Chandra Shamsher visited the British Resident on August 3, 1914 and explained to the Resident the purpose of his visit. He handed over a very important letter which was to be communicated to the Viceroy of India. This was the declaration of his loyalty, sincerity and devotion to the British, and that he offered to help even before they had formally entered the War. The document read as follows:

'The war cloud looks very threatening. In the event of a continental war Great Britain will in all probability be involved. I have come to

[1] 'On the 1st of June, Wilson's force was strengthened by the Sirmur battalion of Gurkhas (1st Battalion, 2nd Gurkhas) a regiment which later covered itself with glory, and gained an undying name for its gallantry during the siege of Delhi.' Lord Roberts, *op. cit.*, Vol. I, p. 154.
[2] Chandra Shamsher's speech before the Bahadurs, Officers and men, in connection with 'Victory Celebration in Nepal.' *Correspondence Regarding World War I, Basta No. 63.* (N.F.O.K.)

request you to inform His Excellency the Viceroy and through him His Majesty the King Emperor that the whole military resources of Nepal are at His Majesty's disposal. We shall be proud if we can be of any service however little that may be. Though far from the scene of actual conflict we yield to none in our devotion and friendship to His Majesty's person and Empire. We have spoken of our friendship on many occasions. Should time allow, we hope to speak in deeds.

'I may say I am speaking in the double capacity, firstly as the Marshal of the Gurkhas and secondly as Major-General in His Majesty's Army.'[1]

This unusual action was performed at a time when the nations of the Triple Entente were in grave anxiety about which of the hostile alliances was the stronger. The prime minister did not wait to find out the winning side but cast his lot without any bargain. Future events showed how nobly and sincerely he made good his professions of friendship.

The Government of India in thanking him for his offer, said that 'should necessity arise the Government of India would not hesitate to accept it'.[2] British expeditionary forces sent to France were so small, and its casualties in 1914 were so heavy, that the Government of Great Britain relied heavily upon the Indian army for reinforcement in France. Within a few months the war spread to the Middle East. By the end of 1914 the British regular army had been largely destroyed. The offer of help by Nepal was very welcome. The Indian Government sent a strong army which included Sikhs, Pathans, Punjabees and the South Indians. The departure of most of the Indian army soon created a new problem. This was the possibility that a German-Turkish army might invade India in alliance with the Afghans, and that an attack from without might be synchronized with a domestic revolt.[3] Beside widespread recruitment of volunteers from inside India, the government looked to Nepal for help and found a ready response. Nepalese

---

[1] Resident to the Secretary, Government of India, *Foreign and Political Department Secret Internal*, September 1914, Nos. 15–16. (N.A.I.) Memo—3/8/14. The letter is written by Sir Chandra to the Resident: *Basta No. 63.* (N.F.O.K.)

[2] Annual report on the course of events in Nepal during the year 1914–15, by the Resident, *Foreign and Political Secret Internal*, October 1915, Nos. 1–3. (N.A.I.)

[3] See Sir Michael O'Dwyer, *India As I Knew It*, Chapter XV on 'The War Effort of the Punjab', pp. 213–31. London, 1925.
 1914. The Home Government has asked for 21,000 combatant recruits in the last four months of the year; 28,000 were raised, of whom 14,000 came from the Punjab, 3,000 from Nepal, 3,000 from the Frontier and trans-Frontier, and 8,000 from the rest of India.

assistance was not limited to the defence of India: Chandra Shamsher also agreed to send soldiers out of the country to the actual theater of operations. Nepalese assistance took various forms. It could be divided into the following sections: (a) supply of recruits (b) the loan of Nepalese troops (c) help in maintaining the British Gurkha regiments of the Indian army (d) financial and material help, and (e) keeping the Government of India informed about any intrigue against it.

The Supply of Recruits

The supply of recruits to the Indian army had been a sore point between the two governments from the early days of their contact. But from the beginning of Chandra Shamsher's assumption of office, there had been relaxation in this area. Chandra Shamsher allowed more Nepalese to be recruited for the Indian army. During the war Chandra Shamsher became still more generous. Immediately after the outbreak of the war, the British requested more recruits. Chandra Shamsher promptly agreed to provide them. He ordered his officials to use gentle and persuasive methods to induce recruits to enlist because in his opinion this was always the best method. Every precaution was taken not to allow unwilling men to be recruited. The Durbar issued special instructions to all its officials to see that more recruits were collected at different recruiting stations. The Durbar even went so far as to say that those who served the British during the war would be considered to have been in the service of their own country. Persuasiveness and inducements were successful, and by September and October 1914, Nepalese came forward in greater numbers than ever before. This was due to the strong exhortation of the Maharajah and his officials. The result was that 200,000 of the country's best men were recruited during the entire period of the war. This greatly helped the Indian army in keeping its Gurkha battalions up to strength, in spite of heavy losses at the front. The supply of recruits was one of the major contributions of Nepal towards the Great War.[1]

    1915. 93,000 combatants were enrolled, of whom 46,000 were from the Punjab, 14,000 from Nepal, 6,000 from the Pathan areas, and 28,000 from the rest of India.
    1916. 104,000 combatants were enrolled, viz. 50,000 from the Punjab, 15,000 from Nepal, 5,000 from the Pathan tribes, and 32,000 from the rest of India.
By the end of 1916 the Punjab, which had started the war with 100,000 men in the Army, had supplied 110,000 out of the 192,000 fighting men raised in India. The Pathan areas had supplied 14,000; all the rest of India (with eleven-twelfths of the population) only 68,000; while the Nepal State had raised 33,000, making a grand total of 225,000.

[1] 'Nepal and the Great War', a report, *Basta No. 63*. (N.F.O.K.)

Loan of Nepalese Troops to the Government of India.

Soon after the war started the Maharajah decided to keep some 8,000 men in reserve so that if there should be any sudden call for help he could immediately send them to India. The soldiers were given full training in the valley, and later were sent to the border districts to be ready to enter India without any delay. In February 1915, a request came for 6,000 troops and the request was met immediately. Some 7,501 men were sent to India on the third and fourth of March under General Baber Shamsher. Baber Shamsher, the second son of the Maharajah, was appointed Inspector-General of the contingent and was attached to army headquarters in India. Padma Shamsher, a nephew of the prime minister, was appointed as the General in command of the regiments which were sent to the North-West Frontier Province. Another of the Maharajah's nephews, General Tej Shamsher, was appointed commander in the United Provinces. The 7,501 Gurkhas were divided between the North-West Frontier, and the United Provinces. They took garrison duty in India so that additional Indian army soldiers could be sent abroad. A second contingent of 4,000 troops was sent to India in December 1915. The Maharajah assured the Resident that this was by no means the limit to what he was prepared to do. He would send more troops if there should be need for them in case of any emergency. A third contingent was sent to India under the command of Lieutenant-General Kaiser Shamsher, the third son of the Maharajah. A fourth contingent went to India under the command of a half-brother of the prime minister, Major General Sher Shamsher. All these contingents were fully officered and equipped. A total of 4,257 was sent to India in four installments between 1916 and 1918. The first regiment with 658 men went to India in December 1916, the second with 658 men a year later, the third with 779 men in February 1918, and the fourth with 1,800 men was ready to go when the war was about to terminate.[1]

The moral effect on the Government of India was great since its own army was absent in Europe and the Middle East fighting for the British cause. These regiments earned the highest praise in India for behaving in the most disciplined manner and performing their duty as it was detailed to them. A British officer appraised the help rendered by the Nepal Durbar as follows:

'It will be granted therefore that the Nepalese Government behaved with the greatest generosity when in addition to making good all losses by drafts of volunteers from Nepal it sent an allied contingent

[1] *Basta No. 63, op. cit.*, Resident to the Secretary, Government of India, Foreign and Political Department Internal—B, June 1916, Nos. 528–58. (N.A.I.)

of nearly 14,000 excellent troops to help the British Government; and the matter was more magnanimous for Nepal, in sending these contingents, sent her first old regular regiments, thus reducing her own army at a time when the world was at war and when at any moment unforeseen eventualities, requiring the presence of every man in their country, might occur. They are very good shots, expert with the bayonet, most excellent hill-fighters, and in fact, regular first line troops. They are extra-ordinarily well behaved and disciplined—crime being conspicuous by its absence—very pleasant to deal with and like all Gurkhas, the greater the hardships to be suffered the more cheerful they become.'[1]

This appraisal by a British officer was a true description of the Gurkhas who stayed in India to defend it against any eventualities. These four contingents which were sent to India were over and above the recruits whom the Durbar supplied for service overseas. Undoubtedly the help which was provided in the form of manpower to the British Government in India deserved its recognition and gratitude. The Viceroy and the Government were not slow to express this to the Maharajah. In short, Nepal's military help to the British both for the defence of India and to take part in the World War was a record of the greatest devotion, loyalty, cooperation and sincerity which could have been expected from one friend to another in time of need.

Nepal's Help in Keeping the Gurkha Regiments up to Strength

When the war broke out some soldiers of the Gurkha regiments were on leave, visiting their families in Nepal. It was most important to recall them at once, in order to bring their battalions up to strength. Again the Maharajah, Sir Chandra Shamsher, came forward to help the British. Special messengers were sent to each village to inform all those who were on leave of the urgency of the situation, and the necessity of their return at the earliest possible moment to India. Chandra Shamsher made it very plain that those who failed to answer the call would be dealt with in the same way as a soldier of the Nepalese army who failed to rejoin his regiment on receipt of orders in time of war. The prime minister took every possible precaution to see that men of the British Gurkha regiments reached their cantonments in India as quickly as it was possible for them to do so. Their rapid return in great numbers was due to the Maharajah's prompt and energetic efforts. Chandra Shamsher took other measures such as making sure that no Gurkha sepoy should be delayed because of any legal proceed-

---

[1] *Basta No. 63, op. cit.*

ings against him, because of non-payment of taxes or because of family problems, such as litigation and other legal proceedings. Above all he managed to get permission for the Gurkhas to cross the Kala Pani (black water, or the ocean). There were religious scruples against doing this, since a Hindu who crossed salt water broke the laws of his caste. It was due to the influence of Chandra Shamsher that the 'Patia'[1] was granted to those soldiers who went overseas with the permission of the Nepal Government in the service of the Government of India on active duty in the war, and returned immediately after their period of enlistment was terminated. They were to obtain a certificate from a British officer that during their stay overseas they had observed all the rules and regulations of their caste and religion. If they failed to do so, they were excommunicated from their society and caste.[2]

About these brave, loyal and devoted soldiers, General Sir Francis Tuker wrote:

'In the war of 1914–18 the Gurkha soldier's ammunition boot clattered along the roads of France, crunched among the rocks of Gallipoli, Palestine, Baluchistan and the North West Frontier of India, padded the deserts of Suez, Egypt and Mesopotamia, and pounded the weary miles away from Khaniqin to the shores of the Caspian Sea, far from the villages sleeping peacefully on the sunny slopes of Gorkha, the Bara Mangranth, the Limbuana and the Panchthar, "the land of the five tribes" as they call it. Two hundred thousand of them strolled in their careless way into the depots at Ghoom and Gorakhpore to follow the drum whose beat was a call not to be denied by the martial clans.'[3]

Candler, a British war correspondent, had this to say of the gallantry of these hill fighters:

'The hill men of Nepal have stood the test as well as the best. Ask the Devons what they think of the Gurkhas who fought on their flank on the Hai. Ask Kitchener's men and the Anzacs how the 5th and 6th bore themselves at Gallipoli, and read Ian Hamilton's report. Ask Townsend's Immortals how the 7th fought at Ctesiphon; and the British regiments who were at Mahomed Abdul Hassan and Istabulat

---

[1] Patia. Permission given by the Brahmin priest to go overseas and upon their return to be accepted in Hindu society without any religious penalty after performing a certain religious ceremony.
[2] *Basta No. 63, op. cit.*
[3] Tuker, Francis, *op. cit.*, p. 193.

what the 1st and 8th did in these hard-fought fights. Ask the gallant Hants rowers against what odds the two Gurkha battalions forced the passage of the Tigris at Shumtan on February 23rd. And ask the Commander of the Indian Corps what sort of fight the six Gurkha battalions put up in France.'[1]

General Sir James Willcocks said, 'Of the Indians who served with me in France, the Gurkhas were the first in the permanent trenches to bear the shock of a German attack . . .'.[2] Major Northey wrote, 'Nepal suffered some 20,000 casualties on our behalf, and its men fought in every theatre of war, cheerfully enduring tropic heat and the cold of northern winter'.[3] The Gurkhas were amongst the best in the British armies and British generals and officers showered praise on them.

Before they were sent overseas, Chandra Shamsher and the British authorities had detailed and frank discussion on questions such as their pay, military rules and regulations, and whether they should be sent to fight outside India. In a letter to Manner-Smith on January 26, 1915, Chandra Shamsher argued against the idea of sending Nepalese soldiers overseas. He objected because of the belief invariably held in India, or at least in Nepal since the Boer War, that colored troops could not be employed against white troops by European powers fighting among themselves. This was so well known that to discuss it was superfluous. The Maharajah felt too that this step would be unpopular in Nepal and also in the European country where they were sent.[4] Eventually, he was persuaded to agree to the use of the Gurkhas overseas. It was agreed that payment to these soldiers would be at the same rate as was the case during the Indian Mutiny in 1857. As to compensation for total or partial disablement, e.g. loss of a leg, etc., to any individual soldier, they agreed that it could be discussed when the occasion arose.[5] The Prime Minister of Nepal very strongly demanded that Nepal's own regulations and law should be applied to all Nepalese soldiers because he thought that the British military code was so intricate and complicated that it would not be understood easily by the Nepalese. The real reason for his objection was that he objected to Nepalese being made subject to foreign law and regulations. He wrote,

'Above all the extension or application of the British Military law

[1] Candler, Edmund, *The Sepoy*, p. 2. (London, John Murray, 1919).
[2] Landon, *op. cit.*, p. 143.
[3] Northey and Brook, *op. cit.*, p. 269.
[4] Chandra Shamsher to Manner-Smith, Camp Mudbalwa, January 26, 1915, 'Correspondence Regarding War', *Basta No. 63*. (N.F.O.K.)
[5] Chandra Shamsher to Manner-Smith, Nepal, February 26, 1915, *Basta No. 63*.

to our officers and men of the contingent by a preliminary order and notification as proposed, directly opposed to any precedent as it also is, will be regarded as a measure seriously affecting the prestige and status of this country.'[1]

However, these differences were gradually reconciled to the mutual benefit of both parties. Recruits came forward in increasing numbers and were sent overseas with the active and sincere cooperation of the Durbar.

Financial and Material Help by Nepal

Nepal's aid was not confined to providing military manpower. Financial and material help was given on an equally generous scale. The first contribution of money came in September 1914, of Rs. 300,000 ($60,000) to buy machine guns for the Gurkhas of the Indian army. Unfortunately, this large sum was rejected in the beginning by the Viceroy for the particular purpose designated by the prime minister, though later it was accepted and used for other war purposes during the war. The Maharajah permitted it to be placed in the hands of the Commander-in-Chief of India to be used in any way he might think best.[2] Here Chandra Shamsher was wiser than the Governor-General, for the opening battles in France showed that the British infantry battalions were heavily handicapped by their inferiority to the Germans in machine guns. On New Year's day of 1916 and again in January 1917 Rs. 300,000 ($60,000) were presented on each occasion to the Viceroy for use in any way in connection with the war. When the King-Emperor and Queen-Empress of India were celebrating their silver wedding anniversary in 1918 the Maharajah presented Rs. 200,000 ($40,000). While these were the major gifts, there were in addition many small contributions for hospitals and other purposes.[3]

Of the produce of the country 5,000 maunds (40,000 pounds) of cardamons, 84,699 pounds of tea, 200 jackets and 12 great coats were sent for the soldiers. 200,000 broad gauge sleepers free of royalty and 220 sisoo logs were also supplied free of cost, for the railways.[4] Some newspaper published the story that the Maharajah had contributed numbers of Tibetan and Nepalese blankets for the British Gurkha regiments. The statement was false, and when Chandra Shamsher read

---

[1] Chandra to Manner-Smith, Nepal, July 20, 1915, *Basta No. 63.* (N.F.O.K.)
[2] Chandra Shamsher to Manner-Smith, Nepal, September 12, 1914, *Basta No. 64.* (N.F.O.K.)
[3] *Basta No. 63, op. cit.*
[4] *Ibid.*

it, he seized the opportunity to write the following letter to the British Resident.¹

Nepal,
13th December, 1914

'My dear Colonel Manner-Smith,

In the newspapers received here yesterday and the day before, I find a statement made to the effect that a number of Nepal and Tibetan blankets have been offered by me for the use of the British Gurkha Soldiers at the front and accepted by His Excellency the Viceroy. In the absence of any news from you on the subject it makes me anxious to know if the announcement as published by the press is correct. If that be so, I suppose I can put together now some 2,000 (two thousand) pieces of Tibetan and Nepal blankets known respectively as Pakhias and Jhum Radhis and expect to be able to procure some two or three thousand more pieces in the course of a month or so, and I shall be glad to know when and where and to whom they are to be delivered. An early reply will oblige.

With best regards,
Yours very sincerely.
Sd/- Chandra Shamsher.'

Nepal also gave some arms to the British. Thirty machine guns bought from Vickers Armstrong were presented to the King-Emperor in London on the occasion of his birthday in 1915. The same year 340 mechanics from the Nepal Government's arms factories were offered to repair broken arms and to work in the Indian workshops. The services of 71 were accepted out of 340.²

One of the most important items of contribution was the Indian rupees and Nepalese silver coins given by the Durbar and the nobles of Nepal in 1917 and 1918. At this time India was critically short of rupees and of silver for coining purposes. Nepal managed to send to India one crore and one lakh ($200,000) of British Indian rupees and twenty-five lakhs (two and half millions) of Nepalese coins from the government treasury.³ This was very timely assistance, and Nepal gave it as a sincere friend.

War Time Intrigues

War is not fought only on the battlefield. The hidden war of intrigue can sometimes be more dangerous than open warfare. The Nepalese

¹ *Basta No. 64, op. cit.*
² *Ibid.*
³ *Ibid.;* Landon, *op. cit.*, p. 144.

Government kept the British informed about these forms of hostilities also. The Maharajah was in the habit of listening to the radio and he recorded one of the German broadcasts which was intended for the Gurkha soldiers. It stated that the British were the hereditary enemy, and that instead of fighting for them the Gurkha soldiers should seize the opportunity to conquer India.[1]

Beside the radio broadcasts the German Imperial Government also sent letters to the Maharajah Dhiraj and the prime minister of Nepal through the medium of Prince Nasrullah Khan of Kabul, the brother of King Habibullah of Afghanistan, whom, it is believed, he murdered in 1919. Mahendra Partap who was a well-known Indian revolutionary and a German agent also wrote a personal letter to the Maharajah Dhiraj and the prime minister. These letters were sent through an emissary, Teja Singh. All of these letters were written in the month of June 1917. The purport of all was very similar; they stated that the British were bound to lose the war; that Nepal should not help them; that since it was the only kingdom in India which had maintained its independence it should set an example to the whole of India; that Germany would help Nepal to achieve all the goals prescribed by the Germans for Asians; that the whole of Asia would go against the British. The emissary Teja Singh gave additional information to the Durbar about the plans of Afghanistan, Persia, Mehendra Pratap and other Indian revolutionaries. He assured Nepal that the governments of India and Afghanistan were on unfriendly terms. Afghanistan was held up as the model which Nepal should imitate:

'Look at Afghanistan 'how she has been able to conserve her manpower and other resources by keeping aloof from the war. And when opportunity comes she will strike and reap large benefits. . . .'[2]

[1] 'The English are the enemies of your forefathers. They will never wish that you may improve fully or keep your independence. If you are prudent save yourself from rack and ruin by not giving way to the insincere talk of the English or by giving away your troops to them. The English, China and Tibet are your old enemies. Save and protect yourself and taking the whole of India under your hands join it with Nepal. If your troops go to fight the Germans they will never be able to return alive. Drive the English out of India. In case any terrible incident were to take place in Nepal the English will never either protect you or help you. Make your King really understand so that he may not destroy your army. Germany will win: the Feringees will suffer death.' (There was no date, no name, and no place mentioned. This could have been taken from a radio broadcast. This document was found in the Foreign Office of Nepal, Kathmandu, in *Basta No. 63*, which had most of the papers and correspondence on World War I.) *Basta No. 63*. (N.F.O.K.)

[2] Information gathered from conversation with Teja Singh. (*Vide* note of conversation with Resident on September 10, 1917), *Basta No. 77*. (N.F.O.K.)

NEPALESE-BRITISH CO-OPERATION IN WORLD WAR I

The Chancellor of Imperial Germany in his letter to the Maharajah Dhiraj wrote:

'I have come to know that the entire population are trying to set up a big force state by destroying the abominable British rule. In this war of independence the Rajas and people of India look upon you as their leader and it is only through your help that their wishes will be fulfilled.'[1]

About the Amir of Afghanistan the letter said '(he) has drawn his sword on the side of Germany, Austria-Hungary and Turkey to destroy the enemy of India'.[2] All these letters and Teja Singh's information are revealing and valuable documents on German attempts to paralyze India's contribution to the British war effort.[3]

Maharajah Chandra Shamsher took all precautions against intrigues of this nature and had several interviews with the Resident in which he passed on all the information which he had collected about German intrigues for transmission to the Government of India. The Indian Government was very grateful to the Durbar for providing the information and handing over the original letters from the Chancellor of Imperial Germany and Mahendra Pratap. At the same time the Secretary of the Indian Foreign Office was careful to assure Chandra Shamsher that the entire report given in these letters was false. The Government of India had no doubt that similar letters were sent to friends of the British and many Indian princes. According to the Government of India these letters were a part of the general attempt of the Germans to bring about a revolt against British rule. The Secretary further wrote to the Resident for the information of the prime minister that:

'As an illustration of the character of these German agents it may be mentioned that, according to the information in the possession of the Government of India, the head of the German-Indian conspiracy (is) in America. . . .'[4]

About Teja Singh, the Government of India believed that he was really named Kala Singh, and that he was an absconder in the Lahore con-

---

[1] Letter of German Imperial Chancellor to Maharajah Dhiraj of Nepal. (Note of conversation with Resident at interview on September 9, 1917.) *Basta No. 77.* (This letter was a translation into English.) (N.F.O.K.)
[2] *Ibid.*
[3] See Appendix XII.
[4] Secretary to Lt. Colonel S. F. Bayley, Resident, Simla, September 29, 1917, No. 209–I–A (C); *Basta No. 77.* (N.F.OK.)

spiracy case. He could be arrested for his previous crime if the Maharajah wished to keep his promise to him that he would not be denounced to the British as a German agent. However the Government of India felt it was for the Durbar to make the decision.[1] All these intrigues of the Germans had no adverse effect on the Durbar or on the determination of the Maharajah to support the British. The friendly cooperation between the two governments continued until victory was achieved.

This did not mean that they never differed on matters affecting their relations with one another. While the war was in progress there were constant reminders from the Maharajah to the British Government of Nepal's independent status. Other matters arose of which the most important was the question of allowing the Nepalese to cross the ocean and granting them *patia*. But these differences in no way injured their cooperation and they were discussed in an atmosphere of cordiality and friendliness. General Baber Shamsher, Inspector-General of the Nepalese forces in India, visited the Viceroy on January 1, 1916. This interview had no political significance, but was arranged to say goodbye to Lord Hardinge who was leaving India. This conversation was interesting and does give a lasting impression of how greatly the Nepalese enjoyed the company of the Viceroy of India. It also indicates how the Viceroy treated most of the Nepalese Generals.[2] Chandra Shamsher wrote a very strong letter to the Resident, Manner-Smith, on March 4, 1916, in which he set forth his grievances against the Government of India both old and new. He complained that titles had been given to Nepalese Generals without his previous knowledge. In Britain no British subject can accept a foreign title without the Queen's consent. He brought up the old question of the status of Nepal and once more criticized the 1907 edition of the Imperial Gazetteer of India, which had listed Nepal as a 'Native State'. He lamented that the prestige of his country had gone down since he came to power, and he stated that his grievances were all shared by the Bahadurs and Sardars of Nepal.[3] Chandra Shamsher's letter was followed by a meeting between General Baber Shamsher and the Viceroy. The former supported the remonstrances of his father directly to the Viceroy, Lord Hardinge, who was to leave India one month after this meeting.

[1] Secretary to Lt. Colonel S. F. Bayley, Resident, Simla, September 29, 1917, No. 209–I-A (C); *Basta No. 77*. (N.F.O.K.)
[2] See Appendix XIII. Memo of conversation with His Excellency the Viceroy and General Baber Shamsher, January 1, 1916, *Register No. 1*. (This register is in three volumes was maintained by Baber Shamsher from 1914–18. To my knowledge there is no other copy available anywhere but in the Foreign Office of Nepal, Kathmandu.)
[3] Chandra to Manner-Smith, March 4, 1916, *Basta No. 68*. (N.F.O.K.)

In reply to the General's complaint that Tibet was receiving better treatment from the British than Nepal Lord Hardinge assured him that,

'... we look upon Nepal and Nepalese as our old friend and ally, but we don't call Tibet our ally. In fact though it would not be diplomatic for me—yet it is only between you and me—I tell you that we look upon Tibet as a nuisance constantly giving us trouble, no help and secretly playing with China....'[1]

The lengthy interview gave an opportunity to Baber Shamsher to place all the grievances of his father before the Viceroy. The interview closed with an assurance by Lord Hardinge that the British Government had no intention of disrupting the existing friendly relations with Nepal.[2] Afterwards the new Viceroy, Lord Chelmsford, arrived in India. A year later the prime minister of Nepal went to Bankipore, Patna, to have a personal interview with him. After the interview the Maharajah left a note with the Viceroy in which he plainly told him of the services of Nepal to the British government. He emphasized that during his tenure of office he had done much more than any of his predecessors.[3] The new Viceroy again assured the Maharajah of the good intentions of the Government of India.[4] When the Secretary of State for India visited India in 1917, General Baber Shamsher had an interview with him and tried to impress on him the need for arms and ammunition for Nepal.[5] Throughout the period of the war it was noticed that the prime minister and by his order all members of his family tried to impress on the British Government of India the value of their services before and during the war, and at the same time strongly maintained the right to call themselves an independent ally of the British.

The Afghan War and Nepal

The armistice was signed, and the peace conference had just

[1] Memo of conversation with His Excellency and Baber Shamsher on March 27, 1916. (This register was maintained by Baber Shamsher himself in his own handwriting. There is no duplicate copy of it that I know of.) *Register No. 1.* (N.F.O.K.)

[2] See Appendix XIV. Memo of conversation with His Excellency the Viceroy and General Baber Shamsher on March 27, 1916, *Register No. 1, op. cit.* (N.F.O.K.)

[3] Petition handed over by Sir Chandra Shamsher to H.E. the Viceroy of India at Bankipore in a private interview on January 12, 1917 at 11.15 a.m. in the Government House of Bihar and Orissa, *Basta No. 64.* (N.F.O.K.)

[4] H.E. the Viceroy to Chandra Shamsher, Delhi, January 21, 1917, *ibid.*

[5] See Appendix XIII. Memo of conversation between Baber Shamsher and the Secretary of State for India when the latter visited India in 1917, *Register No. II, 1914–19.* (N.F.O.K.)

started when the Amir Habibullah of Afghanistan was assassinated and his son and successor Ammanullah threatened the peace of India. The Maharajah immediately offered the services of his troops,[1] but at first the British kept his offer in abeyance, since they thought that the war would be over in a week or so.[2] The attack turned out to be more formidable than they had anticipated, so that within a week the offer was accepted and the Maharajah was requested to send his troops.[3] The further correspondence between the Resident and the Maharajah clearly shows the sincerity and friendliness of the offer of help. Both the Resident and the Maharajah condemned the action of the Amir of Afghanistan. This time again Nepal was generous in its help. Undoubtedly the war came at a very unwelcome time, because the troops of both the Nepalese and Indian armies had been weakened by four and a half years of heavy fighting. The quality of the Indian army was decidedly inferior to what it had been in 1914, and most of the officers skilled in fighting the Pathans had been killed in France and in other places. Nonetheless the Maharajah managed to send enough help to the British. Fortunately for them the British were able to defeat the Afghans and end the war quietly and quickly.[4]

The report of the final victory of the allies in the World War came to Nepal on November 14, 1918, and this news brought relief to the entire population of the kingdom. A week later on the 21st of the same month, Nepal celebrated the victory with a parade of troops, illumination of buildings, declaring the day a public holiday for all and distribution of food and clothes to the hungry and poor. Maharajah Chandra Shamsher made a long speech on the occasion, in which he reminded the British of the timely help provided by the Durbar. He also thanked the soldiers, the Bahadurs, the noblemen and the general public of Nepal for their help and contribution to a friend and to the cause of justice and truth.[5] Asquith, the prime minister of Great Britain in a Guildhall speech of May 1915 had rightly described the help of Nepal to the British when he said, 'It was not founded on obligation but upon goodwill and sympathy'.[6] The Maharajah in his

[1] Chandra to O'Connor, the Resident, Nepal, April 20, 1919, *Basta No 56*. (N.F.O.K.)
[2] Resident to the Prime Minister of Nepal, April 28, 1919, No. 44–C/12–5 (Secret), *Basta No. 56*. (N.F.O.K.)
[3] Telegram from the Government of India to the Resident, Carrying a Message for the Maharajah, May 6, 1919, *Basta No. 56*. (N.F.O.K.)
[4] Maharajah to the Resident, Nepal, May 8, 1919, *Basta No. 56* (N.F.O.K.); Resident to Maharajah, May 9, 1919, No. 64–C/5–10 of 1919, *Basta No. 56* (N.F.O.K.); *Basta No. 63*. (N.F.O.K.)
[5] 'Victory Celebration in Nepal.' November 21, 1918, *Basta No. 63—B*. (N.F.O.K.)
[6] Asquith's speech in the Guildhall, May 1915, *Basta No. 63—B*. (N.F.O.K.)

speech at the victory celebration emphasized the same point, as the reason why he and his Government supported the British in the war. He spoke with conviction and firmness when he said:

'One and only one consideration made me decide to share the fortunes of our friend in this great war, to sink or swim with them and that was the sacred cause of friendship, a friendship over a century old, to promote which has always been my one aim and intention. The vital interest of the country, the lofty teachings of our Shastras (Hindu sacred writings) and our pride as Kshattriyas (the Hindu warrior caste to which the rulers of Nepal belonged) all, to my humble judgment, demanded that we should make whatever sacrifice was possible at such a time for such a cause.'[1]

Beside this public confession, the hidden reasons for their supporting the British could be to check the British from supporting Tibet more than Nepal; secondly, the Maharajah thought that if he were on the side of the British during World War I, the chances of getting the recognition of Nepal's full independence after the war would become obligatory on the British Government; lastly, that by supporting the British he was indirectly strengthening his position and power in the eyes of the Bahadurs and Sardars of Nepal, because the support of the British for him would be enough to close the mouth of all his opponents. Future events have proved these assumptions well founded; the Maharajah succeeded in getting all he wanted after the war for Nepal, for himself, and for his family.

[1] Maharajah's speech on the occasion of the Victory Celebration on November 21, 1918, *Basta No. 63—B.* (N.F.O.K.)

CHAPTER 6

NEPALESE–BRITISH RELATIONS BETWEEN THE WORLD WARS

With the termination of hostilities in 1918 there developed much closer, friendlier, and more cooperative relations between the two neighbors—Nepal and British India. It was pointed out in the last chapter that Nepal played a more important role in World War I than the Government of India had anticipated. Some issues which both governments had acknowledged to be important but which had been shelved during the war were now brought up for discussion. Other issues which had formerly been a serious problem had been almost forgotten. This was a clear indication that the two countries were moving towards better relations for the future.

The Problem of Pani Patyia[1]

The issue of *Pani Patyia* had been a serious problem for the Gurkha soldiers since 1900 when they were sent to China as part of the international army which captured Peking during the Boxer Rebellion and rescued the Europeans besieged in the embassies. The penalty was not imposed on those men who went to Malta, Perak and some other places but only on those who went to China and subsequently on those

---

[1] '*Pani Patyia* is apparently the ceremony of re-admission to the caste of Gurkhas who have outcasted themselves by going overseas. There is a certain number of Gurkha officers and men who have been overseas on peace duties, e.g. as Orderly Officers to the King and for whom unavailing efforts have been made for many years to get re-admission (to their caste). As stated in the draft which is for approval, their case is now considered hopeless. There is no difficulty about men who go abroad on active service.'
A. N. L. Cater, March 2, 1920.
H. R. C. Dobba, March 2, 1920.
'Memorandum from the Political Department, Government of India to the Secretary of State.' Letter No. 74-M, dated September 9, 1920. *Foreign and Political Department*, October 1920, Nos. 103–5. (Estt. B.) (N.A.I.)

who went to London as orderly officers. The panchayat (association of leaders) of a Gurkha regiment which met on March 20, 1906, decided in favor of granting *Pani Patyia* to all of them who went outside of India for any service but the Brahmins rejected the decision.[1] Even a passionate appeal made by Chandra Shamsher in 1906 to the priests and religious Pandits in the following words, failed to change their determination not to grant *Pani Patyia*:

'I have called you all here together today to help me to decide a question which is important and which presses for an immediate solution. It is a question which is intimately connected with the growth and expansion of our community and upon the proper solution of which depends so much the continued well-being of our community and country.'[2]

The issue was not solved in 1906 and was shelved until 1919 when after the war it again came up for discussion. In 1922, Maharajah Chandra Shamsher wrote to two Maharajahs of India, viz. the Maharajahs of Durbhanga and Banares. Both supported him. They urged that Hindus should be allowed to cross the sea without loss of caste provided they made some contribution to their religion in the foreign land to which they went. They cited the examples of Babu Premnanda, Vivekananda and the followers of the Islamic religion. They hoped that the Maharajah of Nepal would be able to persuade the Hindu priests. The Maharajah of Banares requested the prime minister to treat this subject carefully, since otherwise he thought it would affect the Hindu religion adversely.[3] This discussion among the Hindu Rajahs and their liberal attitude had no effect upon the Brahmin orthodox priests. Therefore, the Brahmin decision of 1920 remained in effect, that no Gurkha could go overseas except on active service without being outcasted; that all of the Gurkha officers and men then in England (some 90 in number but all of them were not King's orderlies) would be outcasted; that except for active service, no drafts could be sent from India to those Gurkha battalions which were then overseas; that except for active service, no Gurkha battalions could, in the future, be

---

[1] Panchayat held by the Gurkha Officers of the 1/4 Gurkhas in respect of the support of Pani Patyia by the Nepal authorities. March 20, 1906, *Basta No. 75*. (N.F.O.K.)
[2] Speech of Maharajah Chandra Shamsher, in April 1906, *Basta No. 75*. (N.F.O.K.)
[3] Chandra Shamsher to Maharajah of Banaras, Nepal, October 27, 1922; Maharajah Durbhanga to Chandra Shamsher, Durbhanga, November 4, 1922; Maharajah Banaras to Chandra Shamsher, November 14, 1922, and February 26, 1923, *Basta No. 75*. (N.F.O.K.)

used anywhere else except in India.[1] Chandra Shamsher was very sympathetic to the Gurkha soldiers but he could not oppose the priesthood of his country. At that time the question for the British Government of India was 'whether in the future Gurkhas should be employed in India only, or to garrison their overseas possessions ?'[2] As always since the Indian Mutiny, the Government of India was afraid to interfere in any way with the religions of India. With the passing of time the question has been answered. Gradually after World Wars I and II more and more Hindus and even orthodox Hindus travelled in European countries. The priest class no more made difficulties on this issue. The King of Nepal and other orthodox enlightened Hindu rulers took the lead in breaking down this old religious rule.

Rewards and Titles

The prime ministers of Nepal from the time of Jung Bahadur to Mohan Shamsher, the last Rana prime minister, were all delighted to receive British titles. Every one of them and their relatives had some title attached to their names. Chandra Shamsher received almost all British titles including military titles.[3] During the First World War he was made an Honorary General in the British Army. After the war Chandra Shamsher accepted, although reluctantly, for his generals and officers the titles of Knight Commander of the Star of India for General Sir Baber Shamsher, and three Knights Commander of the Indian Empire for three other generals. He was not happy on this issue because of a rumor in Nepal as to the grant of titles even before it was known to him. Therefore, he changed some of them and recommended twelve other officers for the title of Companion of the Indian Empire. The reason for this was that the Order of British India and the Indian Meritorious Medal were mostly conferred on subjects of princely States, and might therefore be taken to imply that Nepal would fall into this category. He also asked for twenty Indian Distinguished Service Medals as these had no implications of status and could be conferred on any soldiers serving in India.[4] In return for the assistance

---

[1] Memorandum, No. 74-M, dated September 9, 1920, *Foreign and Political Department*, October 1920, Nos. 103–5. (Estt. B.) (N.A.I.)

[2] *Ibid.*

[3] Chandra's British titles: (KCSI), GCBI, GCMG, GCVO, DCL, Honorary General, British Army; Honorary Colonel, Fourth Gurkhas. Jung Bahadur had only (KCSI), GCB, and GCSI.

Landon, *op. cit.*, p. 245.

[4] W. F. T. O'Connor, Resident to Sir John Wood, Secretary, Political Department, Government of India, No. 63-C dated Camp Raxaul December 31, 1918 (Confidential). *Foreign and Political Department Internal—B Proceedings*, July 1919, Nos. 85–104. (N.A.I.)

provided by the Nepal Government and himself, the Government of India suggested the following rewards for the consideration of the British Government:

(I) the status of Nepal might be so raised as to differentiate it unmistakably from the Indian Native States;
(II) 'His Majesty' might be recognized as the title of the Maharajadhiraj;
(III) the Prime Minister might be addressed as 'His Highness' instead of 'His Excellency';
(IV) the Prime Minister or his representative when visiting India on a mission from the Nepal Government, might be given the title of 'Ambassador' in place of that of 'Envoy';
(V) some additional territory might be given to Nepal on the Philibit border or elsewhere, or some land might be given in perpetuity to the prime minister;
(VI) facilities might be offered to the Nepal Government for purchasing and importing cannons, rifles, ammunition, and warlike stores;
(VII) a gift of magazine rifles and ammunition might be made to the contingent of the Nepalese army when they returned from India to Nepal;
(VIII) a gift of machine guns with ammunition might be made to the prime minister (for his personal protection) at the conclusion of the war or as soon as the guns could be spared.[1]

These recommendations were made because, although the prime minister liked to receive titles for himself and for his relatives or officers, he also wanted rewards that were much more substantial than mere 'status symbols'. He wished to show his people that his policy of giving aid to the Government of India had been of benefit to the country. This in turn would strengthen his position as the virtual ruler of Nepal. He knew that Nepal's generous assistance had put the Government of India under a heavy obligation, and he pressed his advantage with astute diplomacy. These recommendations were made in 1919 and 1920, and by the end of 1923 all but one were accepted by the British Government. In place of additional territory, an annual present of ten lakhs of rupees ($200,000) was granted in 1920. The Maharajah Dhiraj was called 'His Majesty' and the prime minister 'His

[1] 'Summary of discussion on the subject of the honours and rewards which might be conferred on the Maharajadhiraja of Nepal and the Prime Minister for the assistance rendered to the British Government by the Nepal Government in connection with the war.' *Foreign and Political Department Secret Internal Proceedings*, July 1919, Nos. 36–65. (N.A.I.)

Highness' on the ground that he was the Maharajah of the states of Kaski and Lamjang which were part of Nepal. The name of the Residency was changed to 'Legation', the Resident was called the 'Minister', and the Residency surgeon was called 'legation Surgeon'. The former title of 'Durbar' was changed to 'Government of Nepal'. All these changes came in 1919–20.[1] The question of a subsidy of ten lakhs of rupees was debated. The prime minister wanted no conditions attached to it. The wording of the grant was as follows:

'... the annual present of ten lakhs of rupees will be paid in perpetuity unless and until the friendly relations which so happily subsist between the countries are broken off....'[2]

Eventually the original word 'subsidy' was substituted for 'annual present'.[3] Under recommendation VII, the Nepalese contingent was allowed to take back with them to Nepal, in order to mark the debt of gratitude which the Government of India owed to Nepal, all the arms and equipment which they received while serving in India. In all this included 8,000 M.L. rifles, with ammunition and 80 Lewis guns with ammunition.

Recommendation VIII provided four Maxim guns for the prime minister's own protection and with permission that if he wished he could present them to the Nepal Government subsequently.

Treaty of Friendship—1923

Ever since Maharajah Chandra Shamsher first came into power, the vital and fundamental aim of his policy had been the negotiation of a new treaty, replacing the Treaty of Segowlee which would fully and unequivocally recognize the independence of Nepal. This had been

[1] Resident to the officials of the Government of India, September 29, 1920; Secretary, Government of India to Resident, D.O. No. 2607-E.B., October 26, 1920, *Basta No. 68–B;* Note on the talk which H.H. the Maharajah had with Colonel O'Connor on December 15, 1918, *Basta No. 68* (N.F.O.K.): Resident and Government of India's correspondence on the question of changing the name of Residency and others, *Foreign and Political Department External—A;* March 1920, Nos. 1–8; *Foreign and Political Department*, October 1920, Nos. 103–5 (Estt. B.) (N.A.I.) 'Correspondence between Resident and other officials of the Government of India on the question of honours and Rewards to Nepal Government.' *Foreign and Political Department Internal—B Proceedings*, July 1919, Nos. 85–104; *Foreign and Political Secret Internal Proceedings*, August 1919, Nos. 1–6; *Foreign and Political Department Internal—A*, November 1919; Nos. 93–5. (N.A.I.)

[2] Resident to Maharajah, October 16, 1919, *Register No. 1.* (N.F.O.K.)

[3] L. D. Wakely to Government of India, India Office, Whitehall, London, September 8, 1919, P.-4418 (Immediate). *Foreign and Political Department Internal—B Proceedings*, November 1921, Nos. 178–96. (N.A.I.)

sought by all his predecessors from Sir Jung Bahadur onward. Chandra Shamsher decided to achieve his purpose by peaceful and friendly cooperation. In spite of disappointments he never abandoned his policy or changed his tactics. Before he went to England and even more so after his return, he broached the idea to the Resident. The Government of India politely evaded any clear definition of Nepal's status. During the years of World War I, Chandra Shamsher gave unstinted help and at the same time made it clear that his purpose was unaltered. His opportunity came after the war and he then pressed for it because he knew he had put the British under a heavy obligation. The matter was raised in Kathmandu, discussed at length at Delhi, and referred to the India Office in London. Correspondence passed back and forth between three capitals, discussing, debating, and analyzing the pros and cons of a new treaty. It would entail the abrogation of Article VII of the Treaty of 1815 which forbade the Maharajah Dhiraj ever to employ or retain in his service 'any British subject, nor the subject of any European and American States without the consent of the British Government'.[1] The cancellation of Article VII would give Nepal a free hand to employ or retain such a person and to make contacts with any country in the world.

Another question was whether concessions on the importation of arms and ammunition should be granted. For this the Government of India had always had a marked lack of enthusiasm, but the Indian army was anxious about its effect on Gurkha recruiting. The Foreign Department of the Government of India wanted to know whether it could control foreign relations of Nepal, whether Nepal would be allowed to establish diplomatic relations with foreign states, and above all what benefit both parties would obtain from a new treaty which would establish their relations on a basis of close friendship.[2]

---

[1] Aitchison, *Treaties*, Vol. XIV, p. 64 (Edition 1929). See Appendix XVI for the Treaty of 1815–16.

[2] Bray, Secretary, Government of India to Resident Kennion, D.O. No. 372-E.B. Delhi, February 2, 1921; Kennion to Bray, Confidential. D.O. No. 133-C.; Kennion to Government of India, Confidential, Letter No. 19-C, British Legation, Nepal, April 26, 1921; Viceroy to the Secretary of State for India, No. 49, May 26, 1921; Kennion to Government of India, Confidential, No. 1201-E.B., Simla, September 16, 1921; Secretary of State to Viceroy, December 6, 1921 (P. 4957); W. F. T. O'Connor to Government of India.

'Proposed cancellation of Article 7 of the Treaty with Nepal of 1815'; Letter to His Majesty's Secretary of State for India; *Foreign and Political Department Secret External*, No. 49, May 26, 1921. (P. 2637), 1921. (F and P Press-No. 4036–18–5–11–34.) (I.O.L. Microfilm.)

W. F. T. O'Connor to Government of India Confidential. Enclosure No. 7. Letter No. 44-C.C.P., dated Camp *via* Raxaul, January 4, 1922; O'Connor to the Secretary, Government of India, Political Department, Enclosure No. 8. Letter No. 50-C.C.p., dated Camp *via* Raxaul, February 8, 1922 (Confidential);

Sir Arthur Hirtzel, the Under-Secretary of State for India, drew up a draft treaty for the consideration of the Government of India in 1922. In a long memorandum he outlined some of his fears about the new treaty. He was particularly apprehensive that foreign states would open diplomatic relations with Nepal, and suggested that a clause should be inserted which would prevent Communist agents and Indian seditionists from taking shelter in Nepal, because in his opinion Nepal was one of the most powerful Hindu states near India, and might one day decide to side with the Indian nationalists against the British. Hirtzel further advised that the Resident must insist on having some kind of limitation on the quantity of arms and ammunition imported. If possible, he must obtain a letter to be appended to the treaty which would agree that a list of the arms that Nepal wished to import would be submitted before the actual importation took place. Hirtzel pointed out that the demand could be justified on the ground that when Chandra Shamsher asked for the right to import arms he always cited the case of Afghanistan. The limitation he proposed would actually follow the Afghan precedent, which reserved to India the final decision on the quantity allowed to be imported. Hirtzel admitted that the right of the Government of India to limit Afghanistan's imports of arms had been weakened by a letter which Sir H. Dobbs had written to its government. In it he stated that,

'the British Government has no desire to make trifling incidents an excuse for the stoppage of such arms and munitions. It would only be in the event of the Government of Afghanistan showing plainly by its attitude that it is determined on an unfriendly and provocative course of policy towards India contrary to the neighbourly treaty above mentioned, that the latter State would exercise the right of stoppage.'[1]

O'Connor to Bray, Enc. in India Foreign Secretary's No. 36-M. dated June 1, Received June 19, 1922; Nepal, May 16, 1922, O'Connor to Secretary Government of India, Confidential. Enclosure No. 9 Letter No. 17-C; dated Nepal, June 26, 1922; Viceroy to the Secretary of State for India, July 27, 1922.
'Proposed new Treaty with Nepal.' Letter to His Majesty's Secretary of State for India, *Government of India Foreign and Political Department Secret. External*, No. 5-A, July 27, 1922. P. 3317, 1922, (G.M. Press, Simla-No. C151–FD–29–7–22–20–KCM.) (I.O.L. Microfilm.)
For detailed correspondence see *Foreign and Political Department Secret. External*, File No. 97 (External of 1922) and *Foreign and Political Department Secret*, External, File No. 97(2) X Sec. 1923. (N.A.I.). (Note: These two files contained the entire correspondence regarding the New Treaty with Nepal and other matters related to the Treaty of 1923.)

[1] Sir Arthur Hirtzel, Under-Secretary of State for India, *Political and External Files*, J.O.L.M./3/463, Part II, Notes Section, 1922. (I.O.L.) (Microfilm.)

Hirtzel did not advise that a similar letter should be written to Chandra Shamsher. Covering all contingencies Hirtzel suggested that if Chandra Shamsher should ask for a similar letter the Resident should avoid giving it on the ground that it was unnecessary, since the treaty with Nepal was only a treaty of friendship. Chandra Shamsher should be discouraged from sending an envoy to London, but if he insisted it would be rather difficult to refuse. Hirtzel was also of the opinion that a clause on the recruitment of Gurkhas for the Indian army should be included because 'it is after all, mainly because of the Gurkha element in the army that we value the friendship of Nepal'.[1]

At one point in the deliberations the Viceroy in a letter to the Secretary of State for India wrote:

'Our general conclusion, therefore, is that we should endeavour to avoid a fresh treaty with Nepal. We advise that the British Envoy should inform His Highness that we have carefully considered the question of the conclusion of a new treaty; that we feel that none is called for, since the only question outstanding between us is the question of the free import of arms; and that it seems hardly worth while drawing up a fresh Treaty on this score, as we are prepared to grant and guarantee this in a formal letter. . . .'[2]

However, after a lengthy discussion by officials in Delhi and London, a draft treaty was presented to the Prime Minister of Nepal. After full deliberation of the draft by his advisers, the Bahadurs, and the Councilmen of Nepal, the Maharajah returned the draft with some modifications to the Resident on September 10, 1923. The major change was very understandable. It was the complete rejection of Article VI of the draft treaty, which read as follows:

'Neither of the High Contracting Parties will employ subjects of the other without the previous general or special consent of the other High Contracting Parties, and each of the High Contracting Parties agrees to assist the other as here-to-fore with regard to the employment of its subjects by the other High Contracting Party.'[3]

It seems that Chandra Shamsher rejected this Article because he sensed the same limitation here which was embodied in Article VII

[1] Sir Arthur Hirtzel, *op. cit.*
[2] Viceroy to the Secretary of State for India, No. 5-A of 1922, 'Subject; Proposed New Treaty with Nepal', dated July 27, 1922. *Foreign and Political Department*, 1922. (I.O.L. Microfilm).
[3] *Foreign and Political Department*, File No. 97(2)-X Secret, 1923 (Confidential). (N.A.I.)

of the treaty of 1815 (see Appendix XVI), except that it was based on reciprocity. Instead of this article the Maharajah was ready to write a letter which would assure the enlistment of Gurkhas in the Indian army.[1] He also agreed to write a letter to be attached to Article V, on the import of arms, in the terms suggested by Sir Arthur Hirtzel. The letter would promise that when Nepal bought arms and ammunition it would submit a list to the Resident before the importation took place. The final draft submitted by the Maharajah contained only seven articles, and the treaty which was signed was the same as the draft submitted to him except for minor changes in the wording and the rejection of Article VI. Most of the proposals of Sir Arthur Hirtzel were incorporated in the treaty.

The first article of the treaty provided for lasting friendship between the British Government and Nepal and mutual recognition of 'each other's independence, both internal and external'.

This is the usual language of recognition by one independent state of another, and clearly implies the abandonment of any claim of British suzerainty over or protection of Nepal, with the normal consequence of reciprocal diplomatic relations. The second confirmed all the previous treaties and agreements since the Treaty of Segowlee except so far as they had been changed by the present treaty. The third article stated that there would be mutual consultation if any misunderstanding or dispute developed between either and a neighboring state having a common frontier with both, as such friction might lead to unfriendly relations between India and Nepal. It would be the duty of both the Governments to remove any such friction and misunderstanding. In the fourth article each state gave assurance that it would not allow its territory to be used against the other by any third state.

The fifth article was very important. It permitted Nepal to import any amount of arms, ammunition, machinery and factory material and stores, 'required or desired for the strength and welfare of Nepal', from or through British India. This arrangement should hold good for all time as long as the British Government was satisfied that the intentions of the Nepal Government were friendly and that there was no immediate danger to India from such importation. On the other hand the Nepal Government agreed not to export arms itself or to allow private individuals to do so. If the Government of India should become party to any future international regulation of arms and arms traffic, the Nepal Government must comply with the terms of the agreement in order to claim the right to import arms.

[1] *Foreign and Political Department*, No. 97(2)-X Secret, 1923. (N.A.I.)

Attached to this article was a letter written by Chandra Shamsher which embodied the terms advised by Sir Arthur Hirtzel in his memorandum on the treaty.[1] The prime minister agreed that before any arms or munitions were imported the Government of Nepal would give a list of its intended purchases to the British envoy at Kathmandu for transmission to the Government of India. The purpose of this letter was officially stated to be to give the Indian Government information upon which to base instructions to port authorities so that facilities for importation would be provided.

The correspondence of the British officials shows that they expected to use this procedure as a practical means of limiting the importation of arms and munitions despite the unqualified permission in the treaty. In his confidential memorandum Sir Arthur Hirtzel wrote:

'Assuming that the policy is approved in principle, I do not altogether share the Government of India's pessimism as to getting some of the limitations accepted by the prime minister.'

He added:

'I think that a determined attempt should be made to get the prime minister to agree to limit imports to Government purposes, and that Colonel O'Connor should be instructed not to give way on this point without reference home.'

Again discussing the treaty with Afghanistan on arms and munitions, Sir Arthur used the qualifying words, '... as it is assured that the intentions of the Government of Afghanistan are friendly and that there is no immediate danger to India from such importation'. He added: 'for what they are worth, these words or something like them might be embodied in Nepalese treaty'.[2] These arguments of Sir

---

[1] Letter from His Highness the Prime Minister of Nepal to British Envoy at the Court of Nepal. (Regarding Article V and undertaking before the importation of arms and munitions of Indian ports to furnish with a detailed list of the same.)

'Regarding the purchase of arms and munitions which the Government of Nepal buys from time to time for the strength and welfare of Nepal, and imports to its own territory from and through British India in accordance with Article V of the Treaty between the two Governments, the Government of Nepal hereby agrees that it will, from time to time before the importation of arms and munitions at British Indian ports, furnish detailed lists of such arms and munitions to the British Envoy at the Court of Nepal in order that the British Government may be in a position to issue instructions to the port authorities to afford the necessary facilities for their importation in accordance with Article VI of this Treaty.' *Foreign and Political Department External Secret*, File No. 97(2)-X Secret, 1923. (I.N.A.)

[2] Hirtzel, *op. cit.*

Arthur showed the intention of his Government. He himself remarked that 'the Afghan treaty itself is not without words of limitation'.

In actual practice the possession of full details about importations would of course enable the Government of India to consider whether such importations continued to be within the limits of kind and quantity consistent with friendly intentions of Nepal and safety for India. If these limits should be passed, the escape clause of Article V could be invoked to terminate permission to import. Of course the situation could probably be controlled by diplomatic representations without going to such lengths unless a very unusual situation arose. It would therefore seem fair to conclude that the letter of Chandra Shamsher in connection with Article V of the 1923 treaty did afford at least a practical measure of limitation despite the fact that one might interpret the language of the treaty as allowing no restriction unless the treaty itself were abrogated.

According to the sixth article no customs duties were to be levied at British Indian ports on goods in transit to the Nepal Government if a certificate were provided for the customs officer at the port. The certificate must prove that the goods imported were for the use of the state and not for that of private business interests. This concession was further increased by the remission of duty upon trade goods imported at British Indian ports for immediate transmission in bulk to Kathmandu.[1] While the treaty did not give Chandra Shamsher all that he hoped for, at least it gave him a good deal. He looked upon it with justification as the crowning achievement of almost a quarter of a century of diplomatic effort.

The Pioneer, an English language newspaper published in Allahabad, wrote an editorial in 1923 praising the treaty. The editor first of all reminded his readers of the help given by Nepal to the British during the Mutiny, the Tibet mission, the Afghan War, and the Great War, and concluded as follows:

'Nepal thus deserves the greatest consideration at the hands of the British and there will be universal satisfaction both in India and England at the fact that a new Treaty cementing the good relations and friendship which have subsisted between the two Governments has been signed.'[2]

---

[1] See Appendix Treaty of Friendship between Great Britain and Nepal signed at Kathmandu, December 21, 1923, Aitchison, *Treaties*, Vol. XIV, 1929; Landon, *op. cit.*, pp. 152–3; 'Draft Treaty as was proposed by the Nepal Government.' *Foreign and Political External Secret*, File No. 97(2)-X Secret, 1923. (I.N.A.)

[2] *The Pioneer*, Allahabad, Wednesday, December 26, 1923, p. 1.

NEPALESE-BRITISH RELATIONS BETWEEN THE WORLD WARS

In 1924 Percival Landon wrote an article on Nepal which was published in the London *Daily Telegraph*. *The Pioneer* wrote an interesting editorial which commented on it. This read in part:

'India and Her Neighbours'

'The final confirmation of the full independence Status of Nepal was recently given in a Treaty which contained no new provision in reality but merely enshrined a friendship dating as far back as 1816.

'Mr Landon goes so far as to suggest that in the whole field of international relationships, there is no such perfect example of amity between two States. He is not overstating the case for does he not quote a high official of our foreign office at Simla as having said: "We have no policy towards Nepal; we have only friendship." . . . For once it may be conceded that there is an example of graceful language of diplomacy which neither conceals nor disguises.'[1]

One result of the attainment of independence was that Nepal obtained a higher international status than previously. An indication of this was that on March 30, 1925, the French Government sent M. Danial Levi to present the insignia of a 'Grand Officer of the Legion' to Chandra Shamsher at an impressive public ceremony.[2] This was the first time that a European nation had honored the prime minister of Nepal. Previously only Britain and China had conferred a title on him. The League of Nations, too, opened communications with Nepal and invited it to take part in a conference on the abolition of slavery in various countries, including Nepal itself. Chandra Shamsher sent word to the League that he was not interested in attending the conference, since Nepal had already abolished slavery 'with the cooperation of the people and those concerned by the payment of compensation to slave owners'.[3] Under these circumstances 'there appears to be no necessity for Nepal joining the conference of those nations among whom these hated institutions and abominable practices still linger'.[4] At first the Government of India was not wholly pleased that Nepal had come in direct contact with the League of Nations. Later on, however, when the League asked Afghanistan to attend the conference, India decided that it would be better for the British representative to take the initiative

[1] *The Pioneer*, Allahabad, Friday, August 8, 1924.
[2] Landon, *op. cit.*, p. 145.
[3] Chandra to W. H. J. Wilkinson, British Envoy at the Court of Nepal March 5, 1926, *Foreign and Political Department External*, No. 259-X, 1925. (N.A.I.)
[4] *Ibid.*

and to invite Nepal's suggestions and participation in the draft convention of slavery.[1]

In November 1923 there arose a question whether Nepal could take advantage of a clause of the Versailles treaty to bring claims on behalf of Nepalese subjects injured by enemy action during the war. The British envoy to Nepal pointed out that Nepal had engaged in acts of warfare against Germany but was not a signatory of the Versailles Treaty; therefore, technically Nepal might still be at war with Germany. He suggested the difficulty might be circumvented if 'for the purpose of the Peace negotiations Nepal may be regarded as having been included with the British Empire', and inquired whether such a proposal would be 'distasteful to the Nepal Government'. The suggestion was indeed distasteful to the Government of Nepal, which urged that, since it had been associated as an independent state with Britain in the war without having actually declared war, there should be an implication she was also associated in this way in the declaration of peace. If this view should be rejected Nepal was prepared to give a separate notification ending the state of war with Germany, or perhaps to assign the Nepalese claims to a British subject for collection.[2] Chandra Shamsher had won independence for his country, and he did not intend to allow it to be classified as a British dependency.

Agitation Against Chandra Shamsher

In 1920 Chandra Shamsher, like his predecessors had his domestic enemies, but instead of organizing a *coup d'état* they went to British India and from that sanctuary carried on a propaganda war against him. The prime minister complained to the British Envoy about the agitation which was emanating from India and was attempting 'to tamper the loyalty of the troops'.[3] The Maharajah believed that the originators of this movement were the well-known Indian revolutionaries such as Lajpat Rai, Krishna Singh and Ajit Singh.[4] He received many anonymous letters criticising his administration and upbraiding him for the poverty and misery of the people of Nepal. One of the

[1] India Office, London, to Government of India, Delhi, No. P. 4165, Dy: No. 3529, December 3, 1925, *Foreign and Political Department External*, File 259-X 1925. (N.A.I.)

[2] Resident to Deputy-Secretary, Government of India, Delhi, No. 142 (Confidential) Dy: No. 3067. X, Nepal, November 28, 1923; Note from Maharajah, on Nepal's claim on Germany, *Foreign and Political Department*, File 594-X, 1923. (N.A.I.)

[3] Resident to Government of India (Confidential). No. 50-C of 1920, dated July 1, 1920, *Foreign and Political Department External—B*, August 1921, Nos. 120–37. (N.A.I.)

[4] *Ibid.*

letters, written by a Nepalese subject named Ranu Damai, stated that—

'Kami (black-smith), Sarki (shoe-maker), Damai (low-caste people, whose chief occupation is that of a tailor), and Gayan (beggers who beg by singing) are living in such a way as if they have no king. . . . There is no taste to subjects in Gorkha (i.e. Nepal) from your raj (rule). You should therefore give up the raj.'[1]

A newspaper named *Gurkhali* was published in Banares, and each of its issues contained harsh criticisms of the Maharajah. The prime minister tried very hard to persuade the Government of India to punish the agitator or send back the editor to Nepal, but to no avail.[2] The Indian Government was unhappily aware that any attempt to punish agitators who attacked Indian rulers, which would be supported by socialists and liberals in Great Britain, would lead to a violent onslaught by Indian nationalists and the vernacular press. An article 'Nepal Ki Swantantrata' (Independence of Nepal) was published under the name of 'a student of international politics', in Pratap, at Cawnpore on August 22, 1924. It included a short history of Indian–Nepalese relations and ended with the question, 'If Nepal claims to be an Independent State why does it not have ambassadors in Japan, England, France, Germany and America, in the capacity of an Independent Nation.'[3] The same article claimed that 'Nepal is the only Hindu State in the world which can, if it does not fall a victim to the designs of the British Government, become absolutely free and independent within a year or two'[4]. There was a letter to the editor in *Lansbury's Labour Weekly*, which was published in England. It read as follows:

'To His Highness the Maharajah of Nepal. Sir,—You've clicked all right; A pension of £6,000 a year for ever and ever is worth having saves anxiety about your enormous family of children and grandchildren, what? Of course, we granted it to you from the funds of the Government of India for "War services". (I seem to have missed you

---

[1] *Foreign and Political Department External—B*, August 1921, Nos. 120–37.
[2] Resident to Secretary, Government of India, No. 60-C of 1920, August 4, 1920 (Very Confidential) *Foreign and Political Department*, August 1921, Nos. 120–37. (N.A.I.). (This file carries true translations of articles from the Gurkhali newspaper.)
[3] 'Nepal Ki Swatantrata' (Independence of Nepal), by a student of International Politics. *Pratap*, Cawnpore, August 22, 1924. *Foreign and Political Department External*, File No. 229-X, 1925. (N.A.I.)
[4] *Ibid.*

when you passed through London on your way to the front, somehow.) Equally of course, the Indians were not consulted.

Lansbury's.'[1]

Of all the prime ministers of Nepal Chandra Shamsher was the most ambitious, astute, enlightened and shrewd. He bore the attacks of his countrymen who criticized him from outside the country, and held the confidence of his relatives, noblemen, and the Bahadurs (army officers). He did all that he could to raise the status of his country and of himself abroad at the cost of the general public, and of his king. No Rana prime minister of Nepal was completely selfless, and Chandra was no exception to this rule. The object of all of them was to stay in power, first of all for their own benefit, secondly for that of their relatives, thirdly to benefit their friends and supporters, and last of all to help their people and country. None could claim to be an exception to this attitude. However, if Chandra Shamsher's motive was self-serving in seeking independence for Nepal in order to maintain his personal position, it also coincided with the interest of the state. Of all the prime ministers he did most to assure a strong and independent state.

A Lull Before the Storm

The death of Sir Chandra Shamsher brought Bhim Shamsher to the Gaddi (Office) of the prime ministership of Nepal in November 1929. After the negotiation of the Treaty of 1923, most of the issues which had in the past occupied the time, energy and diplomacy of the British Indian Government and Nepal's prime ministers had almost disappeared from the scene. Such questions as independence, the status of Nepal, the importation of arms and ammunition and trade and customs duties had been settled to the satisfaction of both parties. Nepal had nothing to fear from her neighbors since China was distracted by civil war and Tibet was intent on preserving its independence from Chinese control. Chandra Shamsher left a strong administration at home and friendly neighbors for his successors. However, a new phenomenon, nationalism, appeared in India and indeed all over Asia. Its growth was accelerated by World War I. In India the nationalists were hostile to the Indian princes as much as to British rule. Nepal was affected along with the rest of the Indian sub-continent. By the end of World War II nationalism had completely undermined the old form of government to bring a new order in India.

[1] Letter to the Editor, *Lansbury's Labour Weekly*, June 27, 1925. *Foreign and Political Department*, File No. 373-X, Part 2, 1925. (N.A.I.)

In Nepal itself the struggle for power within the ruling class continued as before. In 1930 Bhim Shamsher defeated a murderous attempt on his life by his grandson, and the same year he crushed a minor revolution when a small group of Nepalese in Kathmandu broke into, and stole arms from the arsenal.[1] In 1931 he visited India and the Viceroy, Lord Willingdon, ordered his Foreign and Military Secretaries to go in person to the railway station to meet the Maharajah on his arrival.[2] In a personal interview Lord Willingdon repeated an earlier request that he be allowed to visit Nepal. The Maharajah took the same attitude as his predecessors and politely but firmly declined to allow him.[3] Bhim Shamsher was informed by the Governor-General that the Italian and Chinese Governments wished to confer honors upon him and he decided to accept them.[4] Tuker wrote that Maharajah Juddha Shamsher succeeded his brother Bhim Shamsher at the end of 1931. This would mean that Bhim Shamsher died at the end of 1931.[5] But according to Fisher and Rose, Juddha Shamsher became prime minister in September 1932.[6] Their date seems to be more accurate because Bhim Shamsher visited India in December 1931.[7] Before his death Chandra Shamsher had broached the question of changing the name of the British Minister to its full title 'Envoy Extraordinary and Minister Plenipotentiary'. This was finally accepted by the British Government in 1934 during the rule of Juddha Shamsher. In changing the name of the British Minister at the Court of Nepal the Foreign Secretary wrote,

'The Government of India's views on the general question of upholding Nepal's status as an independent Kingdom (if only as a useful counter devise to Afghanistan) remain as before, and it seems to them as well to accede to the Prime Minister's wishes in this matter.'[8]

The question of appointing a Nepalese Minister at the Court of St James's was also raised by Chandra Shamsher.

---

[1] Tuker, op. cit., p. 204.
[2] Conversation Notes between Bhim Shamsher and the Viceroy, Lord Willingdon, October 15, 1931, Basta No. 42-B. (N.F.O.K.)
[3] Ibid.
[4] Ibid.
[5] Tuker, op. cit., p. 204.
[6] Fisher and Rose, op. cit., p. 14.
[7] Foreign and Political Department, File No. 96(4)-H, 1934. (N.A.I.)
[8] J. C. Acheson, for foreign Secretary to J. C. Walton, Secretary, Political Department, India Office, London. Simla, September 19, 1929, D.O. No. D. 3011-X. Foreign and Political External Secret, File No. 273-X, 1929. (N.A.I.)

'The Government of India dislikes the idea of Nepal being represented in London; first, because it would mean waste of money and time, as regards the actual prosecution of business sheer camouflage; secondly, because of the possibility that this slight opening of the Nepalese door might encourage foreign Powers to endeavour to get the door opened a little wider so as to admit others than ourselves to Kathmandu.'[1]

But finally in 1934 under the prime minister, Maharajah Juddha Shamsher, Nepal appointed its first Minister to the Court of St James's.[2] Nepal was represented at the coronation of King George VI by its foreign minister Kaiser Shamsher.[3]

During Juddha's term of office a serious earthquake took place in India and Nepal. When offered relief by the Indian Government, Juddha Shamsher declined the offer and said, 'if I have not taken too much advantage of the offer it is not because of pride but because of profound sympathy in their (the Indians) own distress'.[4] He wished to gain sympathy of the Indians and for that reason he wanted publicity in India, as is evident from Metcalf's statement. H. A. F. Metcalf, of the foreign and political department of the Government of India wrote to E. C. Mieville, Private Secretary to the Viceroy that 'Daukes and I both think that the Maharajah would be glad to have publicity given to his reasons for declining to accept assistance'.[5]

Juddha Shamsher had to cope with growing hostility from the nationalists, both Indian and Nepalese, against the rule of the Rana family. In 1937 the People's Committee was formed in Nepal; another organization, Nepal Praja Parished, was also in existence for some time. A Bihar newspaper, *Janata*, in 1938 criticized the Rana Government and particularly Juddha Shamsher himself. The agitation against the Rana and in favor of the king was directed from Indian territory.[6] The Rana prime ministers remained helpless against this agitation although they tried to suppress it by force, as the Indian Princes did.

A new development started in the relations between the prime

[1] Davis Bray, *Foreign and Political Department*, New Delhi, December 5, 1929. Confidential D.O. No. 273-K/29, to J. C. Walton, Secretary, Political Department, India Office, London. *Foreign and Political External Secret*, File No. 373-X, 1929. (N.A.I.)
[2] Tuker, *op. cit.*, p. 204.
[3] Ibid.
[4] Juddha Shamsher to Daukes, British Envoy, February 11, 1934; *Foreign and Political Department External*, File No. 39-X, 1934, p. 55. (N.A.I.)
[5] H. A. F. Metcalf to E. C. Mieville, Private Secretary to the Viceroy, February 20, 1934. *Foreign and Political External*, File No. 39-X, 1934. (N.A.I.)
[6] Tuker, *op. cit.*, p. 207.

minister of Nepal and the influential political, social and religious groups of India in the nineteen-thirties. Previously when Nepalese prime ministers visited India they were the guests of the Government of India and they had no contact with any Indian princes or political parties. When Juddha Shamsher decided to visit India in 1935, political, social and religious organizations made overtures to him. Among them were the Hindu Mahasabha, Rajput Prantik, an organization in Delhi, a Gurkha organization named 'Gurkha up Karni Mittra Mandal', the Hindu residents of Delhi, the Maharajah of Patiala, and other ruling princes of India, besides many prominent Hindus of India such as Sir Sri Ram and Dr B. S. Moonje, the former President of the All India Hindu Mahasabha. They expressed the wish either to have a personal interview with the Maharajah or to present an address to him. The Maharajah could not meet any ruling prince owing to lack of time, and also because it would be impolite to meet one and not another. However, he did accept the invitations of some organizations.[1] To Dr Moonje he sent a blunt reply through his secretary which read, 'Thanks for your kind thought of writing. As His Highness's time is all taken up and he is returning soon, you need not take the trouble of coming'.[2] Juddha's interviews with some of the nationalist leaders had no political effect on Nepal or India. But after 1935 this sort of meeting did not take place between Juddha and organizational leaders of India. In fact none of the important political leaders or parties, like the Indian National Congress or the All-India Muslim League, tried to make contact with the Rana group. The Congress leaders in India were mostly interested in Nepal's political leaders, such as the Koirala brothers and others, and they did have contact with them. The result of these contacts came in 1950 when the Rana rule was overthrown.[3] During the rule of Juddha Shamsher a letter was received from Mr

[1] Letters from Honorable Secretary, All India Hindu Mahasabha; Jagdish Singh, President, Surat Singh, General Secretary, Sri Ram Sing, Secretary, Rajput Prantik, Dehli Province; Shib Saran Singh, Narain Singh Thapa, Shobha Singh, Dan Singh Thapa, Pratap Sing Panre, Shil Chand Thakur, Sheo Singh Bhist, Bali Ram, Prem Singh, Rap Singh Pauri, B. S. Thakur, Sharam Singh, Akber Adhikari, on behalf of Gurkha Up Karni Mittra Mandal, January 27, 1935; letter was sent from Birle House on behalf of Hindus of Delhi, January 27, 1935; Sir Sri Ram to the Private Secretary of Maharajah, two letters by Dr Moonje to the Private Secretary of the Maharajah, *Basta No. 43*. (N.F.O.) (last two letters were written on January 26 and 21, 1935, respectively). Maharajah of Patiala to B. J. Glancy, Political Secretary, Government of India. November 20, 1934, *Foreign and Political Department Honours—Br.*, File No. 94 (16)-Honours/1933. (N.A.I.)

[2] Private Secretary of the Maharajah to Dr Moonje, *Basta No. 43*.

[3] This is not the place to discuss this issue in detail. In this connection see, *Politics in Nepal*, by Anirudha Gupta. (Allahabad: Allied Publishers Private Ltd., 1964.)

William H. Dinkins, Executive Officer, Selma University, Alabama, addressed to King Tribhuvan of Nepal, for help in raising some University Fund. The University requested the King to send one book with his autograph in it so that it could be given to one of the university's fund raisers, or to a church as a reward for helping in raising coupons or money.[1] Although the king of Nepal had no importance in those days this shows that even a University in Selam was aware that the attraction of an autographed volume by the king of a mysterious kingdom in the Himalayas would obtain more money or coupons for the University. It is not known whether the king sent the book as requested.

The French again honored the prime minister of Nepal with the insignia of The Grand Cross of the Legion of Honor and also gave the Commander in Chief, Sir Kaiser Shamsher the rank of Grand Officer of the Legion. A special French mission went to Kathmandu for this purpose on May 19, 1934.[2] Juddha Shamsher enjoyed all ceremonies as his predecessors had before him. The decade from 1929 to 1939 was the smoothest, most uneventful, friendliest, and dullest period in the history of British–Nepalese relations. This was no reflection on the personalities or abilities of the two prime ministers, Bhim Shamsher and Juddha Shamsher. The traditional causes of friction had been disposed by Chandra Shamsher in the treaty of 1923. Relations with the Government of India were cordial, and nothing occurred to affect the friendly cooperation of the two administrations.

Also see *Gorkha: The Story of the Gurkhas of Nepal*, by Sir Francis Tuker, Chapters 25 to 29.

[1] William H. Dinkins, Executive Officer, Selma University, Selma, Alabama, U.S.A., to His Majesty the King Tribhuvan, of Nepal, January 5, 1935, Basta No. 61. (N.F.O.K.)

[2] Daukes to Foreign Secretary, Government of India, May 30, 1934. D.O. No. 2759-X/34, No. 2/144-C. *Foreign and Political External*, File No. 229-X, 1934. (N.A.I.)

PART III

THE LAST PHASE AND OTHER PROBLEMS

CHAPTER 7

THE LAST PHASE

Indian–Nepalese Co-operation During World War II
World War II once again brought the British and the Nepalese closer to each other, and during this crisis Nepal came forward with generous help to its friend and ally, the British.

Nepal's Military and Material Help to the British
The generosity and friendship of the Nepalese Government and the gallantry of the Gurkhas in World War I were well remembered by the British Government. During the Second World War, the same help and friendship came from Nepal. The first offer of help came during the Munich crisis when the prime minister Juddha Shamsher made an offer to the Foreign Office in London to send 8,000 picked men of Nepal's Army for garrison duty in India. This move of Juddha Shamsher to offer the help direct to the British Government in London, was to show the independence of Nepal and also to impress on others that Nepal was not like a princely state of India. Chamberlain's government declined the offer since it hoped that peace had been assured by the Munich Agreement. But the following year Germany's invasion of Poland brought about a declaration of war by Great Britain and France. The same offer was then renewed by the prime minister of Nepal. This time it was gratefully accepted by the British Government and the Government of India. The entire staff of the Maharajah started working to implement the offer, and the further training of the troops who were to go to India was started. Details regarding the contingent, financial, organizational, and otherwise, were worked out. By the end of November 1939 General Bahadur Shamsher, the general in command, went to Delhi. General Bahadur and General de Burgh signed an agreement on behalf of the Nepalese and Indian governments.[1] This

---

[1] 'The speech was delivered by the British Envoy, Geoffrey Betham at the Singh Durbar on March 20, 1942.' *Basta No. 54.* (N.F.O.K.)

covered such points as the duties of the soldiers, their strength, the cost, how they would be paid their pension, the grant of honors and awards, the rations to be supplied to them, the maintenance of discipline and the type of military law to which they would be subject, where they should be quartered, how and by whom they would be trained, what should be the procedure of their reception, with what rifles, machine guns, and other equipment they would be supplied, and when, what sort of tentage they would be given, who would supply them with clothing, whether they should bring their own entrenching tools, what should be the charges, who would pay for their transportation, and finally what medical facilities would be given to them.[1] To this agreement three Annexes were attached. Annexe A dealt with the 'rates of allowance paid to the Nepalese contingent by the Government of India in 1915–1918', Annexe B discussed the 'scale of Indian troops' daily rations scale, and Annexe C laid down rules for 'Cadre Training of Nepalese officers and non-commissioned officers'.[2] The most important condition was that the Nepalese contingent would serve in India and would not be called upon to go overseas.[3]

The question of sending the Nepalese troops overseas again came up in a meeting between General Bahadur and the Commander-in-Chief of the Indian army, the British Minister in Nepal, and the Viceroy on December 20, 1941. General Bahadur presented the letter of the Maharajah to the Viceroy which clearly stated that the Nepalese troops should not be sent overseas. The Viceroy wanted to know if there would be any objection to sending the troops to Burma. The first answer of General Bahadur was that it could not be allowed, presumably because there were no roads or railways between Burma and India, and all communication was by sea. General Bahadur explained to the Viceroy that the Maharajah was having trouble on this point with the religious leaders of Nepal. On this the Viceroy said '. . . that in the circumstances, the time had almost arrived to ask Your Highness to take the troops of the Nepalese contingent back to Nepal as the conditions under which they could be employed were so restricted as to make them of little value'.[4] This put General Bahadur in a very delicate position. He replied, 'that if the enemy was at the *frontier of India* he thought that they might go into Burma for a short time'.[5] This incident shows that the Nepalese Government did not

---
[1] Nepalese Contingent for service in India. Conditions of Service. *Basta No. 61.* (N.F.O.K.)
[2] Ibid.
[3] *Basta No. 54, op. cit.*
[4] Geoffrey Betham, British Minister in Nepal to Maharajah Juddha Shamsher, December 21, 1941, No. 2/292-C. *Basta No. 61.* (N.F.O.K.)
[5] Ibid.

want to withdraw their support to the British even if it meant going as far as they could to circumvent the ruling laid down by their Brahmin priests in World War I. Juddha Shamsher's refusal to agree to service overseas applied only to the contingent of the Nepalese army and not to the Gurkhas who had enlisted in the Indian army. This is shown by a speech of Betham, the British envoy at Kathmandu, which he made on March 20, 1942. In it he remarked:

'... I have forgotten to say that on June 16th Your Highness agreed readily to all the Gurkha Regiments of our Army going overseas.'[1]

Presumably, Juddha Shamsher felt that he could not dictate the terms of military service of those of his subjects who had enlisted in the Indian army. Furthermore, he wanted to help the British and not to hamper them. During the first years of the war when Germany was conquering one country after another, the confidence of the Maharajah was not shaken. On June 14, 1940, following the capitulation of France, the Indian Government requested six Gurkha battalions for certain and three more if required, all to be taken from the ten existing Gurkha Regiments. This would entail the enrolment of 7,000 recruits from the recruiting area in Nepal, and an intake of 3,500 men a year would be required as replacements. The prime minister replied that already 14,000 willing recruits were waiting to enlist. On July 22, 1942, there was need for 660 recruits for the 10th Gurkha Rifles, and the Maharajah gladly granted permission for the recruitment. In the same year, on September 16th, the Government of India requested ten more battalions and the Maharajah at once agreed. Within three months recruits had doubled the number of Gurkha battalions of the Indian army.[2] Whenever the Maharajah received a request from the Government of India for Gurkha soldiers he invariably complied with it. He showed complete loyalty to his ally and confidence in ultimate victory.

Besides supplying recruits for the British, recruits for the British Gurkha regiments and Nepalese troops for the garrison in India, the Maharajah sent fifty cigarettes, a photograph of himself with a message on the reverse, a pound of tea, a pound of sugar, and a pound of biscuit to each of the Gurkha soldiers. Even the Bada Maharani (Juddha Shamsher's wife) contributed one lakh of rupees ($20,000) to the Viceroy's war fund, to be divided between the Indian Red Cross Society, the St John Ambulance Association, and the British Red Cross Society. Upon learning through the newspapers that Eastern London had been burned, the Maharajah asked his Minister in London

[1] Betham's speech of March 20, 1942. *Basta No. 61.* (N.F.O.K.)
[2] *Ibid.*

to contribute Rs. 25,000 ($5,000) for the relief of the sufferers. Another lakh of rupees ($20,000) was given to the Viceroy's war fund to be used for the sick and wounded and sufferers in the war. The two junior Maharanis (other wives of the Maharajah) contributed rupees 5,000 ($1,000) to Lady Linlithgow's fund for the purchase of ambulances. On April 15, 1941, on his sixty-seventh birthday, the Maharajah contributed Rs. 15,000 ($3,000) to the St John Relief Fund, 15,000 more to be divided between the widows and orphans of soldiers of the Indian Army, who had been killed and wounded, and £4,560 ($18,240) to the flying squadron fund to provide a canteen for each of the eight squadrons. When Generalissimo Chiang Kai-shek visited India the Maharajah gave Rs. 50,000 ($10,000) to the Chinese Red Cross Fund.[1] Many other small financial contributions to war funds were made by the Maharajah.

At the beginning of the war the Maharajah agreed to the British request for 3,000 walnut trees for the manufacture of rifle butts. Out of the 3,000 trees one thousand were given free of charge as a gift. The Maharajah sent to the Government of India 192 service revolvers, 144 binoculars, 25 Vickers machine-guns and 70 Lewis guns for the use of the regular army, or of the new territorial formations which were being raised in India. When the Government of India needed more railway sleepers the Maharajah was approached. In spite of the fact that all forests of sal-wood had been leased to contractors, the Maharajah managed to send the sleepers from the Morang and Charkos forest areas and also managed to obtain some 800 sal trees.[2] When the British Government decided to requisition all railings from houses in London for making munitions, apart from railings of embassies, the Nepalese Minister voluntarily gave his railings.[3] The provision of soldiers and the contributions in money and kind which have just been described are not a complete list of the help given by Juddha Shamsher. Many other instances could be given of his assistance in providing soldiers and other forms of aid. The examples listed are enough to show the whole-hearted cooperation of Nepal and its prime minister.

The Quit India Movement and the Role of Nepal

The position of Nepal *vis-à-vis* the Government of India was decidedly delicate at a time when most of the leaders of the Indian Nationalist movement were fighting for immediate independence. The Muslim League and its leaders also demanded ultimate independence, but not until their demand for Pakistan was accepted. They did not join the

[1] Betham's speech, March 20, 1942, *op. cit.*
[2] *Basta No. 54, op. cit.*
[3] *Ibid.*

THE LAST PHASE

Quit India Movement sponsored by the Indian National Congress. It was clear that before many years had passed British rule in India would end, and the government would be controlled by the Congress Party. The British could leave India, but Nepal would remain to make terms with the new rulers. Juddha Shamsher feared that they might not be well disposed towards a ruler who had identified himself with the vanished regime. In a letter to the British Envoy in Nepal he expressed his feelings frankly and clearly.

'... Now Sir Stafford [Cripps] has gone a step further with what appears to be a definite plan of the course to be followed. The consideration of the reformed Indian Constitution may possibly have some repercussions on the future foreign relations of India, in which case we have every reason to hope that the British Government will not forget that Nepal has all along stood as a firm friend and ally of Britain never failing to render valuable friendly service from time to time and taking into consideration the removal of the difficulties Nepal is working under.'[1]

When the Congress Party launched a civil disobedience movement in India on August 8, 1942, North Bihar and some parts of the United Provinces which had a common frontier with Nepal were the most disturbed areas. The result was that communications between India and Nepal were completely severed for some weeks. As a rule Juddha Shamsher refrained from any public comment on Indian politics, but on this occasion he condemned the action of the Congress party and called the Congress men 'hooligans'. The prime minister complained to the British envoy that although the Government of India had known that the policy of Congress was to launch a non-cooperation movement in India, yet it took no precautions to keep open a road or railway from India to Nepal or to prevent the civil disobedience movement from crossing the frontier into Nepal. He set forth the policy of his government towards nationalist movements in India in the following despatch:

'It is perfectly well known to the Government of India that the policy of Nepal is one of seclusion. We don't interfere with the internal affairs of India nor do we at all like to poke our nose into the political movements and policies followed in that country.'[2]

He further pointed out that since Nepal was a land-locked state, it

[1] Juddha to Betham, April 1, 1942. *Basta No. 54.* (N.F.O.K.)
[2] Juddha to Betham, Nepal, September 2, 1942. *Basta No. 79.* (N.F.O.K.)

depended upon Indian means of communication for contact with the outer world:

'The Governments of India and Bihar are fully aware that, with all our policy of seclusion, we require to keep at least one main line of communication—our life line, we may say, open.'[1]

Juddha Shamsher went on to say what he thought of the neglect of Nepal's interests with unusual frankness. In addition to his anger over the failure to keep open communications, he believed that the Government of India regarded Nepal as a minor ally whose interests could be disregarded. The material injury suffered was linked in his mind with the psychological grievance of the status of Nepal in the mind of the Government of India. He wrote,

'... Indeed in such circumstances one might be excused if he happens to wonder whether all this indifference was due to the idea that Nepal's friendship is too cheap or that the existence of the British Minister in Nepal is of no consequence to them. I have been harping on the latter point ever since His Britannic Majesty's Envoy Extraordinary and Minister Plenipotentiary was accredited to the Court of Nepal, who though regarded as such by the British Government is evidently treated as no better than a second class Resident by the Government of India.'[2]

In another paragraph of the same letter the prime minister wrote:

'... But to my great disappointment no plane appeared after that for four days consecutively. I can very well realize from what I myself felt what your feeling must have been. It is because in Bihar where I know you are invariably referred to as a Resident and regarded as one of the second class Residents, your word does not carry the weight of a Minister Plenipotentiary. This is indeed humiliating and annoying.'[3]

His continued complaints of being treated badly by the Government of Bihar and India finally brought a soothing reply from the Viceroy. He deeply regretted that Nepal's communications had been disrupted, and he was gratified to observe that in spite of all the difficulties the prime minister had remained unshaken in his friendship.[4]

[1] Juddha to Betham, Nepal, September 2, 1942. *Basta No. 79.* (N.F.O.K.)
[2] Ibid.
[3] Ibid.
[4] Lord Linlithgow to Juddha Shamsher, The Viceroy House, New Delhi, September 17, 1942. *Basta No. 79.* (N.F.O.K.)

THE LAST PHASE

When it became clear in the first part of 1942 that the Japanese army would conquer Burma and attack India, the bulk of the Indian army was stationed along the North West Frontier in anticipation of a German invasion. The army had to be moved from one side of India to the other, and prepare defences to meet the attack which was expected in the autumn after the rainy season ended. The Indian army was too weak to repel the Japanese invasion, and heavy reinforcements were sent from Great Britain. When the civil disobedience movement began in August 1942, the disturbances were so serious that the army on the Burma frontier was cut off from its supply bases in India. The probability is that the Government of India was not able to keep open communications with Nepal, or to spare soldiers to patrol the frontier between it and India.

The prime minister further complained that when the Governments of India and Bihar knew about the Congress civil disobedience movement they took no precautionary measures to guard the frontier between India and Nepal. He was approached by the British Minister to lend him a battalion of the Nepalese army to open up the communication of Raxaul, a border town, with Darbhanga in the East and Segowlee in the South and West, on the Indian side of the frontier, which had been closed by the civil disobedience movement. He explained his refusal as follows:

'I had to refuse, as for one thing among others I did not want to be involved in the internal affairs of India but felt sure that, if the Government of India could not guard my borders, Congress elements and goondas (law breakers) might infiltrate into Nepal unless I strengthened and reinforced my border troops, so I have been busy doing this.'[1]

Juddha Shamsher's attitude during the civil disobedience movement and the earlier section on his assistance to the British during the war show the dual nature of his policy. He maintained the independence and isolation of Nepal and did not interfere in the internal affairs of India. At the same time he and his family prided themselves on their unwavering and generous support of the British Government when it was at war.

On the question of Congress, fugitives who had taken refuge in Nepal after the suppression of the civil disobedience movement, he adopted a policy which was not clear to the Government of India. On January 8, 1943, Colonel Ogilvy wrote a letter to the Commander-in-Chief of Nepal to inform him that some 500 fugitives from Bihar were hiding in Hanumannagar and Biratnagar, and that they were proposing

[1] Juddha to Betham, September 2, 1942. *Basta No. 79.* (N.F.O.K.)

to launch an attack on Biratnagar Police Station.¹ The Commander-in-Chief replied that he had no such information and that 'it seems improbable that there should have been such a concentration without the knowledge of local authorities'.² Betham, the British minister, complained to the prime minister that the Nepal Government had so far been able to arrest only ten out of 435 refugees who had escaped into Nepal territory. They had 'committed acts of sabotage, arson and murder in North Bihar'.³ The British minister hinted diplomatically that it would be to the advantage of the prime minister to arrest the fugitives,

'... indeed the presence of these fugitives from justice in Nepal cannot but tend to cause political upheaval in Nepal, because these men are politically minded in a way which can only be harmful both to Your Highness's Government and to the Government of India.'⁴

In reply to this letter the Maharajah made many excuses and said that he would send fresh instructions to the Hakims (officials) to do their best in this matter.⁵ It is not known why Juddha Shamsher was lenient in arresting these people. The British minister suggested to the prime minister that he should introduce censorship of mail, and the latter accepted the proposal in August 1942:

'... I am indeed very grateful to Your Excellency for the timely suggestion censoring the mails sent through Mir Suba Prakash Man Singh. It was done in the last Great War and I shall do it now also.'⁶

In another letter of November 30, 1942, Betham wrote that the Government of India contemplated establishing the censorship of mail sent to Nepal. It would inform Juddha Shamsher of any discoveries it made of 'subversive anti-Rana elements both in Nepal and India'.⁷ Soon afterwards the office of the censor in India intercepted a letter in Hindi

---

¹ Colonel Ogilvy to the Commander-in-Chief, Nepal, No. 28(42)E/2, January 8, 1943. *Basta No. 79*. (N.F.O.K.)
² Commander-in-Chief to Ogilvy, January 10, 1943. *Basta No. 79*. (N.F.O.K.)
³ Betham to Maharajah, No. 28(42)E/2. British Legation, Nepal, Camp 4 Asoka Road, Calcutta, December 28, 1942. *Basta No. 79*. (N.F.O.K.)
⁴ *Ibid.*
⁵ Maharajah to Betham, Camp Maithali, Near Nawakot, Nepal, January 9, 1943. *Basta No. 79*. (N.F.O.K.)
⁶ Juddha to Betham, Nepal, August 21, 1942. *Basta No. 79*. (N.F.O.K.)
⁷ Betham to Bada Kaji Saheb: 'Owing to the exigencies of conditions obtaining because of the war and enhanced by possible subversive anti-Rana elements both in Nepal and India the Government of India have for some time had under consideration the possibility of introducing a limited secret

which revealed that a certain Baijnath Prasad Sukla had intended to distribute subversive leaflets in Butwal in Nepal territory. The Government of the United Provinces had discovered that the leaflets were also being distributed in Banaras, Sitapur and Bahraich districts.[1] The information accessible in the records is so fragmentary that it is not possible to draw conclusions as to how far the Quit India Movement of 1942 had ramifications in Nepal.

The Governor-General's earlier letter did not remove Juddha Shamsher's conviction that he was looked upon as a second-class ally. In January 1944, he learned that the minister, Geoffrey Betham, would leave Nepal and would be replaced by Lieutenant-Colonel G. A. Falconer of the Indian Political Service. Juddha Shamsher objected to the appointment to Nepal of a man who previously had had a lower rank than that of minister in the Indian Political Service. The Maharajah complained that most of the ministers who were sent to Nepal had not previously held the rank of minister and that they were not treated as ministers after their appointment. Although he finally accepted the appointment of Falconer as British Minister at the Court of Nepal, he lodged a strong complaint with the Government of India. Betham assured him that Falconer was a capable man and had a charming wife who would accompany him to Nepal. Juddha Shamsher relieved his feelings by the following letter to Betham:

'... Looking however into the July Supplement to the Half Yearly List (2nd January 1943) of the Indian Political Service we have found to our great surprise that the selection has gone this time not even to a second class Resident but to a Political Agent, [a rank lower than that of 2nd class Resident] as Lieutenant Colonel G. A. Falconer is said to be in Bhopal since 15th November 1942. Presumably it is from there that he is being posted as Minister in Nepal.'[2]

He went on to say:

censorship of mail passing through Nepal, Raxaul, Forbesginj and Nautanwa post offices, the result of which the Government of India hopes would be of advantage not only to themselves but also to His Highness the Maharajah to whom any information of interest to Nepal desired from this censorship would always be communicated. On this important and delicate question which is of a most secret nature I wish to have a personal discussion with His Highness as soon as possible. British Legation, Nepal, November 30, 1942. *Basta No. 79.* (N.F.O.K.)

[1] Ogilvy to Commander-in-Chief, Nepal, January 11, 1943. *Basta No. 79,* Letter No. 26-C/42. (N.F.O.K.)

[2] Juddha to Betham, Camp Birgunj, January 22, 1944. *Basta No. 66.* (N.F.O.K.)

'Forgive me when I say that circumstances compel me to remark that for all Your Excellency's Uniform and in spite of your 17 gun salute you are shown and seen to be no better than a Resident of the 2nd class.'[1]

The Maharajah made it very clear that this kind of treatment had deeply offended him, and that he hoped that in the future the Government of India would give consideration to what he said.

In the latter part of the war the Maharajah was worried by the possible success of Japan's propaganda. A broadcast had appealed to the Gurkha soldiers to desert and join hands with those who were fighting for freedom. The broadcast made a strong attack on the British.[2] It was similar to the German broadcasts of the First World War. The Maharajah thought the Japanese might have an effect, but the British minister assured him that the Gurkha soldiers had no opportunity of listening to it and that the British Government would soon introduce broadcasts in Gurkhali which would provide an opportunity for the Gurkha soldiers to hear the allied point of view in their own language.[3]

The people and the government of Nepal had strongly objected to British aeroplanes landing at Kathmandu or flying over it. The principal reason was that they did not want aircraft to fly over the Pashupatinath Temple, which was a particularly sacred place of worship in Kathmandu. For that reason they would not have an airfield in Kathmandu. During the non-cooperation movement started in India in 1942, when Nepal was cut off from the rest of the world, the British Minister got permission to build a landing field first on the Birgunj parade ground, and later on when this was found to be unsuitable, in Simra.[4] Both these places are outside Kathmandu and the landing of aircraft in any one of them would not involve an aeroplane flying over the Pashupatinath Temple. Simra is closer to Kathmandu than Birgunj. So the minister suggested to the Maharajah that, 'With a landing ground at Simra and one plane of your own, however small, the moment any emergency such as the recent disgraceful one occurs our plane could carry Your Highness.'[5] With a view to the possibility of an emergency, the landing ground was constructed in Simra and to be used only during the emergency.

[1] Juddha to Betham, Camp Birgunj, January 22, 1944. *Basta No. 66.* (N.F.O.K.)
[2] English translation of a broadcast in Nepali from Rangoon on May 2, 1944. *Basta No. 54.* (N.F.O.K.)
[3] British Minister to the Maharajah, Nepal, July 18, 1944, *Basta No. 54.* (N.F.O.K.)
[4] Betham to General Bahadur, Nepal, April 7, 1944. *Basta No. 79.* (N.F.O.K.)
[5] Betham to Maharajah, Nepal, August 21, 1942. *Basta No. 79.* (N.F.O.K.)

THE LAST PHASE

The award of titles and honors had been one of the lighter touches in every phase of British–Nepalese relations. The discussion generally revolved around how many KCSI, KCIE, or CIE, were to be given and who were to receive them. During the regime of Maharajah Juddha Shamsher, the traditional discussion took place and both he and others received military and civil honors from the British government for their services to the allied cause in World War II.[1] But in addition to this, Juddha Shamsher made a request which was without precedent in the history of Indian–Nepalese relations. In 1941, he politely but unmistakably suggested that Nepal was in sore need of financial and technical assistance and expected the British Government to provide it. He wrote,

'... it is the benefit of the country that should have the first consideration in the acceptance of favours which His Britannic Majesty might graciously be pleased to bestow. As your Excellency knows very well, Nepal stands sorely in need of improvement in her economic condition and is looking eagerly and expectantly to the British Government for such facilities as are calculated to bring about that desired end.'[2]

There is nothing to show whether he ever received any reply to his request. But at least it does show that the Rana ministers thought of the economic problem during their time. This was a departure from the old policy of fighting for status symbols.

For many years large numbers of Nepalese had emigrated to India in search of positions in the army and in the civil service. Most of them became domiciled in India and became British subjects. Periodically prime ministers Juddha Shamsher, then Padma Shamsher who succeeded him in January 1946 and then finally Mohan Shamsher who succeeded Padma in February 1948 wrote to British officials to enlist their help in finding them positions. In 1940, Juddha Shamsher had to ask the Viceroy for fair treatment of the Nepalese who had settled in India. He complained that the Government of India discriminated against them when making appointments to the government services.[3] Juddha Shamsher did not approve of giving King's Commissions (promotion to the rank of officers) to Nepalese subjects who had enlisted in the Indian army. At the same time he objected to discrimination

---

[1] Betham to Maharajah, Camp Raxaul, January 15, 1941; Maharajah to Betham, Nepal, January 19, 1941; Betham to Maharajah, Calcutta, December 27, 1941. *Basta No. 53.* (N.F.O.K.)
[2] Juddha to British Minister, Nepal, February 1, 1941. *Basta No. 53.* (N.F.O.K.)
[3] Maharajah to Juddha Shamsher to Lord Linlithgow, Nepal, April 17, 1940. *Basta No. 56.* (N.F.O.K.)

against Nepalese emigrants who were domiciled in India and had joined the British Gurkha Regiments of the Indian army.[1] The Viceroy tried to appease the Maharajah and informed him that orders had been given to the provincial governments forbidding any form of discrimination.[2] It is not known if this order of the Viceroy was carried out in abolishing discrimination against the Nepalese. A few years later Juddha Shamsher's successor, Padma Shamsher, again complained of the treatment of Gurkhas who were living in India. In May 1947 Padma Shamsher sent a telegram to S. H. Suhrawardy, then Chief Minister of Bengal, asking information why some of the Gurkhas who belonged to the armed police force of Calcutta had been killed. The Chief Minister of Bengal replied that in the Hindu–Muslim communal riots of November 1945 and February 1946, the Hindus did not approve of the impartiality with which the Gurkhas suppressed the disorders and therefore assaulted and killed them. Soon afterwards a new wave of communal riots began in Calcutta, commencing in August 1946, and during this period strangely enough the Gurkhas abandoned their impartiality and took the side of the Hindus, so then they were killed by the Muslims. Suhrawardy assured the Maharajah that the incidents were very few, and he had taken special care to protect the Gurkhas' lives and property.[3] The reason the Government used Gurkhas and not Hindu or Muslim Indian police to put down communal riots was given in Sir Geoffrey de Montmorency's speech in the Punjab Legislative Council on July 18, 1927:

'The experience of the Hindu–Muslim riots in Amritsar and our efforts in posting additional police to that city taught Government that in such circumstances Gurkha policemen were extremely useful. They were efficient for patrolling purpose and likewise they were considered by the inhabitants generally to be impartial. They neither favoured the Hindus nor the Muhammadans. They, therefore, gave the general population a sense of security which other policemen did not give.'[4]

An unprecedented incident took place in 1941, among some of the Gurkha soldiers of the Indian army. General Bahadur reported to

[1] Betham to Maharajah, No. 2–98–C, Nepal, October 5, 1940. Juddha to Betham, Nepal, November 3, 1940. *Basta No. 56.* (N.F.O.K.)
[2] Lord Linlithgow to Maharajah Juddha Shamsher, Simla, August 28, 1940. *Basta No. 56.* (N.F.O.K.)
[3] H. S. Suhrawardy, Chief Minister of Bengal to Maharajah Mohan Shamsher, Prime Minister of Nepal, Bengal Secretariat, Calcutta, May 19, 1947; Mohan Shamsher to Suhrawardy, Nepal, May 30, 1947. *Basta No. 79.* (N.F.O.K.)
[4] Extract from Sir Geoffrey de Montmorency's speech in Punjab Legislative Council on July 18, 1927. *Foreign and Political Department External*, No. 623(4)-X, 1927. (N.A.I.)

THE LAST PHASE

Maharajah Juddha Shamsher on January 6, 1941, that there had been a revolt in the Second Rifles Division. The reason given in his telegram was that the men refused to drink milk purchased from their increased mess allowances and demanded money instead. This disobedience on the part of the Gurkha soldiers raised a serious problem as to what should be done with them. They could not be returned to Nepal because they might communicate a spirit of revolt to the soldiers who were in Nepal. The result is not known. Général Bahadur rightly described this event as 'unprecedented in our military history'.[1] This was the first time that Nepalese soldiers had ever disobeyed an order. They were among the best behaved soldiers in the world. The outcome of this unique occurrence could not be found in the Nepal Foreign Office Papers at Kathmandu.

His Majesty Maharajah Dhiraj King Tribhuvan decided to visit India for sight-seeing and to make a pilgrimage, in 1944. The visit was treated as private and it was at the request of Maharajah Juddha Shamsher that no official functions were held. However, at the request of the Maharajah the British Government gladly agreed to help the Nepal Government in making arrangements for His Majesty's stay in different places in India.[2]

The news of Germany's surrender was officially sent to the prime minister of Nepal. Although the war with Japan was still going on, the scheme for a victory celebration had already been prepared. Juddha Shamsher, who never lost an opportunity to magnify the importance of Nepal, suggested to the British Minister that when the Viceroy broadcast to the people and princes of India, he would appreciate it if he described the assistance given by Nepal as help from a friend and ally. The prime minister seized the opportunity to send telegrams of congratulations to Sir Winston Churchill, King George VI, his own Minister in London, the Viceroy of India, Lord Wavell, and to President Truman.[3] When, after the war, General Baber Shamsher visited the United States in August 1946 he met President Truman and presented to him a letter from the prime minister of Nepal, Maharajah Padma Shamsher. President Truman replied very warmly to the prime minister's letter. Just after the end of the European war Maharajah Juddha Shamsher decided to retire and went to Hardwar, a sacred

[1] General Bahadur's telegram to Maharajah Juddha Shamsher, New Delhi, January 6, 1941. *Basta No. 61.* (N.F.O.K.)
[2] Lieutenant Colonel Falconer, British Minister to Maharajah Juddha Shamsher, Nepal, November 11, 1944; Maharajah to Minister, November 12, 1944. *Basta No. 51.* (N.F.O.K.)
[3] Telegrams to Churchill, King George VI of England, Nepal Minister in London, Viceroy of India, Lord Wavell and Truman. *Basta No. 60.* (N.F.O.K.)

place for Hindus in India.¹ He was succeeded by his brother Padma Shamsher, in January 1946.

The end of the second world war entailed the disbandment of a large number of Gurkha regiments. The Viceroy of India on September 22, 1945, wrote to the prime minister in the following words:

'My Esteemed Friend,

The end of the war with Japan has, as you will realize, completely altered the situation regarding the strength of the army. I have reviewed the situation thoroughly and the Government of India has decided that a considerable reduction in the Fighting Service can now be made.'²

Recruitment had been so heavy that almost all the able-bodied young men had left the country, and this had affected the cultivation of the farms. Demobilization brought its own problems. For example, the question of the rate of exchange between the Indian and Nepalese currencies created serious difficulties, since the returning soldiers brought Indian money with them. Another problem was to find employment for them, and linked with this was their wish for the higher standard of living which they had enjoyed while away from home. Some of them preferred to remain in India. However, their motherland was prepared to welcome them with open arms. The prime minister of Nepal, Juddha Shamsher agreed to the suggestion by the British Minister in regard to the returning of soldiers to Nepal. He suggested that because of the scarcity of transport facilities the movement of the troops returning to Nepal should be left in the hands of the Indian Transport Controller (rather than being handled by the Nepalese). The British Minister in Nepal informed the prime minister that as a token of appreciation and gesture of goodwill, it was proposed, subject to the approval of the British Government which had been sought, that as a gift to Nepal, units of the contingent would be allowed to take with them their military weapons and equipment including ammunition but less motor transport and anti-gas stores (which would be of no use in Nepal), if the prime minister agreed. Juddha Shamsher agreed with both the suggestions.³ The problems created by demobilization were only solved with the passing of time. A study of them lies outside the scope of this book.

[1] Tuker, *op cit.*, pp. 231–2.
[2] 'A friend to another friend.' (Viceroy to the Prime Minister, New Delhi, September 22, 1945.) *Basta No. 60.* (N.F.O.K.)
[3] 'Nepalese Contingent: Note on Conversation with His Highness the Maharajah.' Juddha Shamsher to Falconer, October 2, 1945. *Basta No. 61* and *Basta No. 60.* (N.F.O.K.)

THE LAST PHASE

The end of World War II seems an appropriate date at which to terminate this study of the relations between Nepal and the British Government of India. In 1945 it was clear that the Government of Great Britain would soon transfer what power it still retained to elected Indian leaders, and in 1947 the British regime ended. A few years later the rule of the Rana family in Nepal, which had lasted for a century, was overthrown. Radical changes took place in Nepal's foreign and domestic policies. The termination of the world war marked the approximate end of an epoch. Continuous relations between the two countries began with the war of 1814–16. For long afterwards they were marked by hostility, fear, and suspicion. No Indian or Nepalese official of that period could have believed that they would be transformed into the mutual friendship and confidence of the twentieth century. Credit for the initial marked improvement in the relations between the two governments belongs to Sir Jung Bahadur and his policy of armed help to the British during the Indian Mutiny. Distrust and suspicion continued, however, until nearly the end of the nineteenth century. The twentieth century saw the growth of mutual confidence, loyal cooperation and friendship. Relations between the two governments were summed up in the phrase used in the treaty of 1923, that there should be perpetual peace and friendship between India and Nepal.

CHAPTER 8

GURKHA RECRUITMENT AND THE GOVERNMENT OF INDIA

The principal reason why the Government of India cultivated friendly relations with Nepal was that the country was the homeland of the Gurkhas. The war of 1814-16 gave the British very great respect for their military powers. They began to enlist Gurkhas in the army almost immediately after the conclusion of the war. They proved to be one of the most efficient and valued elements of the Indian army, and eventually there were no less than twenty battalions in the service. When India became independent in 1947 the Government of Great Britain made agreements under which some 14,000 Gurkhas continued to serve in the British army. During the whole period of British rule, however, the desire to attract Gurkha volunteers was the principal reason why the Government of India cultivated friendly relations with Nepal. Sir Arthur Hirtzel, Under-Secretary of State for India, admitted this frankly in a report which he wrote in 1922: '... it is, after all, mainly because of the Gurkha element in the Army that we value the friendship of Nepal'.[1]

Relations between the Indian and Nepalese Governments were sometimes strained, but in the army intense camaraderie always existed between Gurkha privates and the non-commissioned officers and their European British officers.

The term Gurkha is applied to the majority of the inhabitants of Nepal, but strictly speaking it belongs to those races which formed part of the old Kingdom of Gurkha, a comparatively small part of the country. The inhabitants of Nepal consist of different races. A large part are Mongolian in origin. They are divided into the tribes known as Magars, Gurungs, Limbus and Rais. While superficially Hindu they are more Buddhist than Hindu. Then there are the Rajputs who conquered Nepal.

[1] Sir Arthur Hirtzel, *Political and External File*, 1922. (I.O.L.) *op. cit.*

GURKHA RECRUITMENT AND THE GOVERNMENT OF INDIA

These Rajputs were driven out of Rajputana after the capture of Udaipur by the Muslim invaders. Leaving their own home they migrated northwards, and while passing through Kumaon and the adjoining hills they settled near Palpa; from there they gradually extended their rule eastward to Gurkha. The principal town of the old Gurkha Kingdom became the capital of the new state, and the Rajput conquerors became known as the Gurkhas.

Prithvi Narayan, who conquered Nepal in 1768, was the king of this small country. It was he who made Nepal known to the world outside the Himalaya mountains. The Rajputs intermarried with Gurkha women. They include the Khas and Thakur tribes. The Hindu strain is distinguishable, though the Mongol as a rule is predominant. The term 'Gurkha' strictly includes only those people who came from India and settled in Gurkha, and does not include the Bishts, Burathokis, Thakurs, Magars or Gurungs. All these tribes are enlisted in British Gurkha regiments.[1]

The British Indian army and the Gurkha Sepahees had their one and only war in 1814–16. Victory for the British came because numerical superiority and great financial resources forced the Nepalese to sue for peace.[2] The soldiers of the East India Company, who were mostly Hindus, were no match for the Gurkhas in their own mountain terrain.[3] The British won the war, but they came to respect the high quality and fighting spirit of these mountaineers.[4] The British took a realistic attitude and at the close of the war raised the First Gurkha Regiment, Melown Fort surrendered to General Sir David Ochterlony and the entire garrison enlisted in the army of the East India Company.[5] This

---

[1] Captain H. Ramsay, 'Gurkha Recruiting', *Foreign Department Secret—F*, November 1884, No. 234 (N.A.I. Microfilm).

[2] 'Before we come to the contest, their powers of resistance are ridiculed. Their forts are said to be contemptible, and their arms are described to be useless. Yet we find on the trial, that with these useless weapons in their contemptible forts they can deal about death among their assailants, and stand to their defences, notwithstanding the skill and bravery of our army.' Thompson, Edward, *The Making of the Indian Princes*, p. 191, Oxford University Press, London, 1943.

[3] Confidential letter of General Ochterlony to Lord Moira, Vansittart, Eden, *Notes on Gurkhas*; being a short account of their country, history, characteristics, clans, etc., pp. 1 and 20, Calcutta, 1890.

'In some instances our troops, European and Native have been repulsed by inferior numbers with sticks and stones. In others, our troops have been charged by the enemy sword in hand, and driven for miles like a flock of sheep. . . . In this war, dreadful to say, we have had numbers on our side, and skill and bravery on the side of our enemy.' Thompson, Edward, *ibid.*, p. 192; Majumdar, K., *op. cit.* pp. 407–10.

[4] Majumdar, K., *ibid.*, pp. 81–206.

[5] 'File of the Foreign and Military Department Unofficial', dated January

regiment, which was called the Melown Regiment, included mainly Kumaons and Garhwalis who had been under the command of General Amar Sing Thapa during the Nepal war. The second Regiment, called the Sirmoor Rifles, was raised in the early part of 1815 by Lieutenant F. Young. The Kumaon Regiment was raised by Sir R. Colquhoun in the same year. These Gurkhas took service under the British after the fall of Kumaon. Of the three original regiments this was really the oldest as it was raised in late 1814 when Colonel Gardner was attacking Almora. But officially it was raised by Colquhoun just a few days later than the First and the Second Regiments.[1] The first time the Gurkhas saw active service was in 1826 at the siege of Bhuratpore. They also took a prominent part in the Sikh War of 1845 under General Lord Gough.[2] British officers who were posted to Gurkha regiments praised their courage and steadiness in action in the highest terms. Ensign John Shipp described them as 'the bravest of the brave'. He wrote in his memoirs that:

'... I never saw more steadiness or bravery exhibited in my life. Run they would not, and of death they seem to have no fear, though their comrades were falling thick around them for we were so near that every shot told. . . .'[3]

It was Sir David Ochterlony who originated the idea of enlisting Gurkhas in the Company's army, because he had witnessed their performance in the Nepal War and was thoroughly convinced of their fighting spirit. Brian Hodgson, who was the British Resident in Nepal for a long time, wrote about them in the following words:

'In my humble opinion they are, by far, the best soldiers in India; and if they were made participators of our renown in arms, I conceive that their gallant spirit, emphatic contempt to madhesias (people residing in the plains) and unadulterated military habit, might be relied on for fidelity; . . .'[4]

Sir Hugh Gough stated:

'I must pause in this narrative especially to notice the determined hardihood and bravery with which our two battalions of Goorkas,

31, 1882 and January 7, 1882 singed T. F. W. Military Department No. UO to 19-B. *Foreign General—B*, August 1882, Nos. 69–71 (N.A.I.).
[1] Tuker, F., *op. cit.*, p. 298; Landon, *op. cit.*, pp. 190–1.
[2] *Foreign General—B*, August 1882, Nos. 79–71. (N.A.I.)
[3] Tuker, F., *op. cit.*, p. 90.
[4] *Ibid.*, p. 91.

the Sirmoor and Naseree, met the Sikh whenever they were opposed to them. Soldiers of small stature and indomitable spirit, they vied in ardent courage in the charge with the Grenadiers of our own nation and armed with the short weapon of their mountains, were a terror to the Sikhs throughout the great combat.'[1]

Lord Hardinge also praised the Gurkha regiments, and Lord Dalhousie the Governor-General strongly recommended their employment in the Indian Army.[2] The part they played in the Indian Mutiny won them a special mark of distinction. Landon wrote that:

'By G.O.C.C. 379 of 1858 the Sirmoor Battalion (2nd Gurkhas) were granted a third colour in addition to the two in possession and an extra Jemadar was appointed to carry it. This was a special reward for the battalion's extraordinarily gallant services at Delhi in the Mutiny.'[3]

The Gurkhas have very few caste prejudices. As a rule they are very unsophisticated and truthful, but dirty. They love gambling and are generally short-tempered. However, they are quite well-behaved and extremely amenable to discipline. Polygamy was not illegal in Nepal, but a Gurkha seldom had two wives.[4] Captain H. Ramsay described them as:

'... a brave, wild, lazy, ignorant, stupid, roving race of men with a strong natural love for war and sport, but possessing very small aptitude for intellectual employments, which they invariably regard with the greatest dislike'.[5]

Dr Oldfield complimented them as follows:

'... there is not a single instance of a Nepal chief taking bribes from, or selling himself for money to the British or any other State. This loyalty to themselves is only equalled by their loyalty to us during the fiery ordeal of the Mutiny, the records of which, as well as of Ambeyla, of the Kabul Campaign, and many other wars and battles, amply testify the value of the services rendered us by our Gurkha regiments since incorporation in our army in 1815.

[1] Tuker, *op. cit.*, p. 119.
[2] *Ibid.*, p. 120.
[3] Landon, *op. cit.*, Vol. II, p. 191.
[4] Tuker, *op. cit.*, pp. 93 and 121.
[5] Captain H. Ramsay, *Foreign Department Secret—F.*, November 1884, No. 234. (N.A.I.)

BRITISH INDIA'S RELATIONS WITH NEPAL

'Their fighting qualities, whether for sturdy, unflinching courage or enduring élan, are nulli secundus amongst the troops we enrol in our ranks from the varied classes of our Indian Empire, and no greater compliment can be paid to their bravery than by quoting one of their sayings:

Kafar human bhanda manny ramro;
It is better to die than to be a coward.
Written today: "Kafar hone bhanda morne ramro."'[1]

The high opinion universally held about the Gurkhas by army officers and civil servants explains why the Government of India was so anxious to enlist more and more of them in the Indian army.

Source of Recruitment for Gurkha Regiments

In Nepal there are Bisht, Burathoki, Thakur, Newar, Limbu, Karati, Magar and Gurung classes or castes. Gurkhas were added to them after Nepal was conquered by Gurkhas in 1768. Some of them, like the Bishts, Burathokis, Thakurs, Magars, and Gurungs are Hindus while Limbus, Newars, and Kirantis are Buddhists. The Bishts, Burathokis, and Thakurs are of medium caste and eat meat but they will not drink wine. They have proved to be good soldiers but their caste prejudices create extra problems. It is simpler to have soldiers of lower castes like the Gurungs and Magars. They eat meat and drink wine and therefore the higher castes look down upon them. These were the classes most suitable for the British Indian Regiments. Here it must be made clear that in the correct sense of the term the 'Gurkhas' are those who went from India and settled down in the town of Gurkha. The Bishts, Burathokis, Thakurs, Magars, or Gurungs are enlisted in the Gurkha Regiments but are not strictly speaking Gurkhas. Similarly Newars, Limbus, and Kirantis are mentioned as Gurkhas, but very few have been enlisted in the Gurkha Regiments.[2]

The recruits from Nepal come mostly from the Magars and Gurung castes although a few are Bishts, Burathokis and Thakurs. Men of a few other castes are also enlisted. The other source of recruits was the line boys. They were the sons of sepoys of the regiment of Gurkha or Hindustani hill-women. The percentage of the line boys in the army was not more than five, but they were excellent soldiers and more intelligent than recruits from Nepal.[3]

---

[1] Tuker, F., *op. cit.*, p. 94.
[2] Captain H. Ramsay, *Foreign Department Secret—F*, November 1884, No. 234. (N.A.I.)
[3] H. Ramsay, *Foreign Department Secret—F*, November 1884, No. 234. (N.A.I.)

GURKHA RECRUITMENT AND THE GOVERNMENT OF INDIA

Method of Recruiting

The Government of Nepal from the very beginning disliked the idea of their subjects joining the British Army, although it knew that the Government of India was anxious to enlist them. Obviously it was not easy for the Indian army to obtain as many recruits from Nepal as it would have liked to have since the Durbar was most unwilling to allow Europeans to enter the country. The treaties of 1801, 1815, and 1923 were silent on this issue. During the greater part of the nineteenth century the British had only one means of obtaining recruits from Nepal—secretly. The method was not liked by the British nor by the Gurkha Governments, but there was no alternative. Every cold season the Gurkha regiments sent a recruiting party to Gorukpore on the border of Nepal. They established a head-quarters there. Nepalese during the fairs at Bituri, Nipalgunj, Tulsipur and other places came down from the hills to purchase grain and do a little smuggling into India. As the recruiting party was wholly forbidden to enter Nepal, it had to employ secret agents or disguised sepoys to visit the fairs in Nepal and enlist volunteers. They crossed the frontier in small parties and went to Gorukpore to enlist.

This clandestine method was used for a long time but the result was not satisfactory.[1] Every attempt of the Government of India to induce the Nepal Durbar to allow greater facilities for recruiting failed. In spite of the Durbar's official policy of friendship, it never allowed its subjects to enter the British service. British officials became very dissatisfied with attempts to increase the numbers of recruits by using this method since the result was so disappointing.

Maharajah Jung Bahadur had always professed friendly feelings for the British, but when they raised the question of recruiting, or tried to discover the relatives of Gurkhas who had died while in the army in order to return their effects, the Maharajah became most uncooperative. On one such occasion the Maharajah wrote to the Resident:

'I often receive Yaddashts (reminders) from you requesting me to trace the heirs of deceased Goorkhalees, men who had enlisted in the British Army.

'I therefore beg that, in order to obviate such useless annoyance and trouble, you will be so good as to cause such requisitions to be discontinued by representing these circumstances to His Excellency the Viceroy and Governor-General.'[2]

[1] H. Ramsay, *Foreign Department Secret—F*, November 1884, No. 234. (N.A.I.)
[2] Abstract translation of a yaddasht from Maharajah Jung Bahadur, Rana, to the address of Colonel George Ramsay, Resident at Nipal, dated the 11th

Jung Bahadur's attitude was much more uncooperative than that of any of his successors. The Resident, Ramsay, in his report to the Government wrote:

'The Durbar is, and always has been, averse to its subjects entering the British service, and orders have long existed to prevent their doing so without the Minister's previous permission; and a few years ago Maharajah Jung Bahadur went so far as to declare that no sepahees in the British Army, Natives of Nipal, "on leave only from their Regiments," should be allowed to re-enter the country and visit their families, an order which he only withdrew after I had strongly remonstrated against it, and had reported the particular instance that occasioned it for the consideration and orders of the Governor-General.'[1]

The Resident attributed this attitude of the Durbar to a number of unfortunate incidents which had taken place. When Nepalese who joined the British Army without the previous permission of the Durbar, visited Nepal on leave or for other reason, as soon as they crossed the frontier they began to boast about the magnitude of the British power and its superiority to that of Durbar. In one instance a Newar who was in British service returned to Nepal and called himself 'a Goorkha and that his name was Jung Bahadur'. Since a Newar was looked down on by the caste Hindus, for him to call himself by the name of the prime minister was pure insolence. In another incident a Domai, a member of a caste so low that it was not much above that of Mehter (a scheduled caste), was appointed as honorary guard to Bum Bahadur while he was in Almora, India in 1853, by the Commissioner of Kumaon.[2] There were many similar incidents which angered the Sardar and other officials of the Nepal Durbar.

Another possible reason for Jung Bahadur's attitude was that he objected to conferring benefits upon the families of men who had broken the Durbar's orders by leaving Nepal and joining a Gurkha regiment. He would be doing this if he helped the British authorities to trace the heirs of deceased Gurkhas, in order to return the dead men's belongings. Indirectly too the Maharajah would be encouraging those who had left. So to discourage others the prime minister adopted the attitude of refusing to grant the British requests.[3]

of Jeyt sumbut 1923 (corresponding with June 9, 1866). *Foreign Department Political*, July 1866, No. 65. (N.A.I.)

[1] Ramsay to Secretary to the Government of India, in the Foreign Department, with the Governor General, Simla, No. 18 dated June 15, 1866, *ibid.*, No. 64.

[2] Ramsay to Secretary Government of India, *Foreign Department Political*, July 1866, No. 64. (N.A.I.)

[3] *Ibid.*

GURKHA RECRUITMENT AND THE GOVERNMENT OF INDIA

After the death of Jung Bahadur the British Government tried to find some way of solving the problem of obtaining recruits with the sanction of the Durbar. Maharajah Ranodip Singh was also not inclined to be helpful. He issued an order reported by Girdlestone as follows:

'... any person who is detected in an attempt to leave the country for this purpose will be imprisoned, and that the goods, house, and lands of any person so enlisting will be confiscated. It is believed also that any persons who on their return to Nipalese territory are suspected of having served in a British regiment will be severely dealt with.'[1]

One of the informants of the British Resident told him that, 'whereas formerly men caught in Nipal recruiting for us were to be bound and sent back to British territory, they are now to be cut in two'.[2] It was thought possible that this order of the Durbar might be in retaliation for an adverse decision of the Government of India on a request for arms by the Durbar.

The Governments of Nepal and India discussed many schemes for recruiting Gurkhas from Nepal. At first Ranodip Singh would not give way to the British demands and they would not accept his proposals. He put forward different excuses for not allowing recruitment. Finally after a long session of bargaining, discussion and correspondence the following compromise was reached.

The Durbar was prepared:

(a) To make our need of recruits generally known throughout the country, and generally to proclaim that whoever of its subjects is willing to take military service under the British Government, is at full liberty to do so on condition of previously making the local Nepalese District Officer acquainted with his intention.

(b) To give copies of such proclamations, if desired to British Recruiting Agents, who may be on the lookout for recruits near (but on the British side) of the frontier, in order to facilitate their proceedings.

(c) To exert itself to collect recruits, but owing to previous want of success in similar efforts to meet Lord Lytton's requirements, and by reason of the fact that the Nepalese standing army is said to be at present some 700 or 800 men below strength, the Minister wishes it to be understood that he is not sanguine of great results.

[1] Girdlestone to Lyall, Secretary Government of India, No. 3P, Camp Marsewa, January 18, 1880 (Confidential). *Foreign Department Political—A*, July 1880, Nos. 141–58. (N.A.I.)
[2] *Ibid.*

(*d*) To allow pensioners from our Gurkha and Assam Regiments to collect recruits under the Minister's supervision.

(*e*) To permit the Residency Surgeon to examine all candidates, and to accept his opinion concerning physical fitness or otherwise as conclusive.

(*f*) To agree to the training of recruits, as a temporary measure, under the Resident's supervision by the Resident's escort on the Residency parade ground; or the Minister will arrange for such training in accordance with the system now observed in respect of our native troops on his own parade ground by men of the Nepalese army, who have previously served under the British flag.'[1]

Maharajah Ranodip Singh did not, however, allow the British recruiting party to enter the territory of Nepal. It would have been difficult for him to permit it, since none of his predecessors had agreed to the concessions outlined above. The Resident Girdlestone advised the Government of India to offer a few concessions of its own, in the belief that they would induce the Durbar to help the British recruiting party to obtain volunteers. Girdlestone suggested:

1. The grant of breech-loading rifles;
2. Permission to import lead and sulphur for making cartridges;
3. The conferring upon Ranodip Singh of the G.C.S.I., and a salute of 19 guns; and
4. The cession of a strip of land on the frontier of the Terai.[2]

The recommendations were fully discussed by the Foreign Office and the military departments of the Government of India, and the final answer was given by the Viceroy. He decided to make 'a free gift to the Durbar of 800 Sniders with ammunition, whenever 800 Gurkha recruits have been raised for the British service. A similar gift will be made for every additional battalion up to a total of 5,600 recruits.' The second recommendation was also accepted and it was added: 'It is unnecessary that any account of expenditure should be rendered.' Regarding the third suggestion it was decided that the Viceroy would be inclined to make the recommendation if the prime minister should prove able to supply recruits successfully. About the final recommendation of the cession of part of the Terai, the Resident was instructed to say nothing.[3]

---

[1] Girdlestone to Durand, Secretary Government of India, No. 21-P, May 6, 1885 (Conf.), *Foreign Department Secret—E.*, July 1885, No. 37. (N.A.I.)
[2] Durand to the Officiating Resident in Nepal, No. 896-E, Simla, June 9, 1885, *Foreign Secret—E*, July 1885, No. 51. (N.A.I. Microfilm).
[3] *Foreign Secret—E*, July 1885, No. 51. (N.A.I.)

The Resident maintained an uneasy truce with Ranodip Singh because he did not fully carry out the agreement which he made. When Girdlestone went on leave and Colonel Berkeley became the officiating Resident, the situation did not improve. The Nepal Government made proclamation in most of the villages as it had promised, but it was done in such a way that it did not produce the expected recruits. Berkeley suggested that the Government of India should reproach the Maharajah for not implementing the agreement and show its disappointment; or alternatively it should give some further concession as an inducement to cooperate. He also suggested that Ranodip Singh should be invited to Calcutta, to have a frank and cordial talk about recruiting.[1] It was the consensus of opinion that the only way in which recruits could be obtained was through the Durbar. If it created obstacles then the chances of getting any recruits would be slight. The Resident was opposed to the idea of sending a British recruiting party inside Nepal. He argued that this would give an excuse to the prime minister to say that the people of the country did not like the presence of a recruiting party in the country, and so British India would get no recruits.[2] Berkeley's suggestions had no result.

During the lifetime of Ranodip Singh the question of recruiting did not advance beyond the adoption of the six-point agreement, which was not implemented with sincerity. The Resident said on November 4, 1885, eighteen days before the murder of Ranodip Singh, that:

'the Minister does not mean business, but intends by professions and pretences to put off the evil day as long as possible, in the hope that eventually the proposal may be dropped. More than this I am not without fear that the Durbar is actually hindering recruits from coming; and that more harm than good has been done.'[3]

Instead of the proposal being dropped the prime minister was himself dropped from the pedestal.

The emergence of the Shamsher family as the *de facto* rulers of Nepal made some difference in solving the awkward problem of recruiting Nepalese subjects for the British Gurkha regiments. Bir Shamsher came to power not legally (in the Nepalese sense), but by a blood-stained *coup d'état*. This was one occasion in Nepalese–British

---

[1] Berkeley to Durand (Demi-Official) Camp Segowlie, November 10, 1885, *Foreign Department Secret Proceedings—E*, December 1885, K.W., No. 2. (N.A.I.)

[2] *Foreign Department Secret Proceedings—E*, December 1885, K.W., No. 2. (N.A.I.)

[3] Berkeley to H. Durand (Demi-Official) Kathmandu, November 4, 1885, *Foreign Department Secret Proceedings—E*, December 1885, K.K., No. 2. (N.A.I.)

relations when the prime minister of Nepal waited anxiously and nervously for British recognition of his murderous action. It was thought that this was a time when the Government of India could have taken advantage of the situation and gotten everything it wanted. On the other hand, Jung Bahadur's sons and relatives fled to India and put pressure on the Governor-General for help. It was implied that if he would restore them to power they would serve the British and their own interests together. But while the Governor-General sympathized with the sons and relatives of an old friend of the Indian Government, he felt that he could not actively become a party to an internal feud. He made this decision although it was known to the Government of India that the Shamshers were not very friendly to the British. Finally the tense moment of uncertainty was over and Bir Shamsher was recognized as the ruler. In the beginning of his rule he made all sorts of promises, but once he was fully in control of Nepal he tried to avoid fulfilling them. The Resident Girdlestone wrote, 'My conviction is that the present administration has not our interest at heart, and that even if it had its *modus operandi* would be more likely to do us harm than good in the long run'.[1]

The Indian Government had the same suspicion, but it also conceived the idea that if the Gurkhas who were already serving in the Indian Army were to bring their families to India, in the long run part of the recruits who were needed could be obtained by enlisting their children. In this way the British Government would become less dependent on Nepal for Gurkha recruits. Accordingly a proposal to this effect was made to the prime minister. Colonel Berkeley urged its adoption on the ground 'that Nipal would reap [benefit] from the training and the pension which the Nipalese sepoys would obtain . . .'.[2] However the prime minister firmly rejected Berkeley's proposal on the following grounds:

'*1stly*. This proposal (if carried out) will necessitate the departure from Nipal of a considerable number of families at the present time and of more than two or three hundred families annually in future and these will consist of Magars and Gurungs who are scanty in Nipal. For you (British officers) annually enlist more than three or four hundred recruits, consisting more of men of the Gurung and Magar

---

[1] Girdlestone to Cunningham, Official Secretary Government of India, No. 63P, dated Nepal Residency, December 27, 1886, *Foreign Department Secret Proceedings—E*, February 1887, No. 161. (N.A.I.)

[2] Abstract translation of a Yaddasht from the Prime Minister and Commander-in-Chief of Nipal, to the Resident in Nipal, dated the 9th Bhadon, Sumvat 1943 (August 23, 1886), *Foreign Department Secret—E*, December 1886, No. 19 (N.A.I. Microfilm).

clans and less of men of other tribes, in view to the filling up of casualties. It is certain that these will also wish to take their families with themselves.

'*2ndly*. The Nipalese subjects who were enlisted in British regiments, and who were trained in the British service, used on obtaining pension to come back to Nipal for the purpose of joining their families and by serving in the Nipalese army for a while they used to impart instruction to others. If the families of these men go to British India, and make it their home and dwell there, they will have then no necessity at all to return to Nipal.

'*3rdly*. When there remains no necessity for those men to return hither the benefits which it is hoped would accrue to other subjects of this Government through the earning of money in British territory by such men and the spending of it in Nipal after they have obtained pension will not be realized.

'*4thly*. The Darbar has had to overlook and ignore the quarrels which took place between the people and such sepoys as were deputed on recruiting duty, and which resulted from the discontent of the people under extreme pressure that had to be employed in view of complying with the wishes of the British Government for the collecting and bringing forward as many recruits as possible. If, therefore, efforts were to be made at present in this matter, the people of this country being, as a rule, devoid of intelligence would consider that the Darbar, unmindful of its own interests, was using its utmost influence in endeavours to expel also the families of its subjects from this country. Consequently the proposal is not calculated to result in any good to Nipal.

'*5thly*. The benefits which Colonel Berkeley said that Nipal will reap from the training and the pension which the Nipalese sepoy would obtain will thus be illusory.'[1]

This ended another scheme of the Indian Government to keep up the strength of the Gurkha regiments of the Indian army. Bir Shamsher had to some extent kept the promises which he had given to the Indian Government, but in doing so he had used force and coercion. This had not only made recruiting unpopular but had also endangered the popularity of his own Government. The Resident reported this issue to the Government of India.[2]

[1] *Foreign Department Secret Proceedings—E*, December 1886, Nos. 11–21. (N.A.I.)

[2] 'The coercion to which it freely resorted last winter in order to obtain recruits for us is one, though not the most influential, of the causes of the great unpopularity of the present administration. The Shamshers are well aware of

Bir Shamsher was in a quandary. If he tried to please the British, he displeased his own people on whose support his rule depended. On the other hand, he did not want to give any cause of grievance to the British because they helped him during the most critical phase of his life. He wrote to the Resident and pleaded for understanding of his difficulties. He tried first to gain recruits by offering them money, but when this failed he ordered each village to supply a certain number of recruits. The result was that the villagers started fighting with the Durbar's recruiting parties. To cope with this, his administration had to appoint more officials and thus increased Nepal's expenditure. Lastly he was disappointed that out of seven or eight thousand men who appeared before the army doctors, only 2,200 were chosen as answering the standards of height, caste, and age, and were considered as suitable for the service. He begged the Indian army not to insist so exclusively on enlisting only Magars and Gurungs.[1] He further pleaded pathetically, 'My friend; since I have been looking out for means to please the British Government I should not have hesitated to do a thing had it not been beyond my power'.[2] He went even a little further to assure the Indian Government of his sincerity by saying,

'In conclusion I write to assure you that I will again issue encouraging notifications and orders to the Nepalese Officers on the borders to countenance, without fail, such men as wish to accept service under the British Government, and to make it generally known that in the eyes of the Durbar persons who accept the British service will be regarded as though they had accepted service under the Durbar.'[3]

the strong feeling against them, and know that their faction is only tolerated because opposition is so far without a leader. Their rule is founded on terrorism, and there are many of their subordinates, Civil and Military, on whom they can not fully depend. Their own safety suggests that they should not again attempt to press men into our service, and except by undue pressure they are apparently unable to obtain recruits. Their proceedings have had the effect of making our service less popular in Nepal than it used to be, and one result of their highhanded way of supplying men has been that a considerable number of the recruits whom we owe to them have deserted after joining our ranks. Apart from any consideration for the party now in power it is desirable, in our own interests, to avoid any form of coercion in future.'
C. E. R. Girdlestone, Resident in Nepal to W. J. Cunningham, Offg. Secretary to the Government of India, Foreign Department, No. 63P, dated Nepal Residency, December 27, 1886, *Foreign Department Secret Proceedings—E*, February 1887, No. 161. (N.A.I.)

[1] Abstract translation of a yaddasht from the Prime Minister and Commander-in-Chief of Nepal, to the Resident in Nepal. Dated Poos 5th Sumvat 1943 (December 16, 1886), Recd. December 20, 1886. *Foreign Department Secret Proceedings*, February 1887, No. 162. (N.A.I.)
[2] *Ibid.*
[3] *Foreign Department Proceedings—E*, February 1887, No. 162, *op. cit.*

GURKHA RECRUITMENT AND THE GOVERNMENT OF INDIA

The efforts of Bir Shamsher and the Resident's constant reminders to him had a very good result in 1886–87. The Resident reported that the year showed, 'I believe, a far higher return, numerical and proportional, for filling vacancies than that of any previous years; and by dint of the efforts used the percentage of Magars and Gurungs for the line battalions has been more than maintained'.[1] The most important feature of this year was that almost all recruits came of their own free will and were not forced by the Durbar, as was done in 1885–86.[2] Considering the better atmosphere which prevailed in Nepal for recruits, Captain Trench suggested that 'the services of men going on furlough should be made use of while they are at their homes'.[3] The proposal that Magars and Gurangs should be enlisted in the Assam Frontier Police was not approved by the Commander-in-Chief, who felt that these classes should be 'strictly confined to the Gurkha regiments (including the three regiments in Assam) of the regular army . . .'.[4] This gave the impression that recruiting was going on well with little or no difficulty or obstruction.

Encouraged by the success in recruiting Gurkhas, a British army officer brought forward an old idea in new form. Lieutenant Eden Vansittart proposed to the Resident that there should be a recruiting depot in Kathmandu itself. Undoubtedly the depot would be very helpful in the matter of expenses, and the procurement of more and better recruits. There was a medical officer at the Residency who could examine them at the spot, recruiting could go on throughout the year instead of for only part of it, and there were many other advantages. The major recruiting areas like Palpa and Pokhra are very close to the capital of the country.[5] The major issue involved was whether the Durbar would approve this proposal, since of course without its help nothing could be done. Both Durand, the Resident, and Vansittart were in favor of such action. Naturally the entire proposal was put before the military and foreign departments of the Government of India for consideration and discussion. The secretary of the Foreign Department wrote that:

[1] Girdlestone to the Secretary Government of India, No. 54P, Nepal, July 29, 1887, *Foreign Department Secret Proceedings—E*, September 1887, No. 113. (N.A.I.)

[2] *Ibid.*

[3] Captain C. Chenevi Trench, 2nd Battalion 5th Gurkhas to the Resident in Nepal, No. 15-R, dated Abbottabad, June 21, 1887, *Foreign Department Secret Proceedings—E*, September 1887, No. 114. (N.A.I.)

[4] The Adjutant-General of India to the Secretary, Government of India, Native Army/Recruiting, No. 3075-B, July 19, 1887, *Foreign Department Secret Proceedings—E*, September 1887, No. 114-19. (N.A.I.)

[5] Lieutenant Eden Vansittart, 5th Gurkhas to Major E. L. Durand (Demi-Official), *Foreign Secret—E*, June 1888, Nos. 38–41. (N.A.I.)

'Setting aside the chance of the Durbar's objecting to the establishment of a recruiting agency at Kathmandu—an objection which, if we thought the step advisable, I presume we should not listen to—I should be inclined to doubt making the place, at first at least, into Headquarters.'[1]

Eventually both the foreign and military departments, the Viceroy, the Commander-in-Chief and other officers of both the departments after discussing the pros and cons of the entire proposal decided that the Resident should place it before the prime minister. It was decided also to appoint Captain Vansittart as Military Assistant to the Resident and not as the recruiting officer. The Resident, Major Durand, wrote to Sir Shamsher that Captain Vansittart had been appointed as military assistant to the Resident because of the pressure of work in the Residency; that he would stay in Kathmandu only for the summer period and during the winter he would carry on his duty as the recruiting officer in Gorukpore; that while Captain Vansittart was in charge of recruiting operations he would not come to Kathmandu in this capacity, and none of his staff would accompany him. If however any recruits presented themselves for enlistment during the summer, he would use his own judgement in allowing them to go before the medical officer and enlisting them. At the same time it was made clear that Kathmandu would not be made a base for recruiting.[2]

The reply from the prime minister, which might have been expected, was as follows:

'In regard to enlisting recruits who may present themselves for enlistment in the Residency during the summer, I am indeed very sorry to say that I am unable to agree to this proposal for reasons already stated in the previous communications of this office on the subject.'[3]

Soon after this proposal was rejected Major Durand, the chief supporter of the idea, was replaced by Colonel H. Wylie as Resident in Nepal. The Residentship of Colonel Wylie has been discussed elsewhere. He

---

[1] Secretary's notes on file, *Foreign Department Secret—E*, February 1892, Nos. 315–20. (N.A.I.)

[2] Proposal to appoint an officer as Military Assistant to the Resident in Nepal in connection with Gurkha Recruiting. Captain E. Vansittart selected for the post. (This file contains the entire proceedings in connection with the establishment of a recruiting depot at Kathmandu. There is no need to mention each file separately.) *Foreign Department Secret—E*, February 1892, Nos. 315–20. (N.A.I.)

[3] *Ibid.*

believed in trying to advance British interests by conciliation and tactful diplomacy. He condemned the scheme of appointing a recruiting officer or military assistant to the Resident in Nepal. Wylie said that,

'If Captain Vansittart comes here with any idea of recruiting, he will come in the teeth of the very strongest protest from the Nepalese Prime Minister, and will probably arouse great ill-feeling throughout the Durbar.'

He agreed with Bir Shamsher that the appointment would produce unpopularity and risk to himself. He argued with the Government of India on the inadvisability of getting a friendly prime minister into trouble. Wylie also disagreed with those who pleaded that the Government of India had gone so far in the matter that withdrawal would be bad for its prestige. He said,

'I do not think we have gone too far to withdraw. We have stated our wishes to the Nepalese Minister, and he has replied by showing us certain grave objections to them.

'Considering all he has done for us in the way of recruiting, we can now say (if necessary) that, after considering these objections and out of personal regard to himself, we will not now press the appointment of Captain Vansittart, but we expect the Maharaja to continue to help us with recruiting, as if, under the present system, the numbers of recruits fall off, we will have to consider whether it will not be necessary to take other steps to ensure a full supply. If a spur is needed this will probably keep him up to the collar.'[1]

Here again Colonel Wylie's diplomacy was successful. After he took over the Residentship in Nepal the Indian army got more recruits than ever before. He even agreed with Bir Shamsher that the Gurkhas who were Indian army reservists should not reside in Nepal. The policy of Wylie was a success, and the army did not have much trouble in getting as many recruits as it wanted. The following statement by Bir Shamsher reported by Wylie gives an idea of the success of the latter's policy:

'From the record in your office you know that the late Maharaja Sir Jung Bahadur and Sir Ranodip Singh Rana had not the courage to supply recruits to the British Government, yet, with the view of

[1] Colonel H. Wylie to A. Tuker (Demi-Official) dated Camp Segowlie, November 13, 1891. *Foreign Department Secret—E*, February 1892, Nos. 315–20. (N.A.I.)

strengthening the basis of friendship with the British Government, I, as far as possible, having explained to and satisfied the Bahadurs and arranged that the ryots (peasants) would not be displeased, have carried on the work with facility.'[1]

Gurkha Recruitment During the Twentieth Century

With the emergence of new leadership in Nepal the situation substantially changed as regards the recruitment of Gurkhas for the Indian army. Chandra Shamsher, who took power in Nepal after exiling his older brother, proved to be a more ambitious, prudent, clearheaded and shrewder politician than his predecessors. Recruiting in the past had been a problem for the British authorities. By the end of the nineteenth century the Durbar had allowed some relaxation, partly because of Colonel Wylie's diplomacy, and partly because Bir Shamsher had too many enemies to fight at home and so decided to be on friendly terms with the British. Chandra Shamsher did not put much obstruction in the way of recruiting because he wished to gain greater favor from the British in order to attain other ends which he had in view. His first concession was to allow 1,800 reservists of Gurkha regiments to live in Nepal. Bir Shamsher in 1893 had refused this concession.[2] Upon his return from England Chandra Shamsher leaned towards British friendship more than before. During the first half of the twentieth century the major work of recruiting was done, during the two great wars, under the two prime ministers, Chandra Shamsher and Juddha Shamsher. Between the two wars and before World War I, recruiting went on without any hindrance from the Durbar.

Recruiting During the Two World Wars

Chandra Shamsher had decided once and for all to help the British during the war without any obstruction, and without even waiting for a request. During his term of office recruitment had expanded until in 1914 there were over 26,000 Gurkhas in the Indian army, including military police and reservists. Immediately after the war started he gave all possible help in recruiting. Orders of the Nepal Government were sent to both Eastern and Western districts of the country with

---

[1] Wylie to the Secretary of Government of India, No. 67P/27E-3099 Nepal, October 3, 1894, *Foreign Department External Proceedings*, March 1894, No. 135–141 (N.A.I.). Translation of a Yaddasht from the Prime Minister and Commander-in-Chief of Nepal, to the Resident in Nepal, No. 261/50–71, dated 29th Bhadon Sumvat, 1950 (September 24, 1893), received September 25, 1893, *ibid.*

[2] 'Grant of permission to Gurkha reservists to reside in Nepal territory in future.' *Foreign Department Secret Proceedings—E*, May 1907, Nos. 92–100. (N.A.I.)

full instructions to the officials to collect as many recruits as possible for Gurkha regiments. Chandra Shamsher opened seven centers where recruits could be collected for final selection, after which they would be dispatched to the Indian border. These centers later increased to ten, located all over the country. To induce volunteers to come forward, a substantial gratuity was granted for the cost of the journey and other expenses. Money was offered to those who would collect recruits. The headmen in the villages were also offered money and other benefits for their help in finding willing recruits.[1] The result was astonishing. By the end of World War I there were twenty battalions of Gurkhas in the Indian army.[2] This was the time when Chandra Shamsher did not say 'No' to any of the British requests. The following letter from the Resident showed his attitude:

'I have been asked to ascertain whether the following proposals for the continuance of Gurkha recruiting throughout the rainy season will meet Your Excellency's approval:—

(1) The temporary depot at Kathmandu to be closed down.

(2) Three Gurkha Officers and 100 selected non-commissioned officers and men to be kept in the recruiting districts of Nepal on recruiting duty with instructions to collect recruits and return to Gorukpore early in September.

(3) Darjeeling depot to be kept open to carry on recruiting Districts of Nepal during rain.

I presume that I may get reply in the affirmative.'[3]

The Maharajah replied, '(I) write to inform you that they are approved'.[4]

Chandra Shamsher went to the extent of offering prisoners for army service. A telegram from the Government of India stated that they would be included in the Army Bearer Corps. The telegram read;

'Offer of prisoners is accepted. Please thank H. E. the Prime Minister cordially. It is proposed to include them all in Army Bearer Corps, where there is great shortage of men.'[5]

So it was decided that the prisoners would be sent to Raxaul and

[1] 'The Supply of Recruits', 1914–18, *Basta No. 63.* (N.F.O.K.)
[2] Tuker, F., *op. cit.*, p. 192.
[3] Manner-Smith to Chandra Shamsher, No. 20120, Nepal, July 1, 1915. *Basta No. 66-B.* (N.F.O.K.)
[4] Chandra Shamsher to Manner-Smith, July 5, 1915, *ibid.*
[5] Government of India to Nepal Residency, April 30, 1918, *Basta No. 66-B.* (N.F.O.K.)

should travel through the Terai at night.¹ Orders were also passed by the Government of India and transmitted by the Durbar to the Nepal villages that all those who were 'absconders and deserters' would not be punished and their services would be accepted if they returned to their regiments.²

During World War II the British needed even more help as it was a larger and more complicated war than the earlier one. Fortunately for them there was a prime minister in Nepal who was much more willing than even Chandra Shamsher to assist. But there was a difference between Nepal of 1914–18 and that of 1939–46. Since the treaty of 1923, almost all conflicts between the two governments had been settled. Nepal was acknowledged to be an independent state, which was what the Nepalese had always wanted. This strengthened the hands of Juddha Shamsher in helping the British during World War II. A letter from him to General Sir Claude Auchinleck, Commander-in-Chief, on March 11, 1945, will suffice to show the help rendered as regards Gurkha recruits by the Nepal Durbar:³

11th March, 1945

'My Esteemed Friend,

'It was indeed a great pleasure to receive your Excellency's kind letter NO. 50670/Rt. g.I (a) (2) dated 22nd February 1945 and to learn therefrom that the demand of 12,000 Gurkha recruits required during 1944–45 season has already been met in full. I suppose I need hardly write to tell your Excellency how deeply gratified I was at the news that my earnest efforts to make the required number of recruits available this time also had been crowned with success. What little wealth Nepal has is in her manpower, with that she has readily come forward as ever to the help of her great friend and ally during this war and her sons have not failed to show to the world of what stuff they are made. The fact that of the 20 Victoria crosses awarded to the Indian Army during this war 9 have been won by the Gurkha Brigade goes to prove it without doubt. The 2nd Battalion 5th Royal Gurkha Rifles having won 3 V.C.s created a record and it deserves our hearty congratulation on it.

'The information that during the 1945–46 recruiting season Your Excellency would not require more than 5,000 recruits to maintain the

---

¹ Copy of a letter No. 4775C, dated May 27, 1918, from the Recruiting Officer for Gurkhas, Gorukhpore to the Resident in Nepal, *Basta No. 66-B*. (N.F.O.K.)

² Chandra to Colonel Bayley, September 26, 1918; Bayley to Chandra, November 26, 1918, *Basta No. 66-B*. (N.F.O.K.)

³ Juddha to General Sir Claude Auchinleck, Commander-in-Chief of India, March 11, 1945, *Basta No. 56*. (N.F.O.K.)

GURKHA RECRUITMENT AND THE GOVERNMENT OF INDIA

Gurkha units has been noted. Every effort will of course be made to make that number available when the time for that comes. Heavily recruited as the country has been during the last 5 years I am afraid the quality of the recruits that would then be available would be rather poorer. In our army too we are feeling the pinch and recourse has had to be taken to fill up vacancies with recruits of lower standard and that too with much difficulty.'

Sir Francis Tuker stated that the twenty battalions of World War I, eventually expanded to forty-five during World War II.[1] An anticlimax came when the Commander-in-Chief of India wrote to the prime minister that he wanted to reduce recruitment, which he hoped would help the Durbar in maintaining its manpower. That brought to an end the story of recruiting during the war.[2]

Gurkhas in Other Services

The story of the Gurkha's bravery and dependability had not only been recognized in other parts of the world, they were greatly sought after, in the different provinces of India, in the princely states and in Burma. They were needed too for civil work such as tea gardens, railway police, factories, etc.

As far back as 1891 Rampur State was forbidden to employ Gurungs and Magars. Kashmir had nine companies of Gurkhas in the Kashmir Imperial Service Corps and three companies in the regular army of the state.[3] There were other states which were also interested in employing Gurkhas. But the Government of Nepal objected and informed the Government of India that it deprecated the encouragement of such

---

[1] Tuker, F., *op. cit.*, p. 217.

[2] 'It is with greatest pleasure that I am now able to inform Your Highness that, as a result of further detailed examination of the manpower situation I am in a position to reduce my demand for Gurkha recruits for the year 1945-46 to 2,000 only. This will be ample to maintain existing Gurkha Rifle Regiments at full strength.

'In your letter of 11th March 1945 you stated that your country's wealth lies mainly in her manpower, and it is therefore a matter of very considerable satisfaction to me that I am able to do something towards conserving the vital resources of a staunch and noble ally who has given so unstintingly in the past.'

General Sir Claude Auchinleck, Commander-in-Chief of India to Maharajah Sir Juddha Shamsher, Prime Minister of Nepal, D.O.N. 50670/Rtg. I (A) (2), New Delhi, June 30, 1945, *Basta No. 56*. (N.F.O.K.)

[3] Forwarded for an expression of the view of the Government of India, a copy of a letter from the Military Secretary to the Kashmir Council regarding the question of enlisting Gurkha Recruits for the Army of the Jammu and Kashmir State. *Foreign External-A*, May 1891, Nos. 1-3. (N.A.I.)

employment for the simple reason that it was a drain on the manpower of Nepal. The Resident also recommended that:

'... in the interest of our own British Gurkha regiments the time had come to place a check on the admission of any of the best fighting classes, which would be included (1) Gurungs, (2) Magars, (3) Thakurs, (4) Rais, and (5) Limbus, into the Assam and Burma military police or in the Kashmir Imperial Service Infantry'.[1]

This was finally agreed and the Durbar was notified. The Nepal Durbar had also objected to mixing the Gurkhas with other races of India in the army. The Resident assured the prime minister, 'that any enlistment of Jharwas into the Indian Army would be quite distinct and separate from enlistments into Gurkha regiments'.[2]

The Resident submitted a memorandum in May 1925 that the Nepal Government desired that steps should be taken to secure that (a) no person who wished to return should be detained in India; (b) the recruitment of Gurkhas of the fighting castes should be absolutely prohibited in industries of any kind; and (c) non-fighting Gurkha castes might be employed in the mines but due protection should be given to them.[3] Similarly the Government of Nepal objected to other practices such as Gurkhas going to Singapore and other places as a labor force. The Gurkhas who did so generally settled down in those places. The Government of India took special care to meet these demands of the Government of Nepal.

All this proved the importance of the Gurkhas as a great fighting force. It should be noticed that the Government of India gradually abandoned or quietly shelved most of its demands on Nepal except for the recruitment of Gurkhas. For instance the Durbar was not pressed to admit Europeans or to remove restrictions on the Resident's freedom of movement. This proves the truth of the statement made in 1922 by Sir Arthur Hirtzel, the Under-Secretary of State for India, that it was 'after all, mainly because of the Gurkha element in the Army that we value the friendship of Nepal'.[4]

[1] Foreign Department File Notes, *Foreign Department Secret Proceedings—E*, September 1908, Nos. 485–97. (N.A.I.)
[2] Resident to the Prime Minister, Camp Darjeeling, No. 47, October 24, 1919, *Basta No. 67.* (N.F.O.K.)
[3] *Memorandum* by the Resident to the Government of India, dated May 1925, *Basta No. 66-B.* (N.F.O.K.)
[4] Sir Arthur Hirtzel, *Political and External File*, August 25, 1922. (I.O.L.)

CHAPTER 9
NEPAL, CHINA, TIBET

Early Contacts

The relations between these three states during the early period can be summarized briefly. Early in the sixth century Nepal (which at that time had very different boundaries from those of today) became feudatory to Tibet.[1] Charles Bell wrote that:

'The connection between Tibet and Nepal, both socially and politically, is long and intimate. It was in large measure from Nepal that the early Tibetan kings received the Buddhist religion. For Nepal, though warmer than their own country, was habitable for Tibetans; whereas the climate of the torrid plains of India exacted too heavy a toll of lives from the dwellers in the cold uplands, when these came down to study the new religion. Tibetan armies appear to have overrun the territory of Nepal from time to time, and probably in concert with Nepalese, to have invaded northern India. The victorious Tibetan king, Song-tsen Gam-po, took not only a Chinese, but also a Nepalese, princess as his wife.'[2]

This at least indicates that Tibet in those days was a powerful and independent kingdom. This relationship of Nepal with Tibet continued until the ninth century. With the collapse of Tibet by the end of the ninth century, Nepal drifted slowly into the Indian sphere of influence.[3] According to W. W. Rockhill, regular relations between China and Tibet started in the seventh, eighth, and ninth centuries. He wrote:

'Tibet was at the height of its power. During that period of its history

---

[1] 'Historical Note on Relations between Nepal and China.' This document is the property of the Secretary of State for India in Council (Confidential), *File No. B. 176*, 1910 (I.O.L. London, Microfilm); Levi, Sylvain, *op. cit.*, Vol. II, p. 52.
[2] Bell, Charles, *Tibet Past and Present*, p. 231, Clarendon Press, 1924.
[3] 'Historical Note on Relations between Nepal and China', *op. cit.*

it carried its victorious arms far into India, Central Asia and China. In the last named country it had time and again overrun a large part of the present provinces of Kan-su, Ssu-ch'uan and Yun-nan, had even entered Ch'ang-an-fu, the capital of the T'ang emperors, and placed for a time, on the throne of China a prince of its choice. During that period the Tibetans were the allies of the Caliphs of Baghdad and supported them with their arms. This period is marked, on the part of the rulers of China, by extreme friendliness for Tibet; its kings were given imperial princesses as wives, treaties of alliance were made with them, and every assistance rendered to introduce Chinese culture into the country and draw closer its political and commercial relations with the Empire.'[1]

George Patterson wrote:

'According to Chinese writers, the first record of Chinese contact with Tibetans refers to fighting between the two in 2220 BC when the Emperor Shun drove San-meaous tribesmen into a region called San-wei, which later Chinese scholars identified as constituting three parts of Tibet.'[2]

However, George Patterson further wrote that Western scholars were unanimous in dismissing Chinese records of this period as of little or no value. He does support the view of other scholars that regular contact with Tibet and China began in the seventh century.[3] The influence of China did not appear in Nepal until the end of the fourteenth century. This was the beginning of a regular exchange of presents between the two countries which lasted until 1427.[4] However, this did not make Nepal a vassal state to China. China was the strongest power in the Far East and claimed suzerainty over the weak states on her frontier, such as Thailand, Burma, etc.[5] In the latter year the Emperor Huien-ti's mission to Nepal met with no response, and relations seem to have been interrupted until the beginning of the eighteenth century. In the meantime Nepal had divided into three kingdoms, of which China, by its conquest of Tibet in the reign of the Emperor Kang-hsi (1662–1722), became the powerful neighbor. The three Nepalese kings thought it prudent in 1731 to send to the Emperor Yong Tcheng a

[1] Rockhill, W. W., *The Dalai Lamas of Lhasa and Their Relations with The Manchu Emperors of China 1644–1908*, p. 1 (Oriental Printing Office, Leyden, 1910). Reprinted from the *T'oung-Pao*, Series III, Vol. I, No. 1.
[2] Patterson, George N., *Tibet in Revolt*, pp. 17–18. London, 1960.
[3] Ibid., p. 18.
[4] 'Historical Note on Relations between Nepal and China', op. cit.
[5] Vella, op. cit., pp. 112–13.

gold-leaf petition and 'tribute' consisting of local products. It does not appear whether this tribute was rendered a second time.[1]

Under the leadership of the Gurkha King Prithvi Narayan Shah, Nepal was consolidated into one kingdom in 1769. This was the time when the three countries, China, Tibet, and Nepal became clearly distinct from one another. They were the only three powers in those days in this particular area. In the spring of 1788, the Gurkha ruler of Nepal, on the pretext that Tibet had increased customs dues on salt and had illegally exported to Nepal, and also because of controversies over currency and debased coinage, suddenly crossed the frontier of Tibet and occupied Nielam, Tsongka, and Kirung. The Tibetan and the Chinese troops were unable to resist them, and the Tibetans, with the approval of the Chinese General Pa-Chung secured their withdrawal by secret arrangement promising to pay an annual tribute.[2] Rockhill further wrote:

'The Chinese General then reported to the Emperor of China that Gorkha chief only wishes to send a tribute mission to China, and that he had settled the little frontier incident without the loss of a single soldier or spending of a single tael. The Gorkha mission was thereupon allowed to proceed to Peking, and the Emperor in blissful ignorance of the attack on the Tibetan frontier, sent the Gorkha Raja on dismissing it a patent of King.'[3]

When the Tibetan Government refused to pay the tribute to Nepal according to the 1788 agreement, the Nepalese invaded Tibet with an army of 18,000 in 1791 from Nielam, took the position held by the small Chinese and Tibetan forces, and without meeting any opposition, captured Shigatse on September 28th and sacked Tashilhunpo.[4] But soon after this success the Nepalese slowly retreated, having learned a Chinese army was coming to Tibet's help.

This was the first time that both sides appear to have turned to the East India Company for help. In 1792 Lord Cornwallis received a memorial from the Gurkha Government and a letter from the Dalai

[1] 'Historical Note on Relations between Nepal and China', op. cit.
[2] Rockhill, op. cit., p. 51.
[3] Ibid. 'The annual tribute was fixed at 300 Tibetan shoes of sycce, equivalent to 9600 Chinese taels. The Gorkha agreed to evacuate Nielam, Tsongka and Kirung, and pledged themselves never to cross the Tibetan frontier. The Emperor on learning of this agreement annulled it and ordered the condign punishment of Pa-Chung; he escaped it, however, by drowning himself.' (Quoted by Rockhill on page 51, footnote 1 from Tung-hua Ch'uan-lu, Ch'ien-lung CXIV, 29b–30).
[4] Rockhill, op. cit., p. 51.

Lama. It was by no means a happy occasion for the East India Company. Lord Cornwallis replied to both that the Company wished:

'... to maintain the most cordial and friendly terms with all the powers in India, and sensible of the wisdom of this conduct, they are careful not to infringe the rules of friendship, by interference in a hostile manner in the dispute prevalent among foreign powers, except when self-defense, or wanton attacks oblige them. . . .'[1]

To the Rajah of Nepal he specially wrote:

'But, however this line of conduct is in general the policy of the English government; the connexion that has been formed with the Emperor of China renders a due observance of it still more necessary. The English company have for many years carried on extensive commercial concerns with the subjects of the Emperor of China by sea, and have actually a factory established in his dominions. I am confident that this argument will satisfy you that a compliance with your request, to assist you with a military force against the Rajah of Lassa, who is dependent on the Emperor of China, would be not only an infringement on the general policy of the English government, but also a measure inconsistent with the connection that has so long prevailed between the Company and the Emperor. Desirous, however, that harmony and peace should be preserved among those who are the friends of the Company, I shall be very happy if my amicable interference can in any shape contribute to re-establish them between the Lassa and you, and shall be ready to use it in the way of a friend and mediator between you.'[2]

The Chinese General sent his comment on the letter of Lord Cornwallis to the Emperor of China. Rockhill gives it as follows:

'When last year I summoned all the chiefs of tribes to send troops to stop the trouble, I had in view the desirability of diminishing the strength of the Gorkhas, without counting particularly on the aid of the foreign barbarian soldiers. But here we have this headman of the Pëling receiving the summons from your Majesty's Minister with every sign of the profoundest respect. The greatness of our Emperor's fame has been proclaimed afar, it is wafted back from the most distant seas. This tribe which trades at Canton and has always experienced the gracious kindness of the Imperial Court, spontaneously tells the Gorkhas that Tibet has been for ages a dependency of China and that

[1] Kirkpatrick, *op. cit.*, pp. 349–52.
[2] *Ibid.*, p. 350.

they must not seek a quarrel with it. How profoundly just and right are these words....'[1]

Lord Cornwallis sent Colonel Kirkpatrick to mediate, but before he arrived the Chinese, in several sharp engagements, defeated the Nepalese and advanced to a very short distance from Kathmandu, the capital of Nepal. At this point, the Gurkhas being most desirous of concluding peace, the victorious general stopped hostilities 'on return of all the loot taken from Tashilhunpo, and of the Gurkha agreement to send a tribute mission every five years to Peking'.[2] The Chinese source speaks of the Nepal Rajah as 'having relinquished all his conquests in that quarter, and formally recognized the paramount authority of the Emperor of China over the Nepal dominion'.[3] E. H. Parker was quoted in the document on 'Historical Note on Relations between Nepal and China', as giving a synopsis of a decree by the Emperor issued in 1792, after the war, in which the following passage occurs:

'On the whole (the Gurkha's) submission is more humble than that of the usurping King of Annam, and perhaps, hearing of his recent visit to Peking they may be induced also to come later on. Under these circumstances I will pardon them and withdraw.... As matters stand, the success is not such that I can celebrate a formal triumph in the temple. If, therefore, the plunder taken at Tashilhunpo is returned, with Shamarpi's corpse and retainers, you may accept their offers. They can send tribute on the same footing as Annam, Siam, Burma, and Korea.'[4]

The East India Company did not gain anything from the Himalayan crisis. The Chinese strengthened their hold on Tibet much more firmly than before. The result was that Tibet was almost closed to trade with British India. Furthermore the Chinese did not like the attempt of the East India Company to intervene in the Tibetan–Nepalese dispute. So when in 1793 the British tried to obtain closer relations with China they failed.[5] The British problem was to handle the Himalayan crisis so that it would not affect their trade relations with China at Canton. They realized that China treated Nepal and Tibet as her vassal states, and naturally any interference from the East India Company in the

[1] Rockhill, *op. cit.*, p. 62.
[2] Rockhill, *op. cit.*, p. 52, Extract from a demi-official letter from the Residency in Nepal, to the Foreign Secretary, May 26, 1904. *Foreign Department Secret Proceedings—E*, August 1904, Nos. 160-1. (N.A.I.)
[3] Rockhill, *ibid.*, p. 52.
[4] 'Historical Note on Relations between Nepal and China', *op. cit.*
[5] Majumdar, K., *op. cit.*, pp. 441–8.

affairs of these states would have an adverse effect on the attitude of the Chinese Government. On the other hand the Company did not possess any clear information about the exact relationship between Nepal and China. However, it was Nepal's aggressive policy which had led to this Himalayan crisis.[1]

In 1799 the Nepalese King Rana Bahadur requested and received from the Chinese Emperor royal rank for his son and eventual successor. But the attitude of the Chinese seems to have been one of indifference. For example, the Emperor Kienlung had given instructions to his successor in 1796 that he should not interfere with Nepal's affairs unless it should become an absolute necessity.[2] In later days also China maintained indifference towards Nepal. Parker wrote that in 1815:

'When the Nepalese tried to force China's hand by saying that the English would probably disapprove of tribute being sent to China, the Emperor said (i.e. to the Amban at Lhasa): "Tell them you dare not report this language to me. As a matter of fact they can join the Feringhi rule if they like, so long as they send tribute, and so long as the Feringhi[3] do not cross the Tangut frontier." '[4]

[1] Nepal was henceforth obliged to send a quinquennial tributary mission to China. The obligation was faithfully carried out until 1852. Between 1852 and 1866 no mission was sent due to ill treatment meted out to these missions by the Tibetans, on their way to Peking through Eastern Tibet.
After 1866 Nepal sent missions to China in 1877, 1886, 1894, 1906 and 1908. Finally in 1911, the missions were officially discontinued by Nepal. In return for the tribute Nepal received rich goods from the Chinese Emperor. The tributary missions did not mean Nepal's subjection to Chinese political control. China never claimed direct control over Nepal's policies, although Nepalese paid deference to her great name and power. Nepal's relations with China were never the same as Tibet's relations with China. A Chinese garrison was stationed in Lhasa, whereas China had no such garrison posted in Nepal. By 1866 China's power in Tibet had decayed so much that it could not enforce its claim to suzerainty. Also there was danger of British India coming to the help of Nepal if China tried to reimpose its control. So the only reason for sending missions after 1866 was the valuable presents given by the Chinese Emperor. The periodical sending of an embassy to the court of the Chinese Emperor was not a genuine sign of submission by the governments of the frontier states. They paid little or no attention to Chinese orders. Nepal's tributary status was like that of various other dependencies of China, such as Korea, Annam, Siam, and Burma. Generally see Majumdar, K., op. cit., Fisher and Rose, op. cit., Lee, Daniel J., 'Nationalist China Re-establishes Relations with the Kingdom of Nepal', China Weekly Review, 55: 148–49, December 27, 1930 and 'Chinese Mission to Nepal', China Weekly Review, 70: 400, November 17, 1934.
[2] 'Historical Note on Relations between Nepal and China', op. cit.
[3] 'Feringhi' is a Persian version of an Urdu word meaning 'the English people'. It had been used by Muslims and later adopted by the Indians.
[4] Parker, E. H., 'Nepal and China', op. cit., p.72; 'Historical Note on Relations between Nepal and China', op. cit.

NEPAL, CHINA, TIBET

Maulvi Abdul Qadir after his return from Nepal, in his report of 1795 said that shortly after the war of 1788–92 the Chinese did try to exercise some political sway over Nepal, but the latter was wholly opposed to it.[1]

After the war of 1791–92, which rescued Tibet from the Gurkhas, the Chinese Emperor decided to reform the whole administration of Tibet and to take effective control of the reins of government in order to prevent any further repetition of expensive expeditions.[2] It was only after 1793 that the Chinese Amban in Tibet took an active part in the administration of the country. The result of this active interest was that:

'The Colonial office of Peking (Li-fan-yüan) has the general superintendence of Tibetan affairs, but it is the governor-general of Ssŭ-ch'uan who is the immediate superior of the Amban. To him the Amban reports his actions; of him he asks instructions, even sends him copies of his despatches to Peking.'[3]

After introducing administrative changes the interest of the Chinese in Tibet began to wane. When conflict between Nepal and Tibet broke out again in 1854 the Chinese did not come to Tibet's help. The Manchu Emperor was no longer as powerful as he was in 1792.[4] Once more Nepal proved that it was stronger. The Tibetans were badly defeated, and a treaty was signed between the two governments. The preamble to the treaty is said to have stated that 'We further agree that the Emperor of China is to be obeyed by both states as before'.[5] The prime minister of Nepal challenged the accuracy of this translation in 1910 and according to a revised translation made by Major O'Connor, a British official, the correct wording of the preamble was, 'Both parties, paying respect as always before to the Chinese Emperor'.[6] The second article of this treaty further acknowledged the overlordship of China, by stating that, 'The State of Gurkha and of Tibet have both borne allegiance to the Emperor of China up to the present time'.[7] In 1858 soon after this treaty was signed, the prime minister of Nepal received a Mandarin's button and the title 'General in Chief of the Army, truly

---

[1] Majumdar, K., *op. cit.*, pp. 442–8.
[2] Li, Tieh-Tseng, *Tibet Today and Yesterday*, p. 53 (New York, 1960).
[3] Rockhill, W. W., *Land of the Lamas*, p. 291 (London, 1891).
[4] Sanwal, B. D., *Nepal and the East India Company*, pp. 284–5, Bombay, Asia Publishing House, 1965.
[5] Treaty between Nepal and Tibet in March 1856, *Foreign Internal—B*, February 1894, No. 204–8 (N.A.I.)
[6] 'Historical Note on Relations between Nepal and China', *op. cit.*
[7] Treaty between Nepal and Tibet in March 1856, *op. cit.*

brave prince and Prime Minister'.[1] This at least gives the impression that after the Nepalese–Tibetan war of 1854–56 the relations between the Chinese, Nepalese and Tibetans were outwardly friendly, although a fairly long interval elapsed before another Nepalese mission was sent to Peking. Yet until 1852, the Nepalese mission had been maltreated by the Chinese authorities and the people of Eastern Tibet. Jung Bahadur told the Resident that because of the mistreatment of the Nepalese mission in 1852 he waged war against Tibet.[2] He was indignant at the misbehavior of the Chinese Amban and had decided not to send any more tributary missions. His anger continued through 1857 and 1862, when missions would in the ordinary course have been sent to Peking.[3] By 1866, however, he had changed his mind, for he said that he had received:

'... several overtures from the Umbah of Lhassa inviting him to re-establish the relations that formerly existed between their two countries, and promising, upon the part of the Emperor, that any future Mission that may be sent to him by the Goorkha shall be received with high honour and consideration.'[4]

The Government of India had no objection and considered that 'the Nipalese Durbar is, of course, at liberty to act in this matter as it may think proper'.[5]

The mission which was sent by Jung Bahadur in 1866, after a lapse of twelve years, was believed to have met with the same maltreatment as the earlier ones. At least the Resident reported to the Government of India in 1867 that the Durbar seemed to be preparing for war against Tibet.[6] Although the conflict was smoothed over in 1866, a fresh trouble started in 1873. Jung Bahadur insisted that his representative would not return to Lhasa 'without some assurance that there shall not be a repetition of this and former outrages'.[7] His condition for the

---

[1] Levi, S., *op. cit.*, Vol. I, p. 185. (Daniel Wright, *History of Nepal*, p. 40, 1958 gives the date for the above title 1873 instead of 1857 as cited in S. Levi.)

[2] Ramsay to the Secretary, Government of India, Foreign Department, with the Governor-General, No. 15, June 9, 1866. *Foreign Department Political*, June 1866, Nos. 163-4. (N.A.I.)

[3] Ramsay to Secretary Government of India, Foreign Department, No. 15, June 9, 1866. *Foreign Department Political*, June 1866, Nos. 163-4. (N.A.I.)

[4] *Ibid.*

[5] *Ibid.*

[6] Lawrence, Resident to the Secretary, Government of India, No. 2-P, May 22, 1871, *Foreign Department Political—A*, July 1871, Nos. 100-5. (N.A.I.)

[7] Under-Secretary Government of India to Resident, Nepal, No. 2199-P, September 18, 1873, *Foreign Department Political—A*, October 1873, Nos. 67-9. (N.A.I.)

renewal of diplomatic relations with Tibet was 'a formal pledge in writing that a Nepalese Envoy shall henceforth be secure from ill-treatment in Lhasa'.[1] The Resident in Nepal was informed by his Government that 'you should do all in your power by friendly advice to prevent the outbreak of hostilities, and to further the re-establishment of friendly relations between the two countries: beyond this you should be careful not to interfere'.[2] War was averted between Nepal and Tibet in 1873 but once again strained relations between the two countries were reported. It was the opinion of the Resident that because of the superiority of Tibet in arms, Jung Bahadur decided not to go to war. Otherwise he would have regarded the new outrage as an 'additional *casus belli* and declared war'.[3] Due to the strained relations, the British Commissioners in the border areas reported many rumors including a report that Sikkim felt that 'Nipal was the aggressor'.[4] Mr Edgar, the Deputy Commissioner at Darjeeling, stated that:

'... he was informed that for some time past frequent confidential communication had been carried on between the Deb Raja of Bhootan and Sir Jung Bahadoor, with the object it was believed of a united attack on Tibet.'[5]

This report could not be confirmed by the Government of India, and it was doubted whether it could be true.

One of the major reasons advanced for the Tibetan–Nepalese conflict was that the Tibetans did not want closer relations between China and Nepal. The Tibetans believed that the regular mission from Nepal to China could be dangerous to their independence.[6] Charles Bell quoted many Tibetan authorities who believed that Nepal wanted to see China strong in Tibet in order to be able to play China off against Britain.[7] Lönchen Shatra, the Prime Minister of Tibet, told Bell that:

'... when Chao Erh Feng was advancing in Tibet, (Nepalese) constantly advised the Tibetan Government to abstain from opposition. By this bad advice, Chinese troops were enabled to enter Tibet.'[8]

[1] Under-Secretary, Government of India to Resident, *Foreign Department Political—A*, October 1873, Nos. 67–9. (N.A.I.)
[2] *Ibid.*
[3] 'Memorandum as to State of relations between Nipal and Tibet, and of affairs in Tibet according to the most recent information', *Home Department Political—A*, October 1874, No. 97, K.W. (N.A.I.)
[4] *Ibid.*
[5] *Ibid.*
[6] *Ibid.*
[7] Bell, Charles, *Tibet Past and Present*, op. cit., p. 236.
[8] *Ibid.*, p. 236.

He further said:

'When the last Nepalese Mission visited Peking, they were loaded with presents by the Chinese Government, and the Empress Dowager herself granted them a special interview. The Mission were delighted with the treatment that they received, and praised the Chinese Government highly on their return.'[1]

This Nepalese attitude could be explained on the assumption that they probably felt that a certain amount of Chinese influence in Tibet would help them. In case the Tibetan Government did not do what they wished, they could appeal to the Chinese Amban at Lhasa. On the other hand Sir Francis Younghusband in the postscripts of the preface of his book *India and Tibet* wrote:

'The conclusion of this famous authority (Rockhill) on Tibet, that the Tibetans have no desire for total independence of China, but that their complaints have always been directed against the manner in which the local Chinese officials have performed their duties, is particularly noteworthy.'[2]

The British Resident's influence played an important part in localizing and narrowing down the conflict. He suggested to Jung Bahadur that the Tibetans wished the Nepalese Vakil (diplomatic representative) to be changed, and the Resident saw no difficulty in sending a better man to conduct relations between the two states. This was agreed by Jung Bahadur, who decided to adopt a conciliatory attitude towards Tibet.[3] This helpful attitude of the British Resident had been expected by the Tibetans also. One of them told Bell:

'We Tibetans realize that Nepal is too small for her population and that she might endeavour to seize Tibetan districts near the Nepal frontier on some pretext or other. But we do not think she will do so at present, as she has much to lose; and we hope also that the British Government would prevent their ally from acting in that way.'[4]

It was really regrettable that constant friction existed between two neighbors, Nepal and Tibet. Similar examples of conflict existed in other parts of Asia, for example, Japan and Korea, or China and

---

[1] Bell, Charles, *op. cit.* p. 236.
[2] Younghusband, Francis, *India and Tibet*, p. viii, London: John Murray, 1910.
[3] *Foreign Department Political—A*, October 1874, No. 97, K.W., *op. cit.*
[4] Bell, *op. cit.*, pp. 237-8.

Tibet. Jung Bahadur was of the opinion that in any war between Tibet and Nepal the Chinese would come to the aid of Tibet. He also wanted to find out whether the Government of India would support Nepal against China.[1] There were also rumors that Nepal was trying to create a rift between India and Tibet. If the Government of India had given encouragement to Jung Bahadur against Tibet he would have gone to war. But the British attitude was clear enough: they wanted to maintain peace. If they could do this the war would not spread, the northern border would be quiet, and China would not have any pretext for entering the conflict. Once again war was avoided; but the cause of conflict remained to be solved. The Government of India had given wide latitude to Nepal in its relations with China and Tibet. During the war of 1854–56, it remained strictly neutral. India's problem was that if Nepal became involved directly with China it would be difficult for the British to remain aloof. Therefore they wanted above all to maintain peace and avoid trouble.

The British Minister to China, Sir T. Wade, obtained possession of an enlightening document of which he informed the British government. It disclosed that in 1860 the Emperor of China issued a secret decree which was never published. The decree showed that the Russian Consul at Kulja (Ili) had urged the Chinese to induce the Gurkhas to revolt against the British in India, 'in order to embarrass the operations then being conducted against Pekin under Lord Elgin'.[2] The scheme came to nothing because the Chinese Emperor mistrusted the Russians. Sir T. Wade considered that the authenticity of the decree, describing the attempt of the Russian Consul, was 'beyond dispute'.[3] Unfortunately he did not attach the secret decree itself to his letter to the Secretary of State for Foreign Affairs. He went on to write that the Chinese Military Governor of Ili improved upon this plan and suggested that the Russians should first attack India and at the same time Nepal should attack India.[4] Sir T. Wade said that this was the time when the Russian Minister at Peking was 'insisting with violent language upon a demarcation of the frontier in the territories pertaining to the province of Kirin'.[5] The answer to this Russian proposal came directly from the Chinese Government to the Governor of Ili and read that 'the Russians, English and French were all united by a

---

[1] *Foreign Department Political—A*, October 1874, No. 97, K.W., *op. cit.*

[2] 'Office Note. Proposed Mission from Nepal to China', *Foreign Secret Department*, September 1876, Nos. 129/33 K.W. (From His Majesty's Minister in Peking, dated May 24, 1876. (N.A.I.)

[3] *Ibid.*

[4] *Ibid.*

[5] *Ibid.*

common understanding.'¹ The Chinese felt that if the proposed attack on India were successful the Russians would occupy the country and would leave China alone. Furthermore, if the proposal should seem to have originated from China the first thing the Russian barbarians would do would be to inform the English, 'representing us as the mischief makers, so that in actual fact we should be made fools of by the barbarians'.² The Governor of Ili was told to reply to the Russians if this proposal were again put forward by them:

'that the policy of the celestial dynasty, in the exercise of its control over outer nations, is based upon good faith and uprightness, and that it stands altogether aloof from insidious acts of treachery, the result of which must give rise to war.'³

Sir T. Wade wrote that perhaps the most important part of the decree 'is that concerning the relations between Nepal and British India:'⁴

'Nipal . . . is subject to the English barbarians. Were we to propose that it should place its resources at our disposal for an attack upon India, it would be certain to decline the giving offence to the English, and the only result would be to open the door to their [the English] demands and reclamations.'⁵

This decree underlines two important factors. Firstly, the Chinese made it very clear that in their foreign policy they did not intrigue with one European power against another, because they distrusted all of them and avoided entangling alliances with any of them. Secondly, they confirmed their earlier indifference towards Nepal. They were determined to avoid any proposal to Nepal which might invite British reprisals against China.

After the failure of the Nepalese mission of 1866 no embassy could be sent to China in 1871 because of famine conditions in Shansi and Shensi provinces. In July 1878 the Chinese authorities in Tibet informed the Emperor that the Nepalese Mission had now arrived, and delivered a petition from the ruler of Nepal which expressed the desire 'of his wild subjects to become civilized'.⁶ The Chinese officials

---

¹ *Foreign Secret Department*, September 1876, Nos. 129/33, K.W., *op. cit.*
² *Ibid.*
³ *Ibid.*
⁴ *Ibid.*
⁵ *Ibid.*
⁶ Memorial from Heng-Hsun, Manchu, Commander-in-Chief, in Szechwan and Ting Pao-Chen, Governor General of Szechwan, reporting the arrival in Szechwan of tribute-bearing Envoys from Nepal. From the manuscript Edition

received orders from the emperor to 'Let the Nipalese Envoys be permitted as is customary, to come to Peking; and let the Manchu Commander-in-Chief and his colleagues send instructions along the road that proper attention be shown them'.[1] The memorial which was sent by the Manchu Commander-in-Chief in Szechwan made it very clear that he had received a petition from the Rajah of Nepal for sending the tributary mission. It should be noticed that it was Nepal which always requested permission from the Chinese to be allowed to send a mission. The actual wording was a traditional formula for sending the petition with high sounding words which meant nothing. They were intended to exalt the emperor's importance. To the Chinese the use of such phraseology in a petition was very important. If a Rajah did not employ similar terms of humble abasement before the majesty of the emperor when writing to him, in all probability the letter would have been returned. Rockhill gives one such example. He wrote:

'The Emperor of Japan in AD 600 addressed a letter to the Emperor Wen-ti of the Sui Dynasty, which began: "The Son of Heaven of the country of the rising sun, to the Son of Heaven of the country of the setting sun." The Chinese Emperor was so indignant at this that he ordered the letters to be returned to the sender.'[2]

This shows their sensitiveness in the matter of addresses. The prime minister of Nepal always made it a point to inform the British Resident of his intentions of sending a mission, and the British never objected. The Viceroy's opinion was that the Nepal Government had not been among the 'feudatories to the Indian Empire'. It had the power of 'making war, entering into treaties and sending embassies, without let or hindrance from the British Government', and so the Governor-General of India had no *locus standi* to interfere with the proposal of the Durbar to send the usual mission to China.[3] This had always been the attitude of the Indian Government. Because of its friendly relations with Nepal, it had no reason to apprehend that this periodical interchange of presents with China would lead to complications. Nepal tried to please both British India and China.

Nepal had always assured the Government of India that the tributary

of the Peking Gazette, March 24, 1879. *Foreign Secret Department*, June 1879 Nos. 22–5. (N.A.I.)

[1] *Foreign Secret Department*, June 1879, Nos. 22–5, *op. cit.*
[2] Rockhill, W. W., *Diplomatic Audiences at the Court of China*, p. 6, London: Luzac & Co., 1905.
[3] T. H. Thornton, Officiating Secretary, Government of India, Foreign Department, to H. E. Sir T. F. Wade, Her Majesty's Minister Peking, No. 1713, Simla, July 25, 1876, *Foreign Secret*, September 1876, No. 131. (N.A.I.)

mission was only an old custom and that it had the very practical aims of obtaining free access to China and bringing back tax free goods from there. After the assassination of Maharajah Ranodip Singh, Bir Shamsher, who was responsible for the murder, sent a dispatch in the name of the Maharajah Dhiraj to inform the Emperor of China of the murder, and to request for his new prime minister or Ko-chi the same title of 'Valiant Prince', and the 'uniform which was given by the Emperor'[1] to the deceased.

For centuries past, similar letters had been sent by weak states which were near China. Their significance was merely that a ruler whose power was uncertain hoped to strengthen his position by receiving formal recognition from the emperor of the largest and oldest state in Asia. Bir Shamsher was at least as anxious to receive the endorsement of the Government of India. In forwarding the petition, the Chinese Resident at Lhasa wrote that Nepal 'has long been enrolled among the tributary states of the Empire, that its people have the reputation of being fierce and violent, and that its Chiefs are constantly engaged in quarrelling and fighting'.[2] The Chinese official inquired 'whether these favours shall be granted, according to precedent, as a means of keeping control over the country'.[3] The sentence just quoted shows that although China claimed suzerainty over Nepal, its retention of this position was dependent on the acquiescence of the nominal tributary state. The prime ministers of Nepal time and again had assured the Government of India that the Tribute Mission was merely a traditional form, and the servile abasement and humble obedience expressed by the tribute letter was only the immemorial diplomatic formula required when one addressed the emperor of China. It meant nothing so far as their political relations were concerned.[4]

The following is a translation of the tribute letter as rendered into Chinese by the memorialists:

'Your Majesty's humble servant Pijet'ipipikaerhmashenghsiehjetseng kapahatujesaha, Erdeni Prince of the Gurkhas, performing nine prostrations, presents upon his knees a memorial of respectful greeting before the Throne of His August Majesty, whose nourishing kindness

[1] Sir J. Walsham, British Minister, Peking, to the Viceroy of India, No. 58, Peking, August 23, 1886. *Foreign Secret—E*, October 1886, No. 352. (N.A.I.)
[2] Tribute Mission from Nepal to China, dated April 11, 1887. Memorial from Imperial Residents in Tibet to the Emperor of China, April 8, 1887. *Foreign Secret—E*, March 1888, No. 20. (N.A.I.)
[3] *Foreign Secret—E*, March 1888, No. 20, *op. cit.*
[4] The wording of the Tribute Letter assured the emperor that the ruler of Nepal was 'less than the dust beneath thy chariot wheel'. Chinese protocol also dictated that the emperor address the independent emperor of Annam as, 'O, tail of a rat'.

is like the overspreading vault of heaven or the rays of the sun and moon, who extends his fostering care to a myriad of kingdoms, whose longevity is as enduring as the mountain of Hsu-mi (round which the sun and moon revolve). Most Great, Most Honorable Manjusiri Boddhisattwa.

'Your humble servant is required to send tribute once in five years, and he should this year despatch a Kochi and others reverently to bear this tribute to Pekin and there make offering thereof. He has now reverently and carefully prepared these offerings in full tale, and has made selection of a tribute and assistant tribute envoy in the persons of the Kochi Jelapikaerhmajena, chief envoy, and Sardar Tijek'omanla, assistant envoy, with headmen high and low, who leave the town of Yangpu (Katmandu) on this 5th day of the 7th moon of the 12th year (August 4th, 1886), reverently bearing the said offerings.

'On former occasions whenever events have occurred in your humble servant's domain requiring reference to the Throne, such reference has always been made through Their Excellencies the two Residents in Tibet, to whom petitions have been presented. He has accordingly now petitioned Their Excellencies, requesting them to address Your Majesty on his behalf, making due allowance for the distance of Nepal from the capital and your servant's ignorance of the formalities of the celestial court, also giving due and full consideration to the sincerity of your humble servant in his leaning towards civilization.

'Ever since the ancestors of your humble servant tendered their allegiance to the celestial court this allegiance has always been sincere, and all that your humble servant can do is with single heart and mind, and with due reverence and respect humbly to implore Your August Majesty to remember that his predecessors were good men and true. Your servant is young in age and fears that he may be guilty of mistakes in what he does. Regard your humble servant as a slave, and extend your bounty and leniency to him as such, that he may for ever be the humble recipient of the heavenly bounty for which he will be infinitely grateful.

'He addresses this memorial upon his knees after performing nine prostrations on this 5th day of the 7th moon of the 12th year of Kuang Hsu (August 4th, 1886) and respectfully offers a piece of cloth of gold as an accompaniment to this tributary letter.'[1]

In its assurance to the British about the tribute letters to China, Nepal might have added that Great Britain did not acknowledge itself to be a tributary state when the ambassador of King George II, Lord McCartney

---

[1] Translation of the tribute letter as rendered into Chinese by the memorialists. *Foreign Secret—E*, March 1888, No. 19–24. (N.A.I.)

in 1793, and Lord Amherst in 1816, humbly prostrated themselves before the Emperor of China in order to gain more favorable terms of trade.[1] On this question Rockhill in his book *Diplomatic Audiences at the Court of China*, wrote:

'With Ward's failure in 1859 the first phase of this long fought battle came to an end. In it the Chinese had scored victories over the Arabs, Russians, Dutch, Portuguese, British and Americans, and in the middle of the nineteenth century the Western world had no reason to believe that China would ever depart from its successfully enforced demand that foreign envoys should prostrate themselves before the Emperor in compliance with the immemorial custom of the country and of Asia generally.'[2]

A New Trend on the Part of British India

The Government of India had never approved whole-heartedly of the tribute mission, which acknowledged a Chinese suzerainty that was purely nominal, although it had not made any serious objection to it. It particularly disliked the fulsome profession of inferiority required by immemorial custom in the Tribute letter. Previously it had made no objection, but in 1889 a new development occurred which brought matters to a head. The Resident informed the Government of India that a Chinese Mission was coming to Nepal.[3] The Secretary of the Foreign Office called it 'very undesirable', while admitting 'I am afraid we cannot help'.[4] He prophesied that 'sooner or later we shall have trouble with China all along the Himalayas'.[5]

Previously it had been Nepal which had sent tribute missions because they brought benefits such as valuable presents. But on this occasion it was China which was sending an embassy to Nepal. The Government of India was concerned to know what this portended, but it felt that protest was unwise since this would show that it attached importance to the Chinese move. The Resident at Kathmandu was informed that the Government 'do not look with favour upon any dealings with the Chinese on the part of Nipal'.[6] Little information exists about what took place during the visit of the Chinese mission.

[1] Rockhill, W. W., *op. cit.* (For a detailed discussion of this controversial issue see Chapter 2.)
[2] *Ibid.* (See also Chapter 3.)
[3] 'Foreign Office File Notes', *Foreign Secret—E*, August 1889, Nos. 27-8. (N.A.I.)
[4] *Ibid.*
[5] *Ibid.*
[6] *Ibid.*

Probably the indifference professed by the British Government of India forced the Maharajah of Nepal to consider the difficulties in which diplomatic relations with China might involve him.

After 1889 the Government of India took a rather more serious view of these missions and tried to keep an eye on them. When the next embassy from Nepal went to China in 1894, the British Minister in Peking took alarm over the wording of the tribute letter. He pointed out that the ruler of Nepal 'is therein represented as the devoted and submissive vassal of the Emperor of China' and added:

'The uncertainty at present attaching to the political condition of China appears to me to render it of importance that the relations between Nepal and China should be clearly defined, and that a shadowy claim of suzerainty should not be interpreted as constituting a real state of vassalage.'[1]

Lord Salisbury shared this view, and after he had clearly ascertained from the Indian Government that the language used in the Tributary letter was traditional and was believed to date from the end of the eighteenth century, the British Minister at Peking was instructed to speak to the Chinese Government. Accordingly the British Minister informed Prince Cheng and other ministers of the Government of China that:

'the submissive expressions in the letters from Nepal . . . are not regarded by Her Majesty's Government as an acknowledgement of vassalage, or indeed anything more than a purely formal and complimentary style of address.'[2]

The Chinese Ministers for a time discussed among themselves that 'Nepal had for many years past been a tributary to China'.[3] Eventually the question was dropped without a decision being reached.

Tibet–Nepal Conflict a Periodic Affair
Conflict between Nepal and Tibet became routine. The relations between the two governments were not friendly because the Tibetans felt that Nepal had acted in an unjust and highhanded way towards

---

[1] Sir Frederic O'Connor, British Minister at Peking to Lord Salisbury, Secretary of State, Letter No. 164 of April 30, 1895. 'Historical Note on Relations between Nepal and China', *op. cit.*
[2] 'Historical Note on Relations between Nepal and China', *op. cit.*
[3] *Ibid.* Also see Mission from Nepal to China. Question of the subordination of Nepal to China. *Foreign Secret—E*, September 1895, Nos. 116–30, K.W. This file from the National Archives of India contains the complete discussion

them.[1] After an interval of several years, upon one or another pretext each tried to find excuses to go to war. It was as much a routine as the periodic mission of Nepal to China. In 1893 Nepal stopped the import of salt from Tibet. This was not liked by the Tibetans and relations became strained. Fortunately, before the conflict spread any further it was settled without war or serious trouble of any kind.[2] On the question of British policy towards Tibet and Nepal, Bell wrote:

'And, as India takes upon herself the right of self-government which she claims, and takes upon herself also, as a natural corollary, the duty of self-defence, it will fall to responsible Indians to consider their attitude towards Nepal, Tibet and China.

'Meanwhile, it should be a cardinal object of British policy to work as far as possible for a good understanding between Tibet and Nepal. For the friendship of both is necessary to us and ours to them. Both depend on us to a greater or lesser degree for protection and for munitions of war.'[3]

When in 1896 friction again developed between Nepal and Tibet, the Government of India prevented it from developing into an open hostility. But India needed sufficient time to prepare herself to mediate in the dispute between Nepal and Tibet. To reach a peaceful settlement India wanted to discuss the issue with the Chinese Government.[4] At the same time the Government of India informed the Secretary of State for India of its idea of consulting China on the Tibet–Nepal issue.[5] But he did not approve the proposal.[6]

After 1896 there were a few more quarrels between Nepal and Tibet which needed British intervention. The Government of India debated what policy to follow in future if a serious conflict should take place between the two states. Opinions varied in the foreign office as to the best course to follow. It was at this time that the Indian Government was contemplating sending the mission of Colonel Younghusband to Tibet. The consensus of opinion was that Nepal 'except in a very limited sense . . . possesses the unrestricted right of levying war'.[7] Consequently it should settle its own quarrels with Tibet, as

on the above mentioned issues. The letter of the King of Nepal to the Chinese Emperor called Nepal a 'Vassal state' of China. See Appendix XIX.
[1] Bell, op. cit., 237.
[2] Foreign Secret Despatch—E, December 1893, Nos. 38–43. (N.A.I.)
[3] Bell, op. cit., pp. 241–2.
[4] Foreign Secret Proceedings—E, July 1896, Nos. 74–129. (N.A.I.)
[5] Foreign Secret Proceedings—E, November 1896, Nos. 127–62. (N.A.I.)
[6] Ibid.
[7] Foreign Department Secret Proceedings—E, July 1903, No. 21. (N.A.I.)

it had done in the past.¹ This repeated the decision of the Governor-General in 1854 that if Nepal fought Tibet, India had no *locus standi* to prevent it.² There was no doubt that Nepal 'had practically placed herself in the position of an ally of the Indian Government'. One official, S. M. Fraser, thought 'it will be our duty to see that she does not suffer for it'.³ It was also suggested that the Government of India 'may foresee as an outcome of the war with Tibet a permanent improvement in our formal relations with Nepal'.⁴ Nepal had helped the British government a little earlier at the time of the Younghusband mission to Tibet. The Tibetans had taken note of this and they did not conceal their resentment that Nepal had ignored its treaty obligation to them. A few years later they reminded Charles Bell that Nepal had a treaty with them, and through it she had gained a favourable position in Tibet. They complained that

'In return for these privileges the Nepalese undertook to come to our assistance whenever our territory was invaded, but this undertaking they have consistently ignored. They did not help us during the British military expedition to the Chumbi Valley in 1888, nor during that to Lhasa in 1904; they did not help us in our recent contest (1912) with China.

'We realized that it was difficult for them to fulfil their promise when the British came, for they appear to be in alliance with your people. But they are bound to help us against China....'⁵

Chandra Shamsher was afraid that Tibet was intriguing with Russia, and he said that if 'Tibet became independent, Nepal would refuse the suzerainty of China'.⁶ Chandra was rather anxious to go to war because, he said, 'it will employ our troops'.⁷ In December 1902, Chandra Shamsher visited India and had an important interview with the Viceroy in which they discussed the issue of Russian intrigues in Tibet. Chandra clearly told the Viceroy he would not like to see a foreign power in Tibet because the latter would then try to avenge

---

¹ *Foreign Department Secret—E*, October 1903, Nos. 129–30. (N.A.I.)
² *Ibid.* Also see *Foreign Department Secret Proceedings*, August 1904, Nos. 160–1. (N.A.I.)
³ S. M. Fraser, Foreign Office File Note, *Foreign Department Secret Proceedings—E*, August 1904.
⁴ *Ibid.*
⁵ Bell, *op. cit.*, p. 238.
⁶ Notes on an interview with Maharajah Chandra Shamsher, Prime Minister of Nepal, on July 9, 1902, *Foreign Department Secret Proceedings—E*, September 1902, No. 132. (N.A.I.)
⁷ *Ibid.*

her former defeat at the hands of Nepal.¹ Chandra Shamsher spoke frankly to the Viceroy and told him:

'... that he regarded the interests of Nepal as entirely bound up with the British Government in India, and that his Government would be prepared to endorse and actively support any action which the British Government might consider necessary for the protection of those joint interests.'²

At this time the news came that the Dalai Lama had sent an Envoy Dorjieff to the Czar of Russia who had been received by him on June 23, 1901.³

All this information about the Russian intrigues in Tibet convinced the Government of India that it should send a mission to Tibet if Russia tried to do so. They first sounded the opinion of Nepal's prime minister on the question. The result of the meeting was favorable for the British. Both Nepal and the Indian Government looked on the Russian intrigues in Tibet with alarm. About Nepal's offer of help, to the British mission to Tibet, Colonel Younghusband wrote, 'The attitude which the Nepalese Government would take under the circumstances was a matter of considerable importance to us, and no doubt of much questioning of themselves.'⁴ The mission was offered 500 yaks, and later a further offer of 8,000 yaks, blankets, and coolies. Most important of all Chandra Shamsher wrote to the Tibetans to come to terms with the English. He pointed out that the conclusion of the Treaty of 1816 with the British had been continually advantageous to the Government of Nepal. He praised the British friendliness towards Nepal and the strength Nepal derived from the alliance with the British.⁵

The Anglo-Russian Convention of 1907 clearly accepted the 'suzerainty rights of China in Tibet'.⁶ The first article of the agreement read, 'The two high contracting parties engage to respect the territorial integrity of Tibet and to abstain from all interference in its internal administration.'⁷ This agreement ended Russian attempts to establish influence in Tibet. This agreement also brought to an end any serious

---
¹ Notes on an interview between His Excellency the Viceroy and the Prime Minister of Nepal at Delhi. *Foreign Secret—E*, February 1903, Nos. 1-88. (N.A.I.)
² Ibid.
³ Younghusband, *op. cit.*, pp. 67-70.
⁴ Ibid., pp. 133-4.
⁵ Ibid. pp. 134-5.
⁶ Anglo-Russian Convention signed on August 31, 1907, *op. cit.* (See Appendix XI.)
⁷ Ibid.

danger of war between Nepal and Tibet in future. Their relations with one another, however, continued to be chronically unfriendly, and neither lost any opportunity of causing difficulties for the other.

In the year 1923 the question of Nepalese subjects in Tibet became a serious matter. The prime minister of Nepal demanded that all the male, though not the female, children of the Nepalese fathers and Tibetan mothers be recognized as Nepalese subjects.[1] The Tibetan Government refused this demand. The Maharajah of Nepal threatened armed intervention.[2] The Resident did not take the threat very seriously, but the Indian Government felt it essential to have its own representative in Tibet to deal with the problems of Nepal and Tibet.[3] O'Connor, the Resident, suggested that the British Political Agent in Sikkim should be permitted to visit Lhasa so that he could collect information there.[4] The Resident in Nepal suggested to the Maharajah that these petty disputes arose because of incompetent Nepalese representatives in Lhasa, and that he should send better personnel. The matter was considered further by the Nepal Government. British influence played an important part in keeping the two countries out of war if not out of friction and jealousy. The Resident wrote 'how jealously Nepal regards our relations with Tibet',[5] for after the Younghusband expedition and the cessation of Russian intrigues India's relations with the Dalai Lama became increasingly more friendly. Bell reported the attitude of the Dalai Lama to the Chinese:

'The Chinese Mission was in Lhasa for four and half months in 1920. During that period they were permitted only two interviews with the Dalai Lama; and, before going into the presence of His Holiness, each member's person was unceremoniously searched to make sure that he was not secreting arms.'

In the next sentence he compared it to the Dalai Lama's friendliness towards the British.

'When I took my mission to Lhasa in 1921, I frequently visited the Dalai Lama, who used to rise from his seat, grasp my hand cordially,

---

[1] W. F. T. O'Connor, British Envoy at Nepal, 'Nepal–Tibet Affairs', Serial No. 6, the 2nd (received 10th) October, 1923. (Confidential) *Foreign and Political Department Secret*, File No. 459 (2)-X, 1923. (N.A.I.)
[2] Ibid.
[3] Ibid.
[4] Ibid.
[5] O'Connor to Secretary, 'Nepal–Tibet Affairs', No. 53M, No. 22-C, 3340, July 10, 1922. (I.L.O. Microfilm.)

and make me sit at the same table as himself. The contrast could not have been stronger.'¹

After comparing the Chinese position with that of the British in Lhasa, Bell described how the Nepalese felt about the British Mission in Tibet.

'As mentioned above the Nepalese were uneasy over my Mission to Lhasa. It is perhaps undesirable to quote full details in this connection, but the signs were clear to all who could read them. The idea of a British official coming into personal and friendly contact with the Tibetan Government at Lhasa was naturally distasteful to them. I constantly visited the Dalai Lama and the Tibetan Ministers under conditions of privacy, which left no room for the Nepalese or for anybody else as an intermediary.'²

Bell went on to describe the feelings of the Tibetans toward the British and to contrast these with their attitude toward the Nepalese:

'A prominent Tibetan more than once remarked to me, "Your being here renders the Gurkhas less highhanded than they were. It is seen that you, the representative of a Great Power, observe our laws and customs, and thus it has become more difficult for the subjects of Nepal, a small State, to ignore them." Other Tibetans echoed this view also.'³

It is true that Nepal was not very happy to see that the British had established direct contact with Tibet which used to be only an area of influence. Nonetheless, in all frankness one must agree that Nepal was instrumental in cutting its own throat. Younghusband wrote:

'Thus were Bogle's difficulties still further increased. And in one respect, at least, we have advanced since his day; for the Mission to Lhasa in 1904, instead of being hampered, was warmly supported by the Nepalese. The Dewan of Nepal wrote strongly to the Lhasa authorities, urging them to reason, and his agent at Lhasa was of the greatest assistance to me in my negotiations with the Tibetans.'⁴

Nepal's Relations with China in the First Quarter of the Twentieth Century

After 1895 Nepal did not send a Mission to China for ten years because

---

¹ Bell, *op. cit.*, p. 211.
² *Ibid.*, p. 240.
³ *Ibid.*
⁴ Younghusband, *op. cit.*, p. 22.

of the transport problem and other difficulties. Eventually Nepal decided to resume diplomatic relations and requested the Chinese Residents in Tibet to obtain the permission of the Emperor to send a mission in 1906. This was first reported to the British Government by its Minister in Peking. In forwarding the request of Nepal to the Emperor the Residents wrote that in 1900:

'... an Imperial Edict was received temporarily excusing the Gurkhas, the Lamas of Tibet and the Native Tribes from payment of tribute until such time as the road should be open. These Imperial instructions were duly carried out....

'I have the honour to observe that the Gurkha land is a dependency beyond the border of China and that the tribes have always displayed a loyal devotion to the Throne, further proof of which they now give by their anxiety to send the customary tribute.'[1]

The Government of India was naturally not very pleased with the Nepalese overture, and the Resident at Kathmandu took up the question with the Maharajah. Chandra Shamsher dismissed as 'meaningless' the high-flown language peculiar to Chinese official documents. He explained that the:

'... few presents which the mission carried to Peking are not of much value, *and certainly not in the nature of tribute*. The customary letter which is sent on the occasion, is written in the truly oriental style of exuberant but meaningless politeness and follows a stereotyped rule.'[2]

He pointed out that the mission helped Nepal to gain access to China under very advantageous circumstances and to enjoy free help for many things. He wondered that the presents described were 'as a tribute from Nepal'.[3] He underlined the fact that the mission and the letter had 'very little political significance'.[4]

It is important to note that Max Muller, British Chargé d'Affaires in Peking, wrote to Sir Edward Grey, the British Secretary of State for Foreign Affairs, that:

[1] 'Memorial by the Chinese Residents in Tibet on the payment of tribute by the Gurkhas', sent to the Secretary, Government of India by W. R. Brown, dated CH'ENGTU, December 31, 1905. *Political and External File*, No. 1037 of June 9, 1906. (I.O.L.)
[2] Chandra Shamsher to Manner-Smith, dated April 19, 1906, *Political and External File*, No. 1037 of June 9, 1906. (I.O.L.)
[3] *Ibid.*
[4] *Ibid.*

'... the quinquennial tribute may, as I believe is the case, be looked upon by the Nepalese as a mere compensation for privileges allowed them in Tibet, but is certainly regarded by the Chinese as the offering of a subject.'[1]

The British Government sent a dispatch to Prince Ch'ing warning him not to make 'any administrative changes in Tibet to affect or prejudice the integrity of Nepal or of the two smaller states of Bhutan and Sikkim, and that they are prepared, if necessary, to protect the interests and rights of these three states'.[2] The answer made it very clear how China felt about Nepal just before the revolution of 1911. The Prince stated that the Nepalese:

'... are properly (or originally) feudatories of China and Bhutan and Sikkim are both States in friendly relations with China. In the event of steps being taken in the future for the reorganisation of the internal Government of Thibit, such would have no other object than the advancement of progress and order in Thibetan territory and should not affect those States in any way.'[3]

Sir J. Jordan, the British ambassador at Peking, reported to the Government of India that the Mission of 1906 from Nepal was treated with 'scant courtesy by the Chinese provincial authorities'.[4] The Nepalese envoy was dissatisfied and thought that 'these missions appeared to be of doubtful utility'. He told Sir J. Jordan that he was reporting to the prime minister 'on this subject'. Jordan reported that before leaving the envoy was 'less disposed than on the previous occasion' to advocate the discontinuance of these missions. He expressed the opinion that it was 'promoting friendly relations between Nepal and China in Tibet'.[5] It is correct to say that the gifts sent by Nepal to the Emperor of China were officially described as tribute. The extreme vanity of the Chinese Emperors induced them to apply the same phrase to presents brought or sent by envoys of other States, such as Great Britain, or the Prince of Magadha.[6] Landon quoted Maharajah Chandra Shamsher's opinion on this matter thus:

[1] Max Muller to Sir Edward Grey, letter No. 122, *Political and External File*, No. 16007 of 1906. *India Secret Proceeding*. (I.L.O.)
[2] Max Muller to Prince Ch'ing, April 11, 1910, *Political and External File, India Secret Proceedings*, J.O.L.M/3/463/. (I.O.L.)
[3] Prince Ch'ing to Max Muller, April 18, 1910, *Political and External File, India Secret Despatch Proceedings, op. cit.* (See Chapter 4.)
[4] 'Historical Note on Relations between Nepal and China', *op. cit.*
[5] Sir J. Jordan's dispatch No. 308 of July 7, 1908. Political 3772/08. 'Historical Note on Relations between Nepal and China', *op. cit.*
[6] Landon, *op. cit.*, p. 102.

'This claim—that the deputation proved the vassal character of Nepal—is not only an unwarranted fiction but is also a damaging reflection on our national honour and independence. The missions that proceeded from this country to China were of the nature of embassies from one court to another and have invariably been treated with the honour and consideration due to foreign guests, and their expense was entirely borne by the Chinese Government. The presents they carried for the Emperor can never be regarded as tribute, as they are mere sougats (presents) bringing forth counter presents from the Court of China. They are merely the channel by which we tried to keep up our friendly intercourse with distant China, to express our regard and respect for the Celestial Emperor and to cultivate the good-will and friendly feeling of the Chinese Government, especially on account of our heavy stakes in Tibet.'[1]

A few years later China became a Republic and from that time until today no tributary mission has been sent to China.[2]

In 1913, after the fall of the Manchu dynasty, General Chung, the new Chinese Resident in Lhasa, suggested to Chandra Shamsher that a 'union of Nepal with the Five Affiliated Races of China could be effected; Nepal may be regarded as Nepalese China. . . .'[3] It is interesting

---

[1] Landon, *op. cit.*

[2] According to Landon the last mission to China was sent in 1908. He quoted a letter of March 7, 1924, which he received from the Secretary of the Foreign Minister of China, Dr Wellington Koo.

'Waichiao Pu, Peking.

'Dear Sir,

Referring to your letter of February 22nd and my reply of February 25th, I beg to say that the last tribute from Nepal was in the 34th or last year of Kwang Hsu in the 3rd month (April 1908). No tribute has come under the Republic. In the early days of the Manchu dynasty tribute came once in five years, but on account of the distance between Nepal and Peking it was agreed that they should come once in twelve years instead.

Yours Sincerely,
W. P. Wei.'

According to Fisher and Rose the last mission left Nepal in 1906. Fisher and Rose, *op. cit.*, p. 12.

Sir J. Jordan of British Mission in Peking informed Sir Edward Grey on April 29, 1908, about the arrival of the Quinquennial Mission from Nepal to the Emperor of China. *Foreign Department Secret—E*, October 1908, Nos. 696–777. (N.A.I.)

Daniel J. Lee, a Chinese official, wrote of the last Quinquennial Mission from Nepal to China 'being in 1908'.

'National China Re-establishes Relations with the Kingdom of Nepal', *China Weekly Review*, 55. 148–9, December 27, 1930.

[3] General Chung to Chandra Shamsher, Yatung, February 1913, *Foreign Department Secret External*, August 1913, No. 240–50. (Translation.) (N.A.I.)

to note that General Chung wrote to the President of the Chinese Republic that, 'The relations between China and Nepal during the past several hundred years have been unceasingly more intimate than between China and Tibet'.[1] He suggested that a Chinese 'delegation should be sent to Nepal to explain matters'.[2]

Maharajah Chandra Shamsher rejected General Chung's suggestion in the following terms:

'With regard to the question of Union with the Five Races of China I am sorry that as Nepal is an ancient Hindu Kingdom, desirous of preserving her independence and her separate existence, she cannot entertain the idea of such a union with the Five Affiliated Races said to constitute the Republic of China.'[3]

This reply of Nepal satisfied the Government of India because it was sent with the full knowledge and consent of the British Resident. He wrote that 'a small amendment in the reply suggested by me (vide pencil addition at the end of the memorandum) was acquiesced in by the Prime Minister'.[4] Landon wrote that when in June 1924 he was in Nepal, he discussed the relations of Nepal and China with the Prime Minister Chandra Shamsher. He also told Chandra Shamsher about China's idea of receiving the mission every twelve years instead of five. Landon claimed that the Nepalese Government knew nothing about this suggestion, but he further wrote that the prime minister admitted that 'were the old conditions in China to be restored, Nepal might think once more of sending the traditional mission of courtesy'.[5]

During the remainder of the British period, so far as is known, Nepal had no further relations with China.

The convention between Great Britain and China in April 1906 settled the Tibetan question. The second article read as follows:

'The Government of Great Britain engages not to annex Tibetan territory or to interfere in the adminstration of Tibet. The Government of China also undertakes not to permit any other foreign state to interfere with the territory or internal administration of Tibet.'[6]

A note by Mr W. Lee-Warner of the India Office in 1908 says, 'We

---

[1] General Chung to President of China (Telegram), February 1, 1913, *ibid*.
[2] *Ibid*.
[3] Chandra Shamsher to General Chung, Nepal, March 16, 1913, *Foreign Department Secret External*, August 1913, Nos. 240-50. *op. cit.*
[4] H. L. Showers, Officiating Resident in Nepal, to Secretary, Government of India, No. 27, *op. cit.*
[5] Landon, *op. cit.*, p. 103.
[6] The Convention between Great Britain and China, April 1906, *Political*

have formally recognized the suzerain rights of China in Tibet. To China we should first have to look if we had cause of international quarrel with Tibet'.[1] After the convention of 1906 between Britain and China, the British Government again called a conference of China and Tibet at Simla in 1914 for 'Tibetan negotiations'. Nepal felt dissatisfied since it was not present at this conference. Manner-Smith, the Resident, reported the measures he had taken to deal with its complaints:

'After the failure of the Tibetan negotiations at Simla in July 1914, owing to the obstructive attitude taken by the Chinese Government and their refusal to recognize the initialling of the Convention by their Representative at the Tripartite Conference, I was authorized by the Government of India to communicate unofficially and very confidentially to the Prime Minister in Nepal the purport of the Convention signed by the British and Tibetan Plenipotentiaries and to explain the position to him.'[2]

He assured the prime minister that 'nothing in the convention is intended or will be allowed to affect existing agreements or arrangements between Nepal and Tibet'.

'It was added that in the event of the convention coming into force the Government of India will be prepared to give the Nepal Durbar an official assurance that the existing agreements referred to are not affected and that they will do their utmost to secure that the interests of Nepal arising from these agreements are in no way prejudiced by the operation of the Convention.'[3]

From 1914 to 1947 Nepal appears to have had no relations with China, and further reference to China cannot be found in the archives either of India or of Nepal. Chandra Shamsher had established the independence of his country, and the government of China was fully occupied by troubles at home. The establishment of the Chinese Republic was soon followed by the period of the warlords, when interminable civil wars made China not much more than a geographic expression, like Germany in the later centuries of the Holy Roman

and *External Secret* File No. P.2750/1908, *India: Secret Despatch* (I.O.L. Microfilm). Bell, *op. cit.*, pp. 287–9.
   [1] W. Lee-Warner, 'Tibet Relations with Postal Arrangements', India House, Whitehall, S.W., *Political External Secret* File No. 2750/1908. *India Secret Despatch Proceedings*, Volume 225. (I.O.L.)
   [2] Manner-Smith to the Secretary, Government of India, No. 75C, the 26th (received August 31, 1915), *Foreign and Political Department Secret Internal*, October 1915, Nos. 1–3. (N.A.I.)
   [3] *Ibid.*

Empire. The warlords were succeeded by the government of Chiang Kai-shek. He was fully occupied by civil war against the Communists and the Japanese invasion. Tibet took advantage of China's period of weakness to expel the Chinese garrison and recover its *de facto* independence. During this period the relations between Nepal and Tibet were peaceful but not cordial. The influence of the Government of India was on the side of peace. Its policy was to maintain friendly relations with both Nepal and Tibet, and to preserve peace on its Himalayan frontier. Both Nepal and Tibet were well aware of India's attitude. Neither of them was under her suzerainty, but the geographic fact that they had a common frontier with a state so much more powerful than themselves had an influence upon their policy toward one another.

The attitude of the Government of India toward Tibet was that it had no desire to annex the country or control its administration. Its sole interest was that Russia should not bring Tibet within its sphere of influence, since this might involve a slight, though by no means a serious, threat to India's security. India's policy toward Tibet was determined by the view that the wider the barrier of mountainous and roadless country between the Russian and Indian frontiers the better. This strategic requirement was satisfied by the Younghusband mission and the Anglo-Russian Convention of 1907. The Anglo-Chinese Convention of 1906 added the further assurance that China would not allow any other foreign state to interfere in Tibet. The Government of Great Britain recognized China's overlordship, but this did not trouble them under the conditions which existed in 1906. The Manchu dynasty was so feeble that it could not possibly be a threat to India.

The Government of India would have preferred a Tibet which was entirely independent. When the government of the Dalai Lama expelled the Chinese garrison from Central Tibet in 1912 and again in 1918, and also ejected them from many of their eastern territories and regained and established their independence, the Government of India was very pleased. It would have liked to recognize the independence of Tibet, but it was overruled by the Government of Great Britain on the insistence of the Foreign Office. The Chinese refused to abandon their phantom claim to suzerainty, and the British Foreign Office insisted that the maintenance of friendly diplomatic relations with China required the recognition of China's position. Thereafter the governments of India and Tibet maintained cordial and friendly relations. When the world war broke out in 1914, the Dalai Lama offered his reserve stock of arms—some 2,000 matchlocks—to equip the British army.

The Chinese claim to suzerainty over Nepal is difficult to assess by the standards of Western international law. It was often a matter of nominal or symbolic rather than substantive rights. Similar claims were made by other Asian states, for example, Siam *vis-à-vis* the Malay states of Kedah, Kelantan, and Trengganu. The basis of the claim was that China was larger, wealthier and more powerful than the weaker states bordering on her. She had the prestige of an old and highly developed civilization. When the Government of China was strong, it imposed its rule on the neighboring states. When there was a period of weakness they gradually threw off their vassalage and regained their independence. The Government of China never acknowledged this and continued to assert its nominal claim to suzerainty. For example it claimed the empire of Annam as a vassal state, although the Chinese rulers were driven out over 1,000 years ago. When a strong government reappeared in China, it would if possible re-establish its former overlordship over the weak border states.

Nepal was defeated in 1792 by a Chinese army which had come to the help of Tibet, and accepted Chinese suzerainty. This occurred almost at the end of the period of the strong rulers of the Manchu dynasty. Gradually the power of the dynasty decayed until it was overthrown by the revolution of 1911. This was followed by a period of weaknesses which continued until the rise to power of the present communist government. For two generations, the ruler of Nepal continued to send the tribute mission to Peking every five years. Thereafter, it was sent irregularly, and the practice terminated with the overthrow of the dynasty.

The prime ministers of Nepal never drew up a memorandum on all the reasons for sending the embassy, though sometimes they gave a partial explanation. Presumably, the principal reason was that it was wise to propitiate a more powerful state. Other reasons were that the Emperor did not interfere with the administration of Nepal, and that the tribute mission brought tangible benefits such as valuable presents and trading privileges. Most of the prime ministers obtained from the Emperor the title of 'valiant prince'. Since some of them won power by force, they may have hoped to strengthen their position by receiving the stamp of approval from a ruler whose name still carried a great prestige. As the power of the Emperor became visibly feebler, the tribute missions grew more intermittent until they ceased.

W. W. Willoughby and C. G. Fenwick, in their well documented book, *Types of Restricted Sovereignty and of Colonial Autonomy*, have identified nine categories of states not fully independent, e.g. protected independent states, protected dependent states, guaranteed states, vassal states, etc. They defined suzerainty as:

'In general suzerainty connotes in the suzerain power a supremacy over the protégé or vassal state which is at once less absolute and less juristic or constitutional than that connoted by sovereignty. The so-called vassal state frequently has the status of an autonomous province, its autonomy being conditioned upon the rendering by it of certain services in the way of homage or tribute.'[1]

But these authorities did not, under their definition of suzerainty, classify Nepal as a vassal state of China, in spite of the fact that the latter claimed that Nepal was a tributary state. Neither did they include Nepal under any other category. This apparently means Nepal in their opinion was an independent state. Landon, a leading authority on Nepal, Tibet, and China, wrote as follows:

'There is no question of anything but a complimentary exchange of gifts between China and Nepal, and any tie that may have existed in the past must now be regarded from the Nepalese side in much the same light as the "tribute" which Burma was allowed by Calcutta to send to Peking long after the British annexation (both Burma and Hunza-nagar in the north of Kashmir sent political missions to China after they had admittedly come under British rule); and from the Chinese side in the same light as the nominal claim, put forward by Britain until 1801, that the King of England was also King of France. To this day similar shadowy claims are to be found. Thus the King of Spain, whose territories are very precisely and notoriously defined, still claims to be King of the two Sicilies, of Jerusalem, of the Eastern and Western Indies, of India, and "du Continent Oceanien". But these matters are taken more seriously in the East, and though there was but one more mission sent to Peking after the Darbar of 1903 (Imperial Darbar), and though Chandra expressly denied to the Indian Government that any state of vassalage was thereby either symbolized or implied, it was a good thing that the representative of Nepal should make his formal appearance at the Imperial Darbar among the accredited envoys of independent powers.'[2]

The best proof that Nepal did not voluntarily accept a foreign overlord is the determination with which it defended its independence against any suspicion of British intervention.

[1] Willoughby, W. W., and Fenwick, C. G., *Types of Restricted Sovereignty and of Colonial Autonomy* (Confidential for official use only), p. 9, Washington: Government Printing Office, 1919.
[2] Landon, *op. cit.*, pp. 103-4.

CHAPTER 10

THE INTERNATIONAL STATUS OF NEPAL

Summary and Conclusions
The century and a half history of British–Nepalese diplomatic relations has been like the history of a well tended formal garden, with many beautiful roses—and also many thorns. The 'confluence of the occident and the orient' can be seen through the pages of the government reports telling of their conflicts and their friendly cooperation. Through the generations, British India and Nepal have lived like two brothers who quarrelled on every point but generally cooperated when one needed the other. Though they had heard of each other much earlier, their actual contact came in 1792 when the Gurkhas requested help from the British against the powerful joint might of China and Tibet. The British wanted to help because this was a good opportunity to develop contact with the Himalayan kingdom. But the British were not able to arrive in time to help the Gurkhas on the battlefield. However, all was not lost, since the Commercial Treaty of 1792 between the Gurkha ruler and the British India Government came about as a result of the Gurkhas' invitation. This treaty was the beginning of a relationship which lasted one century and a half.

The internal history of the Nepalese, through the years, has often presented a picture of tragedy and misrule. Especially was this true in Nepal's earlier years, where the overthrow of the Malla King of Kathmandu by Prithvi Nayaran Sah of Gurkha, unfortunately did not lead to the permanent establishment of a capable and strong central government in Nepal. Prithvi Narayan himself was an able ruler, with personal characteristics of bravery, courage and ambition. But he singularly failed to develop a strong successor to power. His death in 1775 brought complete chaos in the country. The feuds and blood lettings among the kings and queens resumed and spread to the courtiers, nobles and Bahadars (military generals), as Nepal's leaders chose sides between the Pandes and the Thapas (the two major factions of that time) and proceeded to fight it out for control of the country. Damodar Pande came to power in 1800 as the first Prime Minister of Nepal, but the jealousy of his rivals forced him out of office before he could stabilize the government.

In 1806, the Pandes were deposed by the Thapas, and Bhim Sen Thapa became Prime Minister from 1806 to 1837. His thirty years of rule created many problems for Nepal. He was an ambitious, patriotic and courageous general who was—and is—regarded as one of the heroes of the Gurkhas. During his prime ministership, he aroused strong nationalist feelings among the Nepalese. His ambitions to extend the boundary of Nepal led him into serious conflict with the East India Company, resulting in the Gurkha War in 1814-16. Despite their outstanding courage and military skill, the Gurkhas lost the war and were compelled to sign the Treaty of Segowlee, in 1816. The Treaty of Segowlee forced a number of changes upon Nepal. Nepal lost some of her territory and agreed to abandon her ambition to conquer additional territory and to live in peace with Sikkim. Second, the treaty opened the door of Nepal wide enough to admit an accredited British Resident to live in Kathmandu, a right which had been discontinued since 1803. Also, Nepal agreed not to take any Europeans or Americans into her service without the prior permission of the Government of India.

Treaty or no treaty however, Bhim Sen Thapa remained as unyielding as ever against any interference from any outside power in Nepal's internal affairs. Thapa was no friend of the British, and he managed to keep the Resident at a distance until Brian Hodgson was appointed to the position in 1829. Unfortunately for Thapa, in spite of his great love for his country he could not control the fighting within the royal palace. Neither was he able to destroy completely his enemies the Pandes. During his thirty years as prime minister he created too many enemies and they eventually became the cause of his downfall. We might speculate that if half the energy and diplomacy he spent to keep the British at a distance had been used against the Pandes, he could probably have done much more for Nepal.

British pressure and influence were felt only when Hodgson came as Resident, seven years before the deposition of Bhim Sen Thapa. There was no doubt whatever that Hodgson played an important part in the internal politics of Nepal. He remained in Nepal from 1829 to 1843, a period which was the most troubled in the internal history of modern Nepal. The kings of that period proved to be weak and incompetent. In the absence of a strong ruler, the rival factions of Pandes and Thapas fought each other for control of Nepal, using every weapon from court intrigue to massacre. Party strife was at its height.

The hatred and jealousy of the two factions knew no bounds. Hodgson did not just watch this game from the side lines. He was, at one time, a spectator, a player on different sides, and sometimes referee as well. While the downfall of Bhim Sen Thapa in 1837 lessened Hodgson's activities, it did not end them completely. In 1842, the newly arrived Governor-General (Lord Ellenborough) decided that he did not approve of Hodgson's policy and subsequently replaced him as Resident. Thus ended the career of a man who was said to know more about Nepal than most Nepalese.

The change in the Residency did not stop the jealousy and fighting for power among the Nepalese. However, the way the government had behaved since the downfall of the strongman, Bhim Sen Thapa, could not go on without resulting in the ruin of the country or the production of another strongman. It was the latter which occurred, when in 1846, out of the blood bath, sprang Jung Bahadur who was to be prime minister for thirty years and whose descendants were to rule the country for another seventy years.

Jung Bahadur was a strong leader who happily had many of the qualities of a sincere patriot. He loved his country and he wanted to do the best he could for it during his rule. When he came to power he looked abroad, but what he saw was not very encouraging. Nepal had three important neighbors, and with all of them Nepal had gone to war and had been defeated (Tibet and China, 1792; British India, 1814-16). He looked to his closest and strongest neighbor, India. There, he found that the personal jealousy and rivalry of the princes of India had led to the East India Company becoming the paramount power. Then he looked within his own country and thought of its immediate past history. Since the death of Bhim Sen Thapa, Nepal had not seen a moment of peace. The earth of Kathmandu had been drenched with the blood of its generals, kings, queens, nobles and its leading citizens. Probably he paused and thought for a moment: was all that happened for the benefit of the country or for personal power and profit? The judgement of history must be: mostly for personal power and profit.

At this time Jung Bahadur received an invitation from the British Government to visit England. He decided to go in spite of the fact that he would lose caste by crossing the ocean. While on this trip in 1850-51, he studied the world beyond his own country. He came to realize the great strength and power of the British Government and also of that of the other European nations, and was impressed.

Upon his return to Nepal, Jung Bahadur began to consider a new policy for his country. Should Nepal follow the path of all those Indian princely states which had been overwhelmed in the storm of colonialism, or should it steer its course in such a way as to survive the storm and then look for the shore? The answer to this question involved the future of Nepal, as well as the survival of his family—and himself.

Jung Bahadur's answer came in the form of a long-term plan for both his family and the country. He outlined his policy as 'overt friendly cooperation with the powerful British, together with the strictest isolation from the European people to the extent of jealousy and of possible discourtesies'. At home, he established a principle of succession through which, whatever happened, a member of his family would succeed him to his position. His ultimate ambition was to save his country from complete British domination so that it would eventually emerge as an independent nation either in his lifetime or in that of one of his descendants.

As long as Jung Bahadur lived he never willingly allowed any of his subjects to join the Indian Army, he never gave permission to the Resident to travel freely in the kingdom, and he never allowed any Resident to play the same game that Hodgson had played during the thirties. During the Indian Mutiny, he helped the British because he could not find a better party with which to make an alliance. In 1854-56 he avenged Nepal's defeat by Tibet and forced Tibet to agree to pay ten thousand rupees annually. Upon his death he left a strong, efficient and established government.

Jung Bahadur Kuwanr (later called Rana) established a hereditary prime ministership which remained in his family for just a little over a century. His successors were Ranodip Singh (1877-85), Bir Shamsher (1885-1901), Deb Shamsher (only for three months), Chandra Shamsher (1901-29), Bhim Shamsher (1929-32), Juddha Shamsher (1932-46), Padma Shamsher (1946-48), and Mohan Shamsher (1948-51). However, it has not been a succession that has passed peacefully from brother to brother as was intended. Jung Bahadur's own brother, Ranodip Singh, was murdered by his nephew, who was also a member of Jung Bahadur's family (but bearing the surname of Shamsher). In this *coup d'état*, Ranodip Singh's family and many other nobles were driven into exile. Subsequently, other prime ministers have been deposed and replaced by more powerful members of the Bahadur-Shamsher family. Tenure of office, to say the least, has not been secure in Nepal.

Considering this period, it can be observed that the recent prime ministers have had to be able and ruthless, the strongest and most capable members of the Rana family. The weaklings had no chance. The Rana rule of succession thus had this great advantage over its predecessors. The intrigues and assassinations for control were confined to the members of one family. They did not involve other noble families and their followers. Moreover this Rana example of the survival of the fittest gave Nepal a century of strong and very capable rulers. Admittedly they looked after their own interests, but also they very shrewdly advanced the interests of Nepal.

Jung Bahadur's policies were more or less followed by his successors. It will be noticed that gradually, with the passage of time, the issues which were listed previously as causes of friction between the governments of India and Nepal had been either forgotten, shelved or solved. For example, the question of commerce, trade, and traders was shelved; the issue of boundaries was solved by an agreement in 1875; the problems of refugees and the surrender and extradition of criminals were solved through different treaties in 1837, 1855, 1866 and 1881; the issues of freedom of movement of the British Residents within the kingdom of Nepal and the visits of the Governors-General to Kathmandu were shelved; and the important issues of the import of arms and ammunition and permission for Nepalese soldiers to go overseas were settled by the practice of the First and Second World Wars, and by the Treaty of 1923 respectively. This progress was made possible because of the cooperation, earnest zeal, sincerity, and friendly but frank discussions by Prime Ministers like Ranodip Singh, Bir Shamsher and Chandra Shamsher, with Residents such as Wylie, Manner-Smith and O'Connor, supported by Governors-General like Lytton (1876–80), Ripon (1880–84), Dufferin (1884–88), Lansdowne (1888–94), Elgin (1894–99), Curzon (1899–1905), Minto (1905–10), Hardinge (1910–16), Chelmsford (1916–21), and Reading (1921–26). These men were instrumental in guiding the destiny of British-Nepalese relations in the latter part of the nineteenth century and the first half of the twentieth century.

In contrast, the policy of a show of strength short of open hostilities advocated by Girdlestone in the early part of his Residentship was based on suspicions and past prejudices. In the later part of his career in Kathmandu, Girdlestone realized his mistake and switched to advocating a policy of mutual understanding combined with strength. But the real credit for Britain's change of policy goes to his successor, Wylie, who urged mutual understanding and respect with trust and conciliation. When this policy was finally adopted by the Government of India, most of the previous misunderstandings vanished before World War I started. Whatever misunderstanding or distrust remained was removed by Chandra Shamsher's generous aid during World War I, followed by British recognition of the Maharajah Dhiraj as 'His Majesty' in 1919, and finally by the Treaty of Friendship in 1923, which recognized Nepal as an independent ally. Article VII of the Treaty of 1815, which forbade the employment of any European or

American without British consent, was abrogated, and Nepal was given a free hand to import arms and ammunition. By 1934 Nepal had direct diplomatic relations with Great Britain. The result of this friendship was visible during World War II, when Nepal granted permission to her subjects to join the British army and also to cross the sea to help the British and the Allies. Certainly this chapter of the story of British–Nepalese relations is one which has few if any parallels in the history of international relations.

Evaluation

The Ranas' rule in Nepal has been bitterly criticized by many on the ground that they played into the hands of the British. Considering the situation, it is unlikely they could have done otherwise. When it was noted that even the stronger state of Afghanistan had to surrender control of foreign affairs to the British as the price of retaining domestic autonomy, Nepal's retention of her domestic autonomy plus relative freedom in foreign affairs is all the more unusual, i.e. the Government of India admitted that Nepal had the right to go to war with Tibet and to maintain diplomatic relations with China, little though it liked this. Granted, there could not be two opinions on the question as to whether the Ranas cared more for their family position than for the country and for the kings. But there was no denying the fact that all through their relations with the British they maintained one important point in their minds and that was the independence of Nepal. The correspondence between the two governments shows this beyond question.

It has also been stated that economic reasons played an important role in Ranas' relations with the British because the British wished to expand trade with Nepal. This was partly true in the very early period of Nepalese–British relations, but soon the British emphasis shifted to the recruitment of Gurkhas for the Indian army and to strategic political and military considerations. In support of these points, a statement from the Indian Foreign Office plus a statement from the office of the Secretary of State for India should help in understanding the situation. Sir Arthur Hirtzel, Under-Secretary of State for India, wrote on August 25, 1922, to the Indian Foreign Office that, '. . . it is, after all, mainly because of the Gurkha element in the Army that we value the friendship of Nepal'.[1] The strategic consideration is best illustrated by the second statement, which was prepared in the Indian Foreign Office in 1919:

'The services rendered by Nepal—in the Mutiny, at the time of the Tibet expedition, and above all in the present war, are a matter of

---

[1] Sir Arthur Hirtzel, *Political and External Files*, I.O.L.M./3/463. 1922.

common knowledge. It is only necessary to mention that without Nepalese good will we should lose, beyond the possibility of replacing, the flower of the Indian Army. But Nepal's importance is not limited to that. Nepal is in a position to exercise a powerful influence in Indian internal politics and, if it were disaffected, the anarchist movement in India would assume a much more serious aspect. Externally this State is important to us from two points of view, (1) it forms a very valuable counterpoise to Afghanistan and Moslem movements to the west and north of Afghanistan, (2) the political situation on our North-East frontier is very unstable. We have released Tibet from China, but Tibet cannot stand alone and we cannot support her very effectively against Chinese aggression. . . .'[1]

The fact was that both the British and the Ranas needed each other for their own selfish ends and national interests. The alliance stood firm because, like all durable alliances, it was based on mutual self-interest.

The major criticism which could be levelled against the Ranas was that they did not take advantage of their alliance with British imperialism to enrich the economic, governmental, and social system of their country. Colonialism and imperialism of the past, as well as of the present, must be condemned. They should not have been brought to any country in the past and should be checked now. While the colonialist and imperialist systems have different forms in different ages, they should be criticized in any form and shape when they are imposed on any country of the world. Nevertheless, some benefits could be derived from them. Comparing the economic, governmental and political systems of those countries which were under the direct British colonial system (like India, Malaya, and Ceylon) with those which claimed independence (like Tibet, China, Nepal, and Thailand), it seems that when they regained their independence, the former countries inherited better economic, governmental and political systems than the latter.

If the Ranas had not carried their policy of isolating Nepal from Western influence to such extreme lengths, they could have used their alliance with India to develop such social services as education, medicine and health, improve their agriculture, and raise the standard of government administration. The army was the one government service in which full advantage was taken of the British connection. But even allowing for the effect of British exploitation, the final result would still have been that after 1950, the condition of Nepal in the fields of

[1] Memorandum, *Foreign and Political Department Secretary Internal Proceedings*, July 1919, Nos. 36–65. (N.A.I.)

economic and the social services would have been much more efficient and modern than was actually the case.

The Ranas failed to do this because they were too jealous of personal position. They probably thought that if the country were modernized, their one-family rule would not last long. Isolationism is commendable provided it is practiced for the betterment of the nation, like the isolationism of the United States of America during the eighteenth and nineteenth centuries. Unfortunately, the Ranas were short-sighted. They had only two policies: to preserve the traditional way of life in Nepal free from outside influences, and to keep their monopoly of power. They achieved both of these aims but the world will not cease justifiably to criticize them.

The Diplomatic Status of Nepal

The diplomatic history of Nepal has been discussed in the preceding pages of this dissertation. In the light of this history, it seems proper to ask what the diplomatic status of Nepal was. This was, of course, a question of limited interest to the British prior to the Treaty of Segowlee in 1815. However, research shows that even from the conclusion of this treaty till the death of Jung Bahadur in 1876, this question was not seriously discussed by anyone, even though the British were not satisfied with their relations with Nepal until the Indian Mutiny was successfully crushed. After 1857, the course of events was satisfactory to Jung Bahadur and to some extent to the British Government of India. Nepal's relations with Tibet, China and the British were then governed by treaties and engagements.

The death of Jung Bahadur brought people of lesser stature to power, and with the passage of time, many new problems arose. These problems and issues made it desirable for Nepal to know where she stood in the community of nations. After Jung Bahadur's death, this issue, or some phase of it, was often discussed in the Indian Foreign Office. Gradually the discussion became more serious and significant, not only for India but also for other parties such as Tibet and China. It soon became evident that the British officials were not sure exactly what was the status of Nepal. Was Nepal under the suzerainty of the British Government, or was it under the suzerainty of China? Was it a semi-independent or a completely independent state? What was its status compared with a state like Thailand or the princely state of Hydarabad? The answers to these questions gradually emerged from these periodic Foreign Office discussions.

As to the issue of suzerainty, it can be said that the characteristics of suzerainty differ according to the arrangements made in each separate case. A Government of India Foreign Office memorandum says,

'All that one can gather is that a State "under suzerainty" is one whose sovereignty is in some degree controlled by another Power, and which is not a "recognized member of the family of nations" for the purpose of International Law.'[1]

William Edward Hall, a British constitutionalist of repute wrote,

'It is not likely that the ancient doctrine of the precedents supplied by protectorates in Europe, weighed much with English statesmen and lawyers when they found it necessary to define the relation of Great Britain towards Eastern states and barbarous communities over which protectorates had been established. It is more probable that the Austinian theory of the indivisibility of sovereignty furnished the influence under which they long persisted in regarding protected states or communities as independent, and which induced them, arguing logically from their premises, to repudiate all possession of power within the territory, whether by way of privilege or obligation, except over British subjects. The territory was foreign, its inhabitants were foreign; over neither therefore could jurisdiction be exercised, still less could it be assumed over subjects of other European states.'[2]

Hall further discussed the issue as follows:

'The mark of a protected state or people whether civilized or uncivilized, is that it cannot maintain political intercourse with foreign powers except through or by permission of the protecting state. Whatever results from this fact is necessary to the relation created by a protectorate; whatever is independent of it descends from some other source. Starting from this point, it becomes at once evident that the

---

[1] 'Question as to whether Nepal is under the suzerainty of the British Crown', *Foreign Department Secret Proceedings*, March 1903, No. 228. Notes, *op. cit.* (N.A.I.)

[2] Hall, William Edward, *A Treatise on the Foreign Powers and Jurisdiction of the British Crown*, pp. 205-6 (Oxford University Press, 1894). Hall explained the meaning which he attached to the phrase 'Eastern States' as follows: 'Among Eastern protected states I do not include the native states within the Empire of India. They form a class apart. With many of them treaties were entered into long ago which, if no subsequent change in the relations so established had taken place, would warrant their being looked upon as independent, save in the one point of incapacity to maintain diplomatic intercourse with any European or Eastern power, or any fellow Indian protected state. Since then, however, sometimes by fresh compact, universally by usage, internal indepen-

interposition of the protecting state between the protected country and foreign powers deprives the latter of the means of exacting redress for themselves for wrongs which their subjects may suffer at the hands of the native rulers or people; and that, as the protecting state interposes voluntarily and for its own selfish objects, it is not morally in a position to demand that foreign governments shall patiently submit to wrongdoing from persons whose natural responsibility it covers with the shield of its own sovereign independence. A state must be bound to see that a reasonable measure of security is afforded to foreign subjects and property within the protected territory, and to prevent acts of depredation or hostility being done by its inhabitants. It must consequently exercise whatever amount of control may be found necessary for the purpose. Naturally this must vary greatly with the degree to which a people is advanced towards civilization, with the readiness with which it lends itself to guidance, with the number and character of the Europeans who visit or reside in the country.'[1]

Sir Henry Jenkyns, another jurist and civil servant, in his book, *British Rule and Jurisdiction Beyond the Seas*, quotes Sir Henry Maine on the question of sovereignty thus:

'It is necessary to the Austinian theory that the all-powerful portion of the community which makes laws should not be divisible, that it should not share its power with anybody else, and Austin himself speaks with some contempt of the semi-sovereign or demi-sovereign states which are recognized by the classical writers on international law. But this indivisibility of sovereignty, though it belongs to Austin's system, does not belong to international law. The powers of sovereigns are a bundle or collection of powers, and they may be separated from another. Thus a ruler may administer civil and criminal justice, may

dence has been invaded to an extent which is no doubt very different in the case of the Nizam from that of the petty chiefs of Kathiawar or the Rajput princelings of the Himalayas; but which everywhere involves the exercise to a greater or less degree of territorial jurisdiction by the paramount power, and implies the reserve on its part of a certain dominant "residuary jurisdiction", and even of the right to disregard the plain terms of the treaties themselves when the supreme interests of the empire are touched, or when the interests of the subjects of the native princes are gravely affected. Were the sovereignty of Great Britain less marked in fact, it would still be impossible to hold that the native states of India preserve so much independence as remains in the hands of an ordinary protected state. From the moment that the Queen was proclaimed Empress of India the sovereign powers which native princes enjoyed, and enjoy, ceased to be relics of their independence; they were kept by sufferance or delegation.'

[1] Hall, *op. cit.*, pp. 218–19.

make laws for his subjects and for his territory, may exercise power over life and death, and may levy taxes and dues, but nevertheless he may be debarred from making war and peace, and from having foreign relations with any authority outside his territory. This, in point of fact, is the exact condition of the native princes of India; and states of this kind are at the present in all the more barbarous portions of the world. In the protectorates which Germany, France, Italy, and Spain have established in the Australasian seas, and on the coast of Africa, there is no attempt made to annex the land, or to found a colony in the old sense of the word, but the local tribes are forbidden all foreign relations except those permitted by the protecting state.[1]

In the opinion of Sir Henry Jenkyns:

'By the exclusion of external relations with foreign powers, the protector is held according to international law to assume the external sovereignty of the protected territory, and the territory becomes what is termed by international writers a semi-sovereign state, or, as Sir T. Twiss prefers to call it, a "protected independent state." '[2]

The arguments given above on the question of suzerainty by leading authorities on international law make it clear that, in fact, the attitude of British officials with respect to the status of Nepal appears not to have been wholly consistent and to have been influenced by what seemed convenient or politic in dealing with particular issues. Perhaps the British officials read into the legal instruments regarding Nepal their sense of the intentions of the British Government with respect to Nepal, and thus did not attempt to reduce all points to writing. The treaty of Segowlee of 1815, for example, permitted some latitude of interpretation. On the one hand, the treaty appears to take for granted the independence of Nepal in those areas she was not required to cede to the British East India Company, as well as providing for reciprocal exchange of diplomatic agents. On the other hand, Nepal had to accept restrictions upon her freedom of action with respect to Sikkim, and with respect to employment of European and American citizens. Also, although it was not expressed, it was probably clear to Nepal that she would not be allowed to enter into commitments with other states unless approved by the British. The Nepalese situation seems, therefore, to be one of nominal independence but actual protection by the British—a form of protectorate which still permitted very substantial

[1] Jenkyns, Sir Henry, *British Rule and Jurisdiction Beyond the Seas* (Oxford University Press, 1902), pp. 166–7.
[2] *Ibid.*, p. 166.

Nepalese autonomy. This probably explains why there was some inconsistency in the titles and courtesies accorded to the Nepalese representatives in India.

The matter of titles and courtesies to Nepalese officials was interesting because it illustrated the status of Nepal in the eyes of the Government of India and the rest of the diplomatic world. For instance, when the question came up in 1887 as to whether the Nepalese representative in Calcutta might be received by the Viceroy, the Secretary of the Government of India wrote that in the case of a previous representative, 'an interview was granted, but only as a concession'.[1] On this occasion also, the interview was granted, but only for a few minutes. These interviews had no significance in themselves, except that the Nepalese wanted to show they also had a diplomatic representative in India, whose status required proper recognition by the British. On the issue of extending diplomatic recognition to official visitors from Nepal, the Government of India on many occasions recognized the official deputed from Nepal as an ambassador. Yet, there was no consistent policy and decisions were made according to the situation. For example, in 1876, Dhere Shamsher came as an ambassador to represent Nepal in the Delhi Assemblage; in notification published in the *Gazette of India*, he was described as 'His Excellency the Ambassador from the Maharajah Dhiraj of Nipal'.[2] In 1878, General Dhere Shamsher was sent by the Maharajah Dhiraj to India with a Kharieta (letter) to the Viceroy. In his reply to the Maharajah Dhiraj's letter, the Viceroy called the General 'an Ambassador'.[3] A curiously contradictory incident developed when Sir Ranodip Singh visited India in 1881. He requested, but was not accorded, the title of ambassador; yet in a later letter (No. 2429-E, dated October 15, 1883), to the Resident in Nepal, a British India government official wrote that 'the Minister in 1881 came as an Ambassador', apparently a retroactive award of the title.[4] In yet another instance, Maharajah Bir Shamsher came to India in 1888 and was accepted as an ambassador without question.[5] Since it was a practice of the British that the representatives from those States who were subordinate to the Government of India were called 'Vakils' or 'Motamids'[6] rather than ambassadors, this suggests that a higher status was accorded the Nepalese as representatives of a formally independent state.

[1] *Foreign Department External Proceedings—A*, February 1887, Nos. 12–16. (N.A.I.)
[2] *Ibid.*
[3] *Foreign Political—B*, April 1879, Nos. 109–11. (N.A.I.)
[4] *Foreign Political—A*, March 1883, Nos. 179–81. (N.A.I.)
[5] *Foreign Secret—A*, August 1889, Nos. 50–1. (N.A.I.)
[6] *Ibid.*

Another interesting instance supporting the position that the British Government generally regarded Nepal as a formally independent state occurred when the Maharajah Dhiraj was invited to attend the Delhi Durbar, which was held on January 1, 1903. Because he could not go personally, he deputed Maharajah Chandra Shamsher to represent Nepal. The question arose as to the title of Maharajah Chandra Shamsher. He wanted to go as an ambassador of his king. But the Government of India, on this occasion, did not accord this favor. In this connection he wrote to the Resident, saying that:

'.... for the uniform cordial and friendly relations subsisting between the two Governments for such a length of time that the exceptional term ambassador has always been used. This is more a matter of favour, mutual regard and understanding of privilege than the comity of nations to which you refer in your letter under reply. Even from that point of view I should think His Majesty the Maharajah Dhiraj by his position as an independent ruler may claim the honour of sending an ambassador.'[1]

Because of this protest it was finally agreed that Chandra Shamsher would be styled simply the 'Prime Minister of Nepal and the Representative of Maharajah Dhiraj'. He decided to take his seat in the block reserved for 'distinguished visitors and Foreign Representatives'.[2] In 1877 Chandra Shamsher's father, Dhere Shamsher, had also been seated in the same block, but had been described as an 'Ambassador'. Chandra Shamsher's protest was made soon after he became prime minister. From the very beginning, he asserted the independence of Nepal, and in the end he won recognition of it.

The matter of extradition of criminals is another gauge of the independence of a country, since extradition matters are generally handled between independent states. In 1884, the Government of India concluded a treaty with Nepal on the question of extradition. But when two criminals who were subjects of Rampur (an Indian Princely State) crossed into Nepal to escape capture, a problem was created as to how their extradition could be demanded. In the opinion of the Secretary of the Government of India, Nepal was not a protected Native State. The problem he said was that 'one is protected, e.g. Rampur and the other is virtually independent, e.g. Nepal. . . .' The foreign office officials agreed that 'the Native protected States should

---

[1] Chandra Shamsher to Colonel Ravenshaw, the Resident, Nepal, June 7, 1902. *Basta No. 47.* (N.F.O.K.)

[2] 'Ceremonials', *Foreign and Political Department Secret*, File No. 96 (4)-H 1934, op. cit.

be considered as regards extradition with Foreign States, as quasi-British territory'.[1]

In contrast to the above, there were several instances in which British legislation was construed as applicable to Nepal apparently in the same way as to princely states of India. Thus a British administrative officer held that 'a native of Nepal is a native of India within the meaning of the Emigration Act of 1883....'[2] Certain extra-territorial jurisdictions by British India over British subjects seem to have been exercised in Nepal as in the princely states:

'By Notification No. 178, dated 23rd September 1874 Nepal was included among the "States of India in alliance with Her Majesty over which the High Court at Calcutta had jurisdiction so far as European British subjects of Her Majesty, being Christians, were concerned. And lastly, Nepal has been included among the "dominions of Princes and States in India in alliance with Her Majesty" for the purpose of Notification under the Income Tax Act, II of 1886, and the Births, Deaths and Marriages Registration Act, VI of 1886 (see Notifications, Nos. 4136–I, dated 16th September 1887, and 1428–E, dated 24th July 1889).'[3]

On all these matters Nepal was given the status of a princely state, not of an independent ally.

In 1902, a case arose concerning the jurisdiction of the High Court of India to issue a commission for examination of witnesses in Nepal. This led the court to consider whether under 'section 503 of the Criminal Procedure Code, as interpreted by the General Clauses Act, Nepal can be described as a State under British suzerainty'.[4] The Honorable Mr C. Brett, Judge of the Calcutta High Court, ruled, 'I believe that it cannot, and that it is nominally a State whose relations with the British Government are determined by Treaty (mainly the Treaty of 1815)'.[5] Mr J. B. Wood, Under-Secretary to the Government of India, accordingly wrote to the Judge, 'You will see there is nothing

---

[1] 'Extradition of two Rampur subjects from Nipal', *Foreign Department Internal—A*, September 1884, Nos. 14–18, *op. cit.*

[2] Denzil Ibbetson, Officiating Secretary Government of India, Revenue and Agriculture Department to the Chief Secretary to the Government of North Western Provinces and Oudh, No. 2771–55, Simla, October 16, 1894, *Foreign Department External—A*, November 1894, Nos. 35–7. (N.A.I.)

[3] *Foreign External Department Proceedings—A*, August 1894, Nos. 144–52. (N.A.I.)

[4] 'Question as to whether Nepal is under the suzerainty of the British Crown', *Foreign Department Secret Proceedings—E*, March 1903, No. 228, Note. (N.A.I.)

[5] *Ibid.*

in it [i.e. the treaty] about suzerainty or control of foreign relations, and I think myself that the legal status of Nepal is that of an independent state not under British or any other suzerainty'.[1] However, Mr Wood wanted to see more papers in this connection before giving a final opinion.

Subsequently, the Registrar of the Calcutta High Court inquired from the Government of India on behalf of Justice Brett:

'What the Honorable Judge wishes to know is whether a commission for the examination of witnesses may be issued, under section 503 (2) of the Criminal Procedure Code, to the Resident in Nepal as representing the British Government in that country. To determine this, it is necessary to know whether Nepal is in "India", as defined in section 3 (27) of the General Clauses Act, i.e. whether it is under the Suzerainty of His Majesty exercised by the Governor-General of India, or an officer subordinate to him. I understand from Mr. Brett that, so far as the present case is concerned, it would be more convenient if Nepal were declared to be in India.'[2]

This inquiry became an important issue and so was discussed exhaustively in the Foreign Office. The Secretary of the Foreign Office stated his opinion,

'... Now there is no doubt that, if we follow the terms of our Treaties with Nepal, we must admit that legally speaking, Nepal has "full sovereignty" and owns suzerainty of no other power. But it would be ridiculous to say that Nepal is, in reality, a sovereign State independent of our control in its external independence, for we certainly should not permit her to make war or conclude an alliance with another Foreign Power except with our concurrence [Author's Note: In 1854-56 Nepal did declare war on Tibet and made a separate Treaty with that country. She did not obtain permission from the British Indian Government.] and the Maharajah is precluded from taking into his service the subject of any European State without the permission of the British Government. I think therefore, that we assert that, for practical purposes, Nepal is under our suzerainty. In any case, it would certainly be inconvenient to declare officially that she is not.

[1] J. B. Wood, Under-Secretary to the Government of India, in the Foreign Department, Calcutta, November 29, 1902, to the Honorable Justice Brett, ibid.
[2] 'Enquiries whether Nepal is or is not under the suzerainty of the British Crown', from the Registrar of the High Court Judicature at Fort William, No. 798, dated the 2nd (received 3rd) December, 1903; No. 228. Notes, op. cit.

'... probably the best way out of the difficulty would be to obtain from the High Court officially their reasons for desiring the required information, and then, when we get their reply, to say that for the purpose of issuing a commission under section 503 (2), Civil Procedure Code, Nepal may be regarded as being "in India".'[1]

Lord Curzon, the Viceroy, thought that the position of Nepal was 'anomalous and peculiar'. He said:

'I hold most questionable that the State is under the suzerainty (admitting an elastic rather than a too stringent definition of the term) of the British Crown.'[2]

He elaborated this statement by adding,

'This is a claim inseparable from political autonomy, which it is my recollection that the Government of India have, at any rate in recent years, if not always, steadily resisted, and from which I believe that we have now persuaded the Nepalese Government to desist.'[3]

In the same context while justifying the suzerainty of the British Government, Lord Curzon wrote,

'If they cannot send an ambassador to us, then they cannot be wholly independent; and if they are not wholly independent, then the degree of their dependence, as marked by this and other symptoms, may, I think, justify the claim of suzerainty being put forward, though I doubt not that if it were academically raised with the Nepalese Darbar, they would energetically contest it.'[4]

On the request of the Viceroy, Mr T. Raleigh of the Government of India Legislative Department gave his opinion that,

'We are justified therefore in saying that in this case "alliance" means what is elsewhere in the statute-book called "subordinate alliance", or

---

[1] 'Enquiries whether Nepal is or is not under the suzerainty of the British Crown.' Office file notes. *Foreign Department Secret Proceedings—E*, March 1903, No. 228. Notes, *op. cit.*

[2] Foreign Department File Notes by Lord Curzon, Viceroy and Governor-General of India, *Foreign Department Secret Proceedings—E*, March 1903, *op. cit.*

[3] *Ibid.*

[4] Lord Curzon notes on the file. *Foreign Department Secret Proceedings—E*, March 1903, *op. cit.*

in other words, that Nepal is under British "suzerainty", although in correspondence with the State we should avoid the use of that embarrassing word.'¹

The advice of Mr Raleigh was considered satisfactory in the Foreign Office, but it was settled that the Government of India should 'try by a personal reference or by demi-official confidential letter to avoid having to give a direct reply on the point while assisting the High Court to serve their commission if they still wish this'.²

In this same period, the issue of suzerainty was raised again by London. Lee-Warner, Secretary, Political Department of the India Office, London, wrote a despatch to the Secretary of the Government of India, inquiring if the Government of India had ever clearly stated its view on this subject.³ Lee-Warner observed that foreign governments such as Japan and Switzerland had applied to the British Foreign Office to allow their nationals to travel in Nepal.⁴ This showed that these nations took for granted that Nepal was under British control. His inquiry started another discussion in the Government of India Foreign Office, who eventually answered his query in the following words:

'It is less stringent than our relations with other Native States; it is more stringent than our Treaty Protectorate over Afghanistan. Whatever its precise nature and definition, it is most important that Nepal should be recognized as falling under our exclusive political control, and that it should continue to be included among the States to which the provisions of our code may be applied.'⁵

The lengthy foreign office discussions were kept secret from the Government of Nepal. Therefore Nepal remained under the impression that, directly or indirectly, the Government of India regarded it as an independent state. But the Nepal Government was not absolutely confident of this, however, and for this reason its prime ministers were always on the alert to defend their claim to independence.

The issue of Nepal's status lay relatively quiet for several years after the above noted exchange of correspondence in 1903, until an unfor-

¹ The opinion of Mr T. Raleigh, Law Member, Government of India, Legislative Department Note. *Ibid.*
² Notes by L. Dane, December 19, 1902, *Foreign Department Secret Proceedings—E*, March 1903, *op. cit.*
³ Lee-Warner to L. W. Dane, London, March 13, 1903; *Foreign Department Secret Proceedings—E*, July 1903, Nos. 20–1. Notes. (N.A.I.)
⁴ *Ibid.*
⁵ *Foreign Department Secret Proceedings—E*, July 1903, Nos. 20–1, *op. cit.*

tunate incident occurred in 1907 which revived the controversy. The *Imperial Gazetteer* of 1907 contained the statement, Nepal 'is a Native State' although the *Imperial Gazetteer* of India in 1903 had described Nepal as an 'Independent State'.[1] This change naturally infuriated the prime minister, Chandra Shamsher, who complained to the Government of India about the description. In a despatch to the Resident, he 'produced the original letter from Lord Dufferin, which was written when he was the Viceroy and Governor-General of India on March 31, 1885. In it Nepal was described as an 'Independent State'.[2] Once more, the officials of the Government of India deliberated on the status of Nepal. It was said that,

'At present, the Government of India recognizes Nepal as falling under their exclusive influence and control, and they regarded the Maharajah as a Native Prince or Chief under the suzerainty of His Majesty exercised through the Governor-General of India. . . .'[3]

But Dufferin also noted that the India Government Secretary of State had not formally and categorically 'accepted this view',[4] even though Lee-Warner's note from the India Office described Nepal as 'a glorified member of the protectorate'.[5] Presumably all these views were considered still consistent with the full autonomy of Nepal which had been definitely pledged by Governor-General Lord Elgin in 1894:

'I desire earnestly to impress upon Your Highness that my principal aim is to employ every means in my power to guard against anything which might suggest or foster the idea that my Government ever have entertained, or will entertain, the intention or design of interfering with Nepalese autonomy.'[6]

Note that Lord Elgin did not specifically say Nepal was independent. Thus, it could be possible that the British Government considered Nepal under British suzerainty, and yet allowed autonomy in practice.

Manner-Smith, the Resident, made an extensive effort to remove the apprehension which Chandra Shamsher felt because of the mistake

---

[1] *Imperial Gazetteer*, p. 58, Vol. IV, Chapter III, 1907; *Imperial Gazetteer*, p. 103, Vol. VII, 1903.
[2] *Foreign and Political Department Secret*, July 1911, Nos. 693–703. (N.A.I.)
[3] Foreign Office Notes. *Foreign Department Secret Proceedings—E*, September 1908, Nos. 457–9. (N.A.I.)
[4] Ibid.
[5] Ibid.
[6] Lord Elgin, Kharieta to Maharajah Dhiraj, May 15, 1894, *Foreign Secret—E*, November 1894, Nos. 127–62. (N.A.I.)

made by the *Imperial Gazetteer*. The Resident had accepted that it was not correct to describe Nepal as a 'Native State' and in time succeeded in partially calming the Prime Minister.[1]

While the 'Gazetteer Incident' passed without further complications, Chandra Shamsher still wanted to clarify the official status of his country. To this end, he advanced a rather startling proposal which Manner-Smith communicated to Sir L. W. Dane, Secretary, Government of India, thus:

'... it is perhaps important that you should know of a suggestion which Sir Chandra Shamsher volunteered to me some time ago, viz. that the Nepal Darbar would be prepared under certain circumstances to come to a definite agreement with the Government of India regarding political subordination in dealing with China on the lines of Article 6 of Engagement No. LIV of 1815 relating to Nepal.'[2]

Chandra Shamsher's motive for offering to accept a subordinate alliance was that he wanted to have an unequivocal guarantee from the Government of India of Nepal's internal autonomy. Nepal had been jealous of Afghanistan's position because although its external relations were controlled by India in return for a subsidy, Afghanistan was treated as fully autonomous in her internal affairs.

Manner-Smith reacted to the Prime Minister's proposal by suggesting that when the Prime Minister made his proposed visit to England in 1908, 'we (the British Government) may be able to secure the control of her external relations as suggested by the Minister'.[3] Later, when Chandra Shamsher was making his preparations for his trip to England, Manner-Smith suggested to his Government that 'the Minister should be treated rather as Sirdar Nasrullah Khan than as an Indian Chief'.[4] The answer of the Government of India was very clear:

'Its [Nepal's] position is really between that of Afghanistan and of the Feudatory Princes, but the question of the exact status of the State is one that should not be raised in correspondence or when Mr.

---

[1] Extract from a letter from the Resident in Nepal, No. 109, dated September 26 (received October 2), 1907, *Foreign Department Secret—E Proceedings*, September 1908.
[2] Manner-Smith to L. W. Dane, No. 139, the 18th (received 24th) August, 1907, *Foreign Department Secret Proceedings—E*, Nos. 457–9, *op. cit.*
[3] Extract from a letter from the Resident in Nepal, No. 109, dated September 26, *op. cit.*
[4] Extract from a note by Secretary, Government of India, dated January 4, 1908. *Foreign Department Secret Proceedings—E*, September 1908, Nos. 457–9, *op. cit.*

Hobhouse visits Kathmandu in January. I am afraid that the Resident is suffering from megalomania about Nepal and may cause trouble.'[1]

Manner-Smith then wrote, advising a policy as follows:

'The policy which I would advocate, however, is one of complete confidence in the good intentions and word of the present Prime Minister, and I would go as far as possible without prejudice to our right of suzerainty in the direction of treating Nepal as a friendly independent State whose interests are wrapped up in our own rather than as a subordinate feudatory whose actions must be watched.'[2]

Manner-Smith further advocated his policy by saying:

'I am Imperialist to the core, but I firmly believe that the way to bind the Native Chiefs to the empire is to treat them as loyal junior partners and not as a lot of naughty school boys, who must be kept in their places and repressed.'[3]

The policy recommended by Manner-Smith was partially adopted, although not immediately. In an interesting sidelight, the Indian Foreign Office noted that Manner-Smith generally used the word 'King', in place of 'Maharajah Dhiraj', in his communications. The Foreign Office informed him that,

'It is preferable to safeguard the use of any expressions which are capable of being viewed as indicating the enjoyment of independence or of the main attributes of sovereignty by Native Chiefs under the suzerainty of His Majesty; and although our Protectorate over Nepal may be less stringent than in the case of other Native States, it is undesirable that such expressions as "King", "throne", "reign", "royal", etc., should be employed with reference to the Maharajah Dhiraj of Nepal in any official document.

'The proper designation of "Maharajah Dhiraj" has, therefore, been

---

[1] *Foreign Department Secret Proceedings*, September 1908, Nos. 457–9, *op. cit.*

[2] Extract from a letter of Manner-Smith to the Secretary, Government of India in the Foreign Department, No. 169, September 26/27 (received October 2), 1907. *Ibid.*

[3] Manner-Smith to Foreign Secretary Government of India, No. 6, Residency Nepal, January 13, 1908. *Ibid.*

substituted wherever the title of "King" occurs in your report, and in Colonel Ravenshaw's note.'[1]

To summarize this period it can be seen that the Government of India did not wish to define the exact amount of independence which Nepal possessed. This is borne out in a confidential letter from the Government to the Resident instructing him that:

'The question of the limitations on the freedom of the Durbar is thus a delicate one which the Government of India would prefer not to reopen unless forced to do so, and as they are not prepared, for military reasons, to allow the Durbar greater freedom than they now enjoy, no communication should be made to the Prime Minister on the subject of the present references.'[2]

At the same time, the Government of India wanted to keep peace with Prime Minister Chandra Shamsher. While it is true that the Government of India had not interfered in Nepalese affairs for many years (save in limiting arms imports), and that it promised to continue this non-interference policy, still it did not want to renounce suzerainty. By using the term 'independent position' to describe Nepal's position, the Government of India meant to indicate the continuation of the *status quo*, namely, the same abstention from interference as previously. The Resident was asked to inform the Maharajah,

'... that the Government of India have no desire whatever to interfere with the 'independent position' which the State of Nepal has hitherto enjoyed, and that they share with His Excellency the earnest hope that the happy relations of friendship and mutual confidence which have existed for so many years will remain forever undisturbed.'[3]

This guarantee was very essential to calm the fears of Nepal. Yet the language seemed to allow the Government of India a means of retreat; it could be interpreted as guaranteeing only the same amount of independence which Nepal had hitherto enjoyed—which the British could well argue had been less than complete.

[1] L. Russel, Deputy Secretary, Government of India, Foreign Department, to Manner-Smith, Simla, August 14, 1905, *Foreign Department Secret Proceedings—E*, September 1905, Nos. 1–4. (N.A.I.)
[2] Secretary, Foreign Department, Government of India to Manner-Smith, No. 775 E–B (Very Confidential), Simla, April 24, 1911, *Foreign and Political Department Secret—E*, July 1911, Nos. 693–703. (N.A.I.)
[3] Secretary to the Government of India, Foreign Department to Manner-Smith, No. 775 E–B (Very Confidential), Simla, April 24, 1911, *Foreign and Political Department Secret—E*, July 1911, Nos. 693–703, op. cit.

The position of Nepal *vis-à-vis* the Government of India, changed substantially after World War I. The unlimited and loyal help provided by Nepal during the war proved the sincerity and good faith of Nepal towards its ally, Britain. The change in relationship was shown in February 1919 when the question was raised whether Nepalese could be given Indian passports. The Government of India decided that,

'Tibet and Nepal are Independent States in close friendly alliance with the British Government; they are thus different from Native States in India, and Tibetans and Nepalese cannot be given Indian passports in the same way as is done to Native States' subjects in common with British Indian subjects.'[1]

When Khan Bahadur Sarfraz Husain Khan, a member of the Central Legislative Assembly, asked the question, 'Does the Government propose to make rules relating to passports for persons entering India from Nepal, Bhutan, and other main north-eastern routes?'[2] the answer of the Government was in the negative. This was a proof of India's confidence in the loyalty of Nepal. The Government of India had no fear that any foreign agents or other opponents of British rule would escape the vigilance of the Nepalese authorities. Therefore passports were considered unnecessary.

A second indication of Nepal's status was shown in the changes made by the British Government in India in the titles of Nepalese leaders. Chandra Shamsher requested the Indian Government in its correspondence to change the title of the King of Nepal from 'His Highness' to 'His Majesty'.[3] Subsequently, the title was changed in 1919 from Maharajah Dhiraj to 'His Majesty the Maharajah Dhiraj of Nepal', and the title of 'Nepal Durbar', was altered to 'Government of Nepal'.[4]

A further indication of Nepal's changed status appears in a memorandum prepared for the British King-Emperor and defining the position of Nepal at the end of World War I. It stated in part:

[1] Decision that Tibetan and Nepalese subjects applying for passports to leave India for other countries should be granted exemption certificates under the defense of India (passport) rules. *Foreign and Political Department General-B*, June 1919, Nos. 231–3. (N.A.I.)

[2] Khan Bahadur Sarfraz Husain Khan, 'Question and Answer for the meeting of the Legislative Assembly on August 29, 1927', *Foreign and Political General*, File No. 788-G, 1927, Nos. 1–3. (N.A.I.)

[3] Memo by Chandra Shamsher to the Government of India, 1916, *Basta No. 68*. (N.F.O.K.)

[4] *Foreign and Political Department Secret Internal Proceedings*, July 1919, Nos. 36–65, *op. cit.*

'Such are the relevant facts. It will be observed (1) that the obligation to receive an accredited minister is reciprocal; (2) that the foreign relations of Nepal are uncontrolled, except to the extent that it will not receive protection if it does not take our advice; (3) that until quite recently it acknowledged the suzerainty of a foreign power. It may be added that the ruler of Nepal has not done homage to the King-Emperor, has not been asked to acknowledge his suzerainty; and that Nepal is therefore not included in the legal definition of India. The one respect in which there has been a formal derogation from the Maharajah's sovereignty is the obligation not to employ Europeans or Americans without the permission of the Government of India.'[1]

The 'Treaty of Friendship between Great Britain and Nepal' was a major landmark in British–Nepalese relations. It removed the last restrictions on Nepal's independence, including the prohibition against Nepal's employing Europeans or Americans without the permission of the Government of India. In the preliminary Treaty discussions, the India Office in London had suggested many restrictions in the draft Treaty to safeguard British interests. One of them was a clause 'to prevent Nepal from being made a base by Bolsheviks and Indian seditionists'. Sir Arthur Hirtzel advised that 'Hitherto there have been no signs of this. But Nepal is the most powerful Hindu state in or near India, and sooner or later it may be a very tempting objective for the disaffected'.[2] With one exception, the restrictions were politely rejected by Chandra Shamsher. Nepal was granted the right to import arms and munitions, but this was accomplished by a note written by Chandra Shamsher on the insistence of the Government of India. It obliged Nepal to submit 'detailed lists of such arms and ammunitions [as it wishes to import] to the British Envoy at the Court of Nepal'.[3] Presumably India wished to decide whether the amount was reasonable.

With the solitary minor restriction noted above, Nepal became completely independent on December 21, 1923. The post-Treaty history of the foreign relations of Nepal has given clear proof of this independence.

The 1923 British–Nepalese treaty had a very understandable effect upon the princes who continued as rulers of feudatory states under the

---

[1] *Foreign and Political Department Secret Internal Proceedings*, July 1919, Nos. 36–65, *op. cit.*
[2] Sir Arthur Hirtzel, *Political and External*, File No. JOLM/3/463, August 25, 1922, *op. cit.*
[3] Note from the Prime Minister of Nepal to the British Envoy at the Court of Nepal. December 21, 1923. Aitchison, *Treaties, Engagements and Sunnuds*, p. 77, Vol. XIV, *op. cit.*

paramount power of the Government of India. In one instance, the Resident in the princely state of Gwalior informed the Indian Government that the Maharajah of Gwalior complained that the friendship of Nepal towards the Government of India 'in no means exceeds the friendship and goodwill that Gwalior has displayed to the Government of India since 1817, and more especially during his father's lifetime and his own'.[1] The reply of the Political Secretary to the Government of India shed a good deal of light on the position of Nepal *vis-à-vis* the Indian States on the one hand, and the Government of India on the other. The letter read as follows:

'IX... While the Government of India are fully mindful of the valuable assistance rendered by the Gwalior Darbar during the Great War, they cannot admit that the nature of the relation subsisting between themselves and the Indian States by virtue of Treaties and general usage are hereby affected.

2. Until recently the status of Nepal may not have been very clearly defined but an examination of the history of British relations with it shows its position has always been peculiar and altogether different from that of an Indian State in that

(i) Article 10 of the Treaty of 1801 lays down that the obligation to receive an accredited Minister is reciprocal;
(ii) the foreign relations of Nepal have never been under the control of His Majesty's Government.
(iii) The ruler of Nepal has never done homage to nor acknowledged the suzerainty of His Majesty the King-Emperor.
(iv) Nepal is, therefore, not included in the legal definition of India.

3. No doubt many ruling Princes like the Ruler of Nepal enjoy full powers of internal administration in so far as their territories are concerned. They have, however, ceded their external sovereign rights to the British Crown which has undertaken to defend and protect the States against all external enemies. They have further jointly and severally admitted certain obligations with a view to cooperation with the Government of India and with one another and in the interests of the good government of the States generally.'[2]

This statement of the status of Nepal was a great deal more definite and unambiguous than earlier pronouncements of the Government of

---

[1] Resident of Gwalior to Government of India, No. 147—P, of En. Gwalior, Residency, January 17, 1924. File No. 51-P (Secret) of En. *Foreign and Political Department*, File No. 51 (Secret), 1924. (N.A.I.)

[2] Political Secretary, Government of India, to L. M. Crump, Resident at Gwalior, 'Subject: Nepal *vis-à-vis* Indian States.' *Foreign and Political Department*, File No. 51 (Secret), 1924, *op. cit.*

India. No doubt the reason for the unusual clarity was that the Political Secretary wished to put forcibly the point that the superior status of Nepal was unique and that the Indian princes could not use it as a precedent in order to demand the same rights for themselves. The Government of India had never been willing prior to the Treaty of 1923 to concede the same points in correspondence with Nepal.

In the same way, a Government of India letter to the British Envoy at the Court of Nepal in 1928 stated that,

'I am directed to inform you that it has recently been decided in connection with the revision of Macpherson's British Enactments in force in Native States, that Nepal, in view of her independent status, cannot be held to be in India within the meaning of the definition in the Interpretation Act and the General Clauses Act.'[1]

and in 1929, when an invitation was sent through the British Envoy in Nepal from the South African Government to the Nepalese Government inviting Nepal to attend the International Geological Congress in Pretoria that same year, the British Envoy in Nepal wrote to the Government of India that 'I have suggested to the Prime Minister of Nepal that the Nepal Government should reply directly'.[2] The same practice was adopted for correspondence between the League of Nations and the Nepal Government.

It was also decided by the Government of India, with the permission of the Indian Office in London, that because of the extreme sensitiveness of the Nepalese Government on the subject of their complete independence,

'... in the future all applications from foreigners, i.e. other than British subjects, to visit Nepal should not be referred by the British Representative in Nepal to the Nepal Government. Colonel Daukes, who was the British Envoy in Kathmandu at the time, ascertained from the Nepal Government that they would prefer such applications to be sent direct to them and not through the British Legation.'[3]

---

[1] Letter to the British Envoy at the Court of Nepal, Kathmandu, No, D-3542-X, -28, dated November 6, 1928 (Confidential). *Foreign and Political.* File No. 229-X, 1928. (N.A.I.)

[2] W. H. J. Wilkinson, British Envoy at the Court of Nepal to the Deputy-Secretary, Government of India, Foreign Department, New Delhi, No. 41 C.P., *Foreign and Political Department,* Government of India, File No. 23-X, 1929. (N.A.I.)

[3] Foreign Office Note, *Foreign and Political External,* File No. 203-X, 1935. (N.A.I.)

The British Foreign Office acknowledged Nepal's independence by changing its foreign service rules. In 1928, the Indian Auditor-General was informed by the Government of India, that 'the Governor-General in Council is pleased to decide that Nepal should be treated as outside India for purposes of the "Foreign Service" rules'.[1] Henceforth, those personnel who were employed by British India to serve in Nepal would be treated as in the Foreign Service of the British Government in India. Thus, all the rules which were applicable to those who were in a foreign country would be applicable to the British Minister in Nepal along with his entire staff.

Nepal's new status received gradual recognition by other foreign countries. In 1929, the French Consul-General visited Nepal, and the Italian Consul and other consuls followed suit. In 1934, Nepal sent its first Minister directly to the Court of St James's in London.

In today's context, the following statement perhaps gives the best definition of the status of Nepal:

'If one were to essay a description of Nepal one might speak of it as a State of High Asia, which is independent *de jure* but *de facto* tends to be drawn into the political orbit of its most powerful neighbour. It is India towards which it is drawn, and the Government of India have shown a certain inclination in recent years to encourage, or at least emphasize the process.'[2]

Nepal–Thailand–Hydarabad Comparison

Further light is thrown on the status of Nepal when it is compared with Thailand and with Hydarabad, one of the largest and most powerful of the princely states of India.

First, we note that Thailand's status in 1903 was described by British officials as 'admittedly an independent state. . . .'[3] In this heyday of imperialism, Thailand's relatively independent status was quite unusual. It is noted that probably the main reason Thailand had managed to retain more than nominal independence was because she was a pawn in the rivalries of the two great European powers, Great Britain and France; neither would allow the other to annex her. But in the process

[1] Unofficial Memorandum: Subject: Question whether Nepal is outside India for the purposes of the 'Foreign Service' rules. V. V. Rao, Assistant Secretary to the Government of India to the Auditor-General, No. F.I-XI- R. I/28, Government of India, Finance Department, *Foreign and Political Department External*, File No. 200-A, 1928. (N.A.I.)

[2] *Foreign and Political Department Secret Internal Proceedings*, July 1919, Nos. 36–65, *op. cit.*

[3] *Foreign Department Secret Proceedings—E*, July 1903, Nos. 20–1, Notes, *op. cit.*

of balancing one great imperialist nation against the other, Thailand was compelled to make considerable cessions of territory to both Great Britain and France and to grant low tax rates, reduced duties and the rights of extra-territoriality, to nationals of European countries.

Prior to World War II, British influence played the dominant though not an exclusive role in shaping Thailand's government's policy. During World War II, the predominant influence was that of Japan, and after the war, the United States. Thailand, though legally a sovereign, independent state, was too weak to avoid the necessity to modify its foreign policies in accord with the wishes of its predominant power at the time. In spite of the foregoing, however, Thailand retained more independence in handling her own affairs with Western powers than Nepal. The principal reason seems to have been that Nepal was land-locked, and the only strong power near her was British India. On the other hand, Thailand bordered on French Indo-China and British Malaya; and owing to her seaports, other foreign nations also had an interest in preserving her independence and their own rights of trade.

Hydarabad (and the other princely States) had, by treaties and engagements, surrendered control of its foreign affairs and defense to the Government of India. Hydarabad was forbidden to employ any European nationals without British consent, and during most of the nineteenth century, it (unlike Nepal) was compelled to rely for its protection upon the Indian Army. It was not permitted to declare war or to have diplomatic relations with any other states, Indian, European or Asian.

Like most of the other princely states, Hydarabad was landlocked and completely surrounded by the territory under direct British rule. The policy of the central government of British India was to develop India as a single unit. For example, an India-wide system of roads and railways was built; the economic system of India was developed as a national system ignoring the boundaries of the princely States; the various social services of the government were extended to the princely states as well as to the provinces of British India, etc. The combined result was the development of the doctrine of 'paramountcy'.

By terms of the original treaties, the control of Hydarabad's internal affairs was left to the Nizam. But as the nineteenth century progressed, the central government of British India increasingly overrode the treaty rights of the Nizam in order to extend the same standard of government to the whole of India, and to promote its economic unity by roads and railways, officials were removed for serious misgovernment and successors appointed by the Government of British India, independent of the wishes of the Nizam.

Nepal had a much greater degree of independence than Hydarabad. It at least retained control of its Asian foreign policy. It maintained an efficient and modern army which, though small, would have given a very good account of itself, considering the mountainous terrain and the very few good roads in Nepal. The doctrine of 'paramountcy' was not applied to it. There was no interference with domestic affairs even when Prime Minister Ranodip Singh was murdered and his relatives killed or driven into India. No pressure was put on the Durbar to introduce the social services of British India, and the Indian road and railway system was not extended into Nepal. The most probable explanation is that the Government of India wished to conciliate Nepal because its chief interest in Nepal was the obtaining of Gurkha recruits for the Indian Army. The Durbar showed again and again that it was determined to maintain Nepal's independence and way of life, and there was nothing to be gained by turning a loyal ally into an enemy. As to extending the Indian road and railway system, there was no economic necessity for this since Nepal was on the extreme northern frontier, and its trade, like that of Tibet, was negligible.

In other points of comparison, it can be noted that the kings of Thailand and Nepal never accepted any foreign titles, but the Head of the State of Hydarabad received titles from the British Government. Thailand, Nepal, and Hydarabad all had their own governments with a head of state, national flags, prime ministers of their own choice, and full internal administration. But here again, the kings of Thailand and Nepal were generally free to select any one they wished for their internal administration without foreign interference though an implied limit existed regarding the Nepalese government. However, there seems no likelihood that the Government of British India would have intervened in the Nepal government unless policies considered inconsistent with the security of India had been adopted. This did not occur.

In the final analysis Thailand, in actual practice, although not in law, had not much more independence than Nepal except in international relations. In this field, unlike Nepal, it was free to maintain diplomatic relations with Western as well as Asian states, subject to the proviso that it could not afford to ignore the policies of neighboring states that were much more powerful than itself. Nepal, on the other hand, was a good deal more independent than Hydarabad. In short, Thailand and Nepal had substantial external independence of action, whereas Hydarabad did not. The present status of all these three countries confirms the above analysis.

In the preceding chapters, the history of British India's relations with the kingdom of Nepal from 1857 to 1947 has been traced, with all its complications and ambiguities. This history provided the materials for an analysis of the diplomatic status of Nepal in the international community. The true nature of British–Nepalese relations during this period are difficult to ascertain. There is no doubt that even the highest officials of the Indian Government were not sure of the correct definition of these relations prior to 1923.

It would seem, however, that Nepal remained a largely independent country throughout its existence. The degree of her independence differed from time to time but she never completely succumbed to the control of any outside power. And she emerged as the sole master of her national destiny in the latter half of the twentieth century.

PART IV

BIBLIOGRAPHY AND APPENDICES

BIBLIOGRAPHY

PRIMARY SOURCES

India Office Library, London
  Government Records, Documents, Secret Correspondence (in English)
    Political and Secret Despatches to India, 1850–1912.
    Home Correspondence, 1850–1912.
    Home Miscellaneous Series.
    Secret Letters and Enclosures from India, 1850–1912.
    India Office Papers. Series of Files, 1902–1911.
    India's Foreign Proceedings, 1850–1912.
    Parliamentary Papers (East Indies). Annual Lists of General Index, 1801–1907.
    Political and External Files, 1850–1912.
    Political and Secret Files, 1850–1912.
  European Manuscripts (includes private and personal papers of British officials, with their numbers in India Office Library, London).
    Papers of Frederick Dufferin, Governor-General of India. (On Microfilm, Reel No. 490–535.)
    Papers of the First Earl of Northbrook, 1884–1888. Correspondence with Marquess of Dufferin. (C. 144.)
    Lytton Collection. Papers of Edward Robert Bulwer Lytton. Papers of Earl of Lytton, Governor-General of India, 1876–1880. (E. 218.)
    Papers of Sir C. Wood Halifax, Secretary of State for India, 1859–1866. (F. 78.)
    Lord Elgin Collection. Governor-General of India, 1862–1863. (F. 83.)
    Papers Related to India, 1832–1914. (Microfilm Reel No. 576.)
    Letters from Mahendra Pratap to Indian Princes. In German and Hindi languages. (E. 209.)
    Letter from German Chancellor to Indian Princes, 1914–1918. (E. 204.)
    Papers of John Morley, Secretary of State for India. (D. 555.)
    Papers of Lord Morley, 1905–1911. (D. 573.)
    Papers of Lord Lansdowne, Governor-General of India, 1888–1893. (D. 558.)
    Sir Charles Bell's Collection. (F. 80.)
  Hodgson Papers
    Some papers of Hodgson, Resident in Nepal. (D. 593.)

Hodgson's Manuscripts. (D. 497.)
Hodgson papers on Microfilm, Reel No. 249, Vol. 1, 16 and 17; Reel No. 250, Vol. 18, 50, 52 and 55: Reel No. 251, Vol. 59 and 74, 35, 36, 38, 39, 45, 106.
British Museum, London
  Ripon's Papers, 1880–1884. (Vol. LXXXVI. Additional Manuscripts 43574–43587.)
National Archives of India, New Delhi
  Government Records, Documents, Secret Correspondence (in English).
    Foreign Political Consultations, 1850–1935.
    Foreign Political Proceedings, 1850–1935.
    Foreign Secret Consultations, 1850–1935.
    Foreign Secret Proceedings, 1850–1935.
    Foreign Miscellaneous Proceedings, 1850–1935.
    Foreign Department Proceedings, Revenue Branch, 1850–1935.
    Foreign Department Proceedings, Revenue and Irrigation Branch, 1850–1935.
    Foreign Department Proceedings, General Branch, 1850–1935.
    Foreign Department Proceedings, External Branch, 1850–1935.
    Foreign Department Proceedings, Secret E Branch.
    Nepal Residency Records.
State Central Record Office, Patna, Bihar, India
  Government Records, Documents, Secret Correspondence (in English).
    English Records of the Patna Commissioner's Office.
    Letters to and from the Government of Bengal.
    District Records of Purnea, Letters Received and Issued.
    District Records of Bhagalpur.
    District Records of Champaran.
Nepal Foreign Office Papers, Kathmandu
  Nepal Government Records, Documents, Secret Correspondence (in English) from 1901–1947.
    Bastas (Bundles) No. 45, 54–A, 64, 63, 67, 55, 42–A, 68, 79, 75, 66, 77, 74, 57, 44, 48, 53, 65–B, 59, 73, 70, 72, 58, 60, 66–B, 43, 6, 71, 46, 50, 51, 42–B, 61, 56, 47, 52 and 65.
    Three Registers in the English language kept by Baber Shamsher (from 1914–18).

SECONDARY SOURCES

British Embassy, Kathmandu
  Father Giuseppe, Prefect of the Roman Mission, *An Account of the Kingdom of Nepal.*
  Register of Newspaper Clippings, two volumes, 1908.
Khuda Buxsh Khan Public Library, Bihar, Patna (in Urdu)
  Gul-I-Rahmat (Rose of Mercy). M. No. 155.
  Imadut-S-Aaddat (Truth of the Nobles). No. 154.
  Ghadar-Ke-Baghi-Ullama (Rebel Priests of the Mutiny). (10466.)
  Alvi, Amir Ahmed, B.A. *Bahadur Sahah Zaffar.* (8.31)

BIBLIOGRAPHY

Husain, Maulvi Syed Abid. *History of Jais* (Allahabad: 1878). Found in Maulvi Abdul Qadir's house in Banaras.

Madan Pursakar Pustakalaya (Library), Patan, Nepal (in Nepali)

Dixit, Kamal (Ed.). *Jan Bahadur ke Vilayat Yatra* (Jung Bahadur's visit to England).

Gyavali, Surva Vikram. *Prithvi Narayan Sah.* (Darjeeling: 1992. V.S.)

Nepali, Chittaranjan. *General Bhim Sen Thapa.* (Katmandu: 2013. V.S.)

BIBLIOGRAPHIES

'Bibliography of India, Nepal, Tibet, Sikkim and Bhutan', *The Journal of Asian Studies*, XVIII, No. 5 (September 1959).

Chattopadhyay, K. P. 'An Essay on the History of Newar Culture', *The Journal of the Asiatic Society of Bengal*, XIX, No. 10 (1923), pp. 465–560. (Includes a comprehensive bibliography on Nepal.)

Fisher, Margaret W. *A Selected Bibliography of Source Materials for Nepal.* Berkeley: University of California, 1956.

Kambara, Tatsu. *Nepal Bibliography.* Cambridge: W. Heffer & Sons Ltd., 1959.

Wood, Hugh B. *Nepal Bibliography.* Kathmandu, 1959.

UNPUBLISHED PH.D. THESES

Kumar, Satish. 'Political System of Nepal under the Ranas, 1845–1901.' New Delhi: Indian School of International Studies, 1961.

Majumdar, Kanchanmoy. 'Indo-Nepalese Relations, 1837–1877.' New Delhi: Indian School of International Studies, 1962.

BOOKS

Aitchison, C. U. *A Collection of Treaties, Engagements, and Sunnuds Relating to India and Neighbouring Countries.* Vols. I (1862), II (1863), V (1864), and XIV (1929). Calcutta: Printed by G. A. Savielle and P. M. Cranenburgh, Bengal Printing Co., Ltd.

Anderson, John. *English Intercourse with Siam in the Seventeenth Century.* London: Kegan Paul, Trench, Trübner and Co., Ltd., 1890.

Anonymous. *The Boundary Question Between China and Tibet.* A Valuable Record of the Tripartite Conference Between China, Britain and Tibet. Held in India, 1913–14. Published in Peking, China, 1940.

Auden, J. B., and Ghosh, A. M. N. 'Preliminary Account of the Earthquake of the 15th January, 1934, in Bihar and Nepal', *Records of the Geological Survey of India*, Vol. LXVIII, Pt. II, pp. 177–239. Calcutta: Government Press, 1934.

Description and statistical data. Illustrated.

Bahadur, Poorna. *Nepal Behind the Screen.* Kathmandu: Nepal Youth League, 1957.

Historical and political sketch of the pre-Rana, the Rana, and the modern period.

Bajpai, Girjai Shankar. 'Nepal and Indo-Nepalese Relations', *Indian*

Yearbook of International Affairs, pp. 3–8. Madras: University of Madras, 1954.
    Brief summary sketch.
Balfour, Patrick. 'Nepal', *Grand Tour; Diary of an Eastward Journey*, Pt. II, Chaps. II and III, pp. 143–71. London: John Long, 1934.
    Journal of the author's tour to Kathmandu in 1934, just prior to the earthquake. Illustrated. Map.
Ballantine, Henry. *On India's Frontier; or Nepal, The Gurkhas' Mysterious Land*. New York: J. Selwin Tait and Son, 1895. 192p. (Also, London: Redway, 1896. 192pp.)
    Journal of the author's tour (with his son) to Kathmandu in 1894 (?). Chapter 16 describes Maharajah Udip Singh's assassination. Illustrated. Map.
Banerjee, Nityanarayan. 'Nepal—The Hindu Kingdom', *The Himalayas, In and Across*, Chap. 6, pp. 146–61. Calcutta: New Bookstall, 1937.
    Superficial description. Illustrated.
Baral, Isvar, and Mazumdar, Debu. *Nepal: 1960–61. Trade and Information Directory*. New Delhi: Nepal Trading Corporation, 5–c/10 Rohtak Road.
Barron, William. *The Princes of India with a Chapter on Nepal*. London, 1934.
Bau, Joshua Mingchien. *The Foreign Relations of China; A History and Survey*. London: Fleming H. Revell Company, 1921.
Bayley, S. F. *Kathmandu, the Capital of Nepal*. Calcutta: Johnston and Hoffman, 1918.
    Descriptive.
Bell, Sir Charles. *Tibet Past and Present*. Oxford: Clarendon Press, 1924.
Bendall, Cecil. *A Journey of Literary and Archaeological Research in Nepal and Northern India during the Winter of 1884–85*. Cambridge: Cambridge University Press, 1886. 100pp.
    Report of a journey in 1885 and discovery of new inscriptions and manuscripts. Illustrated.
Catalogue of the Buddhist Sanskrit Manuscripts in the University Library, Cambridge, with Introductory Notices and Illustrations of the Palaeography and Chronology of Nepal and Bengal. Cambridge: Cambridge University Press, 1883. lvi, 225pp.
    Valuable notes derived from manuscripts, and a description of the manuscripts themselves.
Bowles, Chester. 'Nepal Awakens', *Ambassador's Report*, Pt. IV, pp. 261–95. New York: Harper, 1954.
Bowring, Sir John. *The Kingdom and People of Siam*. London: 1857. 2 vols.
Brown, Percy. *Picturesque Nepal*. London: Adam and Charles Black, 1912.
Bruce, C. G. 'Nepal and Sikkim', *Twenty Years in the Himalayas*, Chaps. I and II, pp. 1–37. London: Edward Arnold, 1910.
    Superficial treatment based on a trip to Kathmandu and Nawakote (1908). Illustrated.

BIBLIOGRAPHY

Camman, Schuyler. *Trade through the Himalayas; the Early British Attempts to Open Tibet*. Princeton, New Jersey: Princeton University Press, 1951. 186pp.
  Covers the period, 1774–1793. Chaps. V and VI discuss the Sino-Nepalese war. Annotated billiography. Footnote references.
Candler, Edmund. *The Sepoy*. London: John Murray, 1919.
  The Unveiling of Lhasa. London: Edward Arnold, 1905.
Cavenagh, Orfeur. *Rough Notes on the State of Nepal, Its Government, Army and Resources*. Calcutta, 1851.
  'The Nepalese Embassy', *Reminiscences of an Indian Official*, Chap. 4, pp. 106–81. London: W. H. Allen, 1884.
  Cavenagh's account of his journey with Jung Bahadur from India to England and back to Kathmandu.
Chaudhuri, K. C. *Anglo-Nepalese Relations; from the Earliest Times of the British Rule in India till the Gurkha War*. Calcutta, 1960.
Coomaraswamy, Ananda K. 'Nepal', *History of Indian and Indonesian Art*, pp. 144–6. London: Edward Goldston, 1927. Brief sketch. Illustrated; plates.
Coupland, R. *Britain and India, 1600–1941*. London: Longmans, Green and Co., Ltd.
Crosby, Sir Josiah. *Siam*. Oxford Pamphlets on Indian Affairs, No. 26, January 1945.
Curzon, Lord. *Frontiers*. Oxford, 1903.
Datta, Kali Kinkar. *Biography of Kuhwar Singh and Amar Singh*. Patna, 1957.
  History of the Freedom Movement in Bihar, Vol. I. Patna, 1957.
  History of the Bengal Subah, Vol. I. Calcutta, 1936.
Davis, Hassoldt. *Land of the Eye*. New York: Henry Holt, 1940. 415pp.
  A rather imaginative and often inaccurate description of Nepal based on the author's journey to Kathmandu in 1939. Illustrated.
  Nepal, Land of Mystery. London: Robert Hale, 1942. 345pp. (Also, London: Readers Union edition, 1943. 308pp.)
Digby, William. *1857, A Friend in Need; 1887, Friendship Forgotten. An Episode in Indian Foreign Office Administration*. London: Indian Political Agency, 1890. 148pp.
  Miscellany on Nepalese history; chiefly an appeal to the British public to condemn the Foreign Office for recognizing Bir Shamsher's 'usurpation of power' in Nepal in 1885.
East India Company. *Papers Respecting the Nepaul War*. London: J. L. Cox, 1824. 998pp.
Edwardes, Herbert B., and Merivale, Herman. 'Some Account of the Kingdom of Nepal...', *Life of Sir Henry Lawrence*, Chaps. XI–XIII, pp. 316–79. London: Smith, Elder and Co., 1873. (May have been issued also in 1872 in 2 vols.)
  Very interesting journal, including personal letters, accounts and other source data.
Egerton, Francis. *Journal of a Winter's Tour in India; with a Visit to the Court of Nepaul*. London: John Murray, 1852. 2 vols., 301pp., 290pp.

Several chapters in Vol. I, pp. 176–251, describe the author's journey to Jung Bahadur's Kathmandu in 1851. Other scattered references to Nepal. Illustrated.

Elwes, Henry John. 'Nepal, 1913–1914', *Memoirs of Travel, Sport and Natural History*, Chap. XIX, pp. 251–7. London: Ernest Benn, 1930
Superficial description of hunting in the Terai. Illustrated.

Fergusson, James. 'Nepal and Tibet', *History of Indian and Eastern Architecture*, Vol. I, Book II, Chap. II, pp. 273–86. New York: Dodd, Mead and Co., 1899. 2 vols. (First and revised editions, London: John Murray, 1891 and 1910.)
Architecture of Nepal ably discussed.

Fleet, J. F. 'The Chronology of the Early Rulers of Nepal', *Inscriptions of the Early Gupta Kings and Their Successors, of Corpus Inscriptionum Indicarum*, Vol. III, App. IV, pp. 177–91. Calcutta: Government Press, 1888.

Forbes-Linsay, C. H. 'Nepal', *India, Past and Present*, Vol. I, pp. 289–94. Philadelphia: Henry T. Coates and Co., 1903.
Brief summary.

Fraser, Captain Hastings. *Our Faithful Ally the Nizam*. London: Smith, Elder and Co., 1865.

Fraser, James Baillie. 'Historical Sketches of Nepal', *Journal of a Tour through Part of the Snowy Range of the Himalaya Mountains and to the Sources of the Rivers Jumna and Ganges*, Pt. I, pp. 1–48, 507–55. London: Rodwell and Martin, 1820.
Description of the War of 1814–16; several appendices supply interesting data on population, military forces, etc. Maps.

Gibbs, H. R. K. *The Gurkha Soldier*. Calcutta, 1943.

Gimlette, G. H. D. *Nepal and the Nepalese*. London: H. F. and G. Witherby, 1928. 261 pp.
British Resident Surgeon's historical and cultural sketch, and his personal experiences from 1883–87, including description of Bir Shamsher's rise to power. Illustrated.

Girilal, Jain. *India Meets China in Nepal*. New York: Asia Publishing House, 1959.

Gleig, G. R. *Memoirs of the Right Honorable Warren Hastings*. London, 1841. 3 vols.

Grant, James. *History of India*. London: Cassell and Co., Ltd., 1890. 2 vols.

Gupta, Anirudha. *Politics in Nepal*. Allahabad: Allied Publishers Private Ltd., 1964.

Hagen, Toni. *Nepal, the Kingdom in the Himalayas*. Berne: Kümmerly and Frey, Geographical Publishers, 1961.

Hall, D. G. E. *A History of South-East Asia*. London: Macmillan & Co., Ltd., 1960. New York: St Martin's Press, 1960.

Hall, William Edward. *A Treatise on the Foreign Powers and Jurisdiction of the British Crown*. London: Oxford University Press, 1894.

Hamilton, Francis (Buchanan). *An Account of the Kingdom of Nepal, and of the Territories Annexed to This Dominion by House of Gurkha*. Edinburgh: Archibald Constable and Co., 1819. 364 pp.

BIBLIOGRAPHY

One of the early histories, extending Nepal to include Bhutan on the east, Pakistan on the west. Illustrated. Maps.

Han, Suyin. *The Mountain Is Young*. London, 1958.

Hermanns, Fr. Matthias. 'The Mountain Tribes of Nepal', *The Indo-Tibetans; the Indo-Tibetan and Mongoloid Problem in the Southern Himalaya and North-Northeast India*, Chap. II, pp. 7–28. Bombay: K. L. Fernandes, 1954.

Tribal customs, folklore, and traditions. Illustrated. Map.

Hodgson, Brian Houghton. *Miscellaneous Essays Relation to Indian Subjects*. London: Trubner and Co., 1880. 2 vols., 407 pp., 348 pp.

Includes six essays on Nepal, reprints of magazine articles.

Hoffmeister, Werner. 'Cathmando', *Travels in Ceylon and Continental India; Including Nepal and Other Parts of the Himalayas, to the Borders of Thibet, with Some Notices of the Overland Route*, Sixth letter, pp. 206–43. Edinburgh: William P. Kennedy, 1848. (Also, a German edition.)

Holmes, Rice T. *History of the Indian Mutiny*. London: Macmillan and Co., Ltd., 1898.

Hooker, Joseph Dalton. *Himalayan Journals; Notes of a Naturalist in Bengal, the Sikkim and Nepal Himalayas, the Khasia Mountain*, etc. London: John Murray, 1854. 2 vols., 408 pp., 487 pp. (Another edition, London: John Murray, 1855. 2 vols., 348 pp., 345 pp. A third edition, Glasgow: The Grand Colosseum Warehouse Co., no date, 1 vol., 574 pp. Text in all editions is the same; illustrations vary.)

Journal of the author's wanderings in 1848–51, mostly in Eastern Nepal and borderlands. Illustrated. Maps.

Hudson, Manley O. *Cases and Other Materials on International Law*. Second Edition. St Paul, Minnesota, 1936.

Hunter, William Wilson. 'Nepal', *The Imperial Gazetteer of India*, Vol. VII, pp. 103–17. London: Trubner and Co., 1881. (Revised Edition—Anon.), Vol. XIX, pp. 25–55. Oxford: Clarendon Press, 1908.

Comprehensive sketch—geography, history, culture, agriculture, trade, etc. Revised edition differs, contains map.

Life of Brian Houghton Hodgson: British Resident at the Court of Nepal. London: John Murray, 1896. 390 pp.

Based on private letters; covers period, 1825–43, in Nepal. Illustrated. Bibliographies.

Hurlimann, Martin. 'Himalayas, Nepal and Tibet', *Asia*, Plates 199–223, pp. 252–54. London: Thames and Hudson, 1957.

Ilbert, Sir Courtenay. *The Government of India*. Third Edition. Oxford: Clarendon Press, 1915.

Inglis, J. (Maori). *Sport and Work on the Nepal Frontier*. London, 1878.

Jenkyns, Sir Henry. *British Rule and Jurisdiction Beyond the Seas*. London: Oxford University Press, 1902.

Karan, Pradyumna P., and Jenkins, William M. Jr. *The Himalayan Kingdoms: Bhutan, Sikkim and Nepal*. Princeton, New Jersey: D. Van Nostrand Co., Inc., 1963.

Nepal, A Cultural and Physical Geography. Lexington: University of Kentucky Press, 1960.

Karunakaran, K. P. *India in World Affairs, February, 1950–December, 1953,* pp. 189–200. London: Oxford University Press (for Indian Council on World Affairs), 1957.
    Relations with Nepal.

Kaye, J. W. *History of the War in Afghanistan.* London, 1851. 2 vols.

Kaye, J. W., and Malleson, G. B. *History of the Indian Mutiny, 1857–58.* London, 1889. 6 vols.

Keith, Arthur B. *Imperial Unity and the Dominions.* Oxford: Clarendon Press, 1916.

The Sovereignty of the British Dominions. London: Macmillan and Co., Ltd., 1929.

Kennion, R. L. 'Recollections of Nepal . . .', *Diversions of an Indian Political.* Chaps. XIII–XVIII, pp. 195–277. London: Blackwood, 1932.
    Tourist's description of hunting in the Terai, of Kathmandu, and of the Armory in Kathmandu.

Khanal, Yadunath. *Reflections on Nepal-India Relations.* Delhi: Rakesh Press, 1964.

Kirkpatrick, W. *An Account of the Kingdom of Nepal* (Being the substance of observations made during a mission to the Country in the year 1793). London, 1801.

Krishnamurti, Y. G. *His Majesty King Mahendra Bir Bikram Shaha Deva,* An Analytical Biography. Bombay: The Nityanand Society, no date.

Landon, Percival. *Nepal.* London: Constable and Co., 1928. 2 vols., 358 pp., 363 pp.
    Popular historical account, pro-Rana bias. Based on a trip to Nepal and earlier works. Illustrated. Maps. Bibliography.

Lhasa. London: Hurst and Blacket, Ltd., 1905. 2 vols.

Landor, Henry Savage. *Tibet and Nepal.* London: A. and C. Black, 1905.

Lee-Warner, Sir William. *The Native States of India.* London, no date.

Leuchtag, Erika. *Erika and the King.* New York, 1958.

Levi, Sylvain. *Le Nepal; Etude Historique D'un Royaume Hindon.* Paris: Ernest Leroux, 1905, 1908. Annales du Musee Guimet; Bibliotheque D'etudes, Tomes XVII, 395 pp.; XVIII, 411 pp.; and XIX, 223 pp. 22 plates.

Nepal. New Delhi, India: Indian School of International Studies Library. 2 vols. (Translated into English from French.)

Levi, Werner. *Modern China's Foreign Policy.* Minneapolis: University of Minnesota Press, 1953.

Li, Tieh-Tseng. *The Historical Status of Tibet.* New York, 1956.

Tibet, Today and Yesterday. New York, 1960.

Lovett, Major A. C. and MacMunn, Major G. G. *Armies of India.* London, 1911.

Macdonald, David. *Tibet.* Oxford Pamphlets on Indian Affairs, No. 30, July 1945.

BIBLIOGRAPHY

Macpherson, J. M. *British Enactments in Force in Native States*. Third edition, revised by O. V. Bosanquet. Calcutta: Government of India, 1914. 6 vols. (Further revisions up to 1929, by G. G. Hooper.)
Several volumes include treaties and other papers relating to Nepal.

Maitri, Phya Kalyan. *Siam: Treaties with Foreign Powers, 1920–1927*. Royal Siamese Government, H. H. Prince Traidos Prabandh, Minister for Foreign Affairs. 1928.

Majumdar, R. C. *The History and Culture of the Indian People*. Bombay: Bharatiya Vidya Bhavan, 1962. 10 vols.

Malcolm, John. *The Political History of India from 1784 to 1823*. London: John Murray, 1826. 2 vols., 593 pp., 324, cccii p.
The 'Nepaulese' war of 1814–16 is described in Vol. I, pp. 442–58; and the 'British Proclamation Previous to the Commencement Hostilities with the Rajah of Nepaul', is given in Vol. II, pp. ccxlix–cclxii. Other scattered references to Nepal. Good source material.

Marcu, Valeriu (trans. Richard Winston). *Accent on Power: The Life and Times of Machiavelli*. New York: Farrar and Rinehart, Inc., 1939.

Markham, Clements R. *Narrative of the Mission of George Bogle to Tibet and of the Journey of Thomas Manning to Tibet*. London: Trubner and Co., 1876. 354 pp. (Second edition, 1879, has 362, cxxxiv pp)
A long introduction contains numerous references to Nepal. Maps.

Mason, Kenneth. *Abode of Snow; A History of Himalayan Exploration and Mountaineering*. London: Rupert Hart-Davis, 1955. 372pp.
Comprehensive and reliable. Includes geography, early history and trade routes, survey studies, and history of expeditions. Illustrated. Maps. Excellent bibliography on mountaineering.

McAuliffe, Paton R. *The Nizam: The Origin and Future of the Hyderabad State*. London: C. J. Clay and Sons. Cambridge: Cambridge University Press, 1904.

McLeish, Alexander. 'Nepal', *The Frontier Peoples of India; A Missionary Survey*, Pt. III, Chap. I, pp. 119–29. London: World Dominion Press, 1931.
Brief superficial sketch. Maps.

Menon, V. P. *The Story of the Integration of the Indian States*. Princeton, New Jersey: Princeton University Press.
The Transfer of Power in India. Princeton, New Jersey: Princeton University Press, 1957.

Mills, Lennox A. 'British Malay, 1824–1867', *Journal of the Malayan Branch of the Royal Asiatic Society*, Vol. III, Part II. Singapore: November, 1925.
Southeast Asia. Minneapolis: University of Minnesota Press, 1964.

Morris, C. J. *The Gurkhas*. Delhi, 1933.

Mukherjee, L. *History of India* (Modern Period). Calcutta: Mondal Brothers & Co. Private Ltd., 54–58 College St., Calcutta 12, India, no date.

'Nepal', *The Historical Record of the Imperial Visit to India, 1911*, pp. 228–33. London: John Murray, 1914.
   Description of the King's hunt in the Terai.
'Nepal', *Encyclopedia Americana*, Vol. 20, pp. 76–77. New York: American Corporation, 1950.
'Nepal', *Encyclopedia Britannica*, Vol. 16, pp. 220–23. Chicago, 1959.
'Nepal and the Basins of the Karnoli, Gunduk and Cosi', *The Highlands of India; Being a Chronicle of Field Sports and Travel in India, with Numerous Full-Page and Text Illustrations, Diagrams, etc.*, Sect. VII, pp. 305–15. London: Harrison and Sons, 1887. (This book is called Vol. II, apparently an afterthought, since the preceding volume of five years earlier is not identified as Vol. I.)
   Travelogue description.
Newall, D. J. F. 'Nepal', *The Highlands of India; Strategically Considered with Special Reference to Their Colonizations as Reserve Circles, Military, Industrial, and Sanitary, with a Map, Diagrams, and Illustrations, etc.*, Sect. VII, pp. 92–101. London: Harrison and Sons, 1882.
   Sketchy description of Nepal, based on excursion into eastern part: also describes borderlands. Illustrated.
Nicholson, A. P. *Scraps of Paper*, India's Broken Treaties, Her Princes, and the Problems. London: Ernest Benn, Ltd., 1930.
Northey, W. Brook, and Morris, C. J. *The Gurkhas, Their Manners, Customs and Country*. London: John Lane, 1928. 282 pp.
   General history and sociological study. Illustrated. Map. Bibliography.
O'Connor, Frederic. *On the Frontier and Beyond, a Record of Thirty Years' Service*. London, 1931.
O'Dwyer, Sir Michael. *India As I Knew It, 1885–1925*. London: Constable and Co., 1925.
Oldfield, H. A. *Sketches from Nipal*. London: W. H. Allen and Co., 1880. 2 vols.
Panikkar, K. M. *Indian States*. Oxford Pamphlets on Indian Affairs, No. 4. London: Oxford University Press, 1942.
   Indian States and the Government of India. London: Martin Hopkinson, Ltd., London, 1932.
   Inter-Statal Law (The Law Affecting the Relations of the Indian States with the British Crown). Madras: University of Madras, no date.
Patterson, George N. *Tibet in Revolt*. London, 1960.
Petech, Luciano. *Mediaeval History of Nepal* (c. 750–1480). Rome: Instituto Italiano Per II Medio Estremo Oriente, 1958. 238 pp.
   Rather thorough research based on study of ancient manuscripts.
Phillimore, R. H. 'Beyond the Barriers' and 'Himalayan Mountains', *Historical Records of the Survey of India; 18th Century* (Vol. I), and . . .; 1800–1815 (Vol. II). Vol. I, Chap. V, pp. 67–77; Vol. II, Chap. VI, pp. 70–90. Dehra Dun: Office of the Geodetic Branch, 1945.

BIBLIOGRAPHY

Notes on early surveys with references to Rennell's work. Other scattered references. Maps.

Powell, E. A. *The Last Home of Mystery; Adventures in Nepal*. London, 1929.

Prinsep, Henry T. 'Nipal War', *History of the Political and Military Transactions in India During the Administration of the Marquess of Hastings, 1813–1823*. Vol. I, Chaps. II–V, pp. 54–213. London: Kingsbury, Parbury, and Allen, 1825. 2 vols. (First published, 1820.)
Excellent source material on the war of 1814–16. Illustrated. Maps.

Rajbanshi, Bhabani Shankar. *Anglo-Nepalese Relations Through the Ages*. Kathmandu: Nepal, no date.

Rana, Pudma Jung Bahadur (ed. A. C. Mukherji). *Life of Maharaja Sir Jung Bahadur of Nepal*. Allahabad, 1909.

Rao, Krishna K. *The Preah Vihear Case and the Sino-Indian Boundary Question*. New Delhi: The Indian Society of International Law, 1963

Ray, H. C. 'Dynastic History of Nepal', *The Dynastic History of Northern India (Early Mediaeval Period)*, Vol. I, pp. 185–234. Calcutta: University Press, 1931. 3 vols.
Good historical sketch, though based on secondary sources. Map. Bibliography.

Regmi, D. R. *Ancient Nepal*. Calcutta, 1960.

Modern Nepal. Calcutta, 1961.

A Century of Family Autocracy in Nepal. Benaras, 1950.

Whither Nepal. Kathmandu, 1952.

Regmi, Mahesh C. *Land Tenure and Taxation in Nepal*, Vol. I and II, Research Series No. 3. Berkeley: Institute of International Studies, University of California, 1963 and 1964.

Roberts, Lord Frederick Sleigh of Kandahar, Field-Marshal. *Forty-One Years in India*. London: Richard Bentley and Sons, 1897. 2 vols.

Rockhill, W. W. *Diplomatic Audiences at the Court of China*. London: Luzac and Co., 1905.

Ed. *Journey to Lhasa and Central Tibet*. London, 1904.

Land of the Lamas. London, 1891.

The Dalai Lama of Lhasa and Their Relations with the Manchu Emperors of China, 1664–1908. Leyden:

Rose, Leo E., and Fisher, Margaret W. *England, India, Nepal, Tibet, China, 1765–1958*. Berkeley: University of California Press, June, 1959.

Ross-of-Bladensburg, John. 'The Story of a Treaty: the Gurkhas War, 1814–1816', *The Marquess of Hastings*, Chap. IV, pp. 63–84. Rulers of India Series. Oxford: Clarendon Press, 1893.
Concise story of the war. Map.

Russell, William Howard. *My Diary in India in the Year, 1858–59*, Vol. II. London: Routledge, Warne, and Routledge, 1860.

Sanghvi, Ramesh. *India's Northern Frontier and China*. Bombay: Contemporary Publishers, 1962.

Sanwal, B. D. *Nepal and the East India Company*. Bombay: Asia Publishing House, 1965.

Shah, Ikbal Ali. *Nepal, the Home of Gods*. London, no date.
Shaha, Rishikesh. *Nepal and the World*. Kathmandu, 1956.
Smith, Thomas. *Narrative of a Five Years' Residence at Nepaul from 1841 to 1845*. London: Colburn, 1852. 2 vols., 294pp., 296 pp.
   General sociological study; covers geography and history, including seven chapters on the war of 1814–16; personal experiences, 1841–45.
Smith, Vincent A. *The Oxford History of India*. Second edition. London: Oxford University Press, 1923.
Smythe, F. S. *The Kangchenjunga Adventure*. London: Victor Gollancz, Ltd., Covent Garden, 1930.
Temple, Richard. *Journals Kept in Hyderabad, Kashmire, Sikkim and Nepal*. London: 1877. 2 vols.
Teng, Ssu-yu, and Fairbank, John K. *China's Response to the West*, A documentary survey, 1839–1923. Cambridge, Mass.: Harvard University Press, 1954.
Thackeray, Col. Sir Edward. *Reminiscences of the Indian Mutiny (1857–58) and Afghanistan (1879)*. London: Smith, Elder and Co., 1916.
Thomas, Lowell Jr. *The Silent War in Tibet*. Garden City, New York: Doubleday & Co., Inc. n.d.
Thompson, Edward. *The Making of the Indian Princes*. London: Oxford University Press, 1943.
Tilman, H. W. *Nepal Himalaya*. Cambridge, 1852.
Tucci, Giuseppe (trans. Lovett Edwards). *Nepal: The Discovery of the Malla*. London, 1960.
Tuker, Francis. 'The Gurkha Brigade' and 'India's Mongolian Frontier', *While Memory Serves*, App. VIII, pp. 624–46.
   Britain's last two years in India and her disposition of Gurkha troops. Other scattered references to Nepal. Illustrated. Maps.
  Gorkha, the Story of the Gurkhas of Nepal. London: Constable and Co., 1957. 319 pp.
   Good history of Nepal. Somewhat critical of contemporary politicians. Illustrated. Map. Bibliography.
Tupper, Charles Lewis. *Our Indian Protectorate*. London: Longmans, Green and Co., 1893.
Vansittart, Lt. Col. Eden. *Notes on Gurkhas; Being a Short Account of Their Country, History, Characteristics, Clans, etc.* Calcutta, 1890. *Gurkhas*. 1906.
Vella, Walter F. *Siam under Rama III, 1824–1851*. Locust Valley, New York: J. J. Augustin Incorporated, Publisher (for the Association for Asian Studies), 1957.
Weir, Tom. *East of Kathmandu*. London: Oliver and Boyd, 1955.
Wheeler, James Talboys. 'Kingdom of Nipal', *Summary of Affairs of the Government of India in the Foreign Department from 1864–69*, Chap. II, pp. 210–26. Calcutta: Office of Government Printing, 1868.
   Important political documents.
  'Nipal History: Ghorka Conquest (AD 1767–1814)', 'Nipal War: Lord Moira (Hastings) (AD 1814–1816)', and 'War Decade: Burma and

BIBLIOGRAPHY

Nipal (AD 1839–1849)', *A Short History of India, and the Frontier States of Afghanistan, Nipal, and Burma*, Chaps. XI, XII, and XXI, pp. 461–76; 571–86. London: Macmillan, 1899. (Also published in 2 vols. by Colliers, New York, 1899; and in 1894 under the title, *A Short History of the Frontier States of Afghanistan, Nipal, and Burma*.)
   Diary of Events in Nipal: 1841 to 1846. Calcutta, 1878.
Willoughby, W. W., and Fenwick, C. G. *Type of Restricted Sovereignty and of Colonial Autonomy*. Washington: Government Press, 1919.
Wilson, Horace Hayman. 'Nepal', *The History of British India from 1805 to 1835*, Vol. II, Bk. II, Chaps. I, II, pp. 1–60; 419–28. London: James Madded, 1858. 3 vols.
   Rather detailed history of this period, with emphasis on war of 1814–16, causes and results.
Wood, W. A. *A History of Siam*. London: T. Fisher Unwin, Ltd., 1926.
Woodyatt, Nigel. 'The Kingdom of Nepal' and 'The Little Man', *Under Ten Viceroys; the Reminiscences of a Gurkha*, Chaps. XII and XIII, pp. 158–88. London: Herbert Jenkins, 1923.
   Brief sketch, emphasis on Kitchener's visit to Nepal, 1906. Scattered references and borderlands described in other chapters.
Wright, Daniel, ed., Singh, Munshi Shew Shunker, and Gunanand. *History of Nepal with an Introductory Sketch of the Country and People of Nepal*. Cambridge: Cambridge University Press, 1877. 324 pp. (Reprint, Calcutta: Susil Gupta, 1958. 208 pp.)
   One of the most thorough and reliable histories. Illustrated. Bibliography.
Younghusband, Francis. *India and Tibet*. London: John Murray, 1910.
   Wonders of the Himalaya. London: John Murray, 1924.

PERIODICALS

Ahmad, Qeyamuddin. 'Early Anglo-Nepalese Relations with Particular Reference to the Principality of the Raja of Makwanpur', *Proceedings of the Indian Historical Records Commission*, 34, Part II: 17–26. (Delhi, 1928.)
Aikin, Arthur. 'Report of the Society of Arts on Specimens of Rice, Wool, etc. from Nepal and Assam', *Journal of the Asiatic Society of Bengal*, 5 (June 1936): 365–71.
Bahadur, Poorna. 'The Strategic Importance of Nepal', *Nepal Today*, 6 (April 28, 1953): 5–7.
Balfour, Edward. 'Nepal' and 'Newars' in *Cyclopedia of India* (2nd edition), 4: 80–85, 61–62.
   Contemporary cyclopedia summary.
Ballantine, Henry. 'The Land of the Gurkhas', *Harper's New Monthly Magazine*, 78 (1889): 467–82.
Brown, Percy. 'The Arts of Nepal', *Journal of the Bihar and Orissa Research Society*, 31 (1945): 8–27.

Bruce, C. G. 'Kingdom of Nepal', *Near East*, 35 (May 2, 1929): 553–54, 587–88.
Campbell, A. C. 'Journal of a Trip to Sikkim in December 1848', *Journal of the Asiatic Society of Bengal*, 18, Part I (1849).
Chakraverti, Bishnupada. 'Maulavi Qader's Nepal Embassy, 1795—a Forgotten Episode', *Calcutta Review*, 86 (January 1943): 43–49.
    Like Kirkpatrick's earlier mission, this one was for opening trade with Nepal.
Cheng uos-tsi (trans. Imbault Hurat). 'The contemporary Chinese history of the campaign', *Journal Asiatique*, 3 (1878): 348.
Choudhary, Radha Krishna. 'Review of Regmi's Ancient and Medieval Nepal', *Journal of the Bihar and Orissa Research Society*, 39 (September 1951): 360.
Choudhury, Roy P. C. 'Early Indo-Nepalese Relations', *Bengal Past and Present*, 74 (July–December 1955): 135–43.
Datta, Kali Kinkar. 'Some Unpublished Letters Relating to Anglo-Nepalese Relations in the Beginning of the 19th Century', *Journal of the Bihar and Orissa Research Society*, 25 (June, September–December 1939): 118–24, 138–52.
Diskalkar, D. B. 'Tibet–Nepalese War, 1788–1793', *Journal of the Bihar and Orissa Research Society*, 19 (December 1933): 355–98.
Fear, M. C. 'India's Himalayan Frontier; Conditions in Nepal', *Far Eastern Survey*, 22 (October 1953): 140.
Fisher, Margaret W., and Rose, Leo E. 'Ladakh and the Sino-Indian Border Crisis', *Asian Survey*, 2, No. 8 (October 1962).
Gupta, H. R. 'Sikh–Nepal Relations, 1839–40', *Proceedings of the Indian Historical Records Commission*, 30, Part II; 52–56. (Hydarabad, 1954).
Gupta, Jayanta Kumar Das. 'Nepal's Relations with the Outer World', *Calcutta Review*, 35 (June 1930): 370–88; 36 (July 1930): 90–101; 36 (August 1930): 233–38.
Hodgson, Brian Houghton. 'Origin and Classification of the Military Tribes of Nepal', *Journal of the Asiatic Society of Bengal*, 2 (May 1833): 217–24.
    'Some Account of the Systems of Law and Police as Recognized in the State of Nepal', *Journal of the Royal Asiatic Society of Great Britain and Ireland*, 1 (1834): 258–79.
    'Route from Kathmandu, the Capital of Nepal, to Darjeeling in Sikkim, Interspersed with Remarks on the People and Country', *Journal of the Asiatic Society of Bengal*, 17 (December 1848): 634–46.
    'On the Physical Geography of the Himalaya', *Journal of the Asiatic Society of Bengal*, 18 (August 1849): 761–88.
    'Route of the Two Nepalese Embassies to Pekin, with Remarks on the Water-shed and Plateau of Tibet', *Journal of the Asiatic Society of Bengal*, 25 (1856): 473–97.
Indraji, Bhagvanlal. 'Some Considerations on the History of Nepal', *Indian Antiquary*, 13 (December 1884): 411–28. (Also, Bombay: Education Society Press, 1885).

BIBLIOGRAPHY

Very good analysis of dynasties.

Jayaswal, K. P. 'An Unrecorded Muhammadan Invasion of Nepal', *Journal of the Bihar and Orissa Research Society*, 22 (June 1936): 81–95.

Account of the invasion by Sultan Shamsuddin (of Bengal) of Kathmandu in AD 1346–49

'Chronology and History of Nepal, 600–800 AD', *Journal of the Bihar and Orissa Research Society*, 22, Part II (September 1936): 161–264.

Kennian, R. L. 'England and Nepal', *Nineteenth Century*, 91 (January 1922): 45–56.

Khanal, Y. N. 'Nepal's Foreign Policy and the United Nations', *Journal of the United Nations Association of Nepal*, 1 (December 1957): 22–25.

Kumar, Satish. 'Nepal and China', *Indian Journal of Political Science*, 24, No. 1 (January–March 1963).

'Chinese Agression and Indo–Nepalese Relations, *United Asia*, 15, No. 11 (November 1963).

Lee, Daniel J. 'National China Re-establishes Relations with the Kingdom of Nepal', *China Weekly Review*, 55 (December 27, 1930): 148–49.

'Prime Minister of Nepal Decorated by China', *China Weekly Review*, 60 (April 9, 1932): 188.

'Chinese Mission to Nepal', *China Weekly Review*, 70 (November 17, 1934): 400. (II.)

Levi, Werner. 'Government and Politics in Nepal', *Far Eastern Survey*, 21 (December 17, 1952): 185–91; 22 (January 14, 1953): 5–10.

'Political Rivalries in Nepal', *Far Eastern Survey*, 23 (June 1954): 102–07.

'Politics in Nepal', *Eastern World*, 8 (November 1954): 10–12.

'Government and Politics in Nepal', *Far Eastern Survey*, 24 (January 14, 1955): 5–9.

'India's Himalayan Border', *Contemporary Review*, 188 (July 1955): 42–43.

'Politics in Nepal', *Far Eastern Survey*, 25 (March 1956): 39–46.

'Note on Books from Nepal', *Pacific Affairs*, 29 (June 1956): 187.

'Political Progress in Nepal', *World Today*, 12 (June 1956): 239–47.

'Nepal in World Politics', *Pacific Affairs*, 30 (September 1957): 236–48.

Meng, C. Y. W. 'China's Interest in the Complications Between Tibet and Nepal', *China Weekly Review*, 52 (April 26, 1930): 329–33.

Mitra, K. P. 'Anglo–Nepalese Treaty of Commerce, 1792', *Bengal: Past and Present*, 61 (July–December 1941): 15–19.

Brief analysis of the treaty.

'Anglo–Nepalese Relations in the Last Decade of the Eighteenth Century', *Proceedings of the Indian Historical Records Commission*, 18. (Delhi, 1942).

'Modernization of Nepal', *The Modern Review*, 66 (September 1939): 250–51.

Parker, E. H. 'China, Nepaul, Bhutan and Sikkim; Their Mutual Relations as Set Forth in Chinese Official Documents', *Journal of the Manchester Oriental Society*, 1 (1911–12): 129–52.

'Nepaul and China', *Asiatic Quarterly Review and Oriental and Colonial Record*, 8 (1899): 72.

Regmi, D. R. 'Sources for a History of Nepal (880–1680 AD)', *Journal of the Bihar and Orissa Research Society*, 28 (March 1942): 24–42.
   Inscriptions, geological surveys, manuscripts, foreign accounts, and coins.

'The First Anglo–Nepalese Trade Pact', *The New Review*, 16 (November 1942): 130–41.

'The Second Trade Mission to Tibet', *The New Review*, 16 (November 1942): 406–11.

'The First Gurkha-Tibet War and Kirkpatrick's Mission', *The New Review*, 24 (November 1946): 361–74.

Rose, Leo E. 'Sino–Indian Rivalry and the Himalayan Border States', *Orbis*, 5, No. 2. (Reprint No. 19. Institute of International Studies, University of California, Berkeley.)

Rundall, F. M. 'Raising of a New Gorkha Regiment in India', *Asiatic Quarterly Review*, 7 (January 1889): 46–73.

Sarkar, S. C. 'Some Notes on the Intercourse of Bengal with Northern Countries in the Second Half of the Eighteenth Century', *Proceedings of the Indian Historical Records Commission*, 13 (1932): 99–109.

Sen, Siva Narayana. 'Nepal and Her Ruler', *The Modern Review*, 68 (September 1940), 277–81. (II.)
   General description of Nepal.

Shah, Ikbal Ali. 'The Value of Anglo–Nepalese Friendship', *Great Britain and the East*, 54 (February 15, 1940) 54: 103.

'A Ruler of Nepal', *Great Britain and the East*, 56 (April 24, 1941): 308.
   Biographical sketch of Jung Bahadur.

Shepard, Gordon. 'Where India Meets Red China High in the Himalayas' *The Reporter*, 19 (September 4, 1958): 29–31.
   Communist threat from the North.

Smith, Vincent A. 'Nepal, Tirhut and Tibet', *Journal of the Bihar and Orissa Research Society*, 3 (December 1917): 555–56.

Thapa, S. P. 'Nepal and Its Ruler', *The Modern Review*, 56 (September 1934): 310–13. (II.)

White, John Claude. 'Nepal: A Little-Known Kingdom', *National Geographic Magazine*. 38 (October 1920): 245–83. (II.)

Wilkinson-Guillemaud, Hugh. 'Nepal and Her Relations to the British Government', *Asiatic Review*, 30 (April 1934): 266–75.

PUBLICITY DEPARTMENT, ROYAL GOVERNMENT OF NEPAL, KATHMANDU

Bahadur, Prakash, K.C. *Hostile Expeditions and International Law.* Department of Publicity, H.M.G., 1962.

Gyawali, S. P. *Friendship on Trial.* Department of Publicity, H.M.G., no date.

BIBLIOGRAPHY

Khanal, Yadu Nath. *On Nepal–India Relations*. Department of Publicity, H.M.G., 1963.
Mahendra, H.M. King. *On to a New Era* (Some Historic Addresses). Department of Publicity, H.M.G., no date.
Nepal–India Friendship (Speeches). Department of Publicity, H.M.G., 1962.
Nepal–China Boundary Protocol. Department of Publicity, H.M.G., 1963.
Policy and Main Objects (of His Majesty's Government). Department of Publicity, no date.
Tuladhar, Tirtha R. *Nepal–China: A Story of Friendship*. Department of Publicity and Broadcasting Ministry of National Guidance, H.M.G., no date.

NEWSPAPERS

British Newspapers
March, April and May 1908

Army and Navy Gazette
Birmingham Post
Black and White
Bolton Journal
British Mercury
British Weekly
Bystander
Christian World
Court Journal
Daily Chronicle
Daily Express
Daily Graphic
Daily Mail
Daily Mirror
Daily News
Daily Telegraph
Dover Times
East Anglican Times
Edinburgh Evening Dispatch
Evening News
Evening Standard
Glasgow Herald
Glasgow Record Mail
Globe
Hearth and Home
Illustrated London News
Ladies Pictorial
Leader Field
Leeds Mercury
London Times
Manchester Guardian

Manchester Weekly Times
Military Mail
Modern Society
Morning Leader
Morning Post
Newcastle Chronicle
Newcastle Journal
News of the World
Onlooker
Pall Mall Gazette
People
Planet
Reading Mercury
Reading Observer
Reading Standard
Referee
Reynolds News
St. Helen's News
Satler
Scotsman
Sheffield Independent
Sheffield Telegraph
Sketch
Sphere
Standard
Tit-Bits
Western Mail
Western Morning News
Westminster Gazette
Yorkshire Observer

Newspapers from Other Countries

U.S.A.
    Buffalo Times   *New York Herald*   *St Louis Post*
                            New York World

France
    Gazette De France

India
    The Friend of India (Serampore, later Calcutta), 1838–78.
    The Pioneer (Allahabad), December 26, 1923–August 8, 1924.

APPENDICES

  I. Commercial Treaty of 1792
  II. Treaty of 1801
  III. Jung's letter to Munnoo Khan
  IV. Engagement of 1839
  V. Ickrar Nameh, 1841
  VI. Assembly address, 1887
  VII. Russian General's letter
  VIII. Verbatim conversation between H.E. the P.M. of Nepal and the Viceroy in 1902
  IX. Chandra's visit to India, 1904
  X. P.M. of Nepal's talk with British leaders in London. All together seven interviews
  XI. Anglo–Russian Convention, 1907
  XII. German and Indian leaders, letters of intrigue during World War I
  XIII. Baber Shamsher's interview with the Viceroy, 1916
  XIV. Baber's talk with the Viceroy, March 27, 1916
  XV. Baber's talk with Secretary of State, 1917
  XVI. Treaty of 1815
  XVII. Treaty of 1923
  XVIII. Tibeto–Nepalese Treaty of 1792. Treaty of 1856.
  XIX. Letter from King of Nepal to Emperor of China
  XX. British–Chinese convention, 1906

APPENDIX I

TREATY of COMMERCE with NEPAUL, 1st March 1792

Treaty authenticated under the seal of Maha Rajah Run Behauder Shah Behauder Shumshere Jung; being according to the Treaty transmitted by Mr. Jonathan Duncan, the Resident at Benares, on the part of the Right Honourable Charles, Earl Cornwallis, KG, Governor-General in Council, and empowered by the said authority to conclude a Treaty of Commerce with the said Maha Raja, and to settle and fix the duties payable by the subjects of the respective States of the Honourable English Company and those of Nepaul, the said gentleman charging himself with whatever relates to the duties thus to be payable by the subjects of the Nepaul government to that of the Company; in like manner as hath the aforesaid Maha Rajah, with whatever regards the duties thus to be payable by the subjects of the Company's government to that of Nepaul; and the said Treaty having been delivered to me (the said Maha Rajah) by Mowlavy Abdool Kadir Khan, the aforesaid gentleman's vakeel, or agent; this counterpart thereof having been written by the Nepaul government hath been committed to the said Khan, as hereunder detailed:

Article 1

Inasmuch as an attention to the general welfare, and to the ease and satisfaction of the merchants and traders, tends equally to the reputation of the administrators of both the governments of the Company and of Nepaul; it is therefore agreed and stipulated, that 2½ per cent shall reciprocally be taken, as duty, on the imports from both countries; such duties to be levied on the amount of the invoices of the goods which the merchants shall have along with them; and to deter the said traders from exhibiting false invoices, the seal of the custom houses of both countries shall be impressed on the back of the said invoices, and a copy thereof being kept, the original shall be restored to the merchants; and in cases where the merchant shall not have along with him his original invoice, the custom house officers shall, in such instance, lay the duty of 2½ per cent on a valuation according to the market price.

Article 2

The opposite stations hereunder specified, within the Frontiers of each country, are fixed for the duties to be levied, at which place the traders are to pay the same; and after having once paid duties and receiving a rowannah thereon, no other or further duty shall be payable throughout each country or dominion respectively.

Article 3
Whoever among the officers on either side shall exceed in his demands for, or exaction of duty, the rate here specified, shall be exemplarily punished by the government to which he belongs, so as effectually to deter others from like offences.

Article 4
In the case of theft or robberies happening on the goods of the merchants, the Foujedar, or officer of the place, shall, advising his superiors or government thereof speedily, cause the zemindars and proprietors of the spot to make good the value, which is in all cases, without fail, to be so made good to the merchants.

Article 5
In cases where in either country any oppression or violence be committed on any merchant, the officers of the country wherein this may happen, shall, without delay, hear and inquire into the complaints of the persons thus aggrieved, and doing them justice, bring the offenders to punishment.

Article 6
When the merchants of either country, having paid the established duty, shall have transported their goods into the dominions of one or the other State, if such goods be sold within such State, it is well; but if such goods not meeting with sale, and that the said merchants be desirous to transport their said goods to any other country beyond the limits of either of the respective States included in the Treaty, the subjects and officers of these latter shall not take thereon any other or further duty than the fixed one levied at the first entry; and are not to exact double duties, but are to allow such goods to depart in all safety without opposition.

Article 7
This Treaty shall be of full force and validity in respect to the present and future rulers of both governments, and being considered on both sides as a Commercial Treaty and a basis of concord between the two States, is to be, at all times, observed and acted upon in times to come, for the public advantage and the increase of friendship.

On the 5th of Rejeb, 1206, of the Hegira, and 1199 of the Fussellee style, agreeing with the 1st of March 1792 of the Christian, and with the 22nd of Phagun, 1848, of the Sunbut Æra, two Treaties, to one tenor, were written for both the contracting parties, who have mutually engaged

APPENDIX I

that from the third Bysack 1849 of the Sunbut Æra, the officers of both States shall, in pursuance of the strictest orders of both governments, immediately carry into effect and observe the stipulations aforesaid, and not wait for any further or new direction.

(True copy and translation)
(Signed) J. Duncan
Resident
Revenue Department.
(A true copy)
(Signed) G. H. Barlow
Sub-Secretary

Aitchison, C. U. *A Collection of Treaties, Engagements, and Sunnuds, Relating to India and Neighbouring Countries.* Vol. II, pp. 195–198. Calcutta: Printed by G. A. Savielle and P. M. Cranenburgh, Bengal Printing Company Limited. 1863.

APPENDIX II

TREATY with the RAJAH OF NEPAUL, 1801

Whereas it is evident as the noonday sun to the enlightened understanding of exalted nobles and of powerful Chiefs and Rulers, that Almighty God has entrusted the protection and government of the universe to the authority of Princes, who make justice their principle, and that by the establishment of a friendly connection between them universal happiness and prosperity is secured, and that the more intimate the relation of amity and union the greater is the general tranquillity; in consideration of these circumstances, His Excellency the Most Noble the Governor-General, Marquis Wellesley, &c., &c., and the Maha Rajah have established a system of friendship between the respective Governments of the Company and the Rajah of Nepaul, and have agreed to the following Articles:

Article 1

It is necessary and incumbent upon the principals and officers of the two Governments constantly to exert themselves to improve the friendship subsisting between the two States, and to be zealously and sincerely desirous of the prosperity and success of the Government and subjects of both.

Article 2

The incendiary and turbulent representations of the disaffected, who are the disturbers of our mutual friendship, shall not be attended to without investigation and proof.

Article 3

The principals and officers of both Governments will cordially consider the friends and enemies of either State to be the friends and enemies of the other; and this consideration must ever remain permanent and in force, from generation to generation.

Article 4

If any one of the neighbouring powers of either State should commence any altercation or dispute, and design, without provocation, unjustly to possess himself of the territories of either country, and should entertain hostile intentions with the view of taking that country, the vakeels on the part of our respective Governments at either Court will fully report all particulars to the head of the State, who, according to the obligations of friendship subsisting between the two States, after having heard the said particulars, will give whatever answer and advice may be proper.

Article 5

Whenever any dispute of boundary and territory between the two countries may arise, such dispute shall be decided, through our respective vakeels or our officers, according to the principles of justice and right; and a landmark shall be placed upon the said boundary, and which shall constantly remain, that the officers both now and hereafter may consider it as a guide, and not make any encroachment.

Article 6

Such places as are upon the Frontiers of the dominions of the Nabob Vizier and of Nepaul, and respecting which any dispute may arise, such dispute shall be settled by the mediation of the vakeel on the part of the Company, in the presence of one from the Nepaul Government, and one from His Excellency the Vizier.

Article 7

So many elephants, on account of Muckanacinpoor, are annually sent to the Company by the Rajah of Nepaul, and therefore the Governor-General, with a view of promoting the satisfaction of the Rajah of Nepaul, and in consideration of the improved friendly connection, and of this new Treaty, relinquishes and foregoes the tribute above-mentioned, and directs that the officers of the Company, both now and hereafter, from generation to generation, shall never, during the continuance of the engagement contracted by this Treaty, (so long as the conditions of this Treaty shall be in force,) exact the elephants from the Rajah.

Article 8

If any of the dependants or inhabitants of either country should fly and take refuge in the other, and a requisition should be made for such persons on the part of the Nepaul Government by its constituted vakeel in attendance on the Governor-General, or on the part of the Company's Government by its representative residing at Nepaul, it is, in this case, mutually agreed that if such person should have fled after transgressing the laws of his Government, it is incumbent upon the principals of both Governments immediately to deliver him up to the vakeel at their respective courts, that he may be sent in perfect security to the Frontier of their respective territories.

Article 9

The Maha Rajah of Nepaul agrees, that a pergunnah, with all the lands attached to it, excepting privileged lands and those appropriated to religious purposes, and to jaghires, &c., which are specified separately in the account of collections, shall be given up to Samee Jeo for his expences, as a present. The conditions with respect to Samee Jeo are, that if he should remain at Benares, or at any other place within the Company's provinces, and should spontaneously farm his jaghire to the officers of Nepaul, in that event the amount of collections shall be punctually paid to him, agreeably to certain kists which may be hereafter settled; that he may appropriate the same to his necessary expences, and that he may continue in religious abstraction, according to his agreement, which he had engraved on brass, at the time of his abdication of the Roy, and of his resigning it in my favour. Again, in the event of his establishing residence in his jaghire, and of his realizing the collections through his own officers, it is proper that he should not keep such a one and other disaffected persons in his service, and besides one hundred men and maid servants, &c., he must not entertain any persons as soldiers, with a view to the collection of the revenue of the pergunnah; and to the protection of his person he may take two hundred soldiers of the forces of the Nepaul Government, the allowances of whom shall be paid by the Rajah of Nepaul. He must be cautious, also, of commencing altercation, either by speech or writing; neither must he give protection to the rebellious and fugitives of the Nepaul country, nor must he commit plunder and devastation upon the subjects of Nepaul. In the event of such delinquency being proved, to the satisfaction of the two Governments, the aid and protection of the Company shall be withdrawn from him; and in that event, also, it shall be at the option of the Rajah of Nepaul, whether or not he will confiscate his jaghire.

The Maha Rajah also agrees, on his part, that if Samee Jeo should take up his residence within the Company's provinces, and should farm out his land to the officers of Nepaul, and that the kists should not be paid according to agreement, or that he should fix his residence on his jaghire, and any of the inhabitants of Nepaul should give him or the ryots of his pergunnah any molestation, a requisition shall be made by the Governor-General of the Company, on this subject, to the Rajah. The Governor-General is security for the Rajah's performance of this condition, and the Maha Rajah will immediately acquit himself of the requisition of the Governor-General, agreeably to what is above written. If any profits should arise in the collection of the said pergunnah, in consequence of the activity of the officers, or any defalcation occurs from their inattention, in either case, the Rajah of Nepaul will be totally unconcerned.

Article 10

With the view of carrying into effect the different objects contained in this Treaty, and of promoting other verbal negociation, the Governor-General and the Rajah of Nepaul, under the impulse of their will and pleasure, depute a confidential person to each other, as vakeel, that, remaining in attendance upon their respective governments, they may effect the objects above specified, and promote whatever may tend to the daily improvement of the friendship subsisting between the two States.

APPENDIX II

Article 11

It is incumbent upon the principals and officers of the two States, that they should manifest the regard and respect to the vakeel of each other's government, which is due to their rank, and is prescribed by the laws of nations; and that they should endeavour, to the utmost of their power, to advance any object which they may propose, and to promote their ease, comfort, and satisfaction, by extending protection to them, which circumstances are calculated to improve the friendship subsisting between the two governments, and to illustrate the good name of both States throughout the universe.

Article 12

It is incumbent upon the vakeels of both States, that they should hold no intercourse whatever with any of the subjects or inhabitants of the country, excepting with the officers of government, without the permission of those officers: neither should they carry on any correspondence with any of them; and if they should receive any letter or writing from any such people, they should not answer it, without the knowledge of the head of the State, and acquainting him of the particulars, which will dispel all apprehension or doubt between us, and manifest the sincerity of our friendship.

Article 13

It is incumbent upon the principals and officers mutually to abide by the spirit of this Treaty, which is now drawn out according to their faith and religion, and deeming it in force from generation to generation and that they should not deviate from it: and any person who may transgress against it, will be punished by Almighty God, both in this world, and in a future state.

(A true translation)
(Signed)   C. Russell,
Assistant Persian Translator.

Ratified by the Governor-General and Council, 30th October 1801, and by the Nepaul Durbar on the 28th October 1802.

SEPARATE ARTICLE of a TREATY with the RAJAH of NEPAUL, concluded at Dinapore, October 26th, 1801.

The Engagement contracted by Maha Rajah, &c., &c., with His Excellency the Most Noble the Governor-General, &c., respecting the settlement of a provision for the maintenance of Purncahir Goonanund Swammee Jee, the illustrious father of the Maha Rajah, is to the following effect:

That an annual income, amounting to Patna Sicca Rupees eighty-two thousand, of which seventy-two thousand shall be paid in cash and ten thousand in elephants, half male and half female, to be valued at the rate of one hundred and twenty-five Rupees per cubit, shall be settled on the said Swammee Jee, commencing from the month of Aughun

1858, as an humble offering to assist in the maintenance of his household; and for the purpose of supplying the said income, that the Pergunnah of Beejapoor, with all the lands thereunto attached, (excepting rent-free lands, religious or charitable endowments, jaghires and such like as specified separately in the account of collections) be settled on the said Swammee Jee, under the following conditions: That, in the event of his residing at Benares or other place within the territories of the Honorable Company, and of his voluntarily committing the collections of the said jaghire to the servants of the Nepaul government, in such case seventy-two thousand Rupees in cash, and elephants to the value of ten thousand Rupees, shall be punctually remitted, year after year, by established kists, to the said Swammee Jee, without fail or delay, so that, appropriating the same to his necessary expences, he may devote himself to the worship of the Supreme Being in conformity to his own declaration, engraved on copper, at the time of his abdicating the Raje and of his bestowing it on the said Maha Rajah; and further, in the event of his establishing his residence upon his jaghire and of his realizing the collections through his own officers, it is requisite that he should not keep in his service fomenters of sedition and disturbance, that he shall retain no more than one hundred male and female attendants, and that he shall not retain about his person soldiers of any description. That for the purpose of collecting the revenues of the aforesaid pergunnahs and for his personal protection, he may have from the Rajah of Nepaul as far as two hundred men of the troops of that country, and the allowances of such men shall be defrayed by the Maha Rajah himself. He must not attempt, either by speech or writing, to excite commotion nor harbour about his person rebels and fugitives from the territories of Nepaul, neither must he commit any depredations upon the subjects of that country. And in the event of such delinquency being established to the satisfaction of both parties, that the aid and protection of the Honorable Company shall be withdrawn from the said Swammee Jee, in which case it shall be at the option of the Maha Rajah to confiscate his jaghire. It is also agreed by the Maha Rajah that, provided Swammee Jee should fix his residence within the Honorable Company's territories, and should commit the collections of his jaghire to the officers of the Nepaul government, in that case, should the kists not be paid according to the conditions above specified, or in the event of his residing upon his jaghire, provided any of the subjects of Nepaul give him or ryots of his pergunnah any molestation, in either case, the Governor-General and the Honorable Company have a right to demand reparation from the Rajah of Nepaul. The Governor-General is guarantee that the Rajah of Nepaul performs this condition, and the Maha Rajah, on the requisition of the Governor-General, will instantly fulfil his engagements as above specified. In any augmentation of the collections from the judicious management of the officers of Swammee Jee, or in any diminution from a contrary cause, the Maha Rajah is to be equally unconcerned: the Maha Rajah engaging that, on delivering over the Pergunnah of Beejapoor to the officers of

APPENDIX II

Swammee Jee, the amount of the annual revenue shall be Patna Sicca Rupees 72,000; that should it be less he will make good the deficiency, and in case of excess, that Swammee Jee be entitled thereto.

(A true translation)
(Signed)   W. D. Knox.

Ratified by the Governor-General and Council, on the 30th October 1801, and by the Nepaul Durbar, on the 28th October 1802.

Aitchison, C. U. *A Collection of Treaties, Engagements, and Sunnuds, Relating to India and Neighbouring Countries.* Vol. II, pp. 198–205, Calcutta: Printed by G. A. Savielle and P. M. Cranenburgh, Bengal Printing Company Limited. 1863.

APPENDIX III

Abstract Translation of a letter from Maharajah Jung Bahadoor to Munnoo Khan—the Nana Rao, and Raja Benee Madoo Buccus dated Koonwar Budi—(September 1859)

From the letter which I have received from you, I know all your circumstances.

When you first came into Nepal, I believed that you wanted an asylum in the Country; but your Troops soon commenced plundering our villages, beating and often killing the ryots, and violating their women. I have therefore now become convinced that such is not your object and that you have merely come here for purpose of plunder and of operation.

But, notwithstanding all your violence, I have hitherto, solely out of consideration for yourselves, put up with all this misconduct upon the part of your followers, but I can not bear it any longer and I require that they shall now lay down their arms at the Towleywa Cutcharrey and proceed quietly to their homes in the British Provinces.

The door of pardon is still open to all who have not committed murders.

If your Troops will not disperse and leave this Country the British forces will soon come up from the Southward and from Westward, and the Gorkhas shall advance from the Northward and from the Eastward and shall attack them, and they will so entirely destroy them that no traces of their existence, not even their names, shall remain.

The British and the Gorkha Government have been at peace and upon most friendly terms for the last 42 years, and we are bound by Treaty with each other to surrender all murderers. For which reason, were you to produce all your riches, we should not attend your requests or do anything that might be likely to lead to misunderstanding with so very powerful a Government. We will show your Troops no mercy whatever.

If your females and children do not desire to leave the Country, we will not force them to do so, but they shall remain in it subject to the conditions formerly made with them, that is they shall hold no communication with their relatives in the plains of India, nor with other persons, British subjects there nor with any one except by our permission.

I will receive no more Urzees (despatches), and will listen to no overtures of any kind either from you Ommeraos (rich people), or from your

APPENDIX III

Troops. So I now write distinctly to warn you not to expect me to do so.

You are now very few in number, you have but few weapons or guns—very little treasure—scarcely any munitions of War—and you have quitted your own Raj; do you suppose that you can fight against the British Government? The British are as powerful as the planet Saturn; you could not gain from them 4 inches of territory even were you to sacrifice the whole of your lives in trying to do so—you may depend upon the truth of this—I am writing it for your benefit—Their Country is the whole of Hindustan.

Even if you formerly thought that we should go to war with a powerful nation like the British and break our Treaties with them out of mere friendship for yourselves, do you think that we could do so now that you have committed every kind of outrage [sic] violence in the Country—have plundered our villages and deprived the wives of our subjects of their Caste?

I advise you to leave this Country and to throw yourselves upon the mercy of the British Government.

(True abstract Translation.)
Sd. H. A. Oldfield.
Honry. Asst. Resident.

Foreign Political Department, 30 September 1859. Nos. 204/6 & K.W. (N.A.I.)

APPENDIX IV

TRANSLATION of an ENGAGEMENT under the Red Seal, in the form of a letter, from MAHA RAJAH OF NIPAL to RESIDENT, dated 6th November 1839

According to your (Resident's) request and for the purpose of perpetuating the friendship of the two States as well as to promote the effectual discharge of current business, the following items are fixed:

1st. All secret intrigues whatever, by messengers or letters, shall totally cease.

2nd. The Nipal Government engages to have no further intercourse with the dependent allies of the Company beyond the Ganges, who are by Treaty precluded from such intercourse, except with the Resident's sanction and under his passports.

3rd. With the zemindars and baboos on this side of the Ganges, who are connected by marriage with the Royal family of Nipal, intercourse of letters and persons shall remain open to the Nipal Government as heretofore.

4th. It is agreed to as a rule for the guidance of both Sircars, that in judicial matters where civil causes arise there they shall be heard and decided; and the Nipal Government engages that for the future British subjects shall not be compelled to plead in the Courts of Nipal to civil actions, having exclusive reference to their dealings in the plains.

5th. The Nipal Government engages that British subjects shall hereafter be regarded as her own subjects in regard to access to the Courts of Law, and that the causes of the former shall be heard and decided without denial or delay, according to the usages of Nipal.

5th. The Nipal Government engages that an authentic statement of all the duties leviable in Nipal shall be delivered to the Resident, and that hereafter unauthorised imposts not entered in this list shall not be levied on British subjects.

(True translation)
(Signed) R. Christie,
Officiating Assistant to Resident.

Aitchison, C. U. *A Collection of Treaties, Engagements, and Sunnuds, Relating to India and Neighboring Countries*. Vol. II, pp. 212–213. Calcutta: Printed by G. A. Savielle and P. M. Cranenburgh, Bengal Printing Company Limited. 1863.

APPENDIX V

TRANSLATION of an ICKRAR NAMEH signed by the GOOROOS, CHOUNTRAS, CHIEFS, &c., &c., of Nipal, dated Saturday, Poos Soodi 9th, 1897, or 2nd January 1841

We the undersigned Gooroos, Chountras, Chiefs, &c., &c., of Nipal, fully agree to uphold the sentiments as written below, *viz.*:

That it is most desirable and proper that a firm and steady friendship should exist and be daily increased between the British and Nipal Governments; that to this end every means should be taken to increase the friendly relations with the Company, and the welfare of the Nipal Government; that the Resident should ever and always be treated in an honourable and friendly manner; that if, nevertheless, any unforeseen circumstance or unjust or senseless proceeding should at any time arise to shake the friendly understanding which ought to exist between the two Sirkars, or to cause uproar and mischief at Khatmandoo, we should be responsible for it.

Signed by 94 Chiefs.

Aitchison, C. U. *A Collection of Treaties, Engagements, and Sunnuds, Relating to India and Neighbouring Countries.* Vol. II, p. 220. Calcutta: Printed by G. A. Savielle and P. M. Cranenburgh, Bengal Printing Company Limited. 1863.

APPENDIX VI

Assembly of Nipal Pashupati Ganchar,[1] Samvat 1934 Margbadi 6th Monday (26th November 1877)

THE Thrice[2] fortunate Maharaja, my brother Jung Bahadoor Rana, GCB and GCSI, Thong Lin Punma Kokang Vang Syan, Prime Minister and Commander-in-Chief, through his achievements acquired the renown of being regarded as brave, wise, and powerful by the whole of Hindustan, Europe, Tibet, and Nipal. This is known to every one. In this age no Hindustani Rana has acquired such celebrity. To the acquisition of this fame by the Maharaja my brother, you his brothers, nephews, officers, Karindas, army, and people have contributed by your zeal and readiness in obediently discharging your duties with one mind. According to the rotation established by the Maharaja my brother, His Highness the Maharaja Dhiraj having granted a sacred Lal Mohar (the Maharaja Dhiraj's seal), I have now received the same dignity of Maharaja. At the death of such a Maharaja as my brother, the pain I felt is known to me only; but the call of duty cannot be put off. We the brothers, nephews, officers, Karindas, army, and people taught by the same Maharaja, my brother, remain unchanged. Of this I am confident.

To-day you all our Jangi, Nizamti (army and police) officers, sepoys, off roll-men,[3] noblemen, merchants of 32 firms, and people, &c., have been assembled on this spot by Maharaja Ran udip Sing Rana Bahadoor, K.C.S.I., in view to your hearing some words that will be of benefit to this State and to the people thereof. Listen and mark.

How extensive is the country of France, what administrative excellence did it enjoy, you must have heard of these things. Such a vast country through want of good sense, there being discord among the army and officers, and disregard of the sovereign's orders, was defeated by Germany. To what humiliation was it reduced; it lost lakhs of troops in men killed; it had to pay three or four hundred crores of rupees; forfeited territory;

---

[1] Here is a clumsy though close imitation of the Royal arms of England. The lion and unicorn are represented by two Lions. They support a shield surmounted by a standard and figures of the sun and moon. On the top is a jewelled head dress or tiara. Sd/- F.H.

[2] NOTE.—This expression 'Sritin' occurs throughout whenever the Minister is referred to. The sovereign is endowed with a preponderance of blessings and is therefore addressed as Sripanch. Sd/- F.H.

[3] NOTE.—This refers to the Dakria men, who were not enlisted at the 'Panjani' or yearly rotation of officers and who, consequently, are waiting for employment in the army. They are distinguished by white clothes and are very numerous. Sd/- F.H.

APPENDIX VI

the capital was plundered and demolished in order that mounds might be constructed round about it. Its King and Minister were led captive away. On the other hand, the German army, officers and subjects, having concord among them and every one respecting the orders of the King, and the Prime Minister, and doing his duty according to orders, Germany vanquished France, which was greater than itself and added to its own glory.

Behold: I give you another instance of very recent date. Hearken. At this moment a war is going on between Russia and Turkey. Russia is much greater than Turkey, yet the officers, troops, and people of Turkey being of one mind and obedient to the orders of the King and the Prime Minister, though engaged in a war with a greater Power than themselves, and having lost officers and sepoys to the number of more than a lakh, yet, I say, they are not discouraged: Nay, to the present hour has their land been saved. Is not this a marvel? Look once more on Hindustan, you behold disunion and want of order. It is only by the aid and kindness of the British Government that the Kingdoms of the Hindustani are continued.

In our country also from the time of Damoder Pande during the tenure of office of Yasoka Pande and the Thapas as Ministers, there was want of concord between the Maharaja Dhiraj, officers, troops, and people; disunion was rampant, every one neglected his duty through laziness and evasion, what was the result? Let the misery endured by officers and people reply. You are sagacious and intelligent. It was the favor of God only which preserved our country.

During the time Maharaja Jung Bahadoor was Minister, there was concord between the Maharaja Dhiraj, officers, troops, and people. They obeyed one order and did their duty with heart and soul. By such means he held the post of Minister 32 years, and having made war upon Tibet, which was compelled to pay an annual tribute to the Gorkha Government, the broken sword of Gorkha was once more erect. The friendship with British Government was strengthened. The country, the troops, and treasury was augmented. This you know full well.

If you act together, strength is your reward. A single thread may be torn by one wrench: many threads bound together into a rope will hold an elephant. A rock cannot be moved even by a crowd of people unless their forces are combined, but a few men pulling in union may move it. This is also known to all.

Recently the post of Prime Minister and the duty of persuading all and bringing them into the right path have devolved upon me, and I address this exhortation unto you so that in accordance with your destiny whatever post and jagir[1] each of you holds, let the duty of that post be done with heart and soul. That I may not have through anger

[1] NOTE.—In Nipal almost every employee, whether Civil or Military, is paid by an assignment of land which he cultivates ordinarily through the Newar peasantry, taking one-half the produce. Even the private soldiers are paid in this way, a fact which makes it impossible to estimate the Gorkhali revenues.

Sd/- F.H.

to do evil to those who perform the Raja's service faithfully, that I may have to increase the rank and jagir of those who do their duty manfully with heart and soul; that I may not have to dismiss or punish those who neglect their duty, or those who do what is not their duty. Such are the prayers which I offer up continually. That you officers, sepoys, noblemen, people, &c., will do your duty faithfully and in union, paying due respect to the salt of Government, and the obligations of the Minister, His Highness the Maharaja Dhiraj, and I have no doubt; Maharaja Dhiraj Surendra Bikram Shah Bahadoor having entrusted to me all the powers in this country, it is my duty to act honestly towards him and to protect this country.

In discharging these duties I must be Dharma Raj to those who do their duty according to law and the regulations with zeal, and Yama[1] Raj to those who evade and neglect their duty. You officers, troops and people are equal in my estimation. Let not anything evil through foolishness be done by you. This is my loving counsel to you. You are wise and intelligent. I have therefore briefly spoken. That every one may enjoy blessings is the desire of the Maharaja Dhiraj and of the Maharaja.[2] You will act accordingly. Thus you confer benefit on both the State and yourselves. If you do so and are true to your salt and your duties, be sure Heaven will protect you.

Foreign Department Secret Proceedings, December 1877, Nos. 93/94 (N.A.I.)

[1] NOTE.—Two names of the God of the dead—to those who are virtuous he is Dharmaraj and grants rewards; to those who are sinful, he is Yamaraj and awards punishment.

[2] i.e. himself, the Minister.

APPENDIX VII

On His Imperial Majesty the Czar of Russia and Asia's Service

To
  Bir Shamsher Bahodour Rana
  One of the Nephews of the late
    Sir Jung Bahadur Rana General.

Sir,
  As the eldest son of Sir Jung Bahadour Rana and General of Nepal Pudum Jung Buhadour Rana and General of Nepal has placed himself under the protection of his Imperial Majesty the Czar of Russia and Asia with the request to be restored to the power and influence in Nepal as the direct descendant and heir of the late Sir Jung Bahadour Rana, whose place you have wrongfully usurped murdering several of your relatives in order to strengthen your hands, I do hereby in the name of His Imperial Majesty the Czar call upon you to surrender to His Highness Pudma Jung Bahadour Rana who will deal with you on terms more favourable than you may expect. If His Imperial Majesty the Czar's forces occupy the country and restore General Padma Jung to power, and in future taking your surrender, as directed, a Russian Army will be sent against you from Bakahara via Thibet.
              I am General
              Yours truly
              General W. W. Sheppards, offg.
known in India as Dr W. W. Sheppard of the Russian Imperial Staff cummanding the Baskir Dinercan His Imperial Highness the Grand Duke Mehails.
              Army of Asia

Foreign Department External—B Proceedings, February 1901, Nos. 327-28. (N.A.I.)

APPENDIX VIII

Verbatim Conversation between His Excellency the Maharaja and His Excellency the Viceroy in 1902

Viceroy:– I am very glad that Your Excellency has been supplying us with the news which you receive from your Representative in Tibet. Has Your Excellency a good Representative there? Is he an intelligent man?

Maharaja:– Yes, he is far better than his predecessor. So far, he has given me satisfaction.

Viceroy:– We never believed that the reports from your Representative were based on any ground but now I am inclined to believe them from what I have heard from the British ambassador at Petersburgh.
(The Foreign Secretary here added:– Also from what Primachin said to our ambassador in Peking. We heard of this only three weeks ago.)

Maharaja:– Since the time I read in the paper about the Tibetan mission to the Tsar, I was very much concerned and have been trying my best to obtain authentic information on the subject. I also wrote officially to the authorities at Lhassa asking them to supply me with a correct account of the reported mission to Lhassa. They in reply denied having any intercourse with Russia but said that there might be some religious mission from countries bordering Russia. Any information which I have received and which was worth communicating to Your Excellency has been reported by me to the Resident. The report of the Representative goes on to say that there are at present at Lhassa some men, Russianized Mongolians if not Russians, who are kept in a secluded monastery. The Representative also reports that the Tibetans have also established a factory for the manufacture of warlike materials and that these suspected men have brought with them some suspicious-looking cases which it was later on reported by the spies to contain modern weapons and ammunition. The arming of Tibet, Your Excellency, is a great danger to Nepal. The Tibetans have great resources to arm themselves.

Viceroy:– The Russians are always saying to every man that the British will one day gobble you up and so you must take our protection. In this way the Russians often send a religious mission and may also receive a similar mission from Lhassa till ultimately it will come to be a political one. I have already reported my views about Tibet to the Home Government and I shall write to Your Excellency when I hear from them in

APPENDIX VIII

reply. If we are compelled to thrust a mission upon Tibet in return for one from Russia, will Your Highness back it?

Maharaja:– Your Excellency, our interest in Tibet is vast. The Tibetans will in the first opportunity try to wipe off the disgrace of their defeat in the last war and if they are well assured and equipped they may any moment discontinue the tribute of Rupees 10,000 to Nepal and put an end to all political and commercial relations with Nepal. If ultimately it is proved that they have been intriguing with Russia and receiving missions from Russia, it should be my duty to protect the interest of my Government.

First of all, I must try to protect our interest by diplomacy and if it fails we must take recourse to arms. In case we have to do anything jointly against Tibet I hope we shall be allowed to take a portion of the country for us to remunerate the present tribute paid by them to us and to compensate for the loss that we may suffer in our commerce. It is meant if we are to take the extreme measure but I hope they will not be so foolish as to rouse the Government of India and produce disastrous results upon them.

The *Viceroy* laughed softly and said:– Then Your Excellency means to back us if it is necessary.

Maharaja:– Yes, Your Excellency, to protect our own interest.

Viceroy:– How many men bring the tribute?

Maharaja:– Sixteen men.

Viceroy:– It is known to everyone in Nepal about the Russian intrigue in Tibet?

Maharaja:– No, Your Excellency. It is kept a profound secret and it is for this reason that I always send an autographed letter on these subjects or letters from the pen of my Private Secretary.

Viceroy:– Do you think the Tibetans superior or inferior to you?

Maharaja:– Till now we consider them our inferior and we can defy them and defeat them if we have to take arms against them. But if they are well armed and well equipped it may be a different thing. I am afraid if the report of the Representative about their importing and manufacturing of arms and warlike materials is correct, in the struggle which is sure to come sooner or later we will be badly cornered. We then hope to be helped by the British Government with arms and ammunition.

Viceroy:– I take Your Excellency for a trusted ally and friend of the British Government. I hope you will form a stable government and I am very pleased to receive information from you from time to time.

Maharaja:– Thank you, Your Excellency, I shall inform the Resident any further information that I may receive worth communicating to Your Excellency.

Viceroy:– Thank you. I have gladly accepted all your assurances of friendship. In your letter to me, Your Excellency makes mention of the prejudices of your countrymen. What are they?

Maharaja:– They are very rude and do not like innovation political or social, however wholesome it may be. For instance, I am at present thinking of running a rope tramway from Bhimphedi to Kathmandu. The people do not like the idea and are against it but I am determined to carry it through provided it is practicable and within our means.

Viceroy:– Do you mean to have the rope tramway at the place where I am told horses are carried in boxes?

(The Resident here explained the distance and the nature of the road and said that horses are not carried in boxes.)

Maharaja:– No. His Excellency is right to a certain extent; though we never carry horses in that way over the road yet we often carry valuable imported English cows in boxes.

Viceroy:– Then my information is correct and Your Excellency will be giving a boon to the people if you will have a tramway in such a rough road.

Maharaja:– It depends upon the cost.

Viceroy:– The prejudices of men are very strange. Even people in India laughed at the idea of my holding this Durbar and they said that it will never take place, but it is now really taking place and everyone is quiet now. Such is the case everywhere.

Basta 47. (N.F.O.K.)

APPENDIX IX

Official Visit of Chandra Shamsher to His Excellency the Viceroy in India, 1904, 23rd January

Viceroy:– My government is grateful to Your Excellency for your assistance to the Tibet mission and I am much obliged to you for what you have done to help me. The information Your Excellency has been supplying me is very useful. Your Representative at Lhassa appears to be a clear and sensible sort of man.

Maharaja:– Yes, Your Excellency. He has given me every satisfaction. I am glad that Your Excellency appreciated so much the information supplied to you. I shall continue to supply it through Colonel Ravenshaw in the same way as I have hitherto done.

Viceroy:– Do not your countrymen know anything about the Tibetan affairs? Perhaps it is no longer a secret with them.

Maharaja:– It was treated as a secret and confidential matter. But since the newspapers have begun to publish about what I had written to the Tibet Government, they have gradually come to know of it. The Tibetans are the most pigheaded race and if they will come to know that I have been giving you information regarding their doings, I am afraid they will take a very unpleasant step against my representative and I think it is to the interest of the British Government to allow this channel of information to remain unsuspected.

Viceroy:– (To the Foreign Secretary:– Be careful that the information given by the Maharaja does not go out.) But do not the Tibetans know that Nepal is friendly to the British? How do your people think of the matter? Are they in favour of the British?

Maharaja:– I think they are because it is to their interest to be friendly with the British in preference to Russia.

Viceroy:– I shall see that Nepali interest is protected. I am much obliged to you for the yaks but am sorry there has been such a heavy mortality among them. (Turning to the Foreign Secretary:– Some 1600, is it not?)

Maharaja:– I am much obliged to you for valuing my services. As we are mutually interested, I cannot do less. Besides, I am always on the lookout for opportunities to prove by my deeds that the assurances I had personally submitted to Your Excellency last year that I would give effect to the words spoken by my predecessors that all the military resources of my country are at the disposal of the Government of India.

I am burning for the day when we, the Gurkhas, shall flash our Khukri on the enemies of England. This idea has not occurred to me only since I took the reigns of the Government of my country but is an old one and Your Excellency will be pleased to find so in reference in Lord Roberts' *Forty-One Years in India.*

Viceroy:– (Smiling) Yes, he refers to you in his book. Has Your Excellency received a reply to your letter to the Tibetan Government?

Maharaja:– The Representative in his last letter reported that the new members of the Council are talking of drafting out a reply and laying it before the Dalai Lama for his sanction. I hope it will come now.

Viceroy:– I hope so.

Maharaja:– I am glad to bring to Your Excellency's notice that in connection with the yak business and other Tibetan matters I have received assistance and advice from your representative, Col. Ravenshaw.

Viceroy:– I am glad to hear it.

(The Viceroy then spoke highly of the Maharaja's education which he said would be very useful in the government of the country and then went on as follows.)

It has enabled you to have good relations with us. Formerly interpreters were required in talking which was not very convenient and no Viceroy and no Prime Minister might have conversed together so long.

Where is His Highness the Dhiraj? Is he quite well?

Maharaja:– Thanks, Your Excellency. He is quite well and arrived at Kathmandu about a week ago.

Viceroy:– Was Your Excellency in camp?

Maharaja:– I was at Birgunj some 13 miles away from the jungle and when I got news of Shikar, I used to go.

Viceroy:– Where is my friend Col. Gil Bahadur?

Maharaja:– He is not here but is in the hill station.

* * * *

Private Visit of His Highness the Maharaja to the Viceroy

Viceroy:– I hope she will improve. Parliament was opened yesterday and they have demanded an explanation from me for my action in this Tibetan mission affair. Have you any objection to my laying before the Parliament the letter of advice you wrote to the Tibetan Government and also its reply if received?

Maharaja:– It has already been published.

Viceroy:– Yes, it has, but it was not from India that the thing was given out. As soon as I saw its publication I wired home at once. But it appeared that someone in the India Office had sold it to the press. Your letter was however quite sensible and as nobody can find fault with us about it, I did not press the matter further.

APPENDIX IX

Maharaja:— I have no objection to its being laid before the Parliament but I must ask Your Excellency that those papers which I had sent confidentially containing news about Tibet sent by our Representative be not published, as the ignorant Tibetans when they will come to know of it may endanger the life and property of my Representative and the Nepalese subjects in Tibet and so place me in an awkward position.

Viceroy:— We don't mean to give publication to them and I shall see that your interests do not suffer in any way in Tibet. Those papers will not be published.

Maharaja:— Thanks for the expression. I leave it to Your Excellency's discretion for the publicity of such papers as you desire to lay before the House of Commons. I have received information from my brother, the Commander-in-Chief from Nepal, that a reply has been received from the Tibetan Government and he is having it translated in our vernacular from the Tibetan language in which it was sent. As soon as it comes to me I will have it translated into English and send the translation to you.

Viceroy:— Thanks. I may lay it before the Parliament, I hope.

Maharaja:— Yes.

Viceroy:— Have you anything to represent to me about Nepal?

Maharaja:— Nothing in particular, Your Excellency. I want the continuance of the favour and goodwill of Your Excellency and Your Excellency's Government whether Your Excellency be in India or England.

Viceroy:— Anything more?

Maharaja:— If Your Excellency has no objection, I want to import a couple of machine guns and 100 Lee Medford rifles for my bodyguard. I should be thankful if Your Excellency will allow me to have them.

Viceroy:— During my course of tour I visited Manipur once and then I was shown a place from where the Residency was bombarded and I enquired where the gun came from which bombarded it. I was told that the Maharaja of Manipur asked Lord Lansdowne to give him four guns for saluting purposes as he was devoted and loyal to the British Government. Lord Lansdowne acceded to the request and he had to give him an explanation afterwards. We may one day have occasion to send our Foreign Secretary to Kathmandu if we want the Nepal Durbar to demand an explanation and he may have to meet, in one of the passes, the very machine guns we may give you now. So I would consider this matter before taking any step.

Maharaja:— We are not like Manipur. Our devotion to the British Government is genuine. We cannot dare to follow a policy secretly or openly which can have an undesirable result and end in our annihilation as an independent and autonomous government.

Viceroy:— We have no intention to interfere with the present state of independence of your country unless compelled by Nepal owing to internal disturbances. We do not wish Nepal to intrigue against the India Government and want a peaceful and stable neighbor in Nepal. I shall have to consider about your wishes as I am not sure how your successor will turn out to be in his friendship toward us.

Maharaja:— Many thanks for your kind and valuable assurances. We shall always remain true to the British throne and I do not wish to have anything that may rouse the suspicion of the Government of India, and if Your Excellency has any objection I do not wish to have them. My object to ask for this is to be frank with the Resident for if I get these machine guns I will show to the Resident the one we have locally made and which we have kept a secret from him.

Viceroy:— I shall consider the matter and had already sanctioned the supply of M.H. cartridges you require for the practice of your troops.

Maharaja:— Thanks, Your Excellency.

Viceroy:— Nepal has never had a Prime Minister so enlightened as you, and India has never had a Viceroy like myself so much interested with the welfare of Nepal. I should very much like to visit the country once.

Maharaja:— I should have considered it a great honour paid to myself and my country but there are certain matters which stand in the way and I do not know how I am to express them to Your Excellency. If Your Excellency will give me permission to lay them before you, I shall do it.

Viceroy:— Yes, do so please.

Maharaja:— It is known to Your Excellency that this question was proposed by you to the late Sir Bir who had established himself valuable concessions from the Government of India as to enable him to import 8,000 rifles, lakhs of cartridges and guns. Besides he had received high considerations from the Government of India and in consequence had been very popular with the officers and men; yet he, I request to submit, was compelled to lay before Your Excellency reasons which stood in the way of meeting with Your Excellency's wishes. So I humbly crave Your Excellency's kind consideration in this matter when I am hardly beyond two-and-a-half years in power and the most bigotted and conservative class of officers are looking suspicious even to the letter daring to show my devotion to the British throne.

Viceroy:— I am told by Col. Ravenshaw that you are well established and very popular and no one will be able to supplant you.

Maharaja:— It is very good of Col. Ravenshaw to lay such a favourable report about me before Your Excellency. My representations are not diplomatic but a real one. I must say it will endanger my position.

Viceroy:— I do not wish to put you to any trouble and risk but I hope when I return from my holiday we will some day meet in Kathmandu.

Maharaja:— Your Excellency, I don't think it can be before many years. (The Viceroy laughed and did not speak further on the subject.)

APPENDIX IX

Viceroy:— What would be the attitude of the Tibetans to our mission? Shall we have to advance further than Gyantse on to Lhassa, or will the Tibetans come to terms with us before they compel us to move forward to Lhassa?

Maharaja:— Well, Your Excellency, I am not quite sure about the attitude of the Tibetans. But the last letter I sent you of our Representative will tell you that the monks are quite against it. They require a good lesson it looks. They are quite ignorant of the extent of the British power as they remain cooped up in their own country. When once they have been given a lesson, they are sure to come to their senses.

Viceroy:— We don't want anything more of them. What we want is the observance of our treaty with them and to see that they do not come under the influence of any foreign European power. You would not like them to be under Russia, nor would you like Russia to be on your northern boundary.

Maharaja:— Nepal's interest is the same as that of India.

Viceroy:— Nepal is still more interested than India in this because Russia will be her next door neighbour if Russia has Tibet herself.

Maharaja:— In this I assume, Your Excellency, that I am always ready to serve our common cause.

(After this, the Viceroy stood to say goodbye and as he shook hands with the Maharaja said, 'I hope to see you stronger and more useful to your country', to which the Maharaja expressed thanks and came out. The Resident being desired by the Maharaja to drive with him came into His Highness's carriage and was dropped at Messrs. Lawrence and Mays. In the carriage, the Maharaja thanked the Resident for making such a favourable report regarding himself before the Viceroy and added that he would not like to have any thing which the Government of India might see some objection to giving him. The Resident replied that the machine guns and the rifles would also come by and by. His Highness then said that he could not understand what Lord Kitchener meant by the Begari System and requested him to inquire and let His Highness know. The Resident replied that he also could not understand what it meant and promised to make inquiries.)

Basta 42. (N.F.O.K.)

APPENDIX X

The Visit of His Highness the Prime Minister, Sir Chandra Shamsher, to England in 1908 (Correspondence and Interviews)

Translation of the petition from His Highness the Maharaja-Dhiraj to His Most Gracious Majesty the King Emperor of India

Petition to His Most Excellent Majesty Edward the Seventh, by the Grace of God, of the United Kingdom of Great Britain and Ireland, and of the British Dominions beyond the seas, King, Defender of the Faith, Emperor of India.

May the dominion and sway of Your Imperial Majesty who as the sun in the Imperial firmament adorns the Imperial Throne of England and India ever grow and flourish!

After due and humble respects, I beg to state that the bright fame of Your Majesty's ever-growing glory, even-handed justice, and high-souled generosity, scattered far and wide like the rays of the sun, combined with the perfectly good relations that have subsisted between the British Government and Nepal for close upon a Century, the peace and prosperity which this country has enjoyed during that period through the benevolence and good will of the mighty British Government and the kind appreciation of our services from time to time by them, embolden me to approach Your Most Gracious Majesty—who is not only the fountainhead of honour and power but also the goal of all ambition—and thus to fulfill the most cherished of our desires. With this object in view and encouraged by the exalted benignity, august consideration and chivalrous magnanimity of Your Majesty, convinced of the continuance of the kindness and goodwill of the mighty British Government as indispensable for the well-being and security of this poor hill country, deeply conscious of the vast power and endless resources of the said Government, sincerely grateful for those favours which are the visible signs of Your Majesty's gracious kindness and condescension, and profoundly thankful to Your Majesty's Government in India for respecting and preserving intact the autonomy of this solitary and remote land of the Gurkhas who are ever ready to defend the fair name and the just and honorable cause of England with their heart's best blood, I beg most respectfully to send Major General Maharaja Sir Chandra Sham Sher Jung Rana Bahadur G.C.S.I. Thong-Lin-PimMa-Kokong Wang-Syan Prime Minister and Marshal of Nepal, to Your Majesty's gracious acceptance, to pay his humble respects on behalf of this Govern-

APPENDIX X

ment and to lay, when he is graciously favoured with an audience, the profound regard and loyal devotion of our sincere and grateful hearts at the foot of that Throne which exercising its sway over thousands and millions is at once the object of universal wonder and admiration. I feel happy to think that Nepal does not present herself as a total stranger to Your Majesty and she treasures with pride the memory of the high honor of Your Majesty's gracious visit some thirty years ago, as a precious and perfumed memento. With a sincere and loyal heart I beg to entertain the hope that Your Majesty will ever be graciously pleased to continue to allow Nepal a place of security under Your Majesty's most exalted benignity as hithertofore and also beg to pray for the continuous increase of Your Majesty's transcendent glory.

By God's grace Your Majesty's glory—the destroyer of enemies—is far-famed and based on a firm and secure footing. Should however any important occasion arise when Nepal's services could be of any use, Sir Chandra Sham Sher Jung eagerly looks forward to have the honor of serving the British Government as in the days of the mutiny of 1857, and fervently hopes to be allowed to place the whole available military resources of this country at the disposal of Your Majesty's Viceroy in India. He will feel highly honored to submit information about this country which Your Majesty may graciously desire to have.

May the sun of Your Majesty's prosperity and glory ever shine in the exalted firmament of Your Majesty's towering eminence.

Dated the 22nd chaitra Friday 1964—3rd April 1908.

N.B. This is translated from a petition in Nepalese and Persian.

To,
His Highness
  Maharaja-Dhiraj Prithvi Bir Bikram
  Shamsher Jang Bahadur Sah Bahadur
    Shamsher Jang,
  Maharaja-dhiraj of
    NEPAL

My Honoured and Valued Friend,

It gave me great pleasure to receive your Highness's Kharita, dated the 4th Bhadon, Samval 1964 (20th August 1907), announcing that Your Highness's Prime Minister, Major General His Excellency Maharaja Sir Chandra Shamsher Jang, Rana Bahadur, GCSI, is desirous of visiting England in the spring of this year in order to pay respects to His Most Gracious Majesty the King Emperor on his own behalf, and on behalf of Your Highness and the Nepal Durbar.

I have much pleasure in informing Your Highness that His Majesty the King Emperor has most graciously signified his willingness to grant the Minister a special audience both on his arrival in, and prior to his departure from England, and that the necessary instructions will be issued in order to facilitate his journey in every possible way.

I concur with Your Highness in thinking that the visit of His Excellency the Prime Minister to England will assist in cementing the cordial and longstanding friendship which exists between the British Government and Nepal.

I take this opportunity to assure Your Highness of my deep interest in all that concerns the welfare of Nepal and of my sincere appreciation of the loyalty and devotion of the Nepal Durbar.

I desire to express the high consideration which I entertain for Your Highness, and to subscribe myself,

Your Highness's sincere friend,
Sd./ Minto
Viceroy and Governor General of India.

Fort William;
The 1st February 1908

Notes of the conversation between His Highness the Maharaja and Lord Morley, The Secretary of State for India, at an interview which took place at the India Office on the 9th May 1908 at 12 noon.

Secretary:– Are you quite comfortable?

Maharaja:– Perfectly at home.

Your Lordship knows that we Gurkhas are true and loyal and devoted friends of the British Government. I assure you that we wish to prove by deed should occasion arise the sincerity of our devotion to the British Throne.

Secretary:– Oh, I have no doubt of that and we will not forget what the Gurkhas did during the dark days of the Mutiny.

Maharaja:– Your Lordship, I hope the kindness and good will which we were so fortunate to enjoy at the hands of your Government will be continued.

Secretary:– No doubt it will, whether it will be this Government, or another Government. I am so sorry that there is no good book on Nepal. I was reading the other day a book on Nepal by Ballentine. In it he spoke very badly of Nepal as well as our administration in India. Who was he?

Maharaja:– He was an American and the book was written some eighteen or twenty years ago.

Secretary:– Oh, I see, he was an American and the Americans are always against our administration in India.

(Lord Morley then spoke about the opinion which Mr. Bryan of America had given in the newspapers some time ago about what he supposed to be the British maladministration in India.)

How do you tax your people?

*   *   *   *

Secretary:– Last year a very important society, the Geographical Society, demanded a pass from me to explore Everest. I refused it. Is it not as you wish me to do?

APPENDIX X

Maharaja:– It was so good of Your Lordship. My object in keeping my country isolated is so that the Gurkhas may continue to respect the British as they have been doing so far. I think I am right when I say that their respect of the British official in their cantonment equals, if it is not greater than, their respect for their sovereign. But if we agree to let a party into our country others will gradually follow and all Englishmen, Your Lordship, cannot be expected to be gentlemen. If unfortunately there may be a quarrel between the British subjects and the Nepalese subjects and if there be frequent association between them in the hearth and home of the Gurkhas, it may breed contempt and they may not respect the British in the same manner as they do now, which would be a dangerous thing for the interest of Nepal.

Secretary:– I quite understand you. I quite understand you. I agree with you. Was not an exploration party sent to Everest?

Maharaja:– Yes, it was, under a native overseer. I have no mind to keep anything secret from the British Government in my country and, if the British Government want, I have no objection to allow native overseers to go through my country to get any information they wish and so it was sent at the instigation of Major Manners-Smith. It has been found out that it is in Nepal.

* * * *

Secretary:– I am so sorry to hear of the bomb outrage in India.

Maharaja:– So am I, Your Lordship. But I hope it will be repressed.

Secretary:– Oh, it will be so hard. We cannot take steps against the whole Indian population. Bombs are so easy a thing to manufacture. Look what strong measures the Russian Government are taking.
(He then spoke of Irish outrages of former days.)

Maharaja:– Yes, it is so. But it is only a beginning and if the ring leaders are sufficiently punished I hope it will be put to a stop.

Notes of conversation between His Highness the Maharaja and His Majesty the King Emperor of India which took place in the first interview at Buckingham Palace on 11th May 1908. (Official audience.)

King Emperor:– I am so pleased to see you.

Maharaja:– It is so kind of Your Majesty to say so. I was really delighted to have this high honor.

King Emperor:– I still remember the shooting I had with your uncle in your country.

Maharaja:– It is so kind of Your Majesty to still remember it. (After a pause . . .) On behalf of His Highness the Maharaja-dhiraj, my country, and myself, I beg to pay Your Most Gracious Majesty our most humble and profound respects.
(The King Emperor bowed.)

I am deeply thankful that the high honor and proud privilege of being in the august presence of the incarnate might and majesty of the

British Empire have been [vouchsafed][1] to me. One of my long cherished desires was to be able to express personally our hearty and loyal devotion to Your Majesty's august person and throne, and I am happy that it has been so happily fulfilled today. I regard it as the happiest moment in my life.

King Emperor:– Thank you. (Turning to Lord Morley) Is it not so, Morley, that the Maharaja speaks English very well? (Turning again towards the Maharaja) Will you introduce your suit?

Maharaja:– Your Majesty, before doing so I solemnly assure Your Majesty that this my sword and all that it commands are ever at your Majesty's services when required.

King Emperor:– Thank you. (To Major Smith) Who are you?

Resident:– I am the Resident in Nepal, Your Majesty.

King Emperor:– Oh. I see you have received a Victoria Cross. Where did you earn it?

Resident:– At Hunza and Nagar.

Notes of conversation between His Highness the Maharaja and Lord Morley, Secretary of State for India, which took place at Mortimer House on the 11th of May 1908 at 4 p.m. on the occasion of a private return call which Lord Morley made on His Highness.

Secretary:– Are you close to the Afridis?

Maharaja:– No, far away from them.

Secretary:– Where are you?

Maharaja:– Our frontier is within twenty-four hours' journey by rail from Calcutta and we are close to Tibet.

Secretary:– When we meet again some day, we will discuss the question of our trade with Tibet. Do you think it will increase?

Maharaja:– It may.

Secretary:– Is your trade with Tibet increasing?

Maharaja:– No. Since the opening of the Darjeeling route, it has been decreasing enormously.

Secretary:– Why?

Maharaja:– Formerly almost the whole of the southern trade of Tibet used to pass through Nepal and now, since the opening of the Darjeeling route, it being nearer than the Nepal route, the bulk of the trade which formerly belonged exclusively to Nepal has passed on to that side.

Secretary:– I had a great quarrel with the Government of India about receiving the last installment of the Tibetan indemnity. They proposed that the last installment should be taken from Tibet and not from China. I told them that, for goodness sake, they should accept the money, let it come from anywhere. At last, to keep up our face, we took the

---

[1] Illegible in the original.

APPENDIX X

money through the Tibetan official. What is the relation of Tibet with China?

Maharaja:— The influence of China over Tibet was on the wane, at the time when Colonel Younghusband's mission went there. Since then, the Chinese are I think trying to exert and have been exercising great influence over Tibet.

Secretary:— How far is Nepal from China? What is the difference between the Buddhist and yourself?

Maharaja:— The Japanese, Chinese, and Tibetans are Buddhists, that is, followers of Buddha, while we are the followers of God Shiva and Vishnu. I am reading your book of the *Life of Mr. Gladstone*.

Secretary:— Oh, I am so glad. Gladstone was a true Christian and a grand man, and commanded a great personality. He attributed the cause of the Indian Mutiny to our not having made as many Christians in India as possible and was in this respect I think somewhat narrow-minded.

* * * *

Notes of conversation between His Highness the Maharaja and Lord Ampthill on May 16, 1908.

Ampthill:— I was very glad that the relation between the two governments was so cordial while I was in India acting as Viceroy.

Maharaja:— I am very glad that Your Lordship thought so.

Ampthill:— Your time of action in the Tibetan affairs was a good one.

Maharaja:— Thanks for your remarks.

Lord Ampthill then remarked that he had heard that Nepal is a beautiful country and that he would like much to see it, to which the Maharaja replied that he could have come while Governor of Madras in which case His Highness would have been pleased to welcome him; but it would not have been possible for His Highness to entertain the plea of bringing him to Nepal while he was a Viceroy. His Highness said that he should think twice before he would give consent to such a proposal, since his people were not so far advanced as to be able to understand the compliment paid to them by the visit.

After returning from Lord Ampthill's place in the carriage, His Highness spoke about the above to Major Manners-Smith and asked him what he thought of His Highness's remarks. The Major said it was a good remark and His Highness explained to him again that it would not be practicable to have a Viceroy in his country as the step would be frought with many risks.

* * * *

Notes of conversation between His Highness the Maharaja and His Excellency the Prime Minister, Mr Asquith, which took place at the latter's residence at Downing Street.

After inquiring about the Maharaja's health, Mr Asquith told Major Manners-Smith that he would like to have a talk with the Maharaja and Major Manners-Smith left the room.

Asquith:– Are you comfortable in your house here?

Maharaja:– I am, thank you very much.

Asquith:– I am glad to hear that the relations between the two governments are so satisfactory nowadays.

Maharaja:– I am so glad to hear such remarks from Your Excellency.

Asquith:– Was not Lord Kitchener in Nepal last year? He was very pleased with what he saw.

Maharaja:– I am glad that I was able to arrange that visit.

Asquith:– Do the Gurkhas who come to India settle there?

Maharaja:– No, they return after their retirement on pension or after resignation. Very few have settled down in India.

Asquith:– We have heard so much of the Gurkhas and we hear that they are very good mountain climbers.

Maharaja:– It is very gratifying to hear such remarks from the head of the British Government.

Asquith:– Has not my Government lately supplied some rifles to your government?

Maharaja:– Yes, Your Excellency, and we are very grateful for it. It will enable us whenever required to place at the disposal of your government an army which may be able to use these rifles properly. So far we have not been in a position to give them sufficient training in musketry. We have no modern weapons. We could neither import nor manufacture modern weapons but thanks to you the rifles given us by your government will help us a great deal to train our army properly. I assure Your Excellency that the Nepalese army will always be at the service of the Government of India.

Asquith:– Oh, we know that.

Maharaja:– We have kept this army simply for that purpose and to defend ourselves and our country from northern neighbours.

Asquith:– I hope you will see me again.

Maharaja:– I shall make it a point to see Your Excellency before my departure.

Asquith:– What do you think of the unrest in India?

Maharaja:– So far it has affected only a section of the people. It has not spread till now and if the authorities deal with it firmly it will be suppressed.

* * * *

Notes of the conversation between His Highness the Maharaja and

APPENDIX X

Lee-Warner, which took place at Mortimer House on the 19th of May, 1908.

(After inquiries about health, et. . . .)

Lee-Warner:– I have heard so much about the Gurkhas.

Maharaja:– I am very glad to hear such remarks. I have read a book which you have written about the native states in India.

Lee-Warner:– I am glad to hear of it.

Maharaja:– Nepal is always a true friend of the British.

Lee-Warner:– Yes, it is so.

Maharaja:– And I can assure you that she will ever remain faithful to her ally. The only thing we want is that our autonomy may be preserved and not interfered with. And then you will find we are always yours.

Lee-Warner:– Yes, we know it. We do not want to meddle with Nepal. What we want is only a good stable government there so that there may be no anxiety from that quarter.

Maharaja:– I think I may have the pleasure of writing to you when I find it necessary.

Lee-Warner:– Certainly. I shall be very glad to hear from you and to be of any help to you.

Basta No. 45. (N.F.O.K.)

APPENDIX XI

Convention between Great Britain and Russia, 1907

Signed at St Petersburg on the 18th (31st) August 1907.

His Majesty the King of the United Kingdom of Great Britain and Ireland and of the British Dominions beyond the Seas, Emperor of India, and His Majesty the Emperor of All the Russias, animated by the sincere desire to settle by mutual agreement different questions concerning the interests of their States on the Continent of Asia, have determined to conclude Agreements destined to prevent all cause of misunderstanding between Great Britain and Russia in regard to the questions referred to, and have nominated for this purpose their respective Plenipotentiaries, to wit:

His Majesty the King of the United Kingdom of Great Britain and Ireland and of the British Dominions beyond the Seas, Emperor of India, the Right Honourable Sir Arthur Nicolson, His Majesty's Ambassador Extraordinary and Plenipotentiary to His Majesty the Emperor of All the Russias;

His Majesty the Emperor of All the Russias, the Master of his Court Alexander Iswolsky, Minister for Foreign Affairs;

Who, having communicated to each other their full powers, found in good and due form, have agreed on the following:

* * * *

Arrangement concerning Thibet

The Governments of Great Britain and Russia recognizing the suzerain rights of China in Thibet, and considering the fact that Great Britain, by reason of her geographical position, has a special interest in the maintenance of the *status quo* in the external relations of Thibet, have made the following arrangement:

Article I

The two High Contracting Parties engage to respect the territorial integrity of Thibet and to abstain from all interference in the internal administration.

Article II

In conformity with the admitted principle of the suzerainty of China over Thibet, Great Britain and Russia engage not to enter into negotiations with Thibet except through the intermediary of the Chinese

Government. This engagement does not exclude the direct relations between British Commercial Agents and the Thibetan authorities provided for in Article V of the Convention between Great Britain and Thibet of the 7th September 1904, and confirmed by the Convention between Great Britain and China of the 27th April 1906; nor does it modify the engagements entered into by Great Britain and China in Article I of the said Convention of 1906.

It is clearly understood that Buddhists, subjects of Great Britain or of Russia, may enter into direct relations on strictly religious matters with the Dalai Lama and the other representatives of Buddhism in Thibet; the Governments of Great Britain and Russia engage, as far as they are concerned, not to allow those relations infringe the stipulations of the present arrangement.

Article III

The British and Russian Governments respectively engage not to send Representatives to Lhassa.

Article IV

The two High Contracting Parties engage neither to seek nor to obtain, whether for themselves or their subjects, any Concessions for railways, roads, telegraphs, and mines, or other rights in Thibet.

Article V

The two Governments agree that no part of the revenues of Thibet, whether in kind or in cash, shall be pledged or assigned to Great Britain or Russia or to any of their subjects.

Annex to the arrangement between Great Britain and Russia concerning Thibet.

Great Britain reaffirms the declaration, signed by His Excellency the Viceroy and Governor-General of India and appended to the ratification of the Convention of the 7th September 1904, to the effect that the occupation of the Chumbi Valley by British forces shall cease after the payment of three annual instalments of the indemnity of 25,00,000 [*sic*] rupees, provided that the trade marts mentioned in Article II of that Convention have been effectively opened for three years, and that in the meantime the Thibetan authorities have faithfully complied in all respects with the terms of the said Convention of 1904. It is clearly understood that if the occupation of the Chumbi Valley by the British forces has, for any reason, not been terminated at the time anticipated in the above Declaration, the British and Russian Governments will enter upon a friendly exchange of views on this subject.

The present Convention shall be ratified, and the ratifications exchanged at St Petersburgh as soon as possible.

In witness whereof the respective Plenipotentiaries have signed the present Convention and affixed thereto their seals.

Done in duplicate at St Petersburgh, the 18th (31st) August 1907.

Bell, Sir Charles. *Tibet: Past and Present.* Pp. 289–91. Oxford: Clarendon Press. 1924.

APPENDIX XII

German and Indian Leaders' Letters of Intrigue during World War I

Translation

Shriman Maharaja dhiraj Paithvi Bir Bikram Jang Bahadur Shah Sahab Bahadur Shamsher Jung, Maharaja Nepal.

    On behalf of the Imperial Government of Germany I tender to Shriman my respectful Compliments and express that friendly feeling which the Imperial Government of Germany entertained towards your renowned ancient Rajput House and the gallant people of Nepal. In all India Nepal is the only Kingdom which has been able to preserve its independence. If before this the German Government had not established mutual relations with you it is only because the British has ever been making strenuous endeavours that the Kingdom of Nepal might not have any relation with any other countries except England and that the honor and prestige of the Kingdom of Nepal might be lowered before this world.

    The war which England, France, and Russia have begun without any regard for the justice and injustice of the Cause, has caused great loss to all these three enemies and by the grace of God your friend on the side of justice Germany, Austro, Hungary and Turkey have gained unparalleled success and owing to this war Germany has got an opportunity to express her sympathy with Nepal.

    Naturally England growth as power in India will adversely affect your sovereign power. It is clear from the history of India, Egypt and Persia that the British ever wish to weaken the independent states and bring them under subjugation. The experience of the Indian Rajas has made it evident that not the least faith should be placed on the promises of the British. You will have been very sorry to hear that the sturdy warrior sons of hilly Nepal are shedding blood on the side of England, though the British cause is one full of unrighteousness and siding with which is against the interest of Nepal and injurious to the future of India. It will therefore surely give you pleasure to know that those Gurkha warriors who have been captured alive while fighting in enemy country are treated by us with friendly hospitality. We hope that those brave men whom we have permitted to return to their own Country may personally report to you in how friendly a manner we have been treating them. I have come to know that the entire population are trying to set up a big free state by destroying the abominable British rule. In this

APPENDIX XII

war of independence the Rajas and people of India look upon you as their leader and it is only through your help that their wishes will be fulfilled.

The illustrious Amir Sahab of Afghanistan, from whose capital town this letter will be sent to your august presence, has drawn his sword on the side of Germany, Austria, Hungary and Turkey to destroy the enemies of India. In your efforts to raise India to her proper high place in the committee of nations, the Imperial Government of Germany and our allies will give their full and hearty support. Germany, Austro, Hungary and Turkey on account of their strong military and financial strength is powerful enough to win this war in the end and to secure victory to their helping allies. This war must never be ended till England is rendered incapable of maintaining her selfish policy through looting conquered nations. The contrary truth against the false reports which our enemies have been disseminating from a long time past about us, is that Germany never tried to establish her sway in Asia. Any efforts that are made towards securing independence of the civilised nations of Asia are always pleasing to Germany. This policy is in keeping with our history, our customs or usages, our foreign relations and our Country's political creed. Germany has ever followed and shall follow these principles scrupulously. Germany and our allies never think of interfering in the internal affairs of independent India in any way. Germany, Austro, Hungary and Turkey will acknowledge as their equal the future Empire of India and will have political and commercial relations with it.

Your and our interests being identical we consider you as our cofighter against the Imperial Power of England and try to give you our thanks.

> Signature of the Imperial Chancellor appears under the letter in German language. This is only a translation.

c/o H.R.H. the Prince Prime Minister
        Prince Nasrullah Khan
              Cabul
           Afghanistan
           15th June 1917 AD

Your Majesty,

I respectfully beg to present to Your Majesty this Imperial letter of H.E. the chancellor of the mighty German Empire.

The address is noteworthy! The Imperial chancellor addresses our premier maharaja by the wellknown title of 'His Majesty' which is only used for the Independent reigning Kings.

I respectfully and heartily congratulate our Premier Sovereign and the main pillar of Hindu faith on receiving this recognition and I sincerely wish that the Kingdom of Nepal may for ever be on this high distinction.

May I also bring to Your Majesty's notice that this Your Majesty's well wisher had to try very hard to get this recognition for our maharaja by the victorious group of Empire.

I however do not ask for myself any reward for my services. My only request is that Your Majesty may so act for the future that India and ancient Hindu Dharma may receive the highest benefit from the present churning of the world.

Your Majesty's well wisher
sd/- M. Pratap
(Brij bari)
Kumar Sahib of Mussan
and
Raja Sahib of Hathras.

For the time being.................... President of the Provisional Government of Hind.

c/o H.R.H. The Prince Prime Minister
Prince Nasrullah Khan
Cabul—Afghanistan
15th June 1917

To, His Excellency,
    The Maharaja Prime Minister
        of Nepal
Your Excellency,

The bearer Captain Teja Singh of my personal staff brings the Imperial letter of the German Government for His Majesty the King of Nepal. I sincerely hope the letter will be duly presented to His Majesty.

I further beg to bring to Your Excellency's notice the exact situation of the world of today which only a travelled and experienced personage like Your Excellency can understand and appreciate.

The fact is that the English and their party is totally hollowed from inside. Now only a cracking skeleton stands and the English are hiding the truth by false news. The whole powerful neutral world which need be counted for the practical purposes is now the bitter enemy of the English and their friends. Sweden, Holland, Switzerland, Spain and Greece of the neutral powers are practically on the side of Germany and her allies. Russia, Your Excellency of course knows, is divided in itself and majority of peoples of Russia are friends of the Germans. I have personally some experience of the Russian feeling and what I say is only from my own experience. All the Persian people as a whole are the bitter enemies of the English. The Afghan Government and the people are deadly against the English and very soon Your Excellency should see the result of this. The feelings of Indians can not be hidden from Your Excellency. All the legitimate sons of India and really God fearing and religious people are the bitter foes of the English.

Under the circumstances it does not behave well to the Kingdom of Nepal to remain friendly or ally of the English. Nepal by its situation is like the crown of India and as such it should protect the holy land and should not side with the blood sucking English—the foes of the holy land and its civilization.

APPENDIX XII

I request Your Excellency therefore to so act in cooperation with other maharajas and people of India that Your Excellency may tomorrow be the Prime Minister of a great Empire. Afghanistan is willing to come to terms with your government. If Your Excellency will be pleased to communicate confidentially to me anything for Afghanistan and Germany and Turkey I shall heartily attend to Your Excellency's communication. By the grace of God Germany has empowered me to work for her in India and has left to me the whole Indian work so far as it concerns Germany and believe me I am entirely at Your Excellency's service.

Your Excellency's Sincere well wisher,
M. Pratap (Brijbari).

N.B.—This letter is duly closed in a sealed envelop and its border bears my signature.

Information gathered from conversation with Teja Singh.

He said: I am a Sikh. My name is Teja Singh and my home was in an obscure village in Ludhiana district—which I left long long ago. I have now come from Khanabad in Afghanistan where the Raja of Hathras, Mahendra Pratap was. I was with him for two months or so. Before that I was in Kabul which I left about a year ago. At that time there was some Australian (Austrian?) officers and above 300 men entered there. They were treated with every consideration and there are no restrictions placed on their movements. They are paid some 2 to 5 rupees each day but I am not sure what the officers used to get. This is the third month of my departure from Khanabad with the letter which I was charged by Raja Mahendra Pratap to deliver to His Highness the Maharaja. The cover of the letter being too cumbrous I left it on the Sarhad on the Yagistam side for facility of carrying the letter itself securely and well concealed. Mahendra Pratap was in Germany when the war broke out. He had left India because of his hatred of Gulami (Servitude). He knows Hardyal Singh, Ajit Singh, Chattopadhaya, Bhagwan Das and others who are, I understand, now living in Germany. I was told that the letter from Germany was written about two years ago. I swear by Heaven above and Mother Earth below that this is a genuine letter. If you doubt believe me an enquiry from or through Shahzada Nasirulla Khan of Kabul will bear out my statement. The Amir has also received a letter like this. I have not seen much of the Amir, but I know Nasirulla Khan well. Nasirulla Khan and Mahendra Pratap are great friends. The latter is treated with great consideration in Afghanistan. From him I have learned that the Amir is sure to fight the British and is only watching his opportunity. The trans-frontier tribesmen too are not well disposed towards the British. A son of Umra Khan who was a refugee in Afghanistan has come to the Khan of Bajoor. He, in league with the Khan of Dir, will very soon reduce Swat into submission as the latter is friendly disposed towards the British. Dir though seemingly friendly to the British is not really so at heart. The policy of the bulk of tribesmen is to subjugate first those clans among them that are friendly disposed towards the British and thus having removed or overcome opposing section from amongst themselves to go against the British. In the transfrontier districts and in Afghan border there are several long standing colonies where disaffected Indian Mohamedans find asylum and whose fighting strength varies from 200 to 2000 fighting men ready to take up arms at any time required. They receive pecuniary help from their co-religionists in India. These and the tribesmen that ride are never in want of good rifles and ammunition which they can and do manufacture at various places. Even a child among them knows how to handle or to put together the parts of a rifle which are dearer to the men than their own children. The newspaper report that the Mahshuda have been subdued by force of arms is a myth. They have been given two lakhs of rupees to keep quiet for two years but I am sure they will not do so for two months even. The rifles which they are said to have surrendered might be out of a thousand which they have looted from the British before. I am sure they, like the other trans-frontier tribesmen, will never part with their rifles. The tribesmen among them can muster not less than a lakh of armed men with 200 rounds of ammunition each. These will open the campaign and when that has weakened the British then Amir will step in with his army and occupy the country up to attack. So far as the Indian are concerned they will not go against them. The political views of the Hindus and Mohamedans have become the same and they are trying for a free and independent India. Matters can be satisfactorily arranged with Sikhs, Jats, Punjabis, and others. It is only with the Gurkhas that we find difficulties. They would not listen to any such proposals. That is why Mahendra Pratap has sent me with the letter and with this verbal message which I beg to deliver. You should carefully consider the situation. You should have no faith in newspaper reports. The British and their allies are weakening day by day. Russia will not fight now. They had stopped fighting for a few months, but 3 or 4 Russian Generals, bribed with English money, wanted to have the fighting renewed only to be killed, caught between the German fire on one side and that of the Russians friendly disposed towards Germany on their back. Why then does Nepal sacrifice her sons in the losing cause of the British? Afghanistan is unfriendly and so is Persia. The internal condition of India is as bad. All true sons of India and faithful men of all religion are dissatisfied with the British. It is only Nepal which is helping the British. The Raja thinks that the British policy is to weaken Nepal just as they have lowered her very much in the eyes of the world. Why then did you do so much to help and why have you sent your troops to India. Look at Afghanistan, how she has been able to conserve her man-power and other resources by keeping aloof from the war. And when opportunity comes she will strike and reap large benefits. What have you got and what you expect to get by having sent out nearly a lakh of your countrymen to fight for the British? Had it not been for this help of Nepal they would never have been able to send such a large army to France. All what you have done for the ungrateful British will go for

APPENDIX XII

nothing. Remember how very much selfish they are. What did Nepal get in the time of the Indian Mutiny for the help which they gave. The land which they gave to you only a portion of what they had wrested from you. Did they not ignore the services of Maharaja Jung Bahadur, rendered by him at that time, and leave his sons in the lurch when they fall upon evil times. You will see how the British bow before the strong and ride rough shod over the weak. Germany is determined to win the war. She will make peace with everyone even today except the selfish British. She will give Belgium her independence as Germany is just and Raja Mahendra Pratap says that Nepal should side with Germany and come to terms with Afghanistan. If you go on helping the British and weaken yourself what you do to save your country in case of eventualities even now and after the war. If you join or sympathize with us Nepal will become the Shahanshah of India. If you do not want to join, at least remain passive and do not help the British. By helping them, as you are doing, with all your resources, when you are under no obligation to do so, you are working not only against your own interest but you are alienating thereby the sympathy and goodwill of the Indians who have such a high regard for Nepal and making enemies of them by acting injuriously to their cause which they have so much at heart. If you communicate confidentially with Mahendra Pratap he will attend to what you may ask him to do. He can arrange everything with Afghanistan and Germany on your behalf, and even send your man to Germany through Afghanistan if you wish to send one, as he is empowered by Germany to do all her work in India. How friendly Germany is towards Nepal will be proved by her treatment of Gurkha prisoners of war. Ultimate victory will remain with Germany and so it is common prudence for Nepal to side with her.

You may believe in British strength, justice and magnanimity but they are like a hollow tree. On the termination of the war, supposing that the British still remained in India, apart from their selfishness what will you get? They will grind India to serve their own ends. Do not expect any other treatment at their hands than what they have dealt out to the Indian Princes and what is now a matter of history. You will simply be sinking lower and lower, become poorer and lose your strength by keeping up your friendship with the British. On the other hand all India looks upon you as its leader and the whole people there are trying to set up an independent Empire. Thirty thousand rifles at Peking intended for them and though these were confiscated others and more will come in their place in time. So if you know your interest and act accordingly at this juncture, you will not only uphold the ancient Hindu Dharma but receive the highest benefit for your country. Your King will become the Shahanshah of India. I have said what I was charged by Raja Mahendra Pratap and leave it to you to act as you may think best. I have spoken the truth. You know the proverb:

        Sahchay mairay Ek chhail
        chuthey Giulay Joye,

i.e., the truthful goes by leaps, the liar counts his steps.

BRITISH INDIA'S RELATIONS WITH NEPAL

Additional information gathered from conversation with Teja Singh:

He said: I have never been in this part of the country before and so have brought my Mohamedan companion with me. He belongs to the Colony of Indian Mohamedans established at Osmas in the Mohamoud country on the North West frontier of India. Osmas is a big Toli (Colony) capable of providing 1500 to 2000 men fit to bear arms. Their present headman or Amir, as he is called, is a descendent of the previous Amirs, the first of whom had emigrated from Patna. He is young and energetic and succeeded his father as Amir on the latter's death about three years ago. I know him. He is very kind to me. This Toli, like to the other three Tolies of Indian Mohamedans has no other source of income except what it gets from the Amir Sahab of Kabul and the contribution made by their co-religionists in India. I understand that all these Tolies together get some £1800 from the Amir for their maintenance. I say pounds because I am told that so many pounds are received. As all others in these Tolies are, the Mohamedan with me is in the service of his own Amir and as such is a member of the fighting unit in his Toli. The Amir of Kabul shows great sympathy with these men in the same way as he does with the tribesmen on the North-West frontier. Indeed without his knowledge or consent no disturbance of fighting ever takes place in that part of the country. Even before the recent Mashud fighting I know the Mashud Zirgahs had come over twice to Kabul. It was only after that the trouble began that side, which led to the undertaking of an expedition by the British. You think the trouble there is ended and the Mahshuda have been subdued. No, no; the fact is that these men, as much as the other tribesmen, bide their time till they get an opportunity, invariably at the instance of or the back [sic] and call of Kabul to create fresh troubles. The Amir of Kabul has gauged correctly the value of the friendship with the British. You doubt the authenticity of the letters I have brought. If a man be sent from here to Kabul he will have the confirmation from Shahzada Nasrullah Khan and possibly also from the Amir, who will be very glad to see your man there. The man can also easily verify what I have told you before about Afghanistan. A firman or passport, which is issued by Nasrullah, is necessary to go there and I shall ask him to send you one. Never mind, even if you do not want it. You may utilise it if it comes or if you are disinclined to do so you can destroy it. It is just possible that the Amir may also write to the Maharaja. I have already told you that Afghanistan is unfavourably inclined towards the British. The ruling Rajas and Maharajas in India as well as the people are also quite disgusted with them. Make enquiries and then you will know the true state of their feelings. An emissary can easily ascertain this fact. No, Gwalior or Patiala may not be the right place to look to at first. To begin with, states like Nabha and Baroda should be approached. Besides there are our two lakhs of Indians outside India scattered all over the world who heartily hate the British. After all the British are not likely to be in India for over a year. Russia is gone and Germany is sure to come out victorious in this struggle. The only regret is that

APPENDIX XII

Nepal, instead of thinking of benefitting from such a situation so favourable to her, has been sacrificing so much for the British, who care to keep or maintain their friendship only so long as it suits them, but which they do not scruple to break or maintain in a way as to place the other party at a disadvantage whenever they find an opportunity for it as has been already seen in so many instances. I see in the Maharaja a firm determination to support them under all circumstances, but, pleased God, may not that time come when you will have to repent for it by the machinations of those very British whom His Highness calls your esteemed friend and by whom, he says, he is firmly resolved to stand, come what may. I am only an ordinary man. But it makes even me feel so sorry to see his infatuation for British friendship. You impress upon me that no hope is to be entertained of Nepal's standing aloof or alienating from the British. But are you not Hindus, made of the same flesh and blood as the other Hindus are? Don't you feel for them, fallen, sunken and trodden as they are? The Kabul Government and the north-west trans-border tribesmen who are sure to come down on the British once a few thousand German troops are in Afghanistan if not before are desirous to win your goodwill and make friendship with you. But for you and your countrymen in India they would have shown their hands to the British even before this. They do not fear the English soldiers nor have any fear of the Indian soldiers. The latter can be won over to make common cause with them. It is the Gurkhas and Gurkhas alone that stand on their way. I leave you to ponder well over this and hope the Amir or Nasirullah Khan will write to you and open your eyes. My intention is to go from here to Kabul. Perhaps Raja Mahendra Pratap by this time has gone to Germany and if it is so, I shall follow him thither. I shall go to Germany via Russia as the way via Russia is difficult one, the journey having had to be done on foot over a long distance. The other toute is easier and more quick. There is a Railway in Russia which has come up to 2 days' marches away from the Afghan border. Taking train there one can get right through by rail to Germany. There will be difficulty in taking that route if there be fighting going on between Russia and Germany. In that case my plan will require a change. But all this will be settled after my arrival in Afghanistan. Raja Mahendra Pratap at one time intended to go to China traveling through the Pamir. But he was stopped by the Commander of the Russian troops that side and was sent back to Afghanistan after some day's detention. The object of his intended visit to China was to make her go against the British. The Russian General, by whom he was stopped and who was friendly disposed towards him, was aware of this.

Basta 77. (N.F.O.K.)

APPENDIX XIII

Memo of Conversation with His Excellency the Viceroy on the 1st January 1916 (with Baber Shamsher)

His Excellency:– Oh no, I know what amount of pains you are taking and I think there is no harm if I tell you that I had actually thought of you and of all your troubles and seeing that your services desired to be duly recognized I thought I must bestow some honor on you and consulted Nepal. They replied that they did not think it desirable and there—I had to stop.

Baber Shamsher:– As a son I would never like to see my father placed in any false and delicate position for my sake, and when I have heard so much from Your Excellency, I really feel much happier than what I would have been if I were the actual recipient of some honour and your gracious words have pinned the decoration on my heart although it has not been pinned on my breast.

His Excellency:– But it was my idea to personally decorate you.

Baber Shamsher:– Your kind words have been enough, Sir. I can't say how deeply touched I have been by your gracious words and on my part I honestly say that I would value a C.S.I. from your hands more than a K.C.S.I. or even a G.C.S.I. from any other body.

His Excellency:– It is so good of you to say so and the very nice way in which you give expression to the friendly feelings you entertain, has touched me deeply.

Baber Shamsher:– It pains me to think that your departure from India is drawing near. Can I expect that Your Excellency will be pleased to remain here beyond March next.

Register I, 1914–19. Maintained by Baber Sham Shamsher. (N.F.O.K.)

APPENDIX XIV

Memo of Conversation with His Excellency the Viceroy on the 27th March 1916

Baber Shamsher:- My father has further instructed me to inform Your Excellency matters which concerned Nepal and himself and which were some time past uppermost in his mind. With their increasing education and knowledge of the outer world, the people and Bhadars of my country have of late been disposed to view with fears and suspicion the treatment of the Government of India towards Nepal and blame my father by saying that the status and prestige of the country has during my father's administration been impaired instead of being improved. They even go so far as to say that even Tibet who pay us an annual tribute and who only some years back was hostile and unfriendly is being looked upon with greater kindness and honorable considerations than Nepal.

His Excellency:- But General, I must say your people, if they have said and thought so, are wrong—They are completely mistaken. We look upon Nepal and the Nepalese as our old friend and ally but we don't call Tibet our ally. In fact though it would not be diplomatic for me—yet it is only between you and me—I tell you that we look upon Tibet as a nuisance constantly giving us trouble, no help at all and secretly playing with China—while we entertain great respect and regard for Nepal, for I do not for a moment see why your people should blame your father and that there [is] any cause whatever for their doing so. The relations between the two governments have greatly improved during your father's regime and I am happy to say that the relations today are as happy and cordial as one can expect. I am fully conscious of the genuine regard and ftiendship which my government entertain for Nepal and your father.

Baber Shamsher:- It is so kind and generous of Your Excellency to say so and as is well-known to Your Excellency, it has been the constant desire and aim of my father, ever since he came to power to remove all possible misapprehensions and distrust in our relations with the Government of India.

(His Excellency interrupted and said, 'I know and realize that.')

And by establishing the most friendly and cordial relations and winning the valued goodwill and confidence of the British Government to firmly secure the integrity and independence of the Country and better its position and status.

His Excellency:- I am sure we have no distrust or misfeelings in our relations which have ever been so cordial and I believe we have always given due attention and consideration and position of Nepal.

Baber Shamsher:– My father greatly regrets the approaching departure of Your Excellency. Such a kind of sympathetic friend of the uniform kindness of interest which Your Excellency has shown towards Nepal has forced him to make this representation, though he did not wish to do so at such a time and his conviction of your kind sympathetic regard makes him hope that Your Excellency will be graciously pleased to leave behind some good words of advice.

His Excellency:– I can assure you, Sir Baber, that it is not necessary and when you write to your father tell him, that I have assured you on behalf of myself and the Government of India that he should entertain no doubts whatever as to the intentions of the Government towards Nepal. We shall, as I believe we have always done, look upon Nepal as our friend and ally and will bear due regard for the position of the country. Tibet—and that's quite different—Tibet and Nepal—they are not in the same category—they can not be compared—they are altogether different—we talk of Tibet like Bhutan, Sikkim and so on—but we never do so of Nepal—also assure your father that we greatly appreciate the valuable help and tell him that I personally entertain great admiration for him.

Baber Shamsher:– I am sure my father will be greatly pleased at and highly thankful to Your Excellency for such a kind message—and allow me [to] thank Your Excellency before I take leave for all your kindness to me, which I am sure I can never and never forget.

His Excellency:– Thank you so much. As I have already said, I greatly value your friendship and I can tell you that the Government of India fully realizes all your present trouble and services.

Baber Shamsher:– It is so generous of Your Excellency to say so, but I do not think I have been able to do anything much.

His Excellency:– Now, let us say good-bye, though it grieves me to do so.

Baber Shamsher:– Though it is a great comfort and consolation to your friends and admirers that after such a completely successful and memorable viceroyalty, Your Excellency is going back and that you will soon be relieved of your great responsibilities and heavy worries, yet, I cannot say how pained I am today to think that I have come to take private leave of Your Excellency. I shall ever remember you with esteem and affection.

His Excellency:– Thank you so much. Your words have touched me greatly.

Baber Shamsher:– May God bless you—is all that I can say now.
(His Excellency then bowed and we said good-bye.)

Signed / Baber.

Register I, 1914-19. Maintained by Baber Shamsher. (N.F.O.K.)

APPENDIX XV

Memo of conversation between Baber Shamsher and the Secretary of State when the latter visited India in 1917

Baber:– I accompanied my father to Europe in 1908 and I was in London for about a couple of months.

Secretary:– I remember that. I was then private secretary to the Prime Minister and I remember some of you coming to Downing Street. Where do you manufacture your rifles and guns and have you got a military college?

Baber:– We have only got a military school, not a college. We can not manufacture any satisfactory rifles not to speak of guns. We are not allowed to import any arms and ammunitions without the sanction of the Government of India. We are indeed very poor in these lines.

Secretary:– After the war, I am sure, we shall consider all those things.

Baber:– The Government of India are fully aware of what we have got and what we have not and what our grievances are. So it is needless for me to take your time by going into details.

Register II, 1914-19. Maintained by Baber Shamsher. (N.F.O.K.)

APPENDIX XVI

Treaty of 1815

TREATY OF PEACE between the HONORABLE EAST INDIA COMPANY and MAHARAJAH BIKRAM SAH, Rajah of Nipal, settled between LIEUT.-COLONEL BRADSHAW on the part of the HONORABLE COMPANY, in virtue of the full powers vested in him by His Excellency the RIGHT HONORABLE FRANCIS, EARL of MOIRA, Knight of the Most Noble Order of the Garter, one of His Majesty's Most Honorable Privy Council, appointed by the Court of Directors of the said Honorable Company to direct and control all the affairs in the East Indies, and by SREE GOOROO GUJRAJ MISSER AND CHUNDER SEEKUR OPEDEEA on the part of MAHARAJAH GIRMAUN JODE BIKRAM SAH BEHAUDER SHUMSHEER JUNG, in virtue of the powers to that effect vested in them by the said Rajah of Nipal.

Whereas war has arisen between the Honorable East India Company and the Rajah of Nipal, and whereas the parties are mutually disposed to restore the relations of peace and amity which, previously to the occurrence of the late differences, had long subsisted between the two States, the following terms of peace have been agreed upon:

ARTICLE 1st

There shall be perpetual peace and friendship between the Honorable East India Company and the Rajah of Nipal.

ARTICLE 2nd

The Rajah of Nipal renounces all claim to the lands which were the subject of discussion between the two States before the war; and acknowledges the right of the Honorable Company to the sovereignty of those lands.

APPENDIX XVI

ARTICLE 3rd

The Rajah of Nipal hereby cedes to the Honorable the East India Company in perpetuity all the undermentioned territories, *viz*.

First.—The whole of the low lands between the Rivers Kali and Rapti.

Secondly.—The whole of the low lands (with the exception of Bootwul Khass) lying between the Rapti and the Gunduck.

Thirdly.—The whole of the low lands between the Gunduck and Coosah, in which the authority of the British Government has been introduced, or is in actual course of introduction.

Fourthly.—All the low lands between the Rivers Mitchee and the Teestah.

Fifthly.—All the territories within the hills eastward of the River Mitchee, including the fort and lands of Nagree and the Pass of Nagarcote, leading from Morung into the hills, together with the territory lying between that Pass and Nagree. The aforesaid territory shall be evacuated by the Goorkha troops within forty days from this date.

ARTICLE 4th

With a view to indemnify the Chiefs and Barahdars of the State of Nipal, whose interests will suffer by the alienation of the lands ceded by the foregoing Article, the British Government agrees to settle pensions to the aggregate amount of two lakhs of Rupees per annum on such Chiefs as may be selected by the Rajah of Nipal, and in the proportions which the Rajah may fix. As soon as the selection is made, Sunnuds shall be granted under the seal and signature of the Governor-General for the pensions respectively.

ARTICLE 5th

The Rajah of Nipal renounces for himself, his heirs, and successors, all claim to or connexion with the countries lying to the west of the River Kali, and engages never to have any concern with those countries or the inhabitants thereof.

ARTICLE 6th

The Rajah of Nipal engages never to molest or disturb the Rajah of Sikkim in the possession of his territories; but agrees, if any differences shall arise between the State of Nipal and the Rajah of Sikkim, or the subjects of either, that such differences shall be referred to the arbitration of the British Government, by whose award the Rajah of Nipal engages to abide.

ARTICLE 7th

The Rajah of Nipal hereby engages never to take or retain in his service any British subject, nor the subject of any European or American State, without the consent of the British Government.

ARTICLE 8th

In order to secure and improve the relations of amity and peace hereby established between the two States, it is agreed that accredited Ministers from each shall reside at the Court of the other.

ARTICLE 9th

This Treaty, consisting of nine Articles, shall be ratified by the Rajah of Nipal within fifteen days from this date, and the ratification shall be delivered to Lieut.-Colonel Bradshaw, who engages to obtain and deliver to the Rajah the ratification of the Governor-General within twenty days, or sooner, if practicable.

Done at Segowlee, on the 2nd day of December 1815.

PARIS BRADSHAW, Lt.-Col., P.A.

Seal.
Seal.
Seal.

Received this Treaty from Chunder Seekur Opedeea, Agent on the part of the Rajah of Nipal, in the Valley of Muckwaunpoor, at half-past two o'clock P.M., on the 4th of March 1816, and delivered to him the Counterpart Treaty on behalf of the British Government.

(Signed) DD. OCHTERLONY,
Agent, Governor-General

MEMORANDUM for the approval and acceptance of the RAJAH OF NIPAL, presented on the 8th December 1816.

Adverting to the amity and confidence subsisting with the Rajah of Nipal, the British Government proposes to suppress, as much as is possible, the esecution of certain Articles in the Treaty of Segowlee, which bear hard upon the Rajah, as follows:

2. With a view to gratify the Rajah in a point which he has much at heart, the British Government is willing to restore the Terai ceded to it by the Rajah in the Treaty, to wit, the whole Terai lands lying between the Rivers Coosa and Gunduk, such as appertained to the Rajah before the late disagreement; excepting the disputed lands in the Zillahs of Tirhoot and Sarun, and excepting such portions of territory as may occur on both sides for the purpose of settling a frontier, upon investigation by the respective Commissioners; and excepting such lands as may have been given in possession to any one by the British Government upon ascertainment of his rights subsequent to the cession of Terai to that Government. In case the Rajah is desirous of retaining the lands of such ascertained proprietors, they may be exchanged for others, and let it be clearly understood that, notwithstanding the considerable extent of the lands in the Zillah of Tirhoot, which have for a long time been a subject of dispute, the settlement made in the year 1812 of Christ, corresponding with the year 1869 of Bikramajeet, shall be taken, and everything else relinquished, that is to say, that the settlement and negotiations, such as occurred at that period, shall in the present case hold good and be established.

3. The British Government is willing likewise to restore the Terai lying between the Rivers Gunduk and Rapti, that is to say, from the River Gunduk to the western limits of the Zillah of Goruckpore, together with Bootwul and Sheoraj, such as appertained to Nipal previous to the disagreements, complete, with the exception of the disputed places in the Terai, and such quantity of ground as may be considered mutually to be requisite for the new boundary.

4. As it is impossible to establish desirable limits between the two States without survey, it will be expedient that Commissioners be appointed on both sides for the purpose of arranging in concert a well defined boundary on the basis of the preceding terms, and of establishing a straight line of frontier, with a view to the distinct separation of the respective territories of the British Government to the south and of Nipal to the north; and in case any indentations occur to destroy the even tenor of the line, the Commissioners should effect an exchange of lands so interfering on principles of clear reciprocity.

5. And should it occur that the proprietors of lands situated on the mutual frontier, as it may be rectified, whether holding of the British Government or of the Rajah of Nipal, should be placed in the condition of subjects to both Governments, with a view to prevent continual dispute and discussion between the two Governments, the respective Commissioners should effect in mutual concurrence and co-operation the exchange of such lands, so as to render them subject to one dominion alone.

6. Whensoever the Terai shall be restored, the Rajah of Nipal will cease to require the sum of two lakhs of Rupees per annum, which the British Government agreed to advance for the maintenance of certain Barahdars of his Government.

7. Moreover, the Rajah of Nipal agrees to refrain from prosecuting any inhabitants of the Terai, after its revertance to his rule, on account of having favored the cause of the British Government during the war, and should any of those persons, excepting the cultivators of the soil, be desirous of quitting their estates, and of retiring within the Company's territories, he shall not be liable to hindrance.

8. In the event of the Rajah's approving the foregoing terms, the proposed arrangement for the survey and establishment of boundary marks shall be carried into execution, and after the determination in concert of the boundary line, Sunnuds conformable to the foregoing stipulations, drawn out and sealed by the two States, shall be delivered and accepted on both sides.

Seal.   (Signed) EDWARD GARDNER,
Resident.

(A true translation)

(Signed) G. WELLESLEY,
Assistant.

SUBSTANCE of a LETTER under the Seal of the RAJAH OF NIPAL, received on the 11th December 1816

After compliments;

I have comprehended the document under date the 8th of December 1816, or 4th of Poos 1873 Sumbut, which you transmitted relative to the restoration, with a view to my friendship and satisfaction, of the Terai between the Rivers Coosa and Rapti to the southern boundary complete, such as appertained to my estate previous to the war. It mentioned that, in the event of my accepting the terms contained in that document, the southern boundary of the Terai should be established as it was held by this Government. I have accordingly agreed to the terms laid down by you, and herewith enclose an instrument of agreement, which may be satisfactory to you. Moreover, it was written in the document transmitted by you, that it would be restored, with the exception of the disputed lands and such portion of land as should, in the opinion of the Commissioners on both sides, occur for the purpose of settling a boundary; and excepting the lands which, after the cessions of the Terai to the Honorable Company, may have been transferred by it to the ascertained proprietors. My friend, all these matters rest with you, and since it was also written that a view was had to my friendship and satisfaction with respect to certain Articles of the Treaty of Segowlee, which bore hard upon me, and which could be remitted, I am well assured that you have at heart the removal of whatever may tend to my distress, and that you will act in a manner corresponding to the advantage of this State and the increase of the friendly relations subsisting between the two Governments.

Moreover, I have to acknowledge the receipt of the orders under the red seal of this State, addressed to the officers of Terai between the Rivers Gunduk and Rapti, for the surrender of that Terai, and their retiring from thence, which was given to you at Thankote, according to your request, and which you have now returned for my satisfaction.

(A true translation)

(Signed) G. WELLESLEY,

Assistant.

SUBSTANCE of a DOCUMENT under the Red Seal, received from the DURBAR on the 11th December 1816

Doorga
Bowanee.

With a regard to friendship and amity, the Government of Nipal agrees to the tenor of the document under date the 8th of December 1816 or 4th Poos 1873 Sumbut, which was received by the Durbar from the Honorable Edward Gardner on the part of the Honorable Company, respecting the revertance of the Terai between the Rivers Coosa and

APPENDIX XVI

Rapti to the former southern boundary, such as appertained to Nipal previous to the war, with exception of the disputed lands.

Dated the 7th of Poos 1873 Sumbut.

(A true translation)

(Signed) G. WELLESLEY,
Assistant.

Aitchison, C. U. *A Collection of Treaties, Engagements, and Sunnuds, Relating to India and Neighbouring Countries.* Vol. II, pp. 205–11. Calcutta: Printed by G. A. Savielle and P. M. Cranenburgh, Bengal Printing Company Limited. 1863.

APPENDIX XVII

Treaty of 1923

TREATY of FRIENDSHIP between Great Britain and Nepal signed at KATMANDU, 21st December 1923, and Note bearing the same date respecting the importation of Arms and Ammunition into NEPAL—1923

(Exchange of ratifications took place at Katmandu on the 8th April 1925)

TREATY

Whereas peace and friendship have now existed between the British Government and the Government of Nepal since the signing of the Treaty of Segowlie on the 2nd day of December 1815; and whereas since that date the Government of Nepal has ever displayed its true friendship for the British Government and the British Government has as constantly shown its good-will towards the Government of Nepal; and whereas the Governments of both the countries are now desirous of still further strengthening and cementing the good relations and friendship which have subsisted between them for more than a century; the two High Contracting Parties having resolved to conclude a new Treaty of Friendship have agreed upon the following Articles:

Article I.—There shall be perpetual peace and friendship between the Governments of Great Britain and Nepal, and the two Governments agree mutually to acknowledge and respect each other's independence, both internal and external.

Article II.—All previous treaties, agreements and engagements, since and including the Treaty of Segowlie of 1815, which have been concluded between the two Governments are hereby confirmed, except so far as they may be altered by the present Treaty.

Article III.—As the preservation of peace and friendly relations with the neighbouring States whose territories adjoin their common frontiers is to the mutual interests of both the High Contracting Parties, they hereby agree to inform each other of any serious friction or misunderstanding with those States likely to rupture such friendly relations, and each to exert its good offices as far as may be possible to remove such friction and misunderstanding.

Article IV.—Each of the High Contracting Parties will use all such

APPENDIX XVII

measures as it may deem practicable to prevent its territories being used for purposes inimical to the security of the other.

Article V.—In view of the longstanding friendship that has subsisted between the British Government and the Government of Nepal and for the sake of cordial neighbourly relations between them, the British Government agrees that the Nepal Government shall be free to import from or through British India into Nepal whatever arms, ammunition, machinery, warlike material or stores may be required or desired for the strength and welfare of Nepal, and that this arrangement shall hold good for all time as long as the British Government is satisfied that the intentions of the Nepal Government are friendly and that there is no immediate danger to India from such importations. The Nepal Government, on the other hand, agrees that there shall be no export of such arms, ammunition, etc., across the frontier of Nepal either by the Nepal Government or by private individuals.

If, however, any Convention for the regulation of the Arms Traffic, to which the British Government may be a party, shall come into force, the right of importation of arms and ammunition by the Nepal Government shall be subject to the proviso that the Nepal Government shall first become a party to that Convention, and that such importation shall only be made in accordance with the provisions of that Convention.

Article VI.—No Customs duty shall be levied at British Indian ports on goods imported on behalf of the Nepal Government for immediate transport to that country provided that a certificate from such authority as may from time to time be determined by the two Governments shall be presented at the time of importation to the Chief Customs Officer at the port of import setting forth that the goods are the property of the Nepal Government, are required for the public services of the Nepal Government, are not for the purpose of any State monopoly or State trade, and are being sent to Nepal under orders of the Nepal Government.

The British Government also agrees to the grant in respect of all trade goods, imported at British Indian ports for immediate transmission to Katmandu without breaking bulk *en route*, of a rebate of the full duty paid, provided that in accordance with arrangements already agreed to, between the two Governments, such goods may break bulk for repacking at the port of entry under Customs supervision in accordance with such rules as may from time to time be laid down in this behalf. The rebate may be claimed on the authority of a certificate signed by the said authority that the goods have arrived at Katmandu with the Customs seals unbroken and otherwise untampered with.

Article VIII.—This Treaty signed on the part of the British Government by Lieutenant-Colonel W. F. T. O'Connor, C.I.E., C.V.O.,

British Envoy at the Court of Nepal, and on the part of the Nepal Government by General His Highness Maharaja Sir Chandra Shumshere Jung Bahadur Rana, G.C.B., G.C.S.I., G.C.M.H., G.C.V.O., D.C.I., Thong-lin Pimma—Kokang-Wang-Syan, Prime Minister and Marshal of Nepal, shall be ratified and the ratification shall be exchanged at Katmandu as soon as practicable.

Signed and sealed at Katmandu this the twenty-first day of December in the year one thousand nine hundred and twenty-three *Anno Domini* corresponding with the sixth Paush, Sambat Era one thousand nine hundred and eighty.

W. F. T. O'Connor, *Lt.-Col.*
*British Envoy at the
Court of Nepal.*

(Under Vernacular translation of Treaty.)
CHANDRA SHAMSHERE,
*Prime Minister and
Marshal of Nepal.*

NOTE

*From the Prime Minister of Nepal, to the British Envoy
at the Court of Nepal*

Nepal, December 21, 1923.

My dear Colonel O'Connor,

Regarding the purchase of arms and munitions which the Government of Nepal buys from time to time for the strength and welfare of Nepal, and imports to its own territory from and through British India in accordance with Article V of the Treaty between the two Governments, the Government of Nepal hereby agrees that it will, from time to time before the importation of arms and munitions at British Indian Ports, furnish detailed lists of such arms and munitions to the British Envoy at the Court of Nepal in order that the British Government may be in a position to issue instructions to the port authorities to afford the necessary facilities for their importation in accordance with Article VI of this Treaty.

I am, etc.,
CHANDRA

To
Lieutenant-Colonel W. F. T. O'Connor, C.I.E., C.V.O., British Envoy at the Court of Nepal.

Aitchison, C. U. *A Collection of Treaties, Engagements and Sunnuds Relating to India and Neighbouring Countries.* Vol. XIV, pp. 75–77. Calcutta: Government of India Central Publication Branch. Revised edition. 1929.

APPENDIX XVIII

TIBETO-NEPALESE TREATY OF 1792

1. That China should henceforth be considered as father to both Nepal and Tibet, who should regard each other as brothers;
2. That after due investigation by the Chinese Government, the full value of the articles plundered at Lhasa would be paid to the Nepalese sufferers by the Tibetan authorities;
3. That all Nepalese subjects, with the exception of armed soldiers, would be permitted to travel, to establish factories and to carry on trade within the jurisdiction of Tibet and China;
4. That if either of the two brotherly States should commence an unprovoked dispute with the intention of possessing the territories of the other, the representatives of the two Governments would report all particulars to the court of Pekin which would finally decide the dispute;
5. That if Nepal be ever invaded by a foreign power, China would not fail to help her;
6. That the two brotherly States would send to China some produce of their country every five years in token of their filial love;
7. That the Chinese Government would in return send to Nepal a friendly present, and would make every necessary arrangement for the comfort of the mission to and from Pekin.

(From the *Life of Maharaja Sir Jung Bahadur* by General Pudma Jang Bahadur Rana, Allahabad, 1909.)

Jain, Girilal. *India Meets China in Nepal*, p. 159. Bombay. Asia Publishing House. 1959.

APPENDIX XVIII (continued)

TREATY BETWEEN TIBET AND NEPAL, 1856

Translation of the Tibetan text

The undermentioned gentlemen, monks and laymen, of the Gurkha and Tibetan Governments held a conference and mutually agreed upon and concluded a Treaty of ten Articles, and invoked the Supreme Being as their witness, and affixed their seals to it. They have agreed to regard the Chinese Emperor as heretofore with respect, in accordance with what has been written, and to keep both the States in agreement and to treat each other like brothers. If either of them violate the Treaty, may the Precious Ones not allow that State to prosper. Should either State violate the terms of the Treaty, the other State shall be exempt from all sin in making war upon it.

(Here follow the names of the signatories and their seals.)

List of Articles of the Treaty

1. The Tibetan Government shall pay the sum of ten thousand rupees annually as a present to the Gurkha Government.

2. Gurkha and Tibet have been regarding the Great Emperor with respect. Tibet being the country of monasteries, hermits and celibates, devoted to religion, the Gurkha Government have agreed henceforth to afford help and protection to it as far as they can, if any foreign country attacks it.

3. Henceforth Tibet shall not levy taxes on trade or taxes on roads or taxes of any other kind on the merchants or other subjects of the Gurkha Government.

4. The Government of Tibet agrees to return to the Gurkha Government the Sikh soldiers captured by Tibet, and all the Gurkha soldiers, officers, servants, women, and cannon captured in the war. The Gurkha Government agrees to return to the Tibetan Government the Tibetan troops, weapons, yaks, and whatever articles may have been left behind by the Tibetan subjects residing at Kyi-ron, Nyanang, Dzong-ga, Pu-rang, and Rong-shar. And on the completion of the Treaty all the Gurkha troops in Pu-rang, Rong-shar, Kyi-rong, Dzong-ga, Nya-nang, Tar-ling, and La-tse will be withdrawn and the country evacuated.

5. Henceforth the Gurkha Government will keep a high officer, and not a Newar, to hold charge at Lhasa.

6. The Gurkha Government will open shops at Lhasa, where they can freely trade in gems, jewellery, clothing, food, and different articles.

APPENDIX XVIII

7. The Gurkha officer is not allowed to try any case arising from quarrels amongst Lhasa subjects and merchants, and the Tibetan Government is not allowed to try any case arising from quarrels amongst the Gurkha subjects and traders and the Mahomedans of Khatmandu who may be residing in the jurisdiction of Lhasa. In the event of quarrels between Tibetan and Gurkha subjects the high officials of the two Governments will sit together and will jointly try the cases; the fines imposed upon the Tibetan subjects as punishments will be taken by the Tibetan official, and the fines imposed upon Gurkha subjects, merchants, and Mahomedans as punishments will be taken by the Gurkha official.

8. Should any Gurkha subject, after committing a murder, go to the country of Tibet, he shall be surrendered by Tibet to Gurkha; and should any Tibetan subject, after committing a murder, go to the country of Gurkha, he shall be surrendered by Gurkha to Tibet.

9. If the property of a Gurkha merchant or other subject be plundered by a Tibetan subject, the Tibetan officials after inquiry will compel the restoration of such property to the owner. Should the plunderer not be able to restore such property, he shall be compelled by the Tibetan official to draw up an agreement to make good such property within an extended time. If the property of a Tibetan merchant or other subject be plundered by a Gurkha subject, the Gurkha official after inquiry will compel the restoration of such property to the owner. Should the plunderer not be able to restore such property, he shall be compelled by the Gurkha official to draw up an agreement to make good such property within an extended time.

10. After the completion of the Treaty neither Government will take vengeance[1] on the persons or property of Tibetan subjects who may have joined the Gurkha Government during the recent war, or on the persons or property of Gurkha subjects who may have so joined the Tibetan Government.

Dated the 18th day of the 2nd month of the Fire-Dragon Year.[2]

Bell, Sir Charles. *Tibet: Past and Present*. Pp. 278–80. Oxford: Clarendon Press. 1924.

---

[1] *Lit.* 'be angry with'.
[2] 1856.

APPENDIX XIX

Letter from the King of Nepal to the Emperor of China
(Translation)

The Erdeni Prince of the Gurkhas, P'i-je-t'i-pi-k'a-erh-ma-sheng-hsieh-je-tseng-k'a-pa-ha-tu-je-sa-ha, in his attitude of an humble vassal, makes nine prostrations before the Throne of the Emperor of China and presents his respectful prayer for the health of His most noble and mighty Majesty, the Wenchu P'usa or Manjusri, whose brilliancy is as the rays of the Sun and Moon, whose care extends to the myriad kingdoms, and whose length of years shall be as enduring as the Hsu Mi Mountain.

In accordance with the custom which prescribes the payment of tribute once every five years, it becomes your vassal's duty to despatch special *Ko-chi* to take it and deliver it to its High Destination. The full complement of offerings has been duly prepared, and is being despatched to Peking by the hands of a Principal and Assistant Envoy named respectively Ko-chi Ying-ta-je-pi-k'a-erh-ma-je-na-pa-ha-tu-je and the Ko-chi Sa-erh-ta-erh-tsu-ta-pi-je-ch'ia-cha-k'a-ch'ieh-ti-je, accompanied by a number of headmen and secretaries who started from Katmandu on the 10th August 1894.

In accordance with the custom which has always prevailed in the past when anything occurred in your vassal's State of submitting petitions to the Throne through the Imperial Resident in Tibet, he has duly petitioned the present Resident and begged His Excellency to graciously bear in mind the distance which separates Nepal from Peking, and make allowances for his unfamiliarity with the usages of the Court of the Heavenly Dynasty. His Excellency was also asked to take into consideration the earnestness of purpose with which your vassal turned towards the civilisation of China and to place His Majesty the Emperor in full possession of the facts of the case.

Ever since you vassal's state in the days of his ancestors yielded fealty to the Celestial Court, its conduct has been characterised by the most complete respect and submission. Your vassal's whole heart and mind are imbued with feelings of circumspection and reverential obedience. He would humbly implore Your Majesty graciously to regard him as a person who has tendered his allegiance and done some service. Should he hereafter fall into any errors, he trusts Your Majesty will look upon him as a slave and extend to him your kindness so that he may continue for ever to be the recipient of the Celestial favours, for which he will be inexpressibly grateful.

APPENDIX XIX

He indites this memorial at Katmandu on the 14th August 1894 and accompanies it with a respectful offering of gold satin brocade
Imperial Rescript. Perused.

Foreign Secret-E, September 1895. No. 116–30 (N.A.I.)

APPENDIX XX

Convention between Great Britain and China, 1906

Signed at Peking on the 27th April 1906. Ratified at London on the 23rd July 1906

Whereas His Majesty the King of Great Britain and Ireland and of the British Dominions beyond the seas, Emperor of India, and His Majesty the Emperor of China are sincerely desirous to maintain and perpetuate the relations of friendship and good understanding which now exist between their respective Empires;

And whereas the refusal of Tibet to recognize the validity of or to carry into full effect the provisions of the Anglo-Chinese Convention of 17th March 1890, and Regulations of 5th December 1893, placed the British Government under the necessity of taking steps to secure their rights and interests under the said Convention and Regulations;

And whereas a Convention of ten articles was signed at Lhasa on 7th September, 1904, on behalf of Great Britain and Tibet, and was ratified by the Viceroy and Governor-General of India on behalf of Great Britain modifying its terms under certain conditions being appended thereto;

His Britannic Majesty and His Majesty the Emperor of China have resolved to conclude a Convention on this subject and have for this purpose named Plenipotentiaries, that is to say:

HIS MAJESTY THE KING OF GREAT BRITAIN AND IRELAND:

Sir Ernest Mason Satow, Knight Grand Cross of the Most Distinguished Order of St. Michael and St. George, His said Majesty's Envoy Extraordinary and Minister Plenipotentiary to His Majesty the Emperor of China;

AND HIS MAJESTY THE EMPEROR OF CHINA:

His Excellency Tong Shoa-yi, His said Majesty's High Commissioner Plenipotentiary and a Vice-President of the Board of Foreign Affairs,

who having communicated to each other their respective full powers and finding them to be in good order and due form have agreed upon and concluded the following Convention in six articles:

ARTICLE I

The Convention concluded on 7th September, 1904, by Great Britain and Tibet, the texts of which in English and Chinese are attached to the present Convention as an annexe, is hereby confirmed, subject to the modification stated in the declaration appended thereto, and both of the High Contracting Parties engage to take at all times such steps as may be necessary to secure the due fulfilment of the terms specified therein.

ARTICLE II

The Government of Great Britain engages not to annex Tibetan territory or to interfere in the administration of Tibet. The Government of China also undertakes not to permit any other foreign state to interfere with the territory or internal administration of Tibet.

ARTICLE III

The concessions which are mentioned in Article 9 (*d*) of the Convention concluded on 7th September, 1904, by Great Britain and Tibet are denied to any state or to the subject of any state other than China, but it has been arranged with China that at the trade marts specified in Article 2 of the aforesaid Convention Great Britain shall be entitled to lay down telegraph lines connecting with India.

ARTICLE IV

The provisions of the Anglo-Chinese Convention of 1890 and Regulations of 1893 shall, subject to the terms of this present Convention and annexe thereto, remain in full force.

ARTICLE V

The English and Chinese texts of the present Convention have been carefully compared and found to correspond, but in the event of there being any difference of meaning between them the English text shall be authoritative.

ARTICLE VI

This Convention shall be ratified by the Sovereigns of both countries and ratifications shall be exchanged at London within three months after the date of signature by the Plenipotentiaries of both Powers.

In token whereof the respective Plenipotentiaries have signed and sealed this Convention, four copies in English and four in Chinese.

Done at Peking this twenty-seventh day of April, one thousand nine hundred and six, being the fourth day of the fourth month of the thirty-second year of the reign of Kuanghsü.

Bell, Sir Charles. *Tibet: Past and Present.* Pp. 287–289. Oxford: Clarendon Press. 1924.

INDEX

Abdul Quadir, 34, 261, 337
Act of 1813, 32; of 1833, 32; of 1784, 31
Afghanistan (and Afghans), 43, 45, 61, 123, 209, 213, 291;
  Amirs of, 44, 151, 193, 196, 373, 375–9; war with Britain, 127, 195–6, 208; status of, 159, 174, 290, 301, 303; import of arms, 173, 176, 204, 207; and World War I, 184, 192, 193, 373–8
Africa, 295
Afridis, 366
Agrawal caste, 97
Alabama (USA), 216
Allahabad, 25, 79, 86, 88, 91, 96, 104, 208
Almora, 236, 240
Alou-d-din, Sultan, 29
Ambeyla, 237
America, 211; Americans, 270, 286, 290, 295, 307; American States, 203; American subjects, 385
Amherst, Lord, 270
Ammanullah, King of Afghanistan, 196
Ampthill, Lord, 367
Anderson, Colonel, 110
Anglo-Chinese Convention (1906), 282, 398–9
Anglo-Russian Convention (1907), 165, 167, 259, 274, 282, 283, 370–1
Annam, 259, 283
arms, importation and manufacture, 106, 107, 113, 122, 123–4, 137–9, 140, 170–9, 203–4, 206–9
Asia, 96, 212, 256, 264, 268, 270, 310, 373; Asiams, 192, 311, 312; Asian States, 283
Asoka, Emperor, 26, 27
Asquith, H. H., 1st Earl of Oxford and Asquith, 196, 367, 368
Assam, 25, 254; Frontier Police, 247; Regiment, 242
Auchinleck, General Sir C., 252
Auckland, Lord, Governor-General of India, 44, 45
Austinian, theory of sovereignty, 293, 294
Austria-Hungary, 193, 372, 373
Ausuph (Asaf) Jah, Nawab, 59
Azamgarh, 77, 78

Baghdad, 256
Bahadurs (Chiefs), 75, 197, 205, 212, 250, 285, 385
Bahadur, Bum, 54, 56, 69, 91, 240
Bahadur, General, 231
Bahadur, Jit, 156
Bahadur, Krishna, 70, 96
Bahadur, Sir, 156
Bahraich, 227
Baji Rao II, 84
Bala Rao, 81–4, 86, 87
Baluchistan, 188
Bangkok, 65
Bankipur (Patna), 195
Barlow, G. H., 339
Beejapoor, 344
Belgium, 377
Benares, 35, 79, 85, 94, 211, 227, 337, 342, 344; Maharajah of, 199
Bengal, 23, 27; Bay of, 64; Lieutenant-Governor of, 107, 122, 181; Nawab of, 31
Berkeley, Colonel J. C., 132, 141, 142–5, 243–5
Betham, G., 226, 227
Bettiah, Maharajah of, 103
Bhatgaon, 28
Bhimphedi, 356
Bhotias, 24
Bhutan, 23, 25, 93, 103, 105, 167, 176, 263, 278, 306; Rajah of, 263
Bhuratpore, 236
Bihar, 23, 78, 224, 226
Biratnagar, 225, 226
Birgunj, 228, 358
Birjis Kader, 84
Bisht, 235, 238
Boer War, 188
Bombay, 105
Bootwul, 82, 86, 227, 385, 387
Boxer Rebellion, 198
Bradshaw, Lieutenant-Colonel P., 384, 386
Brahmins, 83, 85, 87, 97, 199, 221
Brett, the Honourable Justice C., 289, 299
Britain, non-intervention policy with Nepal, 31, 41, 71–2; trade with Nepal, 33–4, 93–8, 113, 119–22, 136–7; troublesome relations with Nepal, 36, 39; war with Nepal,

400

INDEX

Britain—*continued*
36–8; conciliatory policy towards Nepal, 39, 40, 44; and extradition problem, 53, 91–3, 108, 124–7, 157; and rebel fugitives after mutiny, 81–7; and import of arms by Nepal. 106, 107, 113, 122, 123–4, 137–9, 140, 170–9, 203–4, 206–9; Digby's criticisms of policy towards coup d'état of 1885, 141–6; Treaty of Friendship with Nepal (1923), 202–10. *See also under* China, India, Nepal, Tibet, etc., *and* individual Viceroys
Buccus (Bux) Benee Madoo, 346
Buck, E., Director of Agriculture and Commerce, 119
Buddha, 28, 367; Buddhism, 371; Buddhists, 24, 234, 238, 367
Buhram Ghat, 106
Bunyas, 97
Burathokis, 235, 238
Burgh, General de, 219
Burma, 43, 45, 66, 123, 220, 256; British power in, 98, 284; and World War II, 220, 225; Gurkhas in, 253; and China, 259, 284
Burney, Captain H., 66
Bushmat, Pulwan Singh, 76, 79
Bustee, 97
Byers, Captain C. H., Assistant Resident, Nepal, 80, 88, 90, 106

Cabul (*see* Kabul)
Calcutta, 44, 53, 106, 123, 130, 132, 138, 153, 156, 160, 180, 230, 243, 284, 296, 366; High Court, 298, 299
Campbell, A., Superintendent of Darjeeling, 105
Campbell, Sir C., 75, 77
Candler, British war correspondent, 188
Canning, Lord, 74–6, 84, 85, 87, 128
Cape Comorin, 32
Cawnpore, 74, 83, 211
Ceremonials, accorded to Nepalese prime ministers, 108–9
Ceylon, 291
Chait Singh, Rajah, 33
Chandra Gupta, 25
Chattar Manzil, 77
Chelmsford, Lord, 195, 289
Chen, Ivan, 168
Chiang-kai-Shek, 222, 282
China, 43, 96, 291; Nepalese relations with, 28, 54, 60, 64, 134, 149, 164–6, 167–8, 169, 198, 209, 212, Ch. 9 passim, 287, 303, 393, 396–7; East India Company and, 32; Britain and, 33, 64, 98, 111, 164–5, 167, 168–9, Ch. 9 passim, 398–9; and Tibet, 152–4, 157, 165, 167–9, 195, Ch. 9 passim, 285, 290, 292, 366–7, 370–1; Boxer rebellion, 198; Red Cross, 222; and Burma, 259, 284
Ching, Prince, 152, 167, 168, 271, 278
Christians, 86; missionaries, 24
Christie, R., 348
Chumbi Valley, 273
Chung, General, 168, 279, 280
Churchill, Sir Winston, 231
Clive, R., 31
Colquhoun, Sir R., 236
Commander-in-Chief, of India, 190, 220, 248, 253; of Nepal, 47, 49, 225, 226
Commercial Treaty of 1792, 285
Convention, between Great Britain and China, 371, 398; between Great Britain and Tibet, 371
Coosa, river, 385, 386, 388
Cornwallis, Lord, 33, 34, 257–9, 337
Coupland, Sir R., 32
Court of Directors, 74, 92, 384
Crawford, J., representative of Governor-General of India, 65
Cripps, Sir S., 223
Curzon, Lord, 149, 151, 153, 154, 156, 174, 175, 289, 300

Dalai Lama, 150, 152, 153, 155, 156, 257, 274–6, 282, 358, 371
Dalhousie, Lord, 52, 53, 102, 237
Dane, Sir L., 158, 303
Darbhanga, 225; Maharajah of, 181, 199
Darjeeling, 105, 251, 263
Daukes, Colonel, 309
Deb Raia of Bhutan (Bhootan), 263
Delhi, 31, 75, 203, 205, 215, 219, 237; Coronation Durbar, 162, 297
Digby, W., 141–5
Dinkins, W. H., 216
Dobbs, Sir H., 204
Dorjieff, Dalai Lama's envoy, 274
Dufferin, Lady, 143
Dufferin, Lord, 124, 128, 130, 141, 142, 144, 145, 289, 302
Duncan, J., 337
Durand, Colonel H. M., 101
Durand, Major, 133–5, 137, 247–8
Dutch, 64, 65, 270

East India Company, 29, 31–5, 37, 39, 45, 57, 59, 60, 61, 62, 65, 93, 235, 257–69, 286, 287, 295, 337, 340–2, 344, 348, 349, 384, 385, 388

INDEX

Edgar, Deputy Commissioner at Darjeeling, 263
Edmonstone, G. F., 70–3, 76, 102
Edward VII, 162, 362
Egypt, 61, 127, 188, 372
Elgin, Lord, 140, 165, 172, 265, 289, 302
Ellenborough, Lord, 45, 46, 287
England, Jung Bahadur visits, 53; Chandra Shamser visits, 159, 160–3, 175
Entente Cordiale, 1907, 67
Europe, 31, 105, 145, 159, 171, 175, 186, 293, 350,
Europeans, 60, 61, 63, 66, 96–8, 104, 106, 107, 109–11, 117–19, 123, 124, 128, 135, 136, 189, 200, 203, 209, 231, 234, 239, 254, 266, 286–9, 293, 295, 298, 299, 307, 311, 350, 385
extradition, problems of, between Nepal and India, 53, 91–3, 108, 124–7, 157; Treaty of, 93, 297

Falconer, Lieutenant-Colonel G. A., 227
Fatteh Jung (Fatah Jung), 49–51
Feringhee (Christians), 260
Fisher, Margaret, Dr, 70, 213
France, 284, 295, 350, 351, 381, 393; colonial rivalry with Britain, 31, 39, 56, 57, 67; Jung Bahadur in, 53; and Thailand, 64 67, 311; Gurkha battalions in, 183, 188–9, 196; and Nepal, 310
Fraser, S. M., 273
French, 39, 57; French Consul-General, 310

Gallipoli, 188
Ganges, river, 104, 348
Gardner, E., 387, 388
Garwhalis, 236
George VI, 214, 231
Germany, 211, 295, 350–1; and Nepal, 192–3, 210, 372–8
Ghose, N. L., 180
Gillespie, General, 36, 37
Girdlestone, C. E. R., 94, 97, 98, 107, 112, 117–21, 124, 128, 132, 133, 137, 241, 242–4, 289
Giuseppe, Father, 29
Gonda, Rajah of, 80, 82
Gordon, J. D., 108
Gorukpore, 46, 76, 77, 79, 86, 97, 106, 108, 188, 239, 248, 251, 387
Gough, General Lord, 236
Government of India (see under India)

Governor-General (see under India)
Great Britain, 31, 45, 56, 57, 59, 64, 65, 67, 68, 140, 154, 165, 166, 168, 183, 184, 196, 211, 219, 225, 233, 234, 278, 280, 282, 290, 293, 306, 307, 310, 311, 370, 371, 390, 398, 399
Greece, 374
Grey, Sir E., 277
Gunduck, river, 385, 388
Gurkhas (Goorkhas), 28, 29, 36–8, 73, 78, 79, 81, 82, 93, 99, 101, 113, 117, 119, 137, 138, 158, 160, 170, 176, 177, 180, 181, 183, 184, 187, 188–90, 192, 198–200, 203, 206, 211, 219, 221, 228, 230, 231, 235, 236–8, 240, 242, 244, 249, 250–4, 257–9, 262, 265, 276, 277, 285, 286, 290, 312, 358, 364, 365, 368, 369, 372, 379, 385, 395; Army, 73, 75, 77, battalions, 183, 189, 221; brigade, 252; Chiefs, 82; dialect, 89; Gurkhalese, 24, 228; regiments, 158, 185, 187, 190, 230, 232, 235–7, 239, 242, 243, 247, 250, 251; Rifles, 159, 252; soldiers, 30, 37, 44, 64, 74, 235; recruitment of in Indian Army, 113, 133, 136, 205, 234 ff.; definition of, 235; War of, 1814–16, 286
Guroos, tribe, 44, 52, 349
Gurungs, tribe, 24, 234, 235, 238, 244, 246, 247, 253, 254
Gwalior, 308

Habibullah, King of Afghanistan, 192, 196
Hakims (Officers), 226
Haminlto, Ian, report by, 188
Hanumannagar, 225
Harcourt Butter Committee, 63
Hardinge, Lord, 194, 195, 237, 289
Hardwar, 231
Harsha Vardhana, 26
Hastings, Warren, 33
Henvey, F., 113
Himalayas, 23, 120, 170, 216, 235, 270; crisis of, 259, 260; Frontier of, 282; Kingdom of, 161, 183, 285,
Hindus (Hindoos), 81 84 „87, 104, 113 188, 197, 198, 200, 215, 230, 232, 234, 235, 238, 240; Dharma (Faith), 373, 374, 377, Kindom, 24, 87, 280; Mahasabha, 215; and Muslim Communal riots, 230; States, 204, 211, 307; Hindoostan, 81, 139, 347, 350, 351
Hirtzel, Sir A., 204–8, 234, 254, 290, 307

INDEX

Hobhouse, 159, 304
Hodgson, B. M., 40 41, 44–6, 98, 236, 286–8
Holdrich, Brigadier, 82, 83
Holkar, Maharajah, 116
Holland, 64, 374
Holy Roman Empire, 281
Honours, accorded to Nepalese prime ministers, 109, 137, 200, 216
House of Commons, 359
Huien-ti, Emperor of China, 256
Huzrat Mahal, 86
Hydarabad, State of, 56–9, 61, 62, 292, 310, 312; Nizam of, 58–63, 311; relations with British, 63

Ikrarnamah (Ickrar Nameh)—Pledge of Acceptance, 98; *Ikrarnamah* of 1841, text, 349
Ili, 265, 266
Ilyas Shah, 27
Imperial Assembly, Delhi, 1877, 61, 62
Imperial Durbar, Delhi, 1903, 151
Imperial Gazetteer of India, 194, 302, 303
Impey, 114, 117
India, 23, 24, 26–9, 32, 33, 35, 37, 39, 40, 44, 45, 52, 53, 57, 61, 64, 79, 86, 98, 99, 102, 108, 109, 111, 115, 120, 122, 126, 128, 130–2, 134, 138, 145, 150, 153, 158, 160, 161, 164, 168, 171, 172, 178–181, 182, 184–7, 189, 191–6, 199, 200, 201, 204, 206–8, 212–215, 220, 222, 223, 225, 230–2, 239, 244, 253, 255, 265, 266, 272, 273, 281, 282, 284, 289, 291, 296, 299, 300, 307–310, 312, 319, 361–3, 367, 368, 372–8, 383, 391; Government of, 34, 36, 41, 43, 45, 60, 71, 72, 74, 75, 79, 84, 85, 93, 94, 96, 100, 102, 103, 106, 107, 109, 113, 114, 116–20, 122–4, 126, 127, 130, 131, 132, 133, 134, 136, 137, 139, 140, 142, 143, 145, 150–8, 161, 164–71, 173, 174, 176–9, 184, 186, 188, 193–5, 198, 201–4, 207–209, 211, 214–6, 219–26, 228, 229, 232–4, 238, 239, 241, 243–7, 249, 251–4, 262, 263, 265, 268, 270–5, 277–81, 282, 284, 286, 289, 290, 293, 296, 297, 299–303, 305–13, 355, 357, 360, 366, 368, 381, 382, 383; Governor-General of, 31, 34, 43, 44, 45, 47, 48, 49, 52, 53, 61, 62, 65, 70–2, 77, 79–82, 87–92, 96, 100, 103, 104, 106, 109, 110, 113, 118, 119, 123, 128, 130, 131, 133, 135, 171, 190, 213, 227, 237, 239, 240, 242, 244, 267, 273, 287, 299, 302, 340–2, 344, 364, 371, 385, 386; status of princely states, 56–8, 59, 60, 61–4, 111; King Emperor of, 62, 362, 363, 365, 366; Army, 72, 113, 133, 150, 176, 183, 184–6, 189, 196, 203, 221, 225, 229, 230, 234, 235, 237–9, 244, 245, 246, 249–52, 254, 288, 290, 291, 311, 312; Arms Act, 123; Christians, 180; constitution, 223; Mohammedans, 376, 377; Mutiny (1857), 38, 72, 81, 87, 88, 93, 95, 99, 100, 102, 127, 133, 142, 144, 183, 189, 200, 208, 233, 237, 288, 290, 292, 363, 364, 367, 376; National Congress, 215, 223; nationalists, 204, 209, 211, 222; Princes, 39, 72, 103, 110, 116, 140, 193, 212, 214, 215, 253, 372, 377; Ruling States, 23, 37, 38, 39, 45, 56, 57, 62, 64, 68, 72, 113, 124–7, 200, 201, 287, 297, 298, 301, 303, 306, 308–11, 369
Indo-China, 64, 67, 311
International Geological Congress, 309
Iraqi merchants, 94–7
Iswolsky, Alexander, 370
Italy, 145, 295

Jagheer (Jagir, landed property), 86
Japan, 67, 96, 211, 228, 231, 232, 264, 301, 311; Emperor of, 160, 267; invasion of India by, 225
Jaunpur, 77, 78
Jenkyns, Sir H., 294, 295
Jerusalem, 284
Jha, Heera Lal, 50
Jordan, Sir J., 278
Jung Bahadur, Maharajah, Sir, 350, 351, 353; and murder of Matbbar Singh, 48–9, 144; Commander-in-Chief, 49; and Kot massacre, 51; first term as prime minister, 51, 56; co-operation with British India, 51–6, 76; character, 52, 55; aid to Britain during Mutiny, 52, 73–4, 77, 233; visit to England, 53, 109, 161, 287; reforms, 53; resignation, 54, 69; offered crown, 54; his power, 55–6; begins second term, 70–2, 92; Canning accepts offer of help, 75, 76; plot against, 75–6; services acknowledged by British, 77–8; pro-British policy, 79–85, 98–100, 102–3 105–7, 130, 288; and Indian rebel leaders, 79–87; quarrel with Gen. Ramsay, 87–91, 128; ambition to

403

INDEX

Jung Bahadur—*continued*
obtain throne, 99–102; receives knighthood, 100, 109; success and failure of his policies, 107–8, 109–11 287–8; death, 109, 112; and Gurkha recruitment, 239–41; and Tibet, 262–5; letter to Munno Khan, 346–7
Jung, Jit, 130, 131, 143, 145
Jung, Juggut, 112, 115, 116, 131, 145
Jung, Puddum, General, 142, 353

Kabul, 127, 192, 237, 373–5, 378
Kaffirs (Infidels), 76
Kaisar Bagh, 77
Kaisar-i-Hind, 61
Kali, river, 108, 385
Kalwars, 94, 97
Kamrup, Prince of, 25
Kanchenjunga, 23
Kang-hsi, Emperor of China, 256
Karatis, 238
Karnali, river, 23
Karnatakas, 26, 28
Kartapura, 25
Kashmir, 24, 36, 284; Kashmir Imperial Service, 253, 254
Kaski, 54, 55, 100, 112, 202
Kathiawad, 63
Katmandu, 43, 46, 52, 70, 89, 90, 132, 133, 213, 356; valley of, 23, 26, 28; geographical position, 23, 24; holy temple destroyed, 27; kingdom of, 28; Rajah of, 29, 30; Residency in, 35, 39, 166, 286; scientific mission, 69; Lord Roberts' visits, 137; Viceroy suggests visit, 157, 360; Lord Kitchener's visit, 158; French mission to, 216; and aircraft landings, 228; recruiting depot, 247–8, 251
Kedah, state of Malaya, 67
Kelantan, state of Malaya, 66, 67
Kelly, Captain, 81–3
Khan, of Bajour, 375
Khan, of Dir, 375
Khan, Nasrullah, 159, 192, 303, 375, 378, 379
Khan, Sarfraz Ali, 86
Khan, Sarfraz Husain, 306
Khaniqin, 188
Khas, tribe, 235
Khillet (Robe of Honour), 156
Khureeta (Official Letter), 53, 71, 110, 140, 161, 165, 171, 296
Khurtree, Kurbeer, 74
Kienlung, Emperor of China, 260
Kinlock, Captain, 29, 30; expedition, 30, 32

Kirantis, tribe, 24, 28
Kirkpatrick, Colonel, 34, 259; Mission, 34, 35
Kirung, 257
Kitchener, Lord, 158, 159, 188, 361, 368
Knox, Captain, 35, 114, 345
Koirala, brothers, 215
Korea, 259, 264
Kot (Palace) Massacre, 51
Kromchiat, Prince of Thailand, 65
Kshattriyas (Hindu warrior caste) 97, 197
Kumaon, 49, 72, 77, 235, 236, 240; Regiment, 236
Kushans, 26

Lahore, 179, 193
Lakhshmi Devi, Queen of Nepal, 46, 50
Lalia Patan, 28
Lall Mohar (documents bearing King's Red Seal), 70, 350
Lamjung, 54, 55, 100, 112, 202
Landon, Percival, 48, 79, 84–6, 100, 160, 163, 209, 237, 278, 280, 284
Lansdowne, Lord, 138, 139, 140, 171, 289, 359
Lawrence, Major, 46–8, 86, 107
League of Nations, 209
Lee-Warner, 62, 301, 302, 369
Lepchas, tribe, 24
Levi, M. D., 209
Levi, Sylvain, 25
Lhasa, 54, 134, 154–6, 160, 167, 168, 260, 262–4, 268, 273, 275, 276, 279, 354, 357, 361, 371, 393–5, 398; Raja of, 258
Lichhavis (Lichchhavi), 25
Limbuana, 188
Limbus, tribe, 24, 234, 238, 254
Linlithgow, Lady, 222
Loch, W., 141
Logan, J., 32
Lonchen Shatra, Minister of Tibet, 168, 263
London, 46, 53, 67, 84, 104, 109, 123, 157, 160, 161, 163, 171, 175, 191, 198, 203, 205, 209, 212, 214, 219, 221, 222, 301, 307, 310, 383, 399
Lucknow, 44, 75, 77, 79, 86
Lyall, A. C., 112
Lytton, Lord, 241, 289

Macartney, Lord, 269
Macgregor, Brigadier, 79, 88
Mackenzie, G., 88
Mackwanpur, 386
Magar, tribe, 24, 234, 235, 238, 244, 246, 247, 253, 254

INDEX

Mahanahde, river, 23
Maharajah Dhiraj, H. H., and Colonel Ramsay, 87–9, 90; Jung Bahadur's attempt to remove, 100–1, 109; and independence of Nepal, 110; status of, 160; exchanges with King-Emperor, 161, 162; British pledge to, 165; German Government letters to, 192–3; designation as His Majesty, 201, 289, 304; exchange of letters with Viceroy, 296; invitation to Delhi Durbar, 296
Mahendra Pratap, 192, 193, 375–7, 379
Mahpore, 82
Maine, Sir H., 294
Majumdar, K., 84
Majumdar, R. C., 84
Malaya, 64, 291, 311; States, 283
Malla, Jaksha, 28
Malla, Jayprakash, 30, 32
Malla, tribe, 26, 28
Malta, 198
Manchu Empire, 165, Dynasty, 167, 279, 282, 283
Manipur, 174, 175, 359
Manner-Smith, 159, 160, 164, 177, 189, 191, 194, 281, 289, 302–4, 365–7
Mansfield, Sir W., 82
Marathas, 37–40; chieftains, 44
Marley, General, 36, 37
Martini Henry, cartridges, 173; rifles, 178
Marwarees, 95
Mathewson, R. N., 123
Mauriyas, 26
Max Muller, 167, 168, 273
Maxim Guns, 202
McMahon, Sir H., 168
Mechi, river, 23
Meer Alim, 62
Mesopotamia, 188
Metcalf, H. A. F., 214
Middle East, 184, 186
Mieville, E. C., 214
Minto, Lord, 289
Mir Kasim, 29
Misser, Gajraj, 384
Mochulkas (undertakings), 95, 96, 98
Mogul, 27, 29, 31
Mohammedans (see under Muslims)
Mohammed Hoossein, 76, 77, 81, 82
Mohur (Nepalese currency), 97
Moira, Earl of, 384
Mongkuk, Thai King, 66, 67
Montmorency, Geoffrey de, 230
Moonje, Dr B. S., 215

Morang, 222, 385
Morley, Lord, 175, 364, 366
Moti Mahal, 77
Munich Agreement, 219
Munier e-Mulk, 62
Munno Khan, 82, 346
Muslims, 24, 81, 86, 230, 235; All India Muslim League, 215 222
Mutiny, 1857 (see under India, Mutiny of 1857)

Nabob Vizier, 341
Nagarkote Pass, 385
Nakhu Arsenal, of Nepal, 139, 172
Nana, Rao, 376
Nana, Saheb, 74, 82–7
Napoleon III, 67
Navakuta, 29, 48
Nepal, geography, 23–4, 26; population, 23; races, 24, 28; languages, 24; early history, 24–30; and East India Company, 29, 31, 32–3, 34; unification under Gurkhas, 29–30; friendship towards Britain, 34–5, 45, 49, 52, 56, 70, 114, 127–8, 150, 151–2, 153, 155; coolness towards Britain, 36, 39, 42, 115, 128–9; anti-British policy, 43–4; offer of military aid against Sikhs, 49, 52; army of, 49, 58, 64, 122, 140–2, 144, 145, 149–51, 153–60, 162–77, 179, 219–22, 225, 245, 368; King neutralised in politics, 56; prime ministership becomes hereditary office, 56, 129; status of, 56, 58, 59, 60, 68, 109–11, 166, 201–3, 206, 208–10, 213–4, 292–313; British troops allowed to enter, 69; assistance to Britain during Mutiny (1857) 74, 77, 79; British subjects' position, 106, 107, 113, 117, 119; offer of assistance against Russia, 114, 127, 134; co-operation with Britain in World War I, 183–95; and Allied victory, 196–7; co-operation in Afghan War, 196; co-operation with Britain in World War II, 219–22, 228–33. See also under, Britain, China, Tibet, etc.
Newars, tribe, 23, 238, 240
newspapers (Indian and foreign), 161, 179, 180, 208, 209, 211, 214
Nicholson, Sir A., 370
Nicholson, A. P., 63
Nielam, 257
Nipalganj, 239
Norris, 96, 98
Northbrook, Lord, 110

INDEX

Northern Circars, 58
Northey, Major, 49, 189
North-West Frontier (of India), 61, 186, 188, 225, 378
Nursing, General Dhoje, 142, 143
Nyahkote, 82

Ochterlony, Sir D., 36, 37, 137, 235, 236, 238, 386
O'Connor, Colonel, 207, 261, 275, 289, 391, 392
Ogilvy, Colonel, 225
Oldfield, Dr, 49, 73, 83, 237, 347
Oudh, 34, 38, 41, 69, 76, 78, 79, 85, 99; Begum of, 82–4; King of, 76, 109

Pa-Chung, 257
Pakistan, 222
Palestine, 188
Palpa, 76, 235, 247
Panchthar, 188
Pande, Damodar, 35, 36, 42, 286
Pande, Ran Jung, 42, 43, 45
Pandes, 44, 47, 49, 286
Panikkar, K. M., 56, 57, 61, 63, 151
Pani Patyia (Re-admission to Gurkha caste), 198–200
paramountcy, of Britain in India, 83–4
Patan, 28, 64
Pathans, 184, 196
Patiala, Maharajah of, 215
Patna, 44, 71, 96, 122, 195, 378
Patterson, G., 256
Peking, 166, 198, 257, 259, 261, 262, 264, 265, 267, 271, 277, 278, 283, 284, 354, 393, 396, 399
Penang, 65
Perak, 198
Perlis, Malay State, 67
Persia, 192, 372, 376
Philibhit, 201
Plassey, battle of, 31
Pokhra, 247
Poland, 219
Portugal, 56, 64; Portuguese, 270
Premnauda, 199
Pretoria, 309
Prithvi, Bir Bikram Sah, King of Nepal, 117, 118, 363, 371
Prithvi Narayan, King of Nepal, 29, 30, 32–4, 235, 257, 285
Punjab, 30, 32; Punjabees, 184
Pure, Jaykishen, 83
Pushputtee (Pashupati) Nath, Temple of, 87, 228

Quit India Movement, 223, 227

Raghunath, Pandit, 42
Rai, Lajpat, 210
Rais, tribe, 234, 254
Rajendra Lakhshmi, Queen, 34
Raj Guroo (Chief Priest of the State), 75
Rajputana, 235
Rajputs, 44, 234, 235; Rajput Prantik, 215
Raj, Rajeshwari, Queen of Nepal, 35, 36
Raleigh, T., 300, 301
Ramnagar, 44
Rampur, State, 125–7, 253, 297
Ramsay, G., 54–6, 70, 71, 72, 73, 74, 76, 79, 83, 84, 86, 87, 88, 89, 90–3, 95, 101, 102, 105, 109, 128, 240
Ramsay, Captain H., 237
Rana, Bahadur, King of Nepal, 260
Rana, Padma Jung, 54–5, 151
Ranas, 290–2; anti-elements, 226; Family, 56, 64, 129, 200, 212, 214, 233, 288, 289; Government, 214, 215; Minister, 229
Ranbir, D. R., 26
Rapti, river, 108, 385–9
Ravenshaw, 152, 305, 357, 358, 360
Raxaul, 251
Reading, Lord, 284
reforms, 53
Regmi, D. R., 26
Ripon, Lord, 289
Roberts, F. Lord, 137, 158
Rockhill, W. W., 255, 257, 258, 264, 267, 270
Roe, Sir Thomas, 31
Rose, L., 70, 213
Russell, C., 343
Russia, 139; Nepal offers of help against, 114, 127, 134, 135; and Tibet, 150, 152–3, 154–5, 157, 165–6, 173, 273, 274–5, 354, 370–1; intrigues against India, 265–6; and Nepal, 353

Saadat Ali, 34
Sahai, Randhoje, 104
Salar Jung, Sir, 62
Salisbury, Lord, 67, 271
Sapta Gandak, river, 23
Sapta Kosi, river, 23
Saran, district, 386
Schlagintvet, H., 69
Secretary, Government of India, 92, 95, 123, 125, 135, 158, 160, 297, 301, 303
Secretary of State for India, 84, 85, 123, 124, 136, 161, 163, 164, 175, 195, 205, 272, 290, 383

INDEX

Segowlee, Treaty of, 37–40, 108, 202, 206, 286, 292, 295, 385, 386, 388, 390
Shah, Norendro Bikram, 142
Shah, Ram Bahadur, King of Nepal, 33–6, 337
Shah, Shuja, 144
Shah, Surendra Bikram, King of Nepal, 352, 384
Shah, tribe, 26, 28
Shamsher, Baber, 106, 186, 194, 195, 200, 231, 380–3
Shamsher, Bahadur, General, 219, 220
Shamsher, Bhim, 212, 213, 216, 288
Shamsher, Bir, 129, 130, 132, 134, 135, 137, 138–40, 142, 145, 149, 150, 151, 157, 159, 172, 173, 243–7, 249, 250, 268, 288, 289, 296, 353
Shamsher, Chandra, Sir, 288, 391, 392; on states of Nepal, 134, 149; bloodless coup, 149; ambitions, 149–50; policy towards Britain, 150, 151–2, 179–80, 182, 297, 302–3, 306; visits to India, 151, 156, 175, 273, 357; role in Anglo-Tibetan conflict, 152–8; visit to England, 159–163; desire to equip army, 172–5, 177; policy during World War I, 183, 185, 187–194, 196, 289; and problem of *pani patyia*, 198–200; rewards and titles, 200; wins independence, 205–10, 297; agitation against, 210–12; death, 212; and Gurkha recruitment, 250, 251; official visit to Viceroy, 273, 357–61
Shamsher, Deb, 149, 288
Shamsher, Dhir, 109, 115, 117, 122, 129, 132, 151, 296, 297
Shamsher, Judha, 213–5, 219, 221–5, 227, 229, 231, 232, 250, 252, 288
Shamsher, Juggut, General, 115, 116
Shamsher, Kaisar, 186, 214, 216
Shamsher, Mohan, 200, 229, 288
Shamsher, Padma, 186, 229–32, 288
Shamsher, Sher, Major General, 186
Shamsher, Tej, General, 186
Sheoraj, 387
Sheppards, W. W., 150, 151, 353
Shigatse, 257
Shipp, J., 236
Shore, Sir John, 33, 34
Shun, Emperor of China, 256
Siam, 259, 283, 284
Sikhs, 42, 52, 184, 237; First World War, 236; Second World War, 52
Sikkim, 23, 29, 30, 38, 127, 167, 263, 275, 278, 286, 295, 382, 385; Raja of, 136

Simla, 46, 168, 209, 281; Conference at, 168, 169, 179,
Simra, 228
Singapore, 254
Singh, Ajit, 210
Singh, Badri Nar, 83
Singh, Gagan 48–50
Singh, Heera, Lieutenant, 76
Singh, Kedar Nar, 84, 143
Singh, Krishna, 210
Singh, Mathbar, 42, 46–9
Singh, Prakash Man, 226
Singh, Pratap, 33, 34
Singh, Ranjit, Raja, 36, 52
Singh, Ranodip, Sir, 112, 114–24, 127–9, 131, 132, 142, 241–3, 249, 268, 288, 289, 296, 312, 350
Singh, Siddhiman, 84, 86, 110
Singh, Taja, 192, 193
Sino-Tibet, boundary dispute, 168, 170
Sirdars (Officers), 50, 52, 71–3, 75, 83, 95, 99, 100, 102, 177, 194
slavery, 113
Snider, cartridge facory in Nepal, 122, 242
Song-tsen-Gan-po, King of Tibet, 255
Spain, 295, 374
Subarna Prabha, 35
Subsidiary Alliance, 57, 58
Suddur Jungee Kotwalee Cutchery, 94
Suez, 188
Suhrawardy, S. H., 230
Sukla, B. P., 227
Sultan of Kedah, 65; of Mysore, 38
Sundari, Tripura, 36, 41
Sundri Jal Arsenal, 172
Sutleg (Sutlaj) river, 23, 36
Suttee, 113
Swadeshi Movement, 181
Swameejee, P. Goonanund, 343–5
Swat, 375
Sweden, 374
Switzerland, 301, 374

Tai Ping rebels, 54
Tashilhunop, 257, 259
Teesta, river, 385
Telis, 97
Temple, Sir R., 107
Terai, 23, 24, 38, 49, 82, 83, 85, 86, 120, 242, 252, 386–8
Thailand, 56, 64–8, 98, 256, 291, 292, 310–12; King of, 65; Thai Army, 65, 66; Thai-British relations, 66; Thai Government, 65, 67
Thakurs, 26, 28, 235, 238, 254
Thankot, 308

INDEX

Thapa, Bim Sen, 36, 39–43, 46, 100, 113, 286, 287
Thapa, Amar Singh, 236
Thapa, Pirthimon, 180, 181
Thapas, tribe, 285, 286
Thoresby, 52, 188
Tibet, 312, 350; and China, 33, 152–4, 157, 165, 167–9, 173, 195, 212, Ch.9 passim, 285, 290, 292, 366–7, 370–1, 398–9; Nepal and, 33, 39, 54, 60, 64, 123, 152, 159, 164, 174, 197, Ch.9 passim, 287, 288, 290, 292, 299, 354–5, 358, 359, 361, 393–5; Indian trade with, 119; conflict with India, 150, 152; Russia and, 150, 152–3, 154–5, 157, 165–6, 173, 273, 274–5, 354, 370–1; Britain and, 165, 179, 195, 197, 306, 370–1, 381, 382, 398–9; division of, 168
Tigris, river, 188
Tirhoot, district, 386
Toolseepore, 80, 99, 239,
trade between India and Nepal, 33–4, 93–8, 113, 119–22, 136–7, 157
treaties, of 1792, 36, 38, 94; text of, 337 ff; of 1801, 38, 39, 164, 239, 308; of 1815–16, 106, 203, 239, 274, 289, 298; of 1855, 66, 92; of 1860, 108; of 1923, 202, 212, 239, 289, 309; text of, 390 ff; with Bhutan, 93
Trench, Captain, 247
Trengganu, Malay State, 67
Tribhuvan, King of Nepal, 216, 231
Triple Entente, 184
Truman, H. S., 231
Tsongka, 257
Tucker, Sir F., 41, 42, 46, 48, 188, 213, 253
Tupper, C. L., 61
Turkey, 193, 351, 372, 373, 375
Twiss, Sir T., 295

Udaipur, 235
United States of America, 67, 68, 231, 292, 311
Urdu, 63; newspapers, 180
Uttar Pradesh, State of India, 23, 186, 223, 227

Vamshavalis (genealogical Tables), 25
Vansittart, Lieutenant E., 247, 248, 249
Versailles, Treaty of, 195, 210

Wade, T., 265, 266, 270
Wandewash, battle of, 31, 57
Warner, W. L., 281
Washington, 68
Wavell, Lord, 231
Wazir Ali, 34
Wellesley, Lord, 33, 35, 38, 57, 58, 63, 104, 340
Wellesley, G., 387–9
Wen-ti, Emperor of China, 267
Wheeler, General, 74
Willcocks, General J., 189
Willingdon, Lord, 213
Willoughby, W. W., 283
Wood, General, 36, 37
Wood, J. B., 289, 299
World War I, 179, 183, 187, 196–8, 200, 203, 212, 219, 221, 228, 250, 251, 253, 289, 306; World War II, 200, 212, 219, 229, 232, 252, 253, 289, 290, 311
Wright, D., 48
Wylie, Colonel H., 135–41, 145, 149, 171, 172, 248, 250, 289

Yatung, 168
Yong Tcheng, 256
Young, Lieutenant F., 236
Younghusband, Colonel, 150, 156, 174, 264, 274, 276; Mission, 155, 272, 275, 282

For Product Safety Concerns and Information please contact our EU
representative GPSR@taylorandfrancis.com
Taylor & Francis Verlag GmbH, Kaufingerstraße 24, 80331 München, Germany

www.ingramcontent.com/pod-product-compliance
Lightning Source LLC
Chambersburg PA
CBHW052138300426
44115CB00011B/1438